THE CONTEMPORARY
HISTORY OF LATIN
AMERICA

A BOOK IN THE SERIES LATIN AMERICA IN TRANSLATION /

EN TRADUCCIÓN / EM TRADUÇÃO SPONSORED BY THE DUKE–UNIVERSITY OF

NORTH CAROLINA PROGRAM IN LATIN AMERICAN STUDIES

TULIO

HALPERÍN

DONGHI

THE

CONTEMPORARY

HISTORY OF

LATIN AMERICA

EDITED AND TRANSLATED BY

JOHN CHARLES CHASTEEN

DUKE UNIVERSITY PRESS DURHAM AND LONDON 1993

Seventh printing, 2007

© 1993 Duke University Press   All rights reserved

Printed in the United States of America on acid-free paper ∞

Designed by C. H. Westmoreland

Typeset in Trajanus and Trump Mediaeval by Keystone Typesetting, Inc.

Library of Congress Cataloging-in-Publication Data
Halperín Donghi, Tulio.
[Historia contemporánea de América Latina. English]
The contemporary history of Latin America / Tulio Halperín Donghi;
edited and translated by John Charles Chasteen.   p. cm. — (Latin
America in translation/en traducción/em tradução) Includes
bibliographical references and index.
ISBN 0-8223-1356-1 (cl). — ISBN 0-8223-1374-X (pa)
1. Latin America—History   I. Chasteen, John Charles, 1955–
II. Title.   III. Series.   F1410.H23413   1993   980—dc20
93-9884 CIP

*Translation of the books in the series Latin America in
Translation / En Traducción / Em Tradução, a collaboration between the
Duke–University of North Carolina Joint Program in Latin American Studies
and the university presses of Duke and the University of North Carolina,
is supported by a grant from the Mellon Foundation.*

Contents

WORDS, FIRST OF ALL, OF GRATITUDE. Translating a text of history from Spanish to English is never an easy task. As Emilia Viotti da Costa, who courageously decided to absolve a similar task by herself, eloquently commented in the Preface to her *The Brazilian Empire: Myths and Histories* (1985), "The real problem was how to convert a Brazilian prose that is more suggestive than precise, full of long sentences, often written in the passive voice . . . into the short and assertive sentences of the American style." In the case of my *Historia Contemporánea de América Latina,* the problem was compounded because although the book has found its main use in university courses in Latin American history, it had been written with a different audience in mind: those members of the general public who might be attracted to it by informed curiosity for things Latin American. Trusting that the readers would share—to quote again Emilia Viotti—"the same assumptions, the same codes, and the same anxieties and perplexities" that underlay my explorations, I felt even more free to do full justice to "the nuances, the interconnections," and the complexities present in every historical process. Something more than a translation was needed to achieve the metamorphosis of the almost idiosyncratically Spanish American text that resulted from my efforts into a book capable of satisfying American students' demands for clear answers to their precise questions. With reckless generosity, Professor John Charles Chasteen took time from his heavy and exciting intellectual and academic agenda to undertake the difficult task of translating and editing the text with that goal in mind. As a result of his effort, *The Contemporary History of Latin America* now reaches the English-reading public as a different—and I hope better—book than the one known by the readers of the original Spanish version and other translations. For this—and for the good grace with which he entertained (within reason) my pleas for the text that underwent a not always painless metamorphosis—I shall be forever grateful.

Except for the Epilogue, rewritten for the present edition, and for the Bibliographical Essay, prepared especially for it, this is an edited translation of the enlarged thirteenth Spanish edition published in 1990.

Tulio Halperín Donghi
Berkeley, 1993

FOR A QUARTER OF A CENTURY, Tulio Halperín Donghi's *Historia Contemporánea de América Latina* has been the most influential and widely read general history of Latin America in the Spanish-speaking world. Most historians of the region already know its fine-grained interpretation, unparalleled in breadth and ever attentive to the paradoxes of Latin American reality. The special purpose of this English-language version, then, is to make a landmark of Latin American historiography available to a totally new readership.

To produce a book that would read as though originally written for an English-language audience, the transformations of the Spanish text have exceeded those normally indicated by the term *translation*, extending beyond lexicon and syntax to prose conventions and addressing needs specific to new readers who possess less background knowledge of Latin America. Thus, the "lead story" has sometimes been highlighted more vigorously than in the original, which assumed prior familiarity with it, and some matters formerly left implicit have been made more explicit. In addition, a general streamlining occurred as the prose was recast using the shorter sentences and the patterns of paragraphing that are conventional in contemporary English usage. The paragraphs of the original interlock conceptually like links in a chain, a technique involving complex sentences that often reiterate or summarize an earlier idea before proceeding to elaborate on it, while the sentences of the English-language version follow one another more like beads on a string. In this sense, *The Contemporary History of Latin America* has been edited as well as translated. It would have been impossible to undertake such an ambitious task without the benefit of careful monitoring by the author, and I am grateful for his close cooperation throughout the process.

Something is inevitably lost in translation. In this case, the richness of nuance characteristic of the original, its relentless exploration of internal contradictions, nested one inside another, have occasionally been muted by the heightening of primary emphasis and the application of greater forward momentum. Consequently, this translation cannot substitute for consultation of the original on matters of particular interest to specialists. On the other hand, thousands of new readers—many of whom might have been frustrated by a more traditional sort of translation—can now explore a book that has exercised incalculable influence over Latin Americans' understanding of their history.

John Charles Chasteen
Chapel Hill, 1992

FIRST PUBLISHED IN 1967, *The Contemporary History of Latin America* has required a new edition to include what have been, for Latin America, two very long decades since that year. After the process of revision began, it quickly became clear that updating was not enough. These twenty years have thrown a different light on Latin American history, especially on the last half century. Therefore, while I made few changes in the first five chapters of the original version, I decided to rewrite totally the materials covering the period since the crisis of 1929 and to add two more chapters beginning with the Cuban Revolution. The perspective of the last two decades has brought the period of Latin American history after World War II into sharper focus, and, of course, the period during which I first wrote also looks different in retrospect.

The zeitgeist of the 1960s is no longer with us. Gone is much of the optimism created by the great postwar prosperity of the developed world. Gone, too, is some of the impatience then awakened in peripheral countries unable to participate in that prosperity. More than we realized at the time, that optimism underlay both our diagnoses of past ills and our proposed remedies for them. During the 1960s, developmental theories and opposing revolutionary analyses alike rested on assumptions about a happier future seemingly almost within reach. Although neither of those rival faiths dominated this *Contemporary History of Latin America*, rereading makes plain to me how the spirit of the decade colored my own interpretation of those years, since even the grimmest descriptions of current problems revealed the impatient conviction that a solution lay tantalizingly near.

Today that eager confidence in a better future appears clearly as the hallmark of a past era. Need I say that very little of it remains in the new edition? Instead, the new edition must bear the mark of the two decades that have passed since the first appearance of this book, among the most tragic periods in a history rich in tragedies.

What new moral shall we attach to the unfolding story of Latin America or adopt to guide our exploration of its past? The wisdom of disenchantment has replaced the faiths of twenty years ago in their ambition to guide Latin America into the future. I subscribe to no particular version of the current wisdom and propose instead that the future is likely to surprise us. For Latin America, far more than for more settled societies with a longer historical experience, the future will remain an elusive source of political inspiration but an untrustworthy starting point for the study of history.

Tulio Halperín Donghi
Berkeley, 1988

TO WRITE A HISTORY of independent Latin America is problematical indeed. The contrasts of the land itself and the motley variety of Latin American experiences are among the first impressions of outside observers. With understandable caution, Lucien Febvre chose a plural form in his title of the *Annales* volume dedicated to Latin America, *À travers les Amériques latines.* Are there, then, as many different histories of Latin America as there are independent republics? Such a solution has the charm of simplicity, and one finds a score of parallel histories neatly arrayed in many textbooks. However, none of the twenty independent nations provide a unified object of study, as Leslie Byrd Simpson indicated in his synthesis of decades of sagacious research, *Many Mexicos.* From pre-Columbian empires to twentieth-century revolution, multiplicitous Mexicos emerge in the course of time, but owing to the tortured geography of the country, many Mexicos have also always existed simultaneously in the tropical coast, the northern desert, and the central highlands. Similar regional contrasts impose a plural history even on much smaller countries such as Ecuador and Guatemala.

Another obstacle to the creation of a unified history of Latin America lies in the way most scholars have approached the past. Traditional historians have lost themselves in accounts of presidential administrations, partisan politics, and wars. Geographers, sociologists, and anthropologists have emphasized continuities that span centuries of the Latin American past, and Fernand Braudel has shown that history can be the study of continuity as well as change. Such approaches often have created a simple dichotomy between enduring structures and the ephemeral events, be they colorful anecdotes or patriotic narratives, that have absorbed the energies of so many historians. There exists an important middle ground, however, between the clutter of anecdotal narrative and the apparent rigidity of unchanging structures. This is the realm of historical process—coherent, gradual social and economic change—a more problematic historical dimension than either of the other two. Only at the level of social process can a unified interpretation give due attention to enduring patterns without abandoning the problem of historical change.

In the history of modern Latin America, the themes of unity and transformation converge in the region's incorporation into an international economic system with its center in Europe. We will begin with the end of Latin America's original colonial compact with the crowns of Spain and Portugal and follow the process of transformation brought by a new compact with burgeoning industrial powers like Great Britain in the nineteenth century. In the twentieth century, we will observe how this arrangement, too, enters a period of protracted crisis, a search for a new equilibrium in the relationship between Latin America and the international system. As we will see, the tensions of the mid-twentieth century reveal the failure of that search.

In order to provide a coherent picture of this complex process, the field of view must necessarily be carefully limited. No attempt is made here to provide a total history of contemporary Latin America. The reader will not find a profusion of red-letter dates, vignettes on the lives of famous persons, or synoptic treatments of literary and ideological trends. Nor are these the only omissions to which the author has resigned himself. Nevertheless, this *Contemporary History* will not be without some value if it provides historical perspective on the problems of Latin America today—cruel dilemmas that have escaped effective solutions for centuries and that now suddenly attract the alarmed attention of the world.

Tulio Halperín Donghi
Buenos Aires, 1966

CHAPTER I

THE

COLONIAL

HERITAGE

AT THE DAWN OF THE NINETEENTH CENTURY, the traces of conquest were still visible on the Latin American landscape. Nineteenth-century historians who lived in capital cities like Lima, Buenos Aires, or Asunción—cities that seemed to be the direct and enduring result of decisions made by individuals—were fascinated by the triumphs and vicissitudes of the conquistadores. Looking beyond heroes and events, we can discern more enduring realities, contours of social and economic life that link the conquest of the sixteenth century with the independence era of the early nineteenth.

As was well known to the jealous imperial rivals of Spain and Portugal, the Iberian conquerors sought, above all, precious metals. Following the path blazed by its rogue vanguard of conquistadores, the Crown of Castille arranged matters in the West Indies with exactly the same purpose. Beginning roughly in 1500, the nucleus of Spanish settlement remained for two decades in the Antilles, where surface finds of gold produced an early mining boom using Indian labor. The next twenty years, 1520–40, saw the conquest of the Mexican and Peruvian highlands, with their silver mines and dense Indian populations. These areas then became the heartlands of the New World empire of Spain. The catastrophic decline of Indian population caused by epidemics of European diseases put an end to gold production in the Antilles before mid-century, and the volume of silver from Mexico and Peru quickly surpassed gold from the Antilles in the shipments sent from the New World back to Spain. Silver exports permanently passed gold in value as well as volume at the close of the first century of colonization.

By 1600, Spain's empire in the New World had acquired its full extent, and its geographical configuration hardly changed until the wars of independence two hundred years later. The most vulnerable areas of this vast empire organized around the production of silver were its Caribbean and South Atlantic coasts, open to the attacks of rival European empires. Jamaica, among Spain's earliest settlements, was taken over permanently by the British, and the Portuguese advanced their frontiers at the expense of Spain in the South Atlantic. Overall, however, the territory claimed by the Spanish during the sixteenth century remained almost intact by 1810. Observers of the Spanish empire in the eighteenth century were intrigued by, and sometimes indignant about, this spectacle of a vast empire ruled by one of the most archaic nations in Europe.

This surprisingly durable system, designed to produce the largest profit with the least investment, underlay the "colonial compact" binding the New World territories to Spain. How else could one explain why lands producing enough silver to revolutionize the markets of Europe should themselves suffer chronic shortages of coin? Of course, the Crown took quite a considerable portion directly through taxation. The rest of the money in the colonies tended to flow to Spain to pay for imported European goods. Because the colonial market was closed to competition, Spanish merchants could inflate the prices of European goods and maximize their profit margins. The colonial compact also guaranteed the dominance of the privileged mining sector in the economic life of the New World territories as a whole. Obviously, this system had grave consequences for the development of Spanish America. The first of these was the ascendancy of outsiders, agents of the imperial system of taxation and trade, in the economic life of the colonies. The second was the exclusion of almost everyone else— including the miners themselves—from direct participation in the Atlantic economy.

The colonizing power derived clear advantages from this state of affairs, while the descendants of the conquerors had reason to be less pleased. During the first century of conquest, they resisted with an occasional show of force but afterward reconciled themselves to the Crown's organization of Spanish American economic life for the benefit of Spain. The reconciliation was not without its tensions and moments of instability, however, and it existed at all only because the booty of the conquest included people and land along with the precious metals. While tax collectors and merchants carried away most of the gold and silver, the descendants of the conquerors consoled themselves with their control of Indian populations. The highlands of Mexico and Peru became centers of Spanish colonization not only because of their rich mines but also because of the large populations of highland Indians already accustomed to laboring for imperial masters before the arrival of the Spanish.

In addition to facilitating the extraction of forced labor destined for the mines, the complex social organization of highland Indians fit them to be artisans and agriculturalists. The conquerors and their heirs exploited these possibilities in ways that evolved over the course of the colonial period. The conquerors and their immediate heirs often became *encomenderos*, receiving from the Crown a group of tribute-paying Indians to support them. This arrangement declined in the highland centers of Spanish colonization, just as had happened earlier in the Antilles, when Indian populations were decimated by epidemic diseases, and increasingly the heirs of the conquerors controlled the remaining Indians indirectly through royal grants of property. Land and Indian labor, the rewards that the Crown allowed the conquerors to keep for themselves, became the twin pillars of a way of life that carried into the nineteenth century its contradictory traits of opulence and penury. Of course, the new lords of the land did not win their dominions without a struggle. Sometimes the struggle was open and violent, as in mid-sixteenth-century Peru where after open conflict, in return for new oaths of obedience to the Crown, the conquistadores were able to obtain an improvement in the juridical status of enco-menderos. As the decline in Indian population accelerated, landown-ers had to contend with the *mita*, the forced-labor draft of workers sent regularly to textile sweatshops and, inevitably, to those insatiable devourers of Indian manpower, the mines. Long before the true horrors of the mita were added to the "black legend" of Spanish cruelty in the New World, the infamous labor draft had drawn the antipathy of large landowners, Crown officials, and the clergy in the regions where the mita's victims were recruited.

The heirs of the conquerors held sway in broad areas of the coun-tryside, but they did not dominate the colonial economy. However "feudal" might appear the relations between these rural landlords and their serflike populations of Indians, it would be an error to character-ize the colonial social order as feudal. The weight of the primary agricultural sector within the Spanish American economy was much less than might be expected, given the large proportion of the popu-lation involved in agriculture, though that proportion is often exag-gerated. In fact, the organization of the Spanish American economy ef-fectively marginalized the agricultural sector, a process itself partly responsible for the seemingly "feudal" qualities in parts of the coun-tryside. Furthermore, patches of small-scale Spanish agriculture ap-peared very early alongside the larger areas cultivated by tribute-paying Indians. The existence of these smaller farms was the result of the huge demands already placed on Indian labor. Indian agricultural laborers had to produce enough to support a class of minor Indian nobility, Spanish clerics, and Crown officials, as well as the encomendero's family, not to mention their own families. The competing labor requirements of miners and merchants compounded these difficulties.

The demographic collapse that bottomed out in the seventeenth century provoked profound changes in the agricultural sector of the Spanish American economy. From Mexico to Argentina, sheep grazing partly displaced farming because its labor requirements were so much lower. In addition, the arrangement whereby Indian agricultural communities paid a tribute in labor and agricultural products began to be replaced by *haciendas*, large estates where the Indians lived and worked under Spanish supervision. The transformation took place gradually, through a variety of legal pretexts, and it varied from place to place. It occurred most slowly in areas without urban populations because, unlike the tribute-paying Indian communities, the haciendas produced primarily for a market. The strongest and most rapid development of the hacienda system occurred in areas connected by mining and mercantile activities to the trans-Atlantic channels of the colonial economy; the urban populations that grew up around the mines and the centers of trade became the chief markets for agricultural products. Leading in this development was Mexico, at first secondary to Peru in silver exports but better connected in the networks of long-distance trade.

Not even in Mexico, however, did a truly wage-earning work force develop. Wages might be expressed in monetary terms, but payment was mostly in kind. In addition, many rural workers lost their freedom to participate in a wage market because they became indebted to the owner of a hacienda and then could not leave it. Many intermediate stages existed between the tribute system and the fully formed wage system. Commonly, rural laborers received a parcel of land to cultivate for their own families in return for tending the crops of the landowner. Such labor obligations took on a myriad of local variations, as during the transformation of rural Europe centuries earlier.

Though clearly dependent on mining and long-distance trade for its secondhand access to the money economy, the agricultural sector was also able to develop on the lines of a subsistence economy, and mediating between the two economies could be among the most profitable activities in Spanish America. Merchants wanted to keep the door between the two economies only half open. They needed a number of things produced in the countryside: food for the urban population, mules for transport and the mines, and cloth woven in the homes of rural people. They wanted the door open enough to eliminate urban scarcities, but a full opening would force them to compete for the products of the countryside in a wider market. They turned to Crown officials for assistance in regulating the exchange to their advantage. Crown officials instituted the system of *repartimiento* (forced distribution) of goods, in the absence of any more spontaneous exchange, to reduce the isolation of the countryside by royal order. District officials of the Crown began to receive shipments of goods that the Indians under their control were obliged to buy from them. Complaints about what the Indians had to buy—inferior merchandise that had failed to find buyers in urban areas—grew increasingly loud in the eighteenth century. If repartimiento reveals much about the abuse of Indian peasants, it says something as well about the limitations imposed on the power and wealth of the landowning class, who did not share in the benefits reaped by the merchants and officials from the forced distribution of inferior goods. Thus, the subordination of agricultural producers to other interests can be detected not only in a sectoral overview of the colonial economy but also in the remote corners of Spanish America where the predominance of the local landowning class is often thought to have been total.

The relationship between the mining and the commercial sectors varied as much from Peru to Mexico as did the forms of rural production. In Peru, the mine owners of Potosí depended absolutely on capital lent to them by the merchants of Lima, and, though the relentless exploitation of Indian labor in the mines during the eighteenth century responded partly to the gradual exhaustion of the ore, it also represented the attempt of the mine owners to pass along to their workers the pressure they themselves felt from their merchant creditors. Mexican mine owners, in contrast, frequently had enough capital to operate almost autonomously, and when borrowing they normally sought sums that were easily available in Mexico's busier commercial market, without compromising their ability to do business. The Mexican mining sector operated on a fully developed wage system, and European travelers found the mine workers' wages surprisingly high. In the last century of colonial rule, mining production stagnated in Peru and boomed in Mexico. As in the case of the agricultural sector, the differences between Mexico and the rest of Spanish America derived from Mexico's central location in the circuits of the colonial economy, a fact that mitigated for Mexico the negative consequences of the colonial compact.

The colonial compact of the sixteenth and seventeenth centuries underwent significant changes in the eighteenth century when Spain abandoned many of the old restrictions on trade and allowed almost

total freedom of shipping between the Iberian Peninsula and Spanish
America. The architects of empire in Madrid had decided that the
American colonies of Spain had more products to offer than silver
bullion, and they had begun to see a market there for Spanish industries and agriculture. In a number of ways, however, the innovations of
1778–82 upset the delicate equilibrium of interregional trade in the
Spanish colonies. The colonial areas that had dominated parts of the
old closed system now had to compete with the metropolitan economy itself. As a result, eighteenth-century flows of trade altered considerably from former patterns, from the Caribbean to the Río de la
Plata. The landowners of Cuba and Santo Domingo, who formerly had
raised livestock for the Mexican market, now grew tobacco and sugar
for Spanish markets. The cacao (cocoa) planters of Venezuela also
reoriented their exports from Mexico to Spain. In the Río de la Plata,
the Spanish market stimulated the increased slaughtering of cattle for
hide exports. Direct access to trans-Atlantic trade gave rise to the
fragmentation of the Spanish American economy into zones of monoculture that often developed closer contacts with Spain than with
neighboring parts of Spanish America. The process of economic fragmentation had fateful consequences for Spanish America. While tightening its bonds to metropolitan Spain, the liberalization of trade
disrupted the bonds that had bound the disparate parts of Spanish
America to each other.

The new mercantile conquest that swept over eighteenth-century
Spanish America, as Spanish merchants displaced their colonial counterparts from Veracruz to Buenos Aires, was closely linked to changes
occurring in Spain itself. Many at the time decried the monopolistic
tendencies of merchants in the southern Spanish port of Cádiz, long
dominant in the trans-Atlantic commerce. Cádiz had become essentially an entrepôt for merchants from northern Spain, especially Barce-
lona. The rising commercial hegemony of the north was accompanied,
to a degree, by the industrial development that imperial administrators had hoped to encourage through the liberalization of trade, but
ultimately this part of the plan achieved limited success. Eighteenth-
century Spain was unable to supply all the manufactures that the
Spanish Americans wanted, and these had to be acquired from the
more successful manufacturing exporters of western Europe. The new
version of the colonial compact ultimately failed because, instead of
building a stronger trade relationship between Spain and its American empire, it transformed Spain into an unwelcome intermediary
between Spanish America and the dynamic economies of northern
Europe.

Of all Spain's American territories, Mexico (the heart of the vice-royalty of New Spain) was the richest, the most populous, and the most significant to the European economy. The mining boom of the 1700s had made Mexico City the largest and most magnificent urban center of the New World, with mansions and public buildings to rival even the Old World's great capital cities. In the mining region of north-central Mexico—Querétaro, Guanajuato, San Luis Potosí—new, larger mine shafts had been added to the older ones, and the prosperity of these mining centers provided a vigorous market for the cattle raised further north. There, in the Spanish borderlands of North America, lay vast areas very sparsely populated with missions and militia settlers whom the Crown had sent to guard against British and Russian advances from the Pacific Northwest. Because of these origins, the Mexican north was less Indian in its demographic makeup than the central or southern regions. The development of the hacienda system had progressed further in the north than elsewhere, partly owing to the stimulus created by the lucrative market for agricultural products at the mining centers, partly because in the north Spanish ranches could expand onto land not subject to competing claims.

Mine owners, rather than landowners, dominated the society of the thriving northern region and used their wealth to purchase the titles of nobility, openly for sale by an impoverished Crown. Such a title admitted these triumphant nouveaux riches to the highest ranks of the Creole (native-born white) elites in Mexico City, where they were able to vie socially with peninsular Spaniards. Mexican Creoles enriched by the silver of the north, then ennobled by their riches, could be found in Madrid itself, leading a life of luxurious indolence that attracted a mixture of scorn and envy from the peninsular nobility. Understandably, the conspicuous consumption of this new Mexican aristocracy earned the reproach of the nineteenth-century historian, Lucas Alamán, an implacable critic of the late colonial Mexican elite, but Alamán's criticisms were not always well-founded. The miners and merchants may have made ostentatious displays of their accumulated wealth because of their desire for social prestige, but in truth there existed insufficient channels for profitable investment. Operators of northern cottage industries (producing pottery, hand-woven cloth, and articles of copper) were chronically indebted to local merchants, and the merchants who gained so many advantages from the existing system felt little incentive to revamp it totally with large investments of capital. The result was to make northern Mexico, for all its wealth, a satellite area of central Mexico, and only the exceptional productivity of northern mining in this period prevented Mexican mining centers from suffering a debilitating dependence such as that characterizing the relationship between Potosí and Lima.

Likewise, the wealth of northern Mexico could not easily find productive outlets in central Mexico, where Spanish merchants had consolidated their hegemony. Since the commercial reforms of 1778, peninsular merchants based in the chief Mexican port of Veracruz had taken control of highland trading networks. In the late eighteenth century, they diversified their investments into a commercial agriculture that gradually displaced subsistence crops in some of the best lands of the central plateau. An ephemeral boom in wheat cultivation ended due to competition from the newly independent United States after 1795, but the cultivation of sugar, another commercial crop that spread in central Mexico at the time, became a permanent feature of the highland landscape. The network of peninsular merchants also cast its influence over the central area's artisan production, much more important than that of the north. The city of Puebla, southeast of the capital, had long supplied the rough fabrics worn by peasants and workers throughout central Mexico. The middlemen of Puebla controlled the production and distribution of the cloth but were themselves dependent on cash advances and debts owed to the major importers and exporters of Veracruz, the ultimate masters of the central Mexican economy. Meanwhile, the lowlands of the Gulf coast and southern Mexico remained virtually undeveloped, except for scattered towns surrounded by small cultivations of corn, beans, and other subsistence crops.

The rapid growth of the Mexican economy in the second half of the eighteenth century resulted in distortions and polarizations likely to erupt into conflict. To a casual observer, Mexico on the eve of independence might have seemed predominantly a mining country, but the appearance was deceptive. The German traveler Alexander von Humboldt (who visited Mexico during the first decade of the nineteenth century) learned that, year after year, agriculture and livestock generated earnings of thirty million pesos, six or eight million more than the mines. The importance of agriculture remained hidden because so much of it went to local consumption and because Spain sought so avidly to encourage the exportation of the precious metals. Consequently, the Mexican upper class was divided between the owners of silver mines, most of whom were Creoles, and the commercial magnates, most of whom were peninsular Spaniards. The division took institutional form when the mining guild confronted the trade guild, or when the Creole-dominated municipal council of Mexico City challenged peninsular judges appointed by Madrid.

The opulence of miners and merchants contrasted starkly with the misery of the majority of the people, although at the end of the eighteenth century the contrast was a matter of comment only for outside observers. A population of less than three million people in 1750 had more than doubled since then. The growth of Mexico City (with a population of more than 130,000 in 1800) and of the mining centers of the north had added thousands of new consumers to the money economy, but most of the population increase had taken place within the subsistence economy, which daily lost ground to the cultivation of export crops. Money crops like sugar gnawed relentlessly at the land available for subsistence crops like corn and beans, a process that had enduring impact on life in the Mexican countryside. The effects of the process could be discerned at the opening of the independence period in the violent uprisings led by Father Miguel Hidalgo (in the agricultural hinterland of the northern mining centers) and Father José María Morelos (in the agricultural south). Country people, pushed off the land by the extension of export crops, contributed to the swelling populations of towns and cities. The sources of urban employment failed to keep pace with the increase, creating difficult conditions for urban dwellers. Penniless day laborers, finding only sporadic work of any kind, were quick to gather together in angry crowds, while the better-off city folk encountered an uncomfortable shortage of "decent" sources of income in the bureaucracy or the church and became, for that reason, particularly irritated with the preference shown for peninsular candidates in filling such positions. Not so numerous a group as the people from the countryside, the urban population was, however, far more vocal politically. In these ways, the expansion of the Mexican economy steadily increased the pressures that would eventually disrupt it.

Still, Mexico was the most brilliant colonial jewel in the crown of Spain's enlightened despots, the source of two-thirds of the royal revenues extracted from their American empire during the eighteenth century. Spanish merchants had equal cause for enthusiasm, given the manner in which Mexican silver seemed to flow almost spontaneously into their coffers. Among all the colonial possessions of Spain, Mexico was the most prosperous, with a per capita wealth superior to that of the mother country. This fact is all the more astonishing considering that only a tiny part—as little as 5 percent—of the silver from Mexican mines remained in the country. Of the silver exported, possibly half brought nothing in return, and the rest was siphoned out of the Mexican economy by terms of trade that worked systematically to increase the cost of imported goods.

The fastest-growing area of the colonial economy, however, was not Mexico but the Greater Antilles (Cuba, Santo Domingo, and Puerto Rico), which had followed the Caribbean colonies of France, England, and the Netherlands in the intensive cultivation of commercial crops. The destruction of the Haitian sugar industry during the slave rebellion of the 1790s created major opportunities for other producers, and Cuba, which became the refuge of French sugar planters fleeing Haiti, grew fastest of all. The economic transformation of Cuba had begun in the seventeenth century when the cultivation of tobacco emerged as a complement to livestock raising. The fortunes of the tobacco industry fluctuated, however, and the royal monopoly placed on tobacco sales during the last third of the eighteenth century limited the possibilities of expansion. Meanwhile, the sugar industry benefited enormously from a number of international changes. The wars of independence in the United States also opened the Cuban economy to U.S. trade. The French Revolution and the ensuing turmoil in Europe disorganized trading patterns and temporarily slowed the expansion of the sugar industry, but the long-term effect was to boost the process of growth by allowing the Cuban sugar trade to flow outside of the Spanish commercial system. Cuban sugar production increased from less than .5 million arrobas a year in the 1760s to more than 1 million in the late 1780s, then to 2.5 million by 1805. The population of Cuba more than tripled (to approximately 570,000) between the censuses of 1774 and 1817, and the island's port capital of Havana reached a population of 130,000. As a result of slave importations, the black population of Cuba rose to 55 percent. However, many planters had to become deeply indebted in order to build their sugar mills and acquire an enslaved work force. During this period, most Cuban plantations were rather small and technically backward, lacking adequate capitalization and large numbers of slaves. Only around Havana were there plantations with more than one hundred slaves. The Cuban sugar industry would take a long time to create a class of wealthy planters, while the planters' creditors got rich quickly.

Spanish Central America, called the Kingdom of Guatemala, changed much more slowly than Mexico or Cuba. More than half the 1.5 million people in Central America were Indians, less than a fifth were Creoles, and the remainder were of mixed ancestry or black. Most of the Indians lived in Guatemala, the mountainous northernmost province of Central America, a land of sprawling haciendas and Indian communities producing largely for a subsistence economy. El Salvador, in the lowlands to the south, produced Central America's principal export crop, indigo dye for the European textile industry. The ownership of land was not monopolized by large haciendas in these hot lands densely populated by Indians and mestizos. Honduras and Nicaragua, less-profitable provinces dedicated principally to ranching, were inhabited predominantly by people of mixed race. Costa Rica remained the least populated part of Central America, despite the arrival there, in the second half of the eighteenth century, of numerous colonists from Spain who established themselves on subsistence farms in the central valley around the town of Cartago.

Gold was the principal export product of Colombia, then called New Granada, a place characterized by regional diversity then as now. The Andes run through Colombia in three parallel ranges, all high and difficult to cross, creating a large variety of climates, and the rivers that run between are interrupted by barriers to navigation. Bogotá, the capital city, is high up on a chilly Andean plateau then devoted largely to livestock. Bogotá failed to dominate its surrounding regions like other Spanish American capitals. One rival center was the fortified port city of Cartagena on the Caribbean coast, the headquarters of Spanish naval power in that part of the empire. Another rival was the city of Popayán, in the rich sugar-growing region of the upper Cauca River. The gold was panned in the area of Medellín and elsewhere, and its exports had expanded rapidly in the eighteenth century. The geographic diversity of this part of Spanish America led to demographic diversity as well: a population mostly black and mulatto on the coasts, mostly mestizo in the mountainous interior, with a sizable white minority (about a third overall). The inland mining areas had important slave populations, as did the area of Popayán. Large landowners controlled most of the livestock-producing highlands like the area around Bogotá, but elsewhere, near the gold-producing region for example, the property map was more subdivided.

The emphasis on exports of precious metal gave the economic expansion of late colonial Colombia a very traditional cast. In 1788, for example, the value of bullion remitted to Spain reached 1,650,000 pesos, while the combined worth of many minor agricultural exports amounted to only 250,000 pesos. The ensuing years of international naval warfare prevented the collection of reliable figures on the trade, much of which flowed through contraband channels. The contraband trade flowing through English-held Jamaica became increasingly vital in supplying Colombia with European imports during the war years of the late eighteenth century. The structure of officially sanctioned trade, on the other hand, tended to depress all economic activities except for gold mining. Even the highland cultivation of wheat for the internal market could hardly survive because of the imported wheat bought with gold. As a result, the Colombian economy turned inward, and subsistence agriculture and locally oriented artisan production dominated rural areas of relatively dense population, like the mountainous area of Socorro, north of Bogotá. This inward-turned economy enjoyed a certain autonomy from the distortions and fluctuations of Atlantic trade, but it discouraged the growth of urban centers. Although the Colombian population rose toward a million by 1790, there were no cities of more than thirty thousand inhabitants.

Just to the east, Venezuela presented a strong contrast in its openness to the Atlantic economy. Geographically almost as complex as Colombia, Venezuela was better integrated economically. From the Caribbean coast, plantations of cacao scaled the flanks of the coastal mountains and invaded Andean valleys grazed by sheep and goats. Beyond the mountains, the plains of the Orinoco River stretched south, sparsely populated by cowboys and their herds of cattle and mules. This area had always been marginal to the more important settlement area of the coast and mountains, but in the eighteenth century Spanish authorities had tried to encourage, with indifferent success, the growth of a few settlements along the Orinoco River. Together, the regions of Venezuela had only half as many people as Colombia but double the value of products exported: cacao (a third of the total value of Venezuelan exports at more than 4.5 million pesos), followed by indigo, coffee, and cotton. Large landowners using primarily slave labor dominated the agriculture of the coast and the Andean valleys and constituted themselves as the aristocracy of late colonial Venezuela, flush from a triumph over a Spanish trading company in 1778–85. The Guipuzcoana Company, which had enjoyed an officially sanctioned monopoly on the purchase and exportation of Venezuelan cacao, had done very well at marketing cacao in Europe and had thereby stimulated production, but the company had kept most of the profits for itself. Having recaptured a good portion of these profits with the formation of their own merchants' guild, the cacao-planting *Mantuano* aristocracy of Caracas dominated the Venezuelan economy and prospered to the point that some could buy titles of nobility and allow themselves the luxury of a life of ostentation at the Spanish court in Madrid, alongside the silver-rich millionaires of Mexico. The Orinoco plains functioned as part of a more limited trade circuit, sending herds of cattle to feed the cacao-growing areas of the coast, providing more cattle and mules to the Caribbean islands, which no longer raised their own, and shipping some hides to Europe as well. Venezuelans ate meat in quantities that astounded travelers like Humboldt, who noted that the inhabitants of Caracas ate seven and a half times as much meat as the inhabitants of Paris. (Compare this with the diet of corn and beans in Mexico, of rice, beans, and bananas in the Antilles and Central America, of corn and wheat in Colombia, and of corn and potatoes in other parts of the Andes.) Even so, ranching did not offer the same wealth as the cultivation of a tropical export crop like cacao.

Ecuador, then called the Presidency of Quito, presented a sharp dichotomy between the Pacific coast, focused on the port city of Guayaquil, and the Andean highlands, where the capital, Quito, was located. On the coast, the broad valley of the Guayas River produced tropical export crops for the overseas market on plantations using slave labor. This was the fastest-growing region, but the bulk of the Ecuadorian population lived in the highlands. Figures for 1781 show about 30,000 people in the area of Guayaquil and almost 400,000 in the jurisdiction of Quito. Of the coastal people, more than half were black, a third were Indian, and the balance (less than five thousand) were white. The highlands were fully two-thirds Indian, but Quito itself—a city of thirty thousand—as something of a Creole stronghold. The highlands had only tenuous links to the larger economy of long-distance commerce. A few valleys produced some cotton used by local weavers, and the fabrics from these looms might find their way as far south as the Río de la Plata. Some highland wheat found its way to the coast. Such trade resulted in sufficient profit to support the lavish dwellings and scores of servants that the landowners of the Andean region maintained in Quito, but in its basic contours the highland economy remained devoted to subsistence. This relative isolation had allowed the indigenous languages of the Andean highlands to retain their vitality. Unlike Mexico, where the use of Indian languages had become marginal by the eighteenth century, Ecuador saw the continued majority use of Indian languages in broad areas where landowners, priests, and Crown officials might be the only Spanish speakers.

The viceroyalty of Peru had fallen on hard times by the end of the colonial period. The imperial reorganization of the second half of the eighteenth century had dealt Peru a double blow by creating the viceroyalties of New Granada and the Río de la Plata in areas formerly under the administration of Lima and had then added insult to injury by removing the silver mines of Bolivia (then called Upper Peru) from the official preserve of Lima's merchants. As a result, the merchants of Lima lost their sway in the mining economy of Potosí—in decline, but still the richest in South America—and in the commercial circuits that linked the mines to Chile and northwestern Argentina, where the merchants of Buenos Aires replaced those of Lima. A rise in the silver production of the mines that remained under the jurisdiction of Lima constituted only a partial compensation for these losses. The 2.5 million pesos of silver taken yearly from the remaining Peruvian mines at century's end equaled only a tenth of Mexican silver production at the time.

The activity of the mines, including nearly four million pesos of gold production in the Peruvian region of Puno, remained the backbone of the viceroyalty's internal economy and external trade, but there was considerable regional variation. The northern highlands, with long valleys running parallel to the coast, irrigated agriculture, and a considerable mestizo population, had relatively strong trade links, sending mules, textiles, and some agricultural products like olives to Quito and to southern Peru. The strip of desert along the coast was interrupted by oasislike areas of irrigation that produced cotton, sugar, rice, wine, and distilled spirits for markets up and down the Pacific coast from Mexico to Chile. Artisan manufacture of textiles and ceramics had sprung up in connection with the commercial agriculture of the coast. The broad southern highland, with its capital at Cuzco, had been a core area of Indian population since the time of the Incas. The southern highland had agricultural zones and urban commercial centers that served the needs and followed the variable fortunes of the mines, but around them indigenous communities dedicated themselves to mostly subsistence activities, planting corn and potatoes for food, raising sheep and llamas, and weaving their wool into garments. The predominantly subsistence economy of the highlands contrasted with the pattern of large properties, slave labor, and commercial agriculture on the coast. The agricultural laborers of highland Peru had to support not only the Creole landowning class, the church, and the institutions of imperial rule but also a class of privileged indigenous nobility. For their part, highland landowners were socially subordinate to a Lima elite enriched by the commercial agriculture of the coast and by the control of trade throughout the viceroyalty.

The glory of Lima was fading, however. Its population of fifty thousand lagged behind Mexico City and Havana and would soon be passed by Caracas and Buenos Aires as well. Its area reduced by administrative reforms, the viceroyalty as a whole contained little more than a million people (almost two-thirds Indian), a modest number indeed given the former importance of Peru within Spain's New World empire. However much they dominated the regional elites of the viceroyalty, the merchants of Lima were suffering due to Peru's territorial losses and the advances of Spanish commercial houses. As throughout

Spanish America, the bullion from the mines did not accumulate in the Peruvian economy but trickled quickly away to Europe. One plum remaining in the hands of Lima's merchants was the trade in Chilean wheat, since they controlled the fleet of coastal vessels that brought the grain from Chilean producers to consumers in Peru. Formerly their control of Chile's commercial circuits had been complete, but during the second half of the eighteenth century Chilean merchants had begun to receive European imports directly or through Buenos Aires.

Chile, the most remote and isolated of Spanish American lands, had entered a period of modest growth at this time as well. By century's end, its mines produced almost two million pesos annually. In most respects, however, the imperial transformations of the second half of the eighteenth century had hardly touched Chile, and the Chilean economy lacked other export activities with potential for easy expansion. The wheat crop found an adequate market in Lima, but the same could not be said for the possible export products associated with livestock. Chilean ranches could have supplied far more tallow than Peruvians wanted to buy, and Chile could not compete with Argentine exports of hides to Europe because of the greater distance involved. Nevertheless, the population grew more rapidly than the rate of economic expansion would lead one to expect, apparently approaching almost a million inhabitants by 1810. Most Chileans were mestizo or white, and they lived overwhelmingly in rural areas, Santiago, the capital and largest city, having a population of less than ten thousand. This demographic increase spilled onto new agricultural lands as the Chilean frontier advanced south into territory long defended by unsubdued Araucano Indians, and the land and labor arrangements on the frontier closely approximated those of the older rural areas: large properties with tenants who cultivated plots of their own in addition to the crops belonging to the landowner. The Chilean landowning class received an infusion of new blood with the arrival, in the eighteenth century, of Spanish bureaucrats and merchants who married into the upper echelons of Chilean society.

The opposition between native-born elites and newly arrived Spaniards was particularly noticeable because of the homogeneous qualities of the native-born population. As a whole, the Chilean population was profoundly mestizo, combining a predominantly indigenous genetic makeup with a predominantly Iberian cultural makeup. As a result, the distinction between mestizo and white became blurred in Chilean society, and reports concerning the racial makeup of the population vary widely. For example, early nineteenth-century calculations put the mestizo population at 60 percent of the total, while

an enumeration in 1778 found only 10 percent. The number of blacks and mulattoes was small, as generally occurred in areas only tenuously linked to the larger money economy of the empire.

Across the Andes from Chile, on the Atlantic coast, the viceroyalty of the Río de la Plata (composed of modern Argentina, Uruguay, Paraguay, and Bolivia) vied with Venezuela and the Caribbean islands as the part of Spanish America most invigorated by the imperial reforms of the second half of the eighteenth century. The net effect of those reforms had been to redirect the commercial networks of the Bolivian mining complex, along with its satellite areas in Chile and the Argentine northwest, away from Lima and toward the new viceregal capital of Buenos Aires. In fact, the imperial reforms only reinforced a change already under way, since the Atlantic approach had undeniable advantages of a practical nature, and the creation of a new viceroyalty of the Río de la Plata in 1776 functioned above all as a barrier to Portuguese advances in that part of South America. As the administrative center of a vast hinterland, including the mines of Potosí and the politically sensitive frontier bordering Brazil, the port city of Buenos Aires gained suddenly in importance within the Spanish empire, changing with astounding speed from a village of scattered, earthen-walled houses into a bustling replica of a Spanish provincial city.

The growth of Buenos Aires in the late eighteenth century reflected the city's new administrative responsibilities, the proliferation of a reformed imperial bureaucracy, and, above all, the surging expansion of the city's merchant class. In Buenos Aires, as elsewhere in Spanish America, immigration from Spain had contributed to the rapidly rising number of traders, and they were rapidly growing rich thanks to their control of commercial networks that reached as far away as Lake Titicaca in the central Andes. In a good year, the value of the city's exports to Spain surpassed five million pesos, 80 percent of which was silver from the mines of Upper Peru. Between Buenos Aires and Upper Peru lay an archipelago of local commercial, agricultural, and artisanal centers that also fell now into the orbit of Buenos Aires. For centuries, these centers had supplied the mining complex of Potosí with mules, carts, hides, wheat, and wine. Some of them benefited from their new connections to the growing market of coastal Argentina, but others—wheat and wine producers in particular—suffered because those connections suddenly put them in competition with Spanish products easily accessible in the busy port.

The coastal plains around the viceregal capital shared in the late eighteenth-century economic growth of Buenos Aires, but, rather than in the immediate hinterland of Buenos Aires and older settlement areas along the west bank of the Paraná River, the big changes happened in previously unsettled lands to the east of the river, particularly in the area of modern Uruguay, then called the Banda Oriental. West of the Paraná, settlers still battled extremely warlike tribes of plains Indians, who remained a threat after centuries. Until the middle of the eighteenth century, the destructive practice of cattle hunting (as opposed to cattle raising) had decimated the herds of this area. East of the river, however, the indigenous population posed much less of a threat and the herds were more numerous. Many of the Indians of the Banda Oriental were Guaraní who had formerly lived in the famous Jesuit missions along the upper Paraná and Uruguay rivers. After the expulsion of the Jesuits in the 1750s and 1760s, they had drifted onto the plains east of the Paraná, where herds of domestic cattle had run wild and reproduced in profusion on luxuriant natural pastures. In these rich grasslands, people of Guaraní and mixed ancestry became intermediaries between Creole ranchers and more warlike tribes such as the Charruas. They became intermediaries, as well, in the thriving contraband between these Spanish-controlled lands and the Portuguese-controlled lands further north. By the second half of the eighteenth century, the Banda Oriental had become an object of competition between Buenos Aires and the newer port city of Montevideo, as each tried to extend its jurisdiction over the potential wealth of the primitive and dynamic frontier. Montevideo, located across the Río de la Plata the Banda Oriental itself, seemed to have the more natural claim to preeminence there. However, the development of Montevideo had emphasized its function as a naval base, and the city had been slow to sink roots into its hinterland. The new commercial power of Buenos Aires more than compensated for the disadvantages of its location further away.

North of this plains frontier, Paraguay and the Misiones district developed along quite different lines. Since the expulsion of the Jesuits, the Indians of the former missions had entered increasingly into contact with the mestizo settlements of Paraguay, and the cooperative community structure of the Indians had suffered in the process. The population of the Misiones district plummeted as many thousands of Indians emigrated from the district to the cattle frontier. The remaining inhabitants continued to grow cotton and weave it into a rough cloth for export and to collect and export the leaves of yerba mate, a tea that found a market along the length of the Andean region thanks to the Jesuits, who had shipped it as far away as Quito during their administration of the Misiones district. As the yerba mate production of the district declined, that of nearby Paraguay gradually took its place. Paraguayans also became important producers of tobacco, in which they were encouraged by Spanish efforts to resist imports from Brazil. Finally, Paraguayans began to use their own grasslands to participate in the ranching economy of the Río de la Plata.

The main export product of the Platine ranching economy was cattle hides, worth a million pesos a year by the early nineteenth century, and most of the profits went to merchants rather than landowners. The expansion of the ranching economy of the Río de la Plata did not result in an equivalent development of commerce in the Banda Oriental, Misiones, and Paraguay. Commercial interests in Buenos Aires completely dominated the availability of capital and maintained their control over the trade network of the ranching areas through loans that kept their local subsidiaries in debt. So fully did the merchants of Buenos Aires control the ranching economy that the ranchers themselves failed to accumulate comparable wealth even when they produced on a large scale for export with wage labor. The economic and political ascendancy of great landowners in Argentina and Uruguay did not occur until after the wars of independence. Ranching requires comparatively few workers, so the exceptionally high wages were not a barrier to the profitability of ranching. However, the more labor-intensive cultivation of grain in the area near Buenos Aires became increasingly crippled by the cost of labor. The processing of meat, in the form of jerked beef, began on the eve of the wars of independence in the Banda Oriental, but the exports of beef at this time amounted to no more than a tenth of the value of exported hides.

The demographic and economic nucleus of the viceroyalty of the Río de la Plata remained in Upper Peru and in its silver mines, both those of Potosí and the newer mines of Oruro. Around the mines, in sheltered corners of the highlands such as the Cochabamba district, Aymara- and Quechua-speaking Indians cultivated the soil to feed the mining centers and wove fabric in various forms of forced seasonal labor. Mining itself consumed tremendous amounts of labor from Indian communities, which the Crown and the mine owners sought to defend against landowners in need of workers. The burden of Indians who lived in indigenous communities was in some ways heavier than the burden of peons or tenants on a hacienda. In addition to their forced labor in the mines, Indian communities had to support corregidores, priests, and their own nobility. Along with mining centers and Indian villages, there were mercantile cities, of which La Paz was the most important. La Paz lay in an area of dense Indian population and great estates. Its numerous *obraje* workshops and commercial importance derived from the city's function as a link between Upper Peru and Lima, so the late eighteenth-century reorganization of trade—as a result of which much of the mining wealth flowed east toward Buenos Aires—came as a blow to La Paz. In addition to the commercial cities, Upper Peru could support at least one urban center devoted purely to consumption, Chuquisaca (modern Sucre), where the richest mine owners of Potosí and Oruro went with their families to enjoy the climate. Chuquisaca was the seat of imperial and ecclesiastical institutions like an *audiencia* (high court) and a university. The cities of Upper Peru depended directly on the mines. All of them suffered as mining production declined in the late 1700s, and the situation worsened after 1802 when mercury, essential for refining the silver ore, became unavailable because of war in Europe.

The viceroyalty of the Río de la Plata showed such complexity at the end of the colonial period in part because its disparate regions had been shaped into an administrative unit only after a long period of divergent development. Demographic patterns show this clearly. In Upper Peru the white minority remained so tiny that even in the cities Indians and the mestizos had maintained Quechua and Aymara in preference to Spanish, a language that most highland Indians still did not understand at all. In spite of the wealth of the region, the number of black slaves was small. They functioned mostly as house servants and artisans in urban areas. In Buenos Aires and other cities of the Atlantic coastal area, on the other hand, enslaved Africans and their descendants accounted for as much as 30 percent of the population. Census takers did not register the presence of Indians or mestizos apparently because, as in Chile, most had assimilated into the Creole culture. At any rate, European visitors to the Río de la Plata found Indian blood widely diffused in rural areas, where slaves were fewer and Guaraní Indians more numerous. The geographically intermediate regions between Upper Peru and the Atlantic coast, like Cuyo and Tucumán, were racially intermediate as well. Indian communities (as in the highlands) and large numbers of black slaves (as in Buenos Aires) were both rare in the predominantly mestizo populations of the intermediate zones.

Despite the kaleidoscopic variety of Spanish America at the close of the eighteenth century, an increase in social tensions characterized the whole. The steady progress in racial mixing had begun to undermine one of the basic principles of the social order, and increasingly complex caste lines were constructed by the colonial upper classes to maintain a hierarchy that was in danger of collapsing in confusion. The more complex caste system reinforced social distinctions no longer marked by economic differences, preventing the social ascent of urban lower-caste individuals through the army, the church, or the government and otherwise neutralizing the social consequences of wealth acquired by people of mixed blood. Particularly in urban settings, where poor whites and people of mixed blood found themselves competing economically, invidious caste distinctions poisoned the social atmosphere. In the Río de la Plata, we find a Montevidean bureaucrat struggling to defend himself against insistent accusations of mixed blood (which would make him ineligible to hold high office) by acquiring a judicial certification of his pure Spanish ancestry. In Venezuela, the high and mighty Mantuanos saw fit to protest the debasement of racial standards involved in the Crown's sale of certificates of Spanish ancestry to anyone rich enough to buy them. In central areas like the Mexican and Andean highlands, where a deep economic gulf separated the Indians from dominant groups that liked to think of themselves as white, the changing standards worked to justify the status quo. However, by drawing finer racial distinctions for the benefit of those who could claim "purity of blood," the late colonial emphasis on race also threatened those "whites" who had acquired the status in times past, when lineages were not subject to so much scrutiny.

One underlying cause of the fuss over racial categorization was the shortage of viable and respectable livelihoods in the middle and lower levels of late colonial society. Between the rich and powerful, who had no need of "decent" employment, and the masses of poor, who had no hope of it, those who had fallen from fortune or risen from destitution struggled against one another for the very limited social niches available. The result was increasing resentment among modestly well-off people who were unable to find a place at the level of their expectations. Even such a rapidly growing city as Buenos Aires, the economic and administrative center of a vast region of South America, did not provide sufficient employment for its population of forty thousand. People at the bottom of the social hierarchy began to form urban underclasses, able to eke out a meager existence at best. The artisanal activities that might have attracted such people in a different context became a much less attractive alternative in colonial Spanish American cities because free artisans competed economically with enslaved artisans backed by powerful owners eager for profits. Observers of the colonial scene in places as widely separated as Mexico City, Lima, Santiago, and Buenos Aires commented on the "indolence" of urban dwellers of the middle and lower classes, and the most thoughtful of them noted the political dangers of these people with frustrated expectations and no stake in the social order. This characteristic of urban society had a deleterious effect on social relations, detectable in administrative and ecclesiastical life and in literary expression.

The desperate jostling for scarce social resources also explains the growing intensity of Creole resentment against peninsular Spaniards. The Spaniards were unwelcome competitors, and their constant preferment became a further irritant since it was not based on any of the traditional standards of social discrimination. People of mixed race, for example, necessarily expected and had learned to tolerate unequal treatment when competing with white people, but discrimination against Spanish American Creoles had no basis in law or in collective values. The Spaniards were easily isolated targets because immigration to Spanish America from Spain had never been large. In all Spanish America there were probably no more than about 200,000 peninsular Spaniards on the eve of the wars of independence. The concentration of peninsular Spaniards in administrative and commercial activities made them a highly visible group, easily challenged by anyone with broad support among the Spanish American people.

The crowding of the urban population into cities unable to provide employment was only one manifestation of the extremely uneven distribution of population in Spain's New World empire. Mexico alone accounted for almost half of the roughly thirteen million people who lived in Spanish America on the eve of independence, and a large proportion of the inhabitants of Mexico were crowded into the highland valley of Anahuac around Mexico City. The landscape of the Mexican highlands presented population densities similar to those of Europe, but all around it lay vast expanses that remained virtually unpopulated. In some places, such as the deserts of northern Mexico, natural conditions themselves placed severe limits on settlement, but many other areas simply lacked settlers willing to go there and live. Outside of Mexico, excepting the nuclei of dense Indian populations that had preceded the conquest, broad stretches of wilderness constituted the rule. Around 1780, the bishop of Córdoba in Argentina had reason to ask himself whether the habitation of his immense dioceses were so sparse as to make organized social life, religious discipline, and political loyalty completely impracticable. The same question might have been asked about many other areas of Spanish America at the time.

Along with the shortcomings of Spanish colonialism, geography helps explain the discontinuous pattern of Spanish American settlement. Huge mountains created almost insurmountable obstacles to transportation and caused very significant variations of climate within relatively small areas. Rivers provided useful arteries of communication only in exceptional cases—almost nowhere in Mexico, for example. However, the manner of the Spanish conquest and subsequent colonization must bear most of the blame. The conquest contributed to the concentration of settlement by focusing on highland plateaus. The Spaniards settled preferentially in the Mexican and Andean highlands partly because they found cooler climates more congenial to Europeans but principally because these places already supported large populations of fully sedentary Indians who could more easily be integrated into a seigneurial society. Even the economic and demographic expansion of the eighteenth century reproduced in growing areas, such as the Antilles, Venezuela, and the Río de la Plata, the same uneven patterns of settlement that characterized the highland core areas. The city of Buenos Aires had more inhabitants than occupations for them, while in the surrounding countryside a lack of manpower constituted the chief obstacle to faster economic expansion, and similar patterns were emerging in Venezuela.

In the last analysis, these imbalances and contrasts flowed from the social order imposed by Spanish colonization. The unremittingly primitive life of common people in the countryside offered little reward and remained entirely unattractive to most townspeople, not only in the highland areas of Indian peasants and white overlords but also in the newer settlement areas like the Río de la Plata. So it was that the urban poor of Buenos Aires did agricultural work only when forcefully drafted. Their aversion to manual labor, so often attributed to perverse characteristics of the Hispanic cultural heritage, in fact represented an entirely realistic assessment of the obstacles faced by common people competing with slave artisans in the cities and with various kinds of coerced labor in the countryside. The importance of practical considerations may be gauged by the prestige acquired by merchants in spite of cultural traditions as hostile to commercial activities as to manual labor, the operative contrast being that, unlike manual labor, trade was extremely lucrative.

At the beginning of the nineteenth century, the settlements of Spanish America lay separated by tremendous natural obstacles and vast areas that remained virtually uninhabited. Despite the Crown's efforts to protect Mexico against the encroachment of imperial rivals from the north, Spanish settlement remained nonexistent in much of the territory beyond the mining zone. On either side of the route across Panama (long a vital link in the Spanish imperial trading system) stretched a dense tropical wilderness, preventing overland communication between Central and South America. Hostile Indians continued to dominate the tropical lowlands between New Granada and Venezuela and between Ecuador and Peru, forcing the Spanish to take the difficult mountainous routes between these colonies. Where the preferred highland routes narrowed excessively, they might become as tortuous and terrifying as the road through the "knot" of Pasto, between New Granada and Quito. The armies of independence, surging monotonously back and forth across the pages of South American history textbooks, encountered some of their most difficult challenges in deserts and mountains, as when Simon Bolívar crosses the plains of the Orinoco and conquered New Granada by scaling the Andes from behind or when José de San Martín crossed the Andes from Argentina to invade Chile.

Each of these settlement areas, so tenuously connected to the neighboring ones, also lacked internal continuity. Within the viceroyalties of New Granada or the Río de la Plata, essential transportation routes traversed broad areas never entirely subdued until the nineteenth century. Nor were communications easy between the central highland settlements and the ports that served them. Mexico's tableland of Anahuac, the location of the capital and the densest population in the viceroyalty of New Spain, was difficult to reach from both the Atlantic and the Pacific sides, and the ascent from Lima to the highlands of Peru was even more forbidding. Under such conditions, even the most central transportation axis within a territory might demand something akin to heroism on the part of travelers, as observers from Europe frequently commented during their visits in the early part of the nineteenth century. Trackless wilderness and formidable hostile Indians gave particular importance to navigable rivers—especially the Orinoco River through the plains of Venezuela and the Paraná and Paraguay rivers between Santa Fe and Asunción in the Río de la Plata. Such rivers might be better than overland routes, but they still presented very serious obstacles. The Magdalena River, which connected the highlands of Bogotá with the Caribbean coast, abounded in treacherous falls, and the occupants of small river craft looked with some trepidation on the enormous alligators sunning themselves patiently on the muddy banks.

Fortunately, the consequences of these transportation difficulties for the internal cohesion of Spanish America were not as grave as might be expected. As the French anthropologist Claude Lévi-Strauss remarked of the still-archaic parts of Brazil that he encountered in the mid-twentieth century, the general difficulty of communications tended comparatively to favor the most remote regions, because the type of transport that could travel ten miles from a capital city could travel almost anywhere. The sea of mud on the outskirts of the city of Buenos Aires, for example, constituted one of the greatest barriers pampean cart drivers would face on their long trek to the Andes, and not far inland from Lima pack mules became the only viable means of transport. Maintaining this rude system of internal communications was a costly victory, however, in both economic and human terms. Take the transport of wine by mule train from San Juan, in the Andean foothills of western Argentina, up to Potosí. The mule trains followed one of the more frequented routes in the viceroyalty of the Río de la Plata, and along one forty-day desert stretch of it men and mules found no drinking water at all. Perhaps the virtues of heroic resignation, displayed by common and high-born Spanish Americans alike in the face of such perils, should count as an advantage of the system, and despite the terrors of the Magdalena River, viceroys and prelates did arrive in Bogotá safely more often than not.

Nevertheless, whatever the redeeming features of this rough-and-ready transportation system, its economic consequences were grim. In the first place, the system consumed a lot of manpower for muleteers and carters. Around 1800, carters made up a tenth of the population in the prosperous little city of Mendoza, on the route between Buenos Aires and Santiago de Chile. The system consumed animal power and vehicles as well. The working life of mountain pack mules was relatively short, and even on the plains of the Río de la Plata, among the best for carting anywhere in Spanish America, the heavy two-wheeled carts drawn by oxen were jolted to pieces after a small number of trips across the pampa. The carpenters of Tucumán steadily used up local hardwoods to replace the supply of carts, while mule breeders in neighboring regions of the Río de la Plata (and in Venezuela and northern Peru) supplied mules by the tens of thousands. As a consequence of the large amount of resources dedicated to it, transportation remained costly to the economy as a whole.

In sum, the transportation system of late colonial Spanish America managed to keep the whole territory united but left it as economically fragmented as the continent of Europe in 1500. The network of long-distance trade was able to function only with high profits and low volume. Existing patterns of trade were totally insufficient to integrate a thousand local markets, and therefore the energies of most people still flowed into production for themselves, for their neighbors, or for their landlords. Such a transportation system was more appropriate for the era of conquest long past than for a Spanish America divided into areas of large-scale commercial production for overseas markets. The survival of old methods of communication was a reminder of the incompleteness of the transition.

However incomplete the transition, the late colonial reforms had enjoyed moderate success in changing both the direction and the pace of the Spanish American economy. The Spanish Crown's commercial reforms had begun to alter the patterns of interregional trade in Spanish America and encouraged the growth of export economies based on agriculture and ranching alongside the older ones based on mining. The transformation of trade itself was sweeping, but the balance between various productive activities across the Spanish American landscape showed more subtle shifts. Only Venezuela and Cuba had developed export economies completely unassociated with mining. Meanwhile, mining retained its pride of place within the growing economies of Mexico, New Granada, and the Río de la Plata by dominating their exports. A division between the mining sector producing for the overseas market and the agricultural sector producing primarily for local or regional markets remained the rule, despite the exceptions presented by tobacco and sugar from Cuba, cacao from Venezuela and Ecuador, and hides from the Río de la Plata.

The reforms influenced patterns of importation more than patterns of exportation. The liberalization of trade restrictions within the Spanish empire brought Europe significantly closer and lowered the cost of imported manufactures, making possible an increase in the volume of imports. The transformation corresponded to the new role that the colonies were to play vis-à-vis the mother country, a role that they never truly fulfilled. The inhabitants of Spanish America did not become effectively incorporated into a unified imperial market as producers or as consumers. The use of imported consumer goods (cloth especially, hardware, and some food products) did not extend beyond the upper classes. European merchandise was always more difficult to find and more expensive further from the port of entry, and the number of such ports had not increased as much as they might have theoretically under the reforms. Limitations on exports translated into a further limitation on imports. Even the mining sector consumed less than might be expected because of royal taxation and high profits taken by intermediaries. Other producers might be rich in land, corn, or cattle and still be unable to buy many European goods for lack of an export product to earn money with which to buy imports. In Mexico, the shops of northern mining towns were far better stocked with imports than those in centers of livestock production, although they were equally distant from the port of entry at Veracruz. Similarly, early nineteenth-century travelers in the area around Buenos Aires expressed surprise at the rustic dwellings of families who owned many square miles of pasture and thousands of cattle. The travelers often attributed this circumstance to the supposedly barbarous inclinations of the inhabitants, but the shortcomings of the late colonial system of commercialization offer a less jaundiced explanation. Overall, however, despite its shortcomings, the reformed system resulted in slightly more equitable terms of trade between Spain and Spanish America.

Spanish Americans, inclined to qualify the benefits of liberalized trade by pointing out the negative impact of the invasion of Spanish merchants who so widely displaced their Spanish American counterparts in this period, also resented the intrusiveness of a new royal presence designed above all to extract increased revenues for the Crown. As a result of administrative reforms, the Spanish imperial officials tripled tax revenues (from six to eighteen million pesos, approximately) in the second half of the eighteenth century. The new funds made possible larger remissions of money to Spain, as well as the strengthening of the colonies' administrative and military apparatuses, and the years of increased revenues coincided with a number of colonial revolts, all of which included protests against the heavier burden of taxation.

Beyond the extraction of increased revenue, the purposes of administrative reform included important military and political goals. Strategic thinking played a large part in the government reforms of the Enlightenment era, above all in countries outside of the economic centers of western Europe. In Spanish America, the projects aimed at improving colonial agriculture featured a special effort to cultivate hemp to supply cordage for the Spanish navy. As well as being a means to an end, the Spanish authorities viewed administrative reform as an end in itself. They had become as convinced as their most acerbic critics that the present shortcomings of the colonial administration were so grave that they threatened the dissolution of the empire if allowed to continue unremedied.

The defects of the existing system became increasingly evident as administrators rationalized the upper levels of the imperial bureaucracy in Spain. In many cases, the jurisdiction of colonial magistrates overlapped, and superior authorities usually operated from so far away that the resulting conflicts of jurisdiction could not easily be untangled. Viceroys, high-court judges, governors, and corregidores were appointed in Spain, while the members of Creole or Indian town councils were chosen locally. All these officials had complex functions involving civil administration, taxation, justice, and defense, and their functions varied from place to place. The audiencias, for example, combined many other activities with their primary judicial role. Audiencias corresponded directly with the Council of the Indies concerning the promulgation of new initiatives determined by the Crown. The head of some audiencias, like that of Quito, also served as the executive administrator of the area under the jurisdiction of the audiencia.

Viceroys were charged with the administration, taxation, and defense of sprawling territories. Until the eighteenth century, all of Spanish America fell under the authority of two viceroys in Mexico or Peru. Even after the creation of two new viceroyalties in South America, each viceroy held responsibility for a territory too large to be administered effectively without a systematic delegation of authority that the imperial administrative structure did not provide. In the next tier below the viceroys, governors and corregidores (appointed by the Crown, in the first case, and the viceroy, in the second) exercised control over smaller areas. The governors were career bureaucrats who could expect to be transferred from one end of Spanish America to the other, but the corregidores were people of local influence who often paid for the privilege of exercising their office with its lucrative privileges of repartimiento (the forced distribution of goods). The Creole cabildos were municipal institutions patterned after the governing bodies of Spanish municipalities. Originally elected, Creole cabildos followed an evolution parallel to that of their Spanish counterparts in moving toward the permanent cooptation or purchase of membership by powerful families. Creole cabildos exercised administrative and lower-court jurisdiction far beyond the city limits into sparsely populated rural areas. Indian cabildos, on the other hand, existed only in areas of dense indigenous population. Their existence demonstrates the Spanish colonial tendency to delegate direct control over Indian populations to a native elite of preconquest origin, transformed now into a subordinate ally in the project of imperial domination. One finds another manifestation of the same tendency in the minor Indian nobility (called curacas in Peru and caciques elsewhere), who ruled over small groups of Indians in the name of the Spanish Crown and, in compensation, enjoyed a personal exemption from normal tribute payments as well as whatever other benefits they could extract from the Indians under their charge.

The temporary institutions called visitas and residencias added yet another layer of overlapping authority. The visitas were carried out by officials sent from Spain to investigate and resolve disputes concerning the conduct of one or more local representatives of the Crown.

The phenomenon of overlapping and conflicting authority among Crown representatives was an especially common cause of such disputes. The residencias were judiciary procedures carried out routinely upon the completion of a high colonial official's term in office by a magistrate appointed expressly for that purpose. Visitas and residencias occasioned torrents of hotly contradictory allegations. Aware of the limitations on their ability to arrive at the truth in such cases, imperial authorities usually exercised extreme restraint in intervening.

The eighteenth century witnessed numerous jurisdictional changes in the Spanish American empire. Two new viceroyalties were created—the viceroyalty of New Granada in 1717 (abolished in 1724 but reestablished in 1739), followed by the Río de la Plata in 1776. In addition, the administrators of several peripheral regions received greater authority within existing viceroyalties. In this way, Venezuela and Cuba gained more autonomy within the viceroyalty of New Granada; Cuba, Santo Domingo, and Guatemala within the viceroyalty of Mexico; and Chile within the viceroyalty of Peru. Most such modifications responded to the exigencies of imperial defense and took place in areas threatened by outside forces during the course of eighteenth-century warfare among European powers. A third and more ambitious type of reform sought to tighten the control exercised by the Crown throughout the administrative structure of the empire. At the top, a rationalized Ministry of the Indies preempted much of the power formerly held by the lethargic group of retired colonial administrators who composed the Council of the Indies. In Spanish America, the tightening of royal control centered on the most ambitious of the eighteenth-century imperial reforms, the creation of new administrative units known as *intendencies*.

Earlier instituted in Spain itself, the intendencies brought together administrative, fiscal, and military attributes based on a French model, and they represented an important step toward the goal of creating an effective, rationalized colonial bureaucracy staffed, for the most part, by peninsular Spaniards. Most intendants governed territories significantly smaller than the territories of former governors. More rigorous requirements pertained to the appointment of intendants, and they exercised broader powers over the municipal governments in their jurisdictions. Each intendant had a number of subordinates known as *subdelegados* in charge of the intendency's various geographical subdivisions. The rules governing the subdelegados revealed one of the same weaknesses that had plagued the former system, however, since the subdelegados did not earn salaries but instead paid themselves a portion of the tax revenues that they raised in their districts. Despite its drawbacks, this tax farming seemed superior to the system of repartimiento, which tended to disappear as a consequence.

How successful was this complex set of imperial reforms? If intended above all to prevent the collapse of the Spanish empire, the reforms must be judged failures since that collapse occurred relatively soon afterward. Nor did the reforms accomplish many of their lesser goals. Conflict among various colonial institutions only took new forms. Efforts to curb corruption in the colonial administration made at best modest progress. Nevertheless, if we compare the reformed system not only to what preceded it but also to what followed independence, the record appears more impressive. Throughout late colonial Spanish America, the reformed apparatus of government functioned more efficiently. In more than one region, many decades would pass before the governments of new Spanish American nations were able to match the administrative efficacy achieved by the Spanish colonial system on the eve of the wars of independence.

The success of the administrative reforms in imposing true centralized control had been limited from the beginning by the small number of peninsular Spaniards sent to deal with strongly entrenched local interests. Isolated Spanish officials found themselves surrounded by powerful Creole families and unsure of how much support they would receive in their struggle to enforce imperial directives. Even the most dedicated royal representatives often sought the support of one local faction against another, losing part of their administrative independence in the process. Less-dedicated imperial agents simply assumed the protection of the powerful local interests in the area to which they were assigned and profited handsomely from their complicity. The sway of local interests was difficult to resist. Locally powerful families could call on allies in the imperial administrative structure itself to punish the uncooperative Spanish official. They could oppose the official's indictments in the courts with equally scandalous accusations of their own. As a result, neither superior authorities in Spain nor later historians were able to determine whether the official at the center of any particular controversy had increased royal revenues through zealous honesty or ruthless greed. Likewise, one cannot tell whether the chorus of praise surrounding another official resulted from his probity and skill or from his ingratiating submission to dominant local interests. In spite of all the changes, avoiding conflict remained the key to success in the career of a colonial administrator, and provoking the wrath of the locally powerful always meant trouble.

The imperial reforms had also aimed, at least in part, to collaborate in the economic development of the colonies. Thus centralizing administrative reforms were accompanied by others that encouraged the initiative of local organizations such as guilds for mine owners, artisans, or merchants. The guilds (called *consulados* in the case of merchants) represented the interests of their members but also disciplined them and raised money through taxes authorized by the Crown, which was invested in local development projects. Their investments were no doubt more effective than those of the central administration, but the chosen projects logically favored above all the interests of the investing corporation. The mine owners of Mexico, for example, took the initiative in creating the architecturally lavish School of Mines, which the nineteenth-century historian Lucas Alamán subsequently criticized as a typical example of Creole ostentation but which others have praised for achieving an international state of the art in mining technology. The merchants' consulados spent considerable sums of money to build and maintain roads (such as the famous road linking Mexico City to the port of Veracruz and those connecting Buenos Aires to the interior regions of the Río de la Plata), to improve ports and navigation, and to support various kinds of technical education. The consulados also collected information and issued reports on local economic conditions, an activity that complemented similar efforts by royal bureaucrats. Later historians have evaluated these studies in glowing terms, partly because the eighteenth-century technocrats anticipated their own concerns. Their reports provide a glimpse of the desire to foment colonial progress through political power that animated the imperial reformers and also inspired many who eventually became leaders of the independence movements.

The desire to promote technical advancement went hand in hand with the reform of colonial military institutions. In the Río de la Plata, naval officers became the first teachers of mathematics, and military doctors introduced the practice of modern medicine. The military reforms sought to replace a welter of local forces with a much larger, uniformly organized militia and a professional army recruited in Spain. Spanish line soldiers were no longer to be drawn primarily from prisons, and efforts were made to improve the social position of officers by giving them special legal protection and a carefully graduated hierarchy of more than ceremonial importance. Some have found in these measures the roots of the militarism that blossomed after independence, and, though the real explanation must be more complex, the reforms did at least create an army where none had really existed before. Spanish naval installations also expanded in the period. In addition to the gigantic fortified base at Cartagena in New Granada,

Spanish officers and sailors crowded into new bases for naval operations at San Juan and Montevideo on the Atlantic and of Talcahuano on the South Pacific.

Finally, late colonial reformers also turned their attention to that *Church* most pervasive of Hispanic institutions, the Catholic church. Ecclesiastical organization had been firmly in the hands of the monarch since the earliest days of colonization, though the religious orders were less directly subordinated to royal control than the secular clergy. The wealth of the church varied from place to place in Spanish America, but nowhere was it inconsiderable. Mexico presented the greatest concentration of ecclesiastical wealth. Although it may not be true, as liberal polemicists later alleged, that the church owned almost all the land in Mexico, it certainly did own close to half. The situation was less extreme in New Granada and Peru, and still less in more recently settled areas like Venezuela and the Río de la Plata. However, even here the economic power of the church stood out clearly, as in the university city of Córdoba (Argentina) where the monastic orders owned most of the slaves. Overall, the management of ecclesiastical property was fairly efficient despite its critics. Enterprises administered by monastic orders, in particular, did well compared to the properties of private owners. The economic enterprises of the church prospered especially because of stronger links with both metropolitan culture and the money economy. The impact of that advantage could be detected in ecclesiastical ownership of large numbers of slaves and in the church's importance as a supplier of rural credit.

The Catholic church also dominated vast frontier regions from California to the upper Paraná, where its missions constituted practically the only Spanish settlement. Organized principally by the regu- *missions* lar clergy and most notably by the Jesuits, the missions were complex undertakings that fulfilled a crucial geopolitical, as well as evangeli- *Jesuits* cal, function and created relatively closed and autonomous societies on the fringes of the Spanish American empire. The expulsion of the Jesuits in the mid-eighteenth century resulted in the collapse of thriving mission frontiers, the most famous of which were the Guaraní missions of the upper Paraná and Uruguay rivers. The secular clergy and lay administrators who took the place of the Jesuits lacked their ability and their honesty, respectively, and the missions quickly crumbled. This is not the only respect in which the Society of Jesus showed itself uniquely capable of meeting the challenges of the day. The Jesuits organized their productive and commercial activities far more efficiently than did any other religious order, and they contributed some of the essential elements of the Spanish American Enlightenment. After the expulsion of the Jesuits, the secular clergy (composed of parish priests and their superiors) became dominant in the Spanish American church, a development no doubt satisfactory to the Crown, which had more control over the secular clergy, but one which represented a clear decline in the quality of the ecclesiastical presence in Spanish America.

Fortunately, the secular clergy of Spanish America improved as the end of the eighteenth century approached. It had always possessed considerable resources, but, as in Spain, the opulence of the church was spread very unevenly among the many dioceses, and, within each, it clustered around bishops and cathedrals, little affecting the majority of ordinary parishes. Most parish priests supplemented their incomes, especially in Indian lands, by charging their parishioners heavy fees for the performance of sacraments. In early nineteenth-century Tucumán, one comes across the example of a humble country family's funeral expenses to be paid from the inheritance: three plots of land were to be distributed among the heirs, and the house was to remain in the hands of the priest in lieu of payment. The conflictive relationship suggested by this case, fairly typical in the early eighteenth century, became less common as the century progressed, however. By the time of independence, many parish priests enjoyed enough personal prestige, in addition to their supposed heavenly influence and undeniable earthly power, to become political leaders on both sides of the struggle.

The secular clergy did much to collaborate with the reform projects of the Spanish Crown. Most often they simply obeyed as behooved loyal subjects, but sometimes they worked with enthusiasm. There exists a powerful image of the village priest of the time, who, in addition to being the villagers' spiritual pastor, was often their only link to a world of new sciences and techniques. One thinks of the engravings distributed throughout the Spanish American empire, from Buenos Aires to Guatemala, that show a priest carrying in his hands that new instrument of earthly salvation, a lancet for administering vaccinations. The reality was surely more complex and nuanced than this representation, since the secular clergy of Spanish America had the same defects and virtues as the rest of the imperial administration, of which, in many ways, they formed an integral part. There are signs that the church hierarchy tended to devote much attention to the cultivation of mundane bureaucratic careers. The clergy's general docility in the face of royal authority presents one example, and the occurrence of a number of indecorous forms of self-aggrandizement, another. Still, the secular clergy provided one of the principal vehicles of the Enlightenment in Spanish America, better able to transmit renovating impulses than the secular bureaucracy, which was smaller and less trusted by the people. Whatever its limitations, the Catholic church remained, as it had been since the conquest, the right arm of Spanish colonialism in America and the only branch of royal administration that the Spanish Americans themselves did not consider totally alien.

Brazil, even more than Spanish America, had been transformed in the course of the eighteenth century. Until the end of the seventeenth century, Brazil consisted essentially of a sugar-producing core area, located on the northeastern Atlantic coast, surrounded by a periphery that supplied the nucleus with slaves and cattle. The eighteenth century saw an extension of the core inland in the direction of newly discovered gold and diamond fields and an expansion of the periphery to the north and south, extending Portuguese control to tropical forest regions in Amazonia and temperate grasslands in Rio Grande do Sul.

By the early 1700s, the Brazilian sugar economy had entered a long, gradual decline owing in part to forces from outside Brazil. The origins of the decline can be traced to the Dutch invasion and occupation of Pernambuco during the first half of the seventeenth century. Although successfully repelled by Brazilian forces, the invaders took away with them from Pernambuco an understanding of sugar planting that they then applied quite successfully in Dutch territories in the Caribbean. What had been almost a Brazilian monopoly then became a major colonial enterprise of the seaborne empires of the North Atlantic powers—first Holland, then England and France, whose sugar-producing Caribbean possessions were small territorially but powerful economically. The European markets for sugar remained fairly limited in this period, and Brazilian producers suffered from the strong competition of their new rivals in the Antilles. By the end of the seventeenth century, the sugar coast of Brazil had lagged technically and organizationally behind Jamaica and Saint Domingue. From this point on, the Brazilian sugar industry endured two and a half centuries of gradual decline interrupted only when events such as the slave revolt in Saint Domingue devastated its international competitors or when a temporary combination of protectionism and economic growth in other parts of Brazil provided a vigorous internal market for Brazilian sugar.

Contributing to the eclipse of the old core area of Brazilian settlement in the eighteenth century was the loss of a lucrative contraband trade in Spanish silver. During the union of the Spanish and Portuguese crowns between 1580 and 1640, Portuguese merchants had penetrated the trading networks of the viceroyalty of Peru and were able to siphon off a very considerable portion of Spanish silver through the "backdoor" of Potosí—Buenos Aires—to Bahia, the seventeenth-century capital of the Brazilian sugar coast. Displaced Spanish merchants had long denounced the Portuguese traders as New Christians (converts from Judaism—which many were) and lost no time in having them expelled from Spanish American cities when Portugal regained its independence. Forty years later, in 1680, the Portuguese reopened the surreptitious flow of silver through the Río de la Plata by establishing the port city of Colônia do Sacramento across from Buenos Aires. By that time, though, the silver production of Potosí was decreasing, and much of the silver that reached Colônia was shipped directly to Europe, bypassing Bahia.

The weakening of the Brazilian sugar economy in the core area of original settlement had unexpected consequences in the fringe areas, where some settlers still practiced barter with the Indians for dyewood or for small quantities of gold and precious stones, the very earliest form of Portuguese activity in Brazil. One consequence of sugar's decline was the increasing importance of cattle herding in the arid *sertão*, the region inland from the fertile coast of Bahia and Pernambuco that had long provided coastal sugar plantations with meat on the hoof and with oxen. In times of economic slowdown, herding became a preferred subsistence activity. To the north, the coast of Ceará and Maranhão slowly attracted Portuguese settlement associated with the hunt for Indian slaves, but it was to the south of the northeastern sugar coast, around São Paulo, that slave-hunting increased most rapidly in this period. The boundaries of the Captaincy of São Paulo expanded immensely as its slaving expeditions explored vast reaches of the Brazilian interior. The proliferation of both ranching and slaving can be linked to the gradual ebbing of the money economy founded on the cultivation and exportation of sugar. Ranching provided an acceptable way of life that was only loosely linked to the market economy. As for the more intensive hunting of Indian slaves, it responded to the sugar planter's diminishing ability to pay the gold or silver demanded by the trans-Atlantic trade in enslaved Africans. As the fringe areas of Portuguese settlement became more intensively exploited, they expanded Brazil territorially. In 1620, slave hunters from São Paulo began to destroy Spanish Jesuit missions in lands formally part of the viceroyalty of Peru, and they continued to push south and west into Spanish-claimed lands for the rest of the century.

The core and fringe areas of Portuguese settlement in South America produced societies distinct in many ways. Let us consider first the core area of sugar plantations (*fazendas*) dominated by the figure of the *senhor do engenho*, the planter who owned his own grinding mill. The sugar fazendas were worked by large numbers of African slaves (and much smaller numbers of Indian slaves), who contributed to the rapid process of racial mixing and put a lasting African stamp on Brazilian culture. Influenced by their own nostalgia, apologists of Brazilian plantation society have called its social relations patriarchal, and the relations between Brazilian slaves and masters arguably did display a less relentlessly profit-oriented, "rational" exploitation of slave labor than the relations characterized by the plantations of the Antilles. Despite the brutality of the process of transplantation, many elements of African life were able to take root in Brazil. By adding a Christian tint to social and religious traditions brought from Africa, Brazilian slaves were able to conserve much of their culture. In addition, the continued importation of African slaves until the middle of the nineteenth century made Africa a living presence for Brazilians far more than for the people of Jamaica or the United States, for example.

In the Brazilian fringe regions to the north, south, and west of the sugar lands, a different sort of society developed, ethnically more a mix of Indian and Portuguese. The cattle-herding people of the arid sertão fit this description precisely. Ironically, the slave hunters who roamed the tropical forests of the north and the savannas of the south were also mestizos and speakers of an Indian language. As in parts of Spanish America, the imperative to populate and the absence of Portuguese and Spanish women resulted in a variety of demographically fertile polygamous arrangements that horrified more than one European traveler. Life in the fringe areas was simpler and harder for the Portuguese settlers than in the sugar lands. In spite of the slow eclipse of sugar, the planters of the central coast lived in a comparative opulence viewed by the tough cattle barons of the interior with a mixture of envy and scorn.

The whole Brazilian population numbered only about 400,000 at the beginning of the eighteenth century. Slaves were more numerous than Portuguese or mestizos, and these, in turn, outnumbered the Indians. Yet these people had already acquired three million square kilometers of territory for the Portuguese Crown. The huge plateau that underlies much of Brazil presents obstacles at the coast, where there are relatively few harbors or navigable rivers and mountains rise immediately from a narrow coastal plain. Climbing to the edge of the plateau, however, the Portuguese came upon a landscape in which the primary obstacle to be overcome was distance itself. Brazil thus escaped the severe compartmentalization imposed on Spanish America by its geography. The rivers of the Brazilian plateau, passable by canoe

into the heart of the South American continent, became the primary
routes of expansion into the fringe areas. The Rio São Francisco, which
flows a thousand miles through the arid backlands before reaching the
sea north of Bahia, provided a vital artery linking the sugar coast with
the regions to the south where gold was discovered in 1698 by people
from São Paulo.

gold
and
diamonds

The discovery of gold and later diamonds changed the course of
Portuguese settlement in the eighteenth century. The Paulistas who
found gold in central Brazil worked with some success to keep outsiders away for almost a decade. In 1708, however, newcomers clashed
violently with the Paulistas and broke the attempted monopoly of the
mining zone. Thereafter, outsiders streamed in from Portugal, from
the sugar coast, and from its cattle-raising hinterland. Powerful rural
families moved south along the Rio São Francisco, bringing their
slaves to pan for gold in the area named for the mines, Minas Gerais. In
1720, Minas Gerais was removed from the jurisdiction of São Paulo
and became an independent captaincy with its capital at Ouro Prêto,
the first of the architecturally impressive gold-rush cities built in the
mountains. Brazil's new golden wealth also brought a revival of slave
importations and attracted many Portuguese immigrants to the entrepreneurial opportunities surrounding mining. Due to this influx of
people with no parallel in Spanish America, the small Brazilian population climbed toward three million at the end of the eighteenth
century. By that time, Brazil's "gold cycle" had extended its effects far
west into Goiás and Mato Grosso before plunging from boom to bust.
The population that mining had attracted to central Brazil then drifted
away from the splendid baroque mining towns in large numbers to
raise livestock in the semiarid interior. Of the cities that had prospered
from the gold rush, only Rio de Janeiro continued to thrive. The capital
had been moved there from Bahia in 1763 as a concession to the new
demographic and economic importance of the central region, and its
district remained an oasis of rice, cotton, and sugar production.

immigration
in flux

The mining boom of the first half of the eighteenth century further
accelerated Brazil's territorial expansion toward the temperate south
and the equatorial north. In the far south, the well-watered grasslands
of Rio Grande do Sul supported a sort of ranching similar to that
practiced in the neighboring Spanish territories of the Río de la Plata.
The ranchers of Rio Grande do Sul raised mules to supply the transportation needs of Minas Gerais, exported hides to equip the warring
imperial armies of Europe, and produced dried beef rations for the
slaves of the sugar coast, roughly in that order of importance. As for
the extreme north of Brazil, it had long been isolated from the rest by

winds so contrary that for people in Maranhão, the colonial capital at Bahia was a longer voyage away than Lisbon. Maranhão passed through two stages in the eighteenth century. During the first, dominated by the Jesuit missions until they were expelled at mid-century, the principal activity was trade with the Indians of the Amazon basin. During the second stage, Portugal's enlightened despotism created monopoly trading companies to encourage the large-scale commercial cultivation of rice and cotton. The new plantation economy quickly exhausted the supplies of Indian labor and commenced the importation of thousands of African slaves. The sugar economy, meanwhile, had recovered temporarily from its long decline but collapsed at century's end to the production levels of a hundred years earlier.

Until about 1770, in spite of renewed importations of slaves, the sugar coast remained unable to compete with the mining zone for enslaved African labor, while in the Caribbean, French and then British sugar producers continued to reduce Brazil's share of the European market. The textile mills of Europe's industrial revolution stimulated the production of cotton, as did the war of independence in the British colonies of North America, and other warfare between European powers created opportunities for Brazilian agricultural producers in general, except for sugar producers. Although still important, sugar would never again dominate the economy, even given the precipitous decline of gold mining after 1770. At the opening of the nineteenth century, Rio de Janeiro and the peripheral areas of Rio Grande do Sul and Maranhão led a Brazilian economy still reeling from two successive cycles of boom and bust.

The commercial policies of the Portuguese Crown also influenced the economic opportunities of Brazilian producers during the 1700s. Portugal and its colonies had been integrated totally into the British economic sphere early in the period. Brazilian gold, even more than Spanish American silver, found only a brief stopping place in the Iberian mother country before flowing north to the more dynamic European economies across the Pyrenees. As Brazilian historians have pointed out, gold transshipped in Portugal became a notable stimulus to Britain's industrial revolution. Anglo-Portuguese commercial arrangements protected the winemakers of Portugal but not the agricultural products of Brazil, which did not find easy access to the British market. The only effective Crown promotion of Brazilian agricultural expansion occurred under the direction of the Marquis of Pombal. His system of privileged private trading companies succeeded in Maranhão, which had only to enter a waiting market, but a similar monopoly company failed to win a larger market share for the Brazilian sugar producers of the northeast coast. The sugar-planting aristocracy of Pernambuco, for example, had a long history of friction with the merchants of the port city of Recife and refused to cede control of the local market to an overseas trading company. Once the planters of Maranhão themselves had become well established thanks to the stimulus of the official trading company, they began to demand a greater share of the profits of the overseas trade. As a result, in 1789 the official trading companies were disbanded in what many short-sightedly considered a planters' victory.

The Portuguese alliance with Great Britain prevented most of the interruptions of trans-Atlantic communication suffered by the Spanish empire at this time. On the other hand, the later British blockade of Napoleonic Europe and the eventual fall of Portugal to Napoleon's armies dealt heavy blows to the sugar industry after 1800. The vicissitudes of the Brazilian economy can be traced easily in exportation figures. In 1760, near the apogee of gold mining, the value of Brazil's total exports reached almost 5 million pounds sterling, with 2.4 million from sugar and 2.2 million from gold. After fifteen years of declining yields, however, the value of total exports dropped to 3 million in 1776. A very slow recovery followed but, by 1810, the figure had reached only 3.5 million pounds. A variety of agricultural exports were responsible for the gains. In 1814, for example, the value of total exports had risen to about 4 million pounds sterling, with only 1.2 million from sugar and a mere .3 million from gold. Despite its long decline, sugar retained first place in the list of export earnings into the early nineteenth century, and not even in the moment of its greatest splendor did the mining boom dominate the export economy of Brazil to the extent that silver dominated that of Spanish America.

The enduring importance of sugar left a clear imprint on the demography and social organization of Brazil. On the eve of independence, the majority of the population was concentrated along the sugar-growing northeastern coast, where black slaves constituted almost half of all residents while whites composed less than a quarter, Indians less than a tenth, and people of mixed race about a fifth. Brazilian society in this period appeared less divided along rigid caste lines than Spanish American society, mostly because the ubiquitous institution of slavery reduced the need for a caste system to stabilize race relations. The greater importance of immigration originating from the mother country also contributed to distinguish Brazilian race relations from the Spanish American pattern. In terms of social organization, the power of Brazilian sugar and cotton planters closely linked to the Atlantic economy had only minor parallels in Spanish America, where Spanish merchant houses were generally ascendant over land-owners. Economically powerful and politically influential, the plant-ers of the northeast coast and Rio de Janeiro had defeated the hege-monic pretensions of the major Portuguese merchant houses even before independence. The large landowners of other Brazilian regions did not enjoy the same economic preeminence because of their more tenuous links to the Atlantic economy. Their holdings might be even larger, but their products earned less, and unlike the producers of valuable plantation crops, they dealt on disadvantageous terms with merchants involved in long-distance trade. In compensation, however, private armies of mounted retainers endowed the cattle barons of the livestock-raising interior and far south with an autonomous local power base greater than any other in Brazil.

In sum, the relations between Brazilian producers and the Por-tuguese merchants of port cities like Bahia, Recife, and Rio de Janeiro contrasted with the relations between their counterparts in Spanish America. From the earliest settlement of Brazil, a profitable agricul-tural export sector in the hands of a homogeneous landowning class confronted a colonizing power smaller and weaker than Spain. By the end of the colonial period, the landowners of the northeast had the support of local merchants in their fight against the monopoly trading companies that represented the mercantile interests of Portugal. The strongest representatives of trans-Atlantic commerce in the period resided in Rio de Janeiro, which had benefited directly from the gold boom and from a plantation economy more diversified than that of the northeast. Not until the eighteenth century did tiny Portugal succeed in creating a colonial administration comparable to Spain's of the sixteenth century, and the Portuguese ability to impose a cohesive system of mercantile exploitation on its colonies was correspondingly weaker.

Neither the Portuguese nor the Spanish Crown had sufficient resources to carry out the exploration and conquest of the New World alone. Where the Spanish Crown had rewarded the conquerors with grants of Indian labor, the Portuguese Crown had offered grants of land (doações) to private individuals willing to bear the costs of settle-ment in the name of the king. The original pattern of Brazilian settle-ment consisted in a string of private plantation enterprises extending the length of the Atlantic coast. The subsequent transition from pri-vate control in the king's name to direct administration by royal officials occurred much more quickly in Spanish America than in Brazil. The Portuguese Crown sent a royal governor to Bahia in the middle of the sixteenth century but did not buy back all donatory

privileges until the eighteenth century. Furthermore, the extension of
Portuguese royal control over private settlement never achieved the
level of Spanish royal control, so that Brazilian colonial officials had to
behave even more circumspectly than Spanish American officials in
the face of the locally powerful. The Spanish Crown's resounding royal
subjugation of the rebellious conquerors had no Brazilian parallel,
partly because, in the two centuries before the discovery of gold and
diamonds, there was simply less at stake in Brazil. Unlike the encomenderos of Spanish America, Brazilian landowners were not beholden to the Crown for their labor force, which they acquired by
virtue of their buying power in the African slave trade. Nor were
Brazilian planters generally subject to the same kind of juridical uncertainties regarding land tenure that often kept Spanish American hacendados at the mercy of the most recent royal decree. In Brazil, far
more than in Spanish America, wealth and landowning went together.

The concentration of wealth and power among landowners in
Brazil reduced the influence of an administrative structure otherwise
superficially similar to that of Spanish America. Both colonial systems had municipal councils that became the patrimonial strongholds
of local notables, and the officials of royal administration seemed
roughly equivalent. However, the Brazilian system afforded local powers greater autonomy, and they almost always dominated the institutions that royal agents otherwise might have used to subdue them.
When the accelerating rhythm of imperial conflict brought a militarization of Brazilian life in the eighteenth century, regular line troops
dominated the panorama only in the far south. Throughout the rest of
Brazil, the new instruments of coercion were militias organized and
led most often by powerful landowners.

Royal authority often played the role of timid arbiter when opposing groups clashed within Brazil, as in the early eighteenth-century
conflicts in Minas Gerais and Pernambuco. Perhaps the leeway accorded to local power constitutes one of the secrets of Brazil's political
unity after independence (along with a large measure of administrative
continuity), allowing central authority to better adapt to the same
kind of centrifugal forces that broke the more ambitious Spanish system apart. In any case, the Portuguese colonial administrative structure developed more gradually than the Spanish. Not until the period
of union between the Portuguese and Spanish crowns did Lisbon create institutions of colonial administration analogous to those of Seville. In Brazil itself, the most important changes occurred during the
eighteenth century as additional administrative districts were created,

the gold rush populated new areas of the interior, and the colonial capital was moved from Bahia to Rio de Janeiro.

The ascendancy of Brazilian landowners made itself felt in ecclesiastical, as well as administrative, affairs. The Jesuits were the most influential religious order in Brazil, even more predominant than in Spanish America, but they faced tremendous opposition from Brazilian landowners hungry for Indian slaves. The situation has obvious parallels in Spanish America, with the difference that in Brazil the advocates of Indian welfare had stronger enemies and a weaker ally in the Portuguese Crown. Jesuit initiatives among the Indians prospered only in the eighteenth century, and then only in the remote mission frontiers of the Amazon basin. The expulsion of the Jesuits from Brazil in 1759 therefore caused much less disruption than their expulsion from Spanish America a few years later. As for the secular clergy, their subordination to Brazil's powerful landowners appears even clearer. Most priests in the sugar lands lived on plantations, at the behest and under the direct control of the planters in whose chapels they officiated. Employment in such private chapels often went preferentially to a son of the planter, and sons of the landowning aristocrats pervaded the church hierarchy far more than in Spanish America. If a crusading spirit was notably absent in this church that was rather too well integrated into colonial society, abusive immoralities must have been less common than some observers, more zealous than discerning, would have us believe. At least the curates supported by sugar planters had less need to extract exorbitant fees from parishioners for the performance of the sacraments, as was often true in Spanish America.

CHAPTER II

THE CRISIS

OF INDEPENDENCE

(1810–1825)

THE NEW WORLD EMPIRES of Portugal and Spain crumbled rapidly in the early nineteenth century. By 1825, Portugal had lost all of its American territories, while Spain retained only Cuba and Puerto Rico. What brought the long period of colonial rule to such a sudden end? Some historians cite long-term causes going back as far as the time of original conquest, while others emphasize an accumulation of more immediate causes in the second half of the eighteenth century. Our discussion will begin with the more complicated and protracted crisis of independence in Spanish America, turning finally to the Brazilian case for comparative perspective.

In the case of Spanish America, at least, the eighteenth-century imperial reforms failed to reformulate a viable colonial compact. As the reforms opened new opportunities within the colonial economy, they also sharpened people's awareness of the privileged intermediate position reserved for the merchants of the Iberian Peninsula in the trade between Spanish America and the industrializing nations of northern Europe. The wars of independence may be viewed, in that respect, as a struggle by Spanish American producers to acquire better access to overseas markets and secure a larger share of the profits.

The administrative reforms of the same period had created other sources of friction because of their centralizing tendencies and their preference for employing peninsular personnel. While not completely successful, the reformers had made themselves unpopular with Spanish American elites by increasing the efficiency of central control enough to cause serious problems for local interests. The reformers staffed administrative posts with peninsular bureaucrats in an effort to tighten effective imperial control. It was often this augmented control—rather than Creole resentment of the Spaniards' preferment in bureaucratic careers—that constituted the chief irritant for Spanish American elites. The same might be said of the similar resentment

[handwritten margin notes: "XVIII reforms failed"; "tightened imperial control causes resentment"]

directed at the swarm of peninsular merchants who crossed the Atlantic in the second half of the eighteenth century. As they established themselves in port after port and took over trade networks throughout Spanish America, they provoked a widespread enmity among many besides the local merchants directly displaced by their triumph.

One should not, however, exaggerate the tensions resulting from the modest successes of late imperial reform. They raised legitimate concerns for the long-term, perhaps, but hardly presaged the sudden, catastrophic breakdown that in fact occurred. What, then, of another possible explanation for the abrupt cancellation of the recently reformulated colonial compact—the influence of Enlightenment ideas that had steadily gained currency over the course of the eighteenth century?

For the most part, the ideological ferment of the Enlightenment had a less-than-revolutionary impact on political thinking in the Iberian world. New ideas advanced, during much of the century, in the context of scrupulous fidelity to the absolutist crowns that, in spite of all their vacillations, were themselves the leading forces for change. Most criticisms of the colonial order implied no rejection of the monarchy or the ideal of imperial unity, and, far from suggesting a total break with the past among the enlightened thinkers of both the peninsula and its New World colonies, devotion to the reformist sovereign appeared as a rationalized version of older, mystical conceptions of the monarch's role.

By the final years of the eighteenth century, such a vision was not without its skeptics on both sides of the Atlantic. Numerous localized rebellions shook widely separated areas of Spanish America during this period. Though often cited as precursors of independence, there was in fact no direct connection, and most of these revolts displayed only a tenuous link to the new political ideologies. Examined at close range they reveal an assortment of social and economic motivations, many of which do not appear particularly new. Their immediate causes lay most often in tensions created by the administrative reforms—especially the new taxation policies carried out by zealous or greedy bureaucrats—but the response varied greatly from place to place.

The most widespread phenomenon of this kind was the caste war that ravaged Peru in the last two decades of the eighteenth century. Combining nostalgia for the pre-Hispanic past with declarations of loyalty to a Spanish king supposedly ignorant of the abuses committed in his name, the Peruvian rebellions exacerbated existing strains between socioracial groups: Indians against whites and mestizos in Lower Peru, Indians and mestizos against whites in Upper Peru. More than antecedents for the later colonial revolt against Spain, the caste wars provide a clue to the Andean area's obstinate devotion to the loyalist cause; Peruvian elites doubted their ability to dominate the indigenous and mixed-blood population without imperial support.

Other late colonial rebellions managed to present a socially united front, possibly because they were more localized. The *comunero* uprising in the area around the town of Socorro, New Granada, provides an example of this pattern. Because they were localized, however, such rebellions made less impact than did the Peruvian caste conflicts. In many ways, they resembled the scattered small-scale protests that had erupted here and there sporadically since the time of the conquest. Rather than revealing new problems, such episodes betrayed the continuing presence of structural weaknesses that only became more critical as imperial rule encountered new obstacles in the coming years.

Around 1790, however, signs of discontent did appear that we can confidently consider harbingers of the later movements for independence. To the alarm of colonial administrators, seditious initiatives surfaced in cities as far apart as Bogotá (New Granada), where Antonio Nariño produced his Spanish translation of the Declaration of the Rights of Man, Santiago (Chile), where a "French conspiracy" was discovered in 1790, Buenos Aires (Río de la Plata), where French activists appear to have inspired an abortive slave revolt with republican overtones at almost the same time, and Ouro Prêto (Brazil), where a secessionist republican conspiracy had been quashed a few months earlier. All of these rebellions failed. Possibly the most important result of them was the creation of martyrs like Tiradentes, the executed popular agitator of the Brazilian episode, and a crop of political exiles like Francisco Miranda. A friend of Thomas Jefferson and a lover of Catherine the Great (to mention only two of his many exploits), Miranda brought the aspirations of Latin American radicals to the attention of European powers eager to see the dissolution of the Iberian empires. However impressive this cycle of revolts and its heroes, though, the limitations are important to keep in mind. Such movements developed in urban settings while Latin America remained overwhelmingly rural, and they involved very narrow circles of literate people with access to revolutionary ideologies from abroad. Without doubt, their significance has been magnified, first by the imperial officials eager to take credit for repressing them and later by historians seeking precursors of national independence movements.

These ideologically oriented rebellions should be understood, for the most part, as symptoms of a global process destined to undermine the power of the Iberian monarchies in Europe and the New World. Within Spanish America and Brazil, French ideas continued to percolate through urban groups even during the period of relative quiescence that followed the failed conspiracies of the period. As soon as the independence movements started in the second decade of the nineteenth century, petty bureaucrats and parish priests all over Latin America immediately demonstrated a mastery of republican discourse that could only have been acquired over a period of years. Elsewhere in the world, a republican United States and a revolutionary France provided striking precedents for Latin Americans interested in change, while international events brought change ever closer. Amid the great clashes of revolutionary and counterrevolutionary forces abroad in the world, Spain and Portugal exhibited dismaying impotence. At the turn of the nineteenth century, even the most faithful subjects of the Iberian monarchies were forced to contemplate the possibility that those crowns, too, might disappear.

Both Spain and Portugal experienced tremendous difficulties in maintaining contact with their overseas empires. Spain's alliance with revolutionary France in 1795 had particularly disastrous consequences because it brought the Spanish into a long-term conflict with Great Britain. British sea power controlled the Atlantic and constituted an all but insuperable barrier separating Spain from its colonies. The deployment of Spanish military power to the New World became more difficult, and the maintenance of a Spanish commercial monopoly all but impossible. The result was a series of emergency measures authorizing the progressive opening of Spanish American trade, both within the internal routes of the empire and beyond, with neutral powers and their colonies. This lowering of trade restrictions with the outside world contradicted the spirit of earlier reforms and indicated the higher risks of wartime navigation rather than a continuing policy of commercial liberalization.

The Spanish Crown's cautious opening of trade with other countries elicited tremendous enthusiasm in the colonies. Atlantic coast colonies from Havana to Buenos Aires immediately appreciated the commercial advantages of the new arrangement and became increasingly attached to it. Their new isolation from Spanish political and economic power allowed them to explore possibilities of which they had not dreamed before. According to one enlightened economist in Buenos Aires, that city now lay at the very center of world trade and could exploit its geographical advantage using its own resources. The commercial horizons of Buenos Aires had suddenly expanded to include such places as Hamburg, Baltimore, Istanbul, and the sugar

islands of the Indian Ocean. With more imposing powers like England and Spain temporarily absent from trade competition, the South
American port city gained confidence in its own economic potential
and acquired a new sense of how its interests diverged from those of
Spain.

Such grand aspirations soon encountered grand frustrations to
match them. The sea link with Spain was not totally broken until the
British victory at Trafalgar in 1805, and the economy of the colonies as
a whole did not share the windfall profits of merchant speculators in
Spanish American ports during the years of imperial disruption. Even
as Buenos Aires began to fancy itself the center of world trade, it
accumulated vast unsold stocks of one of its most important products,
cowhides. In nearby Montevideo, the stacks of unsold hides towered
higher than the city's modest houses. In the pastures around these two
Platine port cities, the slaughter of animals slowed for lack of an
export outlet. In Cuba, the expanding sugar plantations and coffee
farms faced enormous oscillations in the market price of their products. A disheartening slump began in 1796 and lasted until the end of
the century, when five good years were followed by another slump.
Such unpredictable conditions provoked even more impatience than
the earlier uniform limitations and increased the desire for economic
self-determination on the part of colonial producers and merchants.

Desires for political self-determination also grew as Spain's isolation from its colonies progressively undermined its ability to govern
them. A process of political distancing followed the economic split
between Spain and Spanish America but eventually outpaced it. During the years between 1795 and 1810, the yawning economic and
political gap erased the gains made by the Bourbon Crown in its
attempt to reassert firm control of Spanish America over the course of
the eighteenth century. In the semi-isolation of 1795–1810, while
some Spanish American thinkers surely looked forward to the rupture
of imperial bonds in the hopes of true mercantile autonomy after
independence, the producers who suffered alternating prosperity and
isolation in the last years of the colonial regime often viewed political
independence more as a means to establish new, more reliable links of
economic dependence with European countries other than Spain.

These alternatives had not yet been clearly formulated when imperial warfare in Europe precipitated the process of political independence in America. In 1806, a British expeditionary force appeared
suddenly outside Buenos Aires and captured the city after a brief fight
with the local garrison. The capital of the viceroyalty of the Río de la

Plata had been, on paper at least, one of the chief military centers of Spanish America, and its conquerors won a rich booty in precious metals to be paraded triumphantly through the streets of London. The British were astonished at the reception given them by Spanish officials eager to swear fidelity to a new king and by clergy who preached obliging sermons on the divine origins of all power. Eventually, however, Santiago Liniers, a French-born naval officer in the service of Spain, gathered a force in Montevideo and repelled the British invaders. The next year, a larger British expedition captured Montevideo but failed to recapture Buenos Aires, better defended by militias than it had been by the garrison of regular Spanish troops. Under pressure from the militias, the audiencia of that city removed the Spanish viceroy who had twice fled before the British and replaced him temporarily with Liniers. A tenuous formal legality remained in place, but the substance of colonial rule had disintegrated in Buenos Aires, where the militias had, in effect, unseated a viceroy.

By 1808, Napoleon's occupation of Spain and the imprisonment of the Spanish king, Ferdinand VII, appeared to foreshadow the utter ruin of Spanish imperial power, and within two years the process of political independence had begun throughout most of Spanish America. The French invasion of the peninsula eventually converted Spain's former enemy, Great Britain, into an ally, and the British navy allowed a reopening of the Atlantic lines of communication between the Iberian power and its rebellious colonies. Reestablished communications offered Spanish provisional governments the opportunity to reassert imperial control in Spanish America, but their own war of independence against French occupation left few resources with which to do so.

In Spanish America, Creoles and peninsulars vied for control of caretaker governments set up in the name of the imprisoned Spanish king. Peninsular elements themselves moved to replace Viceroy Iturrigaray of New Spain in 1808 when he appeared ready to allow the Creole-dominated cabildo to form a caretaker government in Mexico City, and the predominantly peninsular audiencia quickly sanctioned the move. In Buenos Aires, Liniers, the French hero who had repulsed the British invasions—now viceroy himself—naturally lost influence when France and Spain became enemies. The peninsular-dominated cabildo of Buenos Aires tried to depose him but failed when the Creole militias rescued his authority at the last moment. Across the Río de la Plata, peninsular officers in control of the garrison of Montevideo formed their own caretaker junta to challenge Liniers's authority. In

Montevideo as well as in Mexico City, peninsular elements themselves had delivered the first blows to the institutions of colonial administration making things change in order that they remain the same.

All over Spanish America, peninsulars and Creoles struggled to control the institutions of legitimate authority, but the initiative quickly passed to the Creoles. In Chile, for example, the death of the royal governor in 1808 allowed Creoles to seat their own candidate for interim governor over the opposition of the audiencia. Although not sympathetic to the more radical Creole plans, the interim governor created a Creole majority in the cabildo of Santiago as a way of strengthening his own hand against the audiencia. Governor, cabildo, and audiencia then battered each other to bits, bringing the irremediable decline of Spanish institutional authority in Chile. In Buenos Aires, the Creole militias were able to force into exile Liniers's main political rival, the peninsular merchant and leader of the cabildo, Martín de Alzaga.

Creoles elsewhere were moving into open rebellion by 1809. One such area was Upper Peru, where the audiencia itself revealed a deep internal split of the sort undermining colonial institutions all over Spanish America. When the president of the audiencia became implicated in the intrigues of the Spanish princess Carlota Joaquina (the sister of Ferdinand VII, married to the Portuguese regent in Rio de Janeiro), the other members of the audiencia set up their own caretaker junta. An uprising of mestizos in La Paz brought a more threatening character to the revolution and led the viceroys in both Lima and Buenos Aires to suppress it with unaccustomed ruthlessness. In Quito that same year, the royal president-intendant was removed from power by a group of Creole aristocrats who assumed power themselves until captured and executed by troops under the order of the viceroy of New Granada. Although the rebels had governed ostensibly in the name of the imprisoned Spanish king, they met reprisals of a severity usually reserved for people of more humble origin.

Institutional infighting and outbreaks of open rebellion prepared the way for the coming revolution. The remaining colonial officials throughout Spanish America revealed the pervasive weakness of the system through their vacillations, as when the viceroy of New Granada allowed himself to be hemmed in by the creation of an advisory junta in 1809. The old institutional framework was crumbling, and even peninsular interests within the colonies began to operate outside that structure. The collapse of these institutions was critical, since the far-flung territories of Spanish America lacked the cohesive force of national community apparent in metropolitan Spain. Neither loyalty

to the imprisoned monarch nor faith in the future order promised by
Spanish resistance governments was able to maintain the unity of a
Spanish America riven by rapidly increasing tensions.

One tension involved redefining the relationship between Spain
and its former colonies. In 1809 and 1810, no end of the French occupation of the Iberian Peninsula was in sight, while the British navy
guaranteed that Napoleon would not be able to extend his conquest to
the Spanish colonies. In 1810, Spanish resistance was finally cornered
in the southern port city of Cádiz. To attract Spanish American support, the regency created in Cádiz offered the colonies an improved
status as overseas provinces with elected representation in a liberalized empire. In economic terms, the British alliance—without which
the anti-Napoleonic forces could not survive—assured the end of the
old Spanish monopoly on trade with Spanish America. The last viceroy of the Río de la Plata himself laid the foundations of the economy
of independent Argentina by authorizing free trade with Great Britain.

The sharpest tension concerned the role that peninsular Spaniards
would continue to play in Spanish America. When Creole elites attempted to displace peninsular merchants and bureaucrats in the initial phases of the crisis, imperial administrators put themselves at
the service of crumbling metropolitan authority. The drastic punishments meted out to Creole rebels in Quito and Upper Peru contrasted
with the conciliatory stance taken later toward the peninsular rebels
who had organized in Montevideo to resist the Creole-backed Viceroy Liniers. By 1809, South American Creoles viewed viceroys, intendants, and audiencias primarily as agents of Spanish supremacy
over the native-born upper classes. This polarization simplified enormously the early stages of the revolution in the southern continent. In
the Antilles and Mexico, on the other hand, other tensions counter-
acted the conflict dividing peninsulars from local Creole elites and
delayed the Creole initiatives toward independence. For Cuban sugar
planters, the Haitian slave revolt had provided a shocking lesson in the
dangers of divisions within the white slave-owning population, while
in Mexico, the Indian and then mestizo uprisings that started the
revolution failed when Creole and peninsular elites joined forces to
suppress the threat from below. Consequently, our examination of
the Spanish American wars of independence will begin with South
America.

In 1810, the anti-Napoleonic forces in Spain entered the next stage
of their seemingly inexorable collapse. By this time, they effectively
governed only the port of Cádiz and its immediate vicinity, including a
few islands in the bay. An angry mob broke up the inept Supreme Junta

of Seville that had failed to avert the disaster, and a regency was formed in Cádiz to take its place. The new government had even more problems than the preceding one. Though the Supreme Junta of Seville had experienced difficulty projecting its authority, the legitimacy of that authority had been widely recognized in the colonies. The newly formed government in Cádiz, on the other hand, was essentially self-appointed, and its claim to legitimacy was much more dubious. The crisis of legitimacy precipitated another moment of self-definition in the Spanish American revolution. In 1808, a wave of Spanish patriotism and loyalty to the Crown had swept the colonies, and in meetings all over Spanish America people had sworn allegiance to the imprisoned Ferdinand VII and to those who governed in his name. Since then, the throne had been vacant for two years, and people had begun to think that it might long remain so. The colonial authorities who claimed to represent the caretaker government in Seville tried to conceal the news of that government's collapse, but without success. As news of the disaster spread, it brought in its wake an escalation of revolutionary activity.

The groups who now constituted themselves as local leaders also presented themselves as loyal subjects of the beleaguered Spanish Crown. For a number of reasons, such leaders were slow to push openly for independence. Great Britain was unlikely to look with favor on such a move because of its Spanish alliance, and, for their part, the leaders of the new round of ad hoc governing bodies viewed themselves not as rebels but as the rightful heirs of an authority that had entered an apparently permanent eclipse. There was no reason for them to emphasize a break with that authority when they intended to use it for their own purposes. Both colonial officials and insurgent leaders now struggled to present themselves as the legitimate heirs of the old order.

The insurgents claimed legitimacy primarily through the institution of the cabildo. Cabildos were not very egalitarian institutions, since membership (when not bought and sold like other colonial offices) was often monopolized by powerful families. At best they represented only the urban minority of the predominantly rural Spanish American population. However, the cabildos had the advantage of being locally constituted, so that their claim to legitimacy had not been undermined by the breakdown of the central government. Though some cabildos were dominated by Spaniards, Creole insurgents could always gain the upper hand by calling a *cabildo abierto*, a town meeting open to the local elite as a whole. In Caracas (April), Buenos Aires (May), Bogotá (July), and finally Santiago, Chile (September), open cabildos established juntas to replace colonial officials.

These royal officials had little choice but to acquiesce. The junta of Buenos Aires gleefully exhibited the "spontaneous" resignation of the viceroy who had obligingly authorized the very assembly that removed him from power. The captain general of Venezuela likewise provided a resignation that became the legal cornerstone of the new order. In both New Granada and Chile, royal officials themselves presided over the formation of the juntas destined to overthrow them. The legal fussiness of this revolution reflected the background of its leadership: lawyers, bureaucrats, and middle-aged merchants dressed up as militia officers.

At this point, the political mobilization of the revolution involved only a tiny part of the population. Creole elites living in capital cities had seized the opportunity to even the score with the peninsular Spaniards with whom they had so long competed at a disadvantage. Their identity as native-born Spanish Americans was now to their benefit, and for a while they could pose as representatives of all their compatriots. In that spirit, they were willing to allow a limited access to power by people of other classes in the name of liberal reform. However, they did not support (nor could most of them imagine) any profound change in the foundations of the political order, much less foresee how their actions gradually would undermine the social order that they hoped to inherit from the agents of the colonial power and the metropolitan economy.

After 1810, these prudent revolutionaries could no longer turn back, even had they so desired. The executions of the year before indicated the consequences of defeat. Wrapping themselves in the mantle of legitimate rule strengthened them against internal challengers, but the decisive battle had still to be won. Royal administrators, clergy, and military officers immediately opposed a Creole movement clearly inimical to their own interests, which depended on the continued vitality of Spanish imperial power. The result was a civil war led by these two opposing factions of the ruling class. Each side quickly sought allies in the larger population. The elite search for allies began, once again, in an entirely traditional manner when the new authorities simply ordered their subordinates to join the revolution. In New Granada and in Chile they encountered little opposition, but the situation was different in Peru, which remained securely under the control of a particularly able viceroy, and in Venezuela and the Río de la Plata, where fighting quickly erupted.

The revolutionary junta of the Río de la Plata formed two military expeditions to extend the revolution throughout its sprawling jurisdiction. Manuel Belgrano, a lawyer and economist whom circumstances had transformed into a military leader, met defeat in his expedition to bring Paraguay under the control of Buenos Aires. Another force managed to take the conservative stronghold at Córdoba (where the resistance was led by the bishop and the former viceroy Liniers) and from there proceeded victoriously through the territory of Tucumán and scaled the Andes to occupy Upper Peru without meeting resistance. In Upper Peru, they made the first major bid to win (rather than simply decree) the allegiance of a broader social base for the revolution by abolishing tribute payments and declaring the total equality of the Indians in a ceremony conducted symbolically amid the pre-Incan ruins of Tiahuanaco. This attempt to reach out to the indigenous population backfired because it sent the Indians' Creole overlords into the arms of the royalists while the indigenous people remained mistrustful of their self-proclaimed liberators.

Eventually, troops sent by the Peruvian viceroy defeated the expedition from Buenos Aires and reclaimed the wealth of Upper Peru for the king, detaining the advance of the revolution at the border between modern Argentina and Bolivia. After 1815, the advanced position of the revolution on the southern side of the line, in Salta, was maintained by the popularly recruited forces of Martín Güemes, using local resources, in an uneasy relationship with the area's commercial and landowning aristocracy. Güemes's mobilization of the rural poor of Salta demonstrated again the willingness of the Buenos Aires revolution to appeal directly for lower-class support. Such willingness owed much to the fact that Upper Peru and Salta lay far from Buenos Aires, and the mobilization of the masses there did not threaten the social dominance of the elites who directed the revolution from the distant port. In areas closer to Buenos Aires, the revolutionary leadership displayed far greater circumspection.

Events in the Banda Oriental showed how much the Creole revolutionaries feared releasing the explosive forces of popular resentment in the name of the revolution of 1810. Montevideo had been the most important Spanish naval base in the South Atlantic, and during the opening phase of the revolution it remained under the control of peninsular military officers stationed there. Under British prodding, both royalist Montevideo and revolutionary Buenos Aires agreed to a temporary occupation of the Banda Oriental by the Portuguese.

By then, the Banda Oriental had experienced a popular rural uprising of more radical social implications than the revolution of Buenos Aires, which supported it initially but feared the "anarchic" tendencies of its leader, José Artigas. When the Banda Oriental was occupied by Portuguese troops with the acquiescence of Buenos Aires, Artigas led the rural populace in an exodus to the province of Entre Ríos. Thereafter, the revolutions of Buenos Aires and the Banda Oriental collaborated uneasily in the fight against the royalists in Montevideo. By 1814, when an expedition from Buenos Aires finally captured Montevideo, Artigas had begun to create an alliance of provincial forces hostile both to the royalists and to Buenos Aires. Within a few months, the provinces of Entre Ríos, Corrientes, Santa Fe, and, briefly, Córdoba had formed a federation under the military leadership of Artigas as "Protector." To the leaders of the revolution of Buenos Aires, Artigas was not only a threat to the cohesion of the revolutionary movement but also the representative of a decidedly more radical version of the revolutionary creed. Only within the Banda Oriental itself did the Artiguista revolution show signs of social radicalism, however, and the excessive fears of Buenos Aires leaders reveal their keen awareness of the dangers that political revolution posed for the social order.

Such difficulties threatened the unity of the leadership in Buenos Aires. The junta constituted to replace the viceroy quickly divided between supporters of Col. Cornelio de Saavedra, the most influential leader of Creole militias in the city since 1807, and his secretary, Mariano Moreno. Saavedra was older, formerly a merchant in Upper Peru, while Moreno was a firebrand who led the way in purifying the revolutionary purpose through such measures as the expulsion of the viceroy and the audiencia, the purge of peninsular elements in the cabildo, and the execution of the royalist opposition leadership in Córdoba. During the critical year of 1810, Moreno's influence had gradually overshadowed Saavedra's, but his drastic expedients convinced many that he intended to create a replica of Jacobin France in the Río de la Plata. Given the conservative inspiration of the Buenos Aires revolution as a whole, the result was mounting opposition to Moreno. Late in the year, when the junta of Buenos Aires incorporated representatives from cabildos in the interior provinces and the radical faction found itself clearly outnumbered by moderates in the new body, Moreno accepted a diplomatic post in London but died during the Atlantic crossing. The triumphant moderate faction then purged the remaining radicals, but the moderates' period of dominance lasted only a few months. Soon they were forced to imitate the radicals by concentrating political power in a triumvirate and mercilessly repressing a royalist conspiracy led by Martín de Alzaga, who was executed on gallows erected in the main square of Buenos Aires. Provincial resistance to the forces of Buenos Aires then inspired a conservative crackdown in the port capital, where the gallows continued their liquidation of dissidents.

By then, officers of the regular army had wrested control of the
revolution from the urban militias who had played such an important
part since the time of the British invasions. Convening secretly in a
lodge organized along Masonic lines, these officers and their political
allies directed the policies of the Buenos Aires revolution until 1819.
Among them were two Creoles recently returned from military service in Spain: the mercurial Carlos de Alvear and the more circumspect José de San Martín. Alvear was the man of the hour. He led the
expedition that defeated the royalist holdouts in Montevideo, becoming chief executive in Buenos Aires upon his victorious return. However, the revolution gave signs of exhaustion when Alvear, who depended increasingly on the army to repress any opposition, began to
consider a reconciliation with Spain, where Ferdinand VII had finally
been restored to his throne following the defeat of Napoleon.

The revolution that now appeared moribund had reached its high
point only shortly before, in the sessions of the Sovereign Assembly of
1813 in Buenos Aires. Reluctant to declare outright independence, the
assembly nevertheless had adopted important symbols of incipient
nationhood: a flag, a seal, and a national anthem. In addition, it had
laid legal groundwork for the new nation by abolishing such colonial
institutions as the Inquisition, titles of nobility, and entailed estates—
and by declaring that the children of slave mothers would no longer be
born slaves. In 1815, however, repulsed by the royalists in Upper Peru,
challenged by the Artiguista confederation in the provinces nearer at
hand, and divided against itself at home, the revolution in Buenos
Aires neared the low point of its first cycle.

The revolution in Chile had run a roughly parallel course in the
years 1810 to 1814. Moderate elements controlled the first stages of
the movement, which became radicalized by the threat of a counterrevolutionary expedition from Peru. To prepare for that eventuality,
Chilean insurgent leaders created an army that very quickly began to
play a leading role in political events—breaking up a royalist conspiracy in 1811 by executing its authors, ousting a number of high officials, and dissolving the audiencia. The radicals oversaw the creation
of a National Congress the following month. When this body displayed more moderate inclinations, the radicals again used the army
to impose their vision on the revolution under the leadership of José
Miguel Carrera, like San Martín and Alvear, a young army officer
recently returned from Spain who belonged to an influential oligarchical family. Many of the group now in control also belonged to the
Santiago aristocracy or were proreform Creole members of the imperial bureaucracy, radicalized by the late colonial crisis, among them

Bernardo O'Higgins, illegitimate son of a Peruvian viceroy, large land-owner and enlightened administrator in southern Chile, and, since 1798, follower of the Venezuelan revolutionary, Francisco Miranda. Having cleared the path for their measures, the radicals led the congress in reforming the administration and judiciary, suppressing the Inquisition, and abolishing slavery.

Factionalism among the radicals themselves undermined the revolution in Chile as in Argentina. The upper-class radicalism dominated by landowners and enlightened bureaucrats like O'Higgins apparently left too little room in the revolution for the young leader who had engineered its victory. Toward the end of 1811, Carrera used the army to establish himself as dictator and appealed to the urban populace for support. Chile's first printing press (imported by a North American sympathizer) was employed to spread the revolutionary gospel with increasing intensity during the next year. Early in 1813, however, a royalist force from Peru landed in the south of Chile, where the revolution had not taken hold. Carrera's revolutionary army marched south to confront the invaders but met repeated defeats during the year and a half of fighting. The triumphant royalists entered Santiago late in 1814, and the remaining revolutionary leaders escaped over the Andes to the Argentine town of Mendoza. In exile, Carrera's radicals and O'Higgins's moderates could dispute the aims of the revolution at their leisure, but it appeared unlikely that either group would have an opportunity to put its ideas into practice.

Far to the north in Venezuela, the fortunes of the revolution fluctuated even more dramatically than in the south. In 1810, Caracas witnessed the establishment of a junta of twenty-three notables, dominated by the cacao-growing landowners of the coastal highlands. The junta eventually found its logical head in the veteran insurgent, Francisco Miranda, but soon showed little enthusiasm for his radical leadership. Miranda organized a revolutionary army and impelled the reluctant revolutionaries to declare their independence from Spain as early as July 1811. As in Argentina and Chile, the revolution controlled the capital city and its environs while other regions—the coastal area west of Caracas and the interior of the country—remained in royalist hands.

Then an earthquake shook Caracas (a sign of divine displeasure, according to the royalists) and heightened political conflicts. The royalist commander of the Coro naval base advanced eastward toward Caracas, encountering only weak resistance from the forces under Miranda, whose will to fight was sapped by his age and by a growing pessimism concerning the whole undertaking. The revolutionary gar-

rison at Puerto Cabello mutinied (despite the attempts of Miranda's
young officer, Simon Bolívar, to put down the insurrection) and joined
the advancing royalists. In the meantime, the fighting had begun to
awaken unrest among slaves on the cacao plantations belonging to
revolutionary leaders (like Bolívar), impressing upon them the hazards
of further civil disruption. The ensuing armistice was marred by the
revolutionaries' surrender of Miranda to the royalists in a murky incident involving Bolívar and others. The "Precursor" was to end his long
and complicated career in a royalist prison, while Bolívar left Venezuela to prepare the next stage of the revolution in New Granada.

The cacao-planting Mantuano aristocracy of Caracas had given
up on the Venezuelan revolution, but others carried on the fight. In
coastal areas east of Caracas, black and mulatto fishermen attacked
Spanish colonists from the Canary Islands, and the colonists responded with a ferocity that became the hallmark of this second stage
of the revolution in Venezuela. After gathering forces in New Granada,
Simon Bolívar returned to Venezuela, made "War to the Death" (no
quarter asked or given) the official policy of his army, and managed to
retake Caracas from the royalists in a matter of months. The victory
was to be a fleeting one. Inland from Caracas, on the tropical plains of
the Orinoco River, the mounted herdsmen called *llaneros* entered the
war on the royalist side, and when they did, they swept all before them.
The Orinoco plains were a cattle frontier, similar in some ways to the
coastal plains of the Río de la Plata, but poorer. The llaneros were
people of thoroughly mixed blood, superb horsemen who worked on
enormous ranches often belonging to absentee landlords. They cared
more for the king of Spain than for their Creole masters, and they
found a leader in an obscure former sailor from Asturias named Tomás
Boves.

The royalist llaneros of Boves drove Bolívar's insurgents out of
Caracas and turned Venezuela into a royalist stronghold. Bolívar escaped to New Granada, then to Jamaica, where he planned another
expedition that the Venezuelan royalists easily repelled. He was soon
back in Jamaica readying himself to leave for another fight, this time
in New Granada. Meanwhile, the future of the Spanish American
revolution appeared dark indeed with the arrival in 1815 of a Spanish
expeditionary force numbering ten thousand soldiers following the
restoration of Ferdinand VII. Disembarking in Venezuela, the veteran
Spanish general Pablo Morillo prepared to march into New Granada
and extinguish the last flickering revolutionary flames remaining in
that part of the continent.

The revolution of New Granada took to an extreme the Spanish

American tendency toward internal divisions. Pasto and Popayán, in the south, were part of the solidly royalist Andean highland bloc that included most of Bolivia, Peru, and Ecuador. However, the counter-revolutionary south did the New Granadan revolution less harm than the dissensions among revolutionaries themselves. The capitaline elite of Cundinamarca, the highland area around Bogotá, preferred to constitute itself as a republic separate from the United Provinces of New Granada. Relations between Cundinamarca and the United Provinces degenerated into civil war until, with Peruvian royalist troops already advancing into New Granada from the south, the forces of the United Provinces under the command of Bolívar emerged victorious. The United Provinces established a central government in Bogotá but remained unable to assure the obedience of the revolutionaries in the diverse localities of New Granada. Bolívar abandoned the struggle when he became convinced that the New Granadan revolutionaries were incapable of working together even in the face of the common enemy. The Spanish army of General Morillo then entered New Granada from the Atlantic, capturing Cartagena and eventually Bogotá. In the northern part of the continent, the flames of revolution seemed to have flickered out.

In 1815, only the southern part of the viceroyalty of the Río de la Plata remained in the hands of insurgents, and the colonial power had begun directly to reassert its presence by sending troops and resources. It appeared that the remaining foci of revolutionary activity would be easily crushed. Why did the Spanish counterrevolutionary efforts fail in the end? Some argue that the violent reassertion of imperial control itself kept revolutionary sentiments alive, but a more conciliatory policy would have encountered tremendous difficulty in maintaining a stable social order without totally eliminating the determined insurgents who persevered in the cause of independence. More important in explaining the failure of pacification efforts were the changes that five years of fighting had brought to Spanish America.

In Venezuela and parts of the Río de la Plata, the escalating violence between patriots and loyalists had raged out of control, threatening to become a race or class war. The situation in most parts of Spanish America was less extreme, but everywhere the revolution had necessitated the creation of increasingly numerous armies in which poor men of color bore arms. The officers were generally Creoles, but advancement in ranks could not be stifled without risk to the armies' fighting spirit, and within a few years mestizos occupied high-ranking positions. These armies had to be equipped and supplied. The hoarded wealth of urban oligarchies, religious orders, and merchant guilds was turned to this new use, along with agricultural assets, especially horses and cattle. Simultaneously, the end of imperial trade restrictions brought about changes as significant as those wrought by the years of civil war.

The economic impact of the first revolutionary cycle had helped undermine the social ascendancy of formerly dominant groups. For one thing, a flood of surplus British production had drastically lowered the cost of manufactured imports in Spanish America, and not only in the patriot-controlled zones, eroding the position of the merchants who had formerly monopolized overseas trade (as well as the business of rural artisans). Governments of revolutionary or royalist persuasion worked to ruin hundreds of magistrates and landowners whose political sympathies aroused suspicion. The systematic proscription of peninsular Spaniards, in particular, decimated the upper classes. The revolution of Buenos Aires extracted repeated forced loans from Spanish residents of the city, while simultaneously forbidding them to exercise small-scale commerce. According to regulations imposed by the patriots, a Spaniard could not serve as the legal guardian of a minor or as the executor of a will. Other regulations prohibited Spaniards from leaving their houses after dark or even riding horseback. No doubt, such measures were not fully implemented in most cases, but the benevolence of the revolutionary authorities must often have had a price.

Many patriot leaders realized that the humiliation of these formerly powerful members of the colonial ruling class weakened the whole social hierarchy, but they had to take the risk since a less rigorous approach had slight chance of success. The royalists themselves, theoretically even more committed to the existing social order, found it equally necessary to adopt measures that tended to undermine that order. In Venezuela, marauding bands of mixed bloods spearheaded the royalist triumph. Neither the revolution nor the counterrevolution could gain a decisive victory without mobilizing the lower classes, and no victory so gained could be without social consequences. Of course, the impact of these years of fighting varied considerably from place to place. The Río de la Plata and Chile were less affected than Venezuela, and the least social disruption occurred in New Granada, where minor clashes among regional oligarchies left intact the supremacy of each in its own bailiwick. Nevertheless, everywhere the effects of the first cycle of revolution had gone beyond the point of possible return to the status quo ante. Many who had not been adversaries of the colonial order before 1810 now had a vested interest in the new opportunities created for them by the years of struggle.

Spanish efforts to repress the revolution thus multiplied the enemies of the old regime while, after the arrival of Spanish expeditionary forces in Venezuela and Peru, the royalists received from Spain less material support than expected. In addition, rivalries sprang up between Spaniards and Creoles within the royalist ranks. Many of the isolated and uncoordinated outbreaks of revolutionary organization had succumbed to the royalist counterattack, leaving more hardened and dedicated revolutionary forces to carry on the fight. The renewed colonial character of the war brought clarity and solidarity to the revolutionary cause. The new stage of the conflict ended the insurgents' vacillating attempts to usurp the preexisting legitimacy of the colonial regime or to mobilize the lower orders. Military solutions now took the place of political ones, and the intricacies of a complex revolutionary process gave way to the simpler lines of a full-scale war.

International events of the immediate post-Napoleonic period were partially favorable to the insurgents. Great Britain did not officially alter its posture of careful ambiguity toward the Spanish American revolution, but it became much more tolerant of arms shipments and volunteers sent by British supporters. In 1814, Britain and the United States had signed a treaty to end the hostilities that had begun between them in 1812, and the South American revolutionaries also hoped to receive aid from their republican neighbors to the north. Though the U.S. government remained officially neutral, it became much easier to purchase arms there as well. After finally acquiring Spanish Florida in 1822, the government of the United States became much less circumspect toward Spain and, the following year, announced its official hostility to projects of imperial reconquest in the Monroe Doctrine. Although the volume of clandestine purchases of weaponry from Great Britain and the United States never amounted to much, its importance to the Spanish American insurgencies shows how limited their resources always were.

The continued violent oscillations of Spanish politics gave further advantages to the revolutionary forces. After recovering his throne in 1813, Ferdinand VII had returned to a Spain ravaged by war and too poor to launch a sustained series of large-scale campaigns against the Spanish American revolutions. Even if the restored monarch had realized the immensity of the challenge (which he apparently did not) he also had to face potent political opposition among the liberal military officers expected to carry out the reconquest of Spain's New World possessions. In 1820, an expeditionary force assembled to put down the revolution in Buenos Aires instead overthrew Ferdinand and proclaimed a new liberal government in Spain. In practice, Spanish liberals were hardly more inclined than the absolutists to allow the independence of Spanish America, though they proposed to secure the loyalty of the rebellious colonies by different methods. Fortunately for the Spanish American revolutionaries, the royalists viewed the liberal government of Spain with profound distrust, making it difficult for them to collaborate effectively against the movements for independence. In many cases (Mexico being the salient example), the specter of liberal revolution in Spain actually reconciled the royalists to a conservative version of independence. By the time that Ferdinand VII was restored once more to his absolutist throne in 1823, the damage had been done. This second restoration of Spanish absolutism, engineered by France, weakened the royalist cause even more by aligning rival Britain firmly against Spain.

The leaders of the second stage of the fighting for South American independence also played an essential role in the eventual victory. The great military campaigns that finally came together like pincers to crush the royalist stronghold in Peru were organized in the northern part of the continent by Simon Bolívar (who had again taken refuge on a Caribbean island when this period began) and in the southern part by José de San Martín, drawing on the resources of the one remaining revolutionary territory in 1815, the Río de la Plata.

San Martín was himself the child of a Spanish official, and his Creole mother came from a family in the service of the Crown as well. Like many sons of respectable families of modest wealth under the old regime, the boy chose a military career. He went to Spain quite young, and his participation in the war against the occupying army of Napoleon provided an important formative influence. In 1812, he returned to Buenos Aires along with a number of other Spanish American officers and there married the daughter of one of that city's richest Creole families associated with the patriot cause. Putting his European experience to work, he trained a corps of horse grenadiers to the rigorous standards of discipline required to carry out complex tactical maneuvers, a discipline until then generally lacking in the improvised armies of both royalists and insurgents. In 1813, troops under his command won a skirmish against a royalist incursion on the banks of the Paraná. In 1814, he briefly commanded the Army of the North, back from its disastrous expedition to Upper Peru, and then directed the revolutionary government of Cuyo in the foothills of the Andes. The arrival of Chilean revolutionaries in that area after their defeats of 1814 helped crystallize San Martín's strategy against the royalist bastion in Peru.

Instead of taking the more direct route through the high tablelands of Upper Peru, San Martín proposed to cross the Andes at a much narrower point, overcome the less formidable royalist forces occupying Chile, and then sail north and attack the viceregal capital of Lima directly. Among the Chilean insurgents who had taken earlier refuge in Mendoza, San Martín allied himself most closely with Bernardo O'Higgins. The two men collaborated effectively because they shared the experience of a Spanish military career and exemplified the integrity and seriousness typical of reform-minded Spanish officialdom at its late eighteenth-century best. San Martín felt only aversion for O'Higgins's more radical rival, the brilliant and ambitious José Miguel Carrera, whose demagoguery he mistrusted.

In preparing his strategy, San Martín counted as well on the help of the government of Buenos Aires, which had recovered quickly from the crisis of 1815. Carlos de Alvear had been deposed by his own soldiers, a new congress had met in Tucumán, and another supreme director had emerged (from the same lodge that supplied so many other leaders to the revolution). This was Juan Martín de Pueyrredón, who pulled together an alliance between the ruling groups of Buenos Aires, Tucumán, and Cuyo against Artigas and his confederated provinces. This alliance moved the revolution gradually to the right because the ruling groups of the interior provinces were markedly more conservative than the leadership of Buenos Aires. The shift can be gauged by the fact that, while the deputies of the 1813 revolutionary congress had addressed each other as "citizen" in French revolutionary fashion, those who met three years later at Tucumán preferred the more traditional "señor." Conservatism was, moreover, in the air, as post-Napoleonic Europe restored a number of the monarchies overthrown during the last twenty years. In Spanish America, the idea of setting up New World monarchies gained currency among military officers who feared the consequences of social and political radicalization during the revolution. In addition, the powerful mercantile interests of Buenos Aires had lost some of their enthusiasm for the new economic order. The price brought by their exports of cowhides plummeted in 1814, and in the mercantile community, they found themselves steadily losing ground to British newcomers.

The Pueyrredón regime faced its greatest challenge in the irreconcilable dissidence of the Artiguista confederation, which maintained its hold on the riverine provinces north of Buenos Aires. To weaken Artigas, the revolution of Buenos Aires had been willing to accept a Portuguese invasion of the Banda Oriental. Between 1816 and 1819, the Portuguese force decimated the ragged army of Artigas and settled down to occupy and, eventually, to annex the province. The rest of the Artiguista confederation was more successful in resisting the advances of armies sent from Buenos Aires. By 1819, the government of Pueyrredón gave clear signs of disintegrating from within, as its proposed centralist constitution received an overwhelming rejection. Pueyrredón called on the army, but support was not forthcoming. At this point, allies of Artigas in the provinces of Santa Fe and Entre Ríos took advantage of the occasion to march on Buenos Aires and oust Pueyrredón. The fall of the Pueyrredón regime can be attributed partly to its determination to achieve victory for the revolution in the transmontane royalist strongholds and partly to the prolonged sacrifices that the campaign required from a people exhausted by a decade of turmoil.

San Martín's army of three thousand crossed the Andes and invaded Chile in early 1817. A quick victory at the battle of Chacabuco opened the way to Santiago, where Bernardo O'Higgins became supreme director of a newly proclaimed Chilean republic. More fighting followed, but after a decisive second victory at the Maipo River, resistance was confined to the southern end of the country, where it smouldered for years afterward without threatening patriot control of Santiago and the central valley of Chile. Recalling the internal dissension that had doomed the first Chilean revolution, O'Higgins imposed an austere, authoritarian rule that did not hesitate to implement the same sort of repressive tactics as the restorationist regime it replaced. Among the dissidents who fell victim to the new republic was Manuel Rodríguez, a guerrilla fighter and hero from the campaign against the royalists.

The next step in San Martín's strategy was to attack Peru by sea, and for that he needed a navy. Two years passed as his tiny flotilla grew to the size needed to transport the army. An adventurous British peer, Thomas Cochrane, directed the patriot navy in its first raids along the Peruvian coast. Finally, in 1820, San Martín embarked with an army of four thousand to liberate Peru, where a royalist force of more than twenty thousand awaited. A frontal assault was obviously out of the question. Instead, San Martín hoped to shake the Creole aristocracy's loyalty to the king by bringing the disruptions of prolonged war home to them as never before. A blockade would hurt them economically, and fighting of any kind would inevitably raise the specter of Indian uprisings in the highlands. When that occurred, he hoped the Peruvian aristocracy would regard a patriot victory as the quickest path to reestablishing the social order.

The revolutionary expedition met some extremely encouraging early successes. Its landing south of Lima sparked a spontaneous rebellion in Guayaquil. Much of the northern Peruvian coast followed, thanks to the leadership of its Creole intendant, whom the royalists had appointed as part of a conciliatory policy toward the Peruvian aristocracy. A campaign in the highlands began to produce the desired unease in Lima (as did news of the eclipse of absolutism due to a constitutionalist revolution in Spain), and in 1821 the royalist commander in chief himself removed the viceroy and established negotiations with San Martín. The two military leaders agreed on the creation of an independent, but monarchist, Peru. The proposal did not satisfy the forces who remained loyal to the king of Spain, but they were at any rate no longer strong enough to prevent San Martín from making a triumphal entry into Lima, where he was proclaimed "Protector" of a liberated Peru.

The new Peruvian state was to be the most conservative of those formed in the cautious climate that prevailed in the independence movement after 1815. To a degree, its conservatism reflected the ideas of San Martín himself, but it also represented an attempt to win over the Lima aristocracy, whose support would be required in the consolidation of the new order. That support became increasingly important as the revolutionary expedition lost momentum in 1821–22. Forces loyal to Spain continued to hold Callao, the port serving the former viceregal capital. Admiral Cochrane had fallen out with the patriot leadership because of a dispute over the spoils of Lima and left to seek more lucrative adventures in the South Pacific. The fighting in the highlands continued, consuming the resources of both sides. San Martín's much smaller army had counted on garnering reinforcements and supplies within Peru, but these had been disappointingly slight. Five years after his expeditionary force had crossed the Andes in its first step toward the liberation of Peru, the defeat of the royalist stronghold in the highlands appeared impossible without further help from outside.

That help could come only from the north, where Simon Bolívar had finally led the revolution to victory in Venezuela and New Granada. After the defeat of the first revolutionary cycle in 1815, Bolívar had returned to Caribbean exile, this time in Haiti, and planned another strategy. In 1816, yet another Bolivarian expedition to Venezuela met with failure. By 1817, on the eve of his triumph, the veteran revolutionary still had no support anywhere on the mainland, his considerable personal fortune had been depleted, and his welcome in Haiti had begun to wear thin. His dauntless determination was an essential ingredient in the success of the independence movement in the northern part of the continent.

Bolívar belonged to one of the oldest families of Caracas, prominent in the cacao-planting aristocracy of the Venezuelan coastal highlands. As a young man, he had shown the precocious energies of so
many other young Creoles, suddenly freed from colonial discipline
and unsure of what to do with their liberty. In 1804, when he was
twenty-one years old, he had experienced the life of a nobleman alongside other cacao-rich Venezuelans in Madrid, had married a young
woman with a background similar to his own, and had returned with
her to Venezuela, where she died within months of a tropical fever.
Before that, he had received a privileged education from his tutor,
Simón Rodríguez, a Venezuelan follower of Jean-Jacques Rousseau,
and from one of the leading Spanish American intellectuals of the period, Andrés Bello. After the death of his wife, Bolívar had returned to
Europe in the company of Rodríguez. While most of his Spanish American contemporaries had a merely theoretical understanding of the
political transformations of the age of revolution in Europe, Bolívar
had experienced them in person. During his travels in Spain, France,
and Italy, he had witnessed the crisis of the old regime, the birth of
republicanism, and the rise of Napoleon Bonaparte. Although he never
pardoned Napoleon for appropriating the revolution for his private
glory, Bolívar believed that the authoritarian and militaristic denouement of the French Revolution had been more than a historical accident. His vision of the future Spanish American revolution was therefore different from that of many of his contemporaries. Unlike San
Martín, who never believed in republics, Bolívar never vacillated in his
republican faith, but his republic would be authoritarian, not liberal.

Bolívar's authoritarian streak was reinforced by social characteristics of the northern revolutionary movement that contrasted with the
revolution in the south. The liberalism of the southern movement
drew on the legalistic and institutional aspects of the Hispanic political heritage, which survived most strongly among the urban elites
who were the heirs of the colonial bureaucracy and magistracy. Urban
elites of Buenos Aires and Santiago permanently influenced the revolutionary process of the south, but in Bolívar's Venezuela, events took
a different course. The patriot cause prevailed in Venezuela only by
cutting its ties with the Mantuano aristocracy of Caracas and relying
on the rural population whose participation was essentially military
rather than political. The rural people of Venezuela had little sympathy for the legal and institutional underpinnings of liberalism. They
responded more to another concept of Hispanic political tradition:
authority whose powers were absolute, but not arbitrary, because they
were guided by justice and virtue. Thus, the theoretical justification of

Spanish absolutism, carefully elaborated by its seventeenth-century ideologues, reappeared in the Bolivarian vision of a virtuous republican leadership wielding unlimited power in defense of liberty. Bolívar eventually extended his hegemony west to Guayaquil and south as far as Potosí, but his most secure power base remained in Venezuela, where the leading guerrilla chiefs, now transformed into generals, were relatively impervious to the seductions of the liberal ideal. If Bolívar's own ideals did not exactly coincide with the reality of the Venezuelan revolution, they at least did not conflict with it.

In 1817, Simon Bolívar was the only leader capable of uniting the many regional chiefs created by the Venezuelan revolution. He had broken with the timid aristocratic revolutionaries of Caracas (partly by threatening to free the slaves who formed the base of their plantation economy) and demonstrated his ability to gain a following among the country people of the Andean region. He now set about broadening his support among the veteran rebels of the coastal region east of Caracas and, most decisively, among the horsemen of the Orinoco plains, who had defeated him in 1814. Entering Venezuela once again with a small force of three hundred men in 1817, the year of San Martín's invasion of Chile, Bolívar finally found the key to victory in an alliance with a new guerrilla chief of the Orinoco plains, José Antonio Páez. The horsemen of Páez were reinforced by the arrival of several thousand volunteers, including a (mostly Irish) Britannic Legion.

The alliance with Páez gave the revolution a base in the Venezuelan interior, but it caused dissension with the llaneros' former adversaries, the veteran patriot fighters of the eastern coast, who were now of secondary importance in Bolívar's strategy. Finding Caracas too well defended, he took his army of three thousand across the Orinoco plains to attack the highlands of New Granada from behind, scaling the eastern slopes of the Andes, catching the royalist defenders of Bogotá by surprise, and shattering them at the decisive battle of Boyacá in 1819. This victory began the formation of the Republic of Colombia (usually called Gran Colombia by historians because it incorporated Venezuela and Ecuador, former dependencies of the viceroyalty of New Granada), which received a provisional institutional structure at the Congress of Angostura at the end of the year. Each of the partially liberated states of the federation would have a vice president in charge of the administrative tasks, while Bolívar, as president and "Liberator," continued the war against the enemy forces still in control of the Venezuelan coast. Meanwhile, news of the liberal revolution in Spain had weakened the cohesion of the royalist cause. In 1821, the Spanish forces abandoned Caracas, and word arrived that Bolívar's lieutenant Antonio José de Sucre had captured Quito. The defeat of the remaining royalist holdouts at Pasto, between New Granada and Quito, completed the liberation of Gran Colombia and freed Bolívar to lead the army south against the royalist bastion in the Andes of Peru.

During the Peruvian campaign, Gran Colombia came close to falling apart. The Congress of Cúcuta in 1821 discarded the federal organization of Angostura and imposed a centralized administration to be directed from Bogotá by Vice President Francisco de Paula Santander. The reformist initiatives of Santander encountered predictable resistance from such vested interests of the colonial order as the church and the slave-owning aristocracy. Merchants and artisans balked at his policy of free trade, which they correctly expected to favor British traders and manufacturers. The leaders of the revolution were hesitant to move too strongly against the conservative interests for fear of opening the door to the kind of social revolution that had occurred in the slave revolt of Haiti, an image never far from the minds of the Creole leadership in the region of the Caribbean.

The northern revolution thus returned to the tradition of moderate reform but was handicapped by the destruction of the previous decade of fighting and the burden of the Peruvian campaign. Nor did Santander have the support that the imperial structure had provided to earlier reformers. In the absence of such support, he could hardly overcome the opposition of the most powerful elements among the governed, who quickly began to send protests to Bolívar and to agitate for more local autonomy. Santander's authority in Venezuela was sharply curtailed by the influence of Páez. In Bogotá, the divisions recalled the first revolutionary cycle, when the United Provinces of New Granada had feuded with the Republic of Cundinamarca. Santander had fought with the United Provinces against Cundinamarca at that time, a circumstance that did not endear him to the populace of Bogotá. Dissidents throughout tottering Gran Colombia pinned their hopes on the return of the Liberator. Without breaking with Santander, whose liberal convictions he did not share, Bolívar tacitly encouraged their appeals.

Such was the situation when Bolívar received San Martín's appeal for aid in the liberation of Peru. Much had changed since 1817, when San Martín had the backing of the Pueyrredón regime in Argentina and when Bolívar, exiled in Haiti, had only determination, boundless energy, and dreams of eventual triumph. In July 1822, when the two liberators met in Guayaquil, Bolívar was the president of Gran Colom-

bia, and San Martín, nominally the Protector of Peru, was Bolívar's
guest in a city the Peruvians claimed as their own. We have no reliable
account of the interview between the two men, but its result was clear.
The price of Bolívar's aid was San Martín's departure from Peru.

San Martín passed the leadership of the Peruvian revolution into
the hands of a weak triumvirate chosen by a constituent convention.
In December 1822, the convention repudiated the negotiations begun
in Europe by San Martín's emissaries, in search of a king for Peru, and
announced the formation of a Peruvian republic, but the deputies
showed more vigor in proclaiming the republic than in prosecuting the
war. The first president, José Mariano de la Riva Agüero, was a Lima
aristocrat only recently converted to the cause of independence. As a
military leader, he showed himself to be more tenacious, but not
substantially more successful, than those who had preceded him.
After the arrival of Gran Colombian forces under the command of
Antonio José de Sucre, a new series of defeats (including the brief
abandonment of Lima by the revolutionary forces) convinced the congress to remove Riva Agüero and replace him with the Marquess of
Torre Tagle, whose credentials within the movement were more convincing. They also requested urgently that Bolívar himself come to
direct the liberation of Peru. Bolívar had been delayed putting down a   *Pasto*
rebellion in Pasto, a part of New Granada where lingering royalist
sympathies were constrained only by bloody repression and mass
deportations. Not until mid-1823 did he reach the Peruvian capital to   *1823 -*
be acclaimed as Liberator with extraordinary military and civil powers *Bolívar*
until the end of the war.   *arrives in*
                                                                        Peru

Bolívar arrived at a critical moment for the independence struggle
in Peru. From its late and lethargic beginnings at the time of San
Martín's invasion, the Peruvian revolution had made slight progress
and now threatened to collapse altogether. The deposed president Riva
Agüero flirted secretly with the royalists, proposing to make a common cause against Bolívar and then seat a prince of the Bourbon
dynasty on the throne of an independent Peruvian monarchy. This
conspiracy was discovered and its author deported. Meanwhile, the
new president, Torre Tagle, engaged in similar negotiations himself
when charged by Bolívar with the task of arranging an armistice. In
early 1824, after a mutiny of the Argentine garrison delivered the port
of Callao into royalist hands, Torre Tagle moved openly into their
camp, along with the vice president and a significant part of the
government. No other urban elite in Spanish America confronted a set
of options so uniformly distasteful as those open to the Creoles of

Lima. As Gran Colombian military domination followed on the heels of Argentine-Chilean occupation, a return to the old regime had come to seem a lesser evil.

Only a string of decisive victories won by Bolívar's army in the highlands saved the Peruvian revolution. Finally, on 9 December 1824, Sucre's force of New Granadans, Venezuelans, Argentines, Chileans, and Peruvians crushed the royalist army at the battle of Ayacucho. The last viceroy of Peru, José de La Serna, was taken prisoner, and his surrender ended the fighting throughout Peru except for around the port of Callao, which did not fall until 1826. In Upper Peru, the partisans of the king held out for a few months after Ayacucho, but Sucre's army soon overcame the last royalist resistance there as well. At the request of the Creoles of Charcas and Potosí, Sucre declared the independence of the Republic of Bolivia in 1825. The new nation named for the Liberator thus escaped the tutelage of Buenos Aires, established by the creation of the viceroyalty of the Río de la Plata in 1776, as well as the renewed domination of Lima, which the vicissitudes of war had made possible once more. Bolivia was the last corner of South America to be liberated. From one end of the continent to the other, bells rang and cannons thundered a salute to the end of the long war for Spanish American independence, which had successfully concluded by this time in Mexico as well.

Mexican independence had taken quite a different course from events in South America, where urban Creole elites initiated the process and, in most places, retained control of it throughout. In Mexico, a similar test of strength between peninsular and Creole elites in 1808 demonstrated the superior strength of the peninsulars. The revolution truly began in an 1810 uprising of rural Indians and mestizos that the Mexican nation would refuse for decades to recognize in its myths of origin. The unexpected protagonist of the movement was the curate of the locality of Dolores, a wealthy parish in the mining area north of Mexico City. Until the time of his protest, Father Miguel Hidalgo had been an unremarkable representative of the enlightened priesthood at the service of innovating late colonial administrations. Hidalgo's superiors approved without excessive enthusiasm his projects ranging from the promotion of silk production to the presentation of works by Molière translated into the native languages, using Indian actors recruited among his parishioners. Whatever his limitations as an insurgent leader, Hidalgo secured a fervent mass following among rural Mexicans of indigenous and mixed blood.

In September 1810, Hidalgo announced his revolution in favor of the king, the true religion, and the Virgin of Guadalupe—and against the Spaniards resident in Mexico. Mine workers joined Hidalgo's rural followers in the capture of the northern mining city of Guanajuato, where the mass killing of Creole and peninsular notables did much to alienate the movement's potential allies among the Creoles. Hidalgo's armed following grew into a multitude of some eighty thousand, perpetually changing in composition. They captured Querétaro, San Luis Potosí, and Guadalajara before suffering a reversal outside of Mexico City. The army that stopped them there, much smaller but better equipped, was itself sorely crippled by the victory, and an assault on Mexico City might yet have succeeded, but Hidalgo decided to retreat and regroup his forces. To his Indian and mestizo followers, the withdrawal confirmed what they had no doubt always suspected—that, despite their momentary success, the old order remained immovable. Hidalgo's army disintegrated during the retreat. Captured in Chihuahua, the renegade priest who had exercised his pastoral mission in peaceful obscurity until the age of fifty and then, for a few months, had been catapulted to the head of a bloody insurrection, recanted in his prison cell and warned others against imitating his bad example. He was then executed.

Hidalgo's final warning was issued in vain. Instead of dissolving, the movement found another regional base and another priest to lead it. Father José María Morelos gathered a following south of Mexico City, where the central highlands slope down to the Pacific Ocean. Gradually, Morelos gained ascendancy over the small groups of insurgents still active after the death of Hidalgo and worked to keep them from settling individually with the royalists. By 1812 his forces controlled much of the southern region, showing greater organization and discipline than Hidalgo had been able to instill. Morelos demanded independence and the suppression of caste distinctions as well as the division of great estates belonging to the royalists. The encroachment of sugar plantations on the subsistence crops of Indian communities, a motivation of the Zapatista insurgency a century later, already formed part of the background of this early stage of the war for Mexican independence.

Eager to provide his revolution with appropriate political institutions, Morelos convoked an insurgent congress, to whose somewhat incoherent instructions he accorded a scrupulous, if suicidal, respect. The failure of this second revolutionary cycle was due partly to the unexpected parliamentary vocation of its leadership but also partly to the increasingly solid opposition it encountered from the upper classes. Moderate in style but radical in content, Morelos's revolutionary program and the independent political base accorded it by his

Indian and mestizo following necessarily pushed peninsular and Creole elites together in opposing it. Their alliance in defense of the established order was more easily maintained than the revolution's mass movement toward an uncharted future, and the upper classes drew on superior resources. The defeat and execution of Morelos in 1815 left only a few smouldering local insurgencies in the south.

In the years after the effective repression of the rural uprisings, a spirit of dissidence reemerged among the Creoles of Mexico City. Soon the Spanish liberal revolution of 1820 gave other, more prominent Creoles new causes for dissatisfaction. As in South America, the fighting of the years since 1810 had created opportunities for social mobility. Creoles had entered the civil, military, and ecclesiastical hierarchies in large numbers. Their new status had solidified their opposition to the kind of revolution led by Hidalgo and Morelos without increasing their desire to remain subject to imperial tutelage.

Surprisingly, the anticlerical policies of the new liberal government in Spain seemed to favor the defeated cause of Hidalgo and Morelos over that of the elite victors. The movements led by two revolutionary priests had marched with religious images at their head, but they had also jeopardized the wealth and position of the ecclesiastical hierarchy. Morelos had even included church lands among those to be divided by the insurgents, driving Mexican bishops unambiguously into the conservative alliance. Now, however, measures similar to those proposed by Morelos had been announced by the Spanish liberals in power across the Atlantic, who moreover appeared willing to make common cause with Spanish American revolutionaries. Such a reconciliation would weaken the forces of absolutism in Spain while encouraging the recognition of Spanish sovereignty in what remained of the empire. The Mexican defenders of the cause of Ferdinand VII had reasons to fear that they would be the principal losers in such a reconciliation.

These apprehensions provoked Agustín de Iturbide, a Creole military officer who had made his career fighting Morelos, to proclaim his "Plan of Iguala," guaranteeing the privileges of the Catholic church and the equality of Spaniards vis-à-vis Creoles in an independent Mexican monarchy to be governed by a Spanish prince. Iturbide's army paraded around the country collecting protestations of support before entering the capital city in triumph. The Plan of Iguala left the choice of Mexico's new monarch to Ferdinand VII (who subsequently refused to designate a new ruler for his rebellious kingdom). In all Mexico, only the garrison of the port of Veracruz remained loyal to the king, and the Captaincy of Guatemala (including all of Central America) soon joined its northern neighbor in declaring independence from Spain.

The Spanish America that emerged from the wars of independence was different from what it had been in 1810 but different, too, from what the revolutionaries had expected. The war itself—its unexpected duration and the fierce polarization that it brought to some areas—constituted a major cause of the difference, and the case of Brazil provides a valuable point of comparison in this regard.

Brazil's independence came without the violent struggle that ravaged Spanish America. To a degree, looser colonial bonds between Portugal and Brazil had prepared the way for a less disruptive separation. Since the seventeenth century, Portugal had ceased to dominate its own colonies economically as they moved together into the commercial orbit of Great Britain. In the late eighteenth-century period of imperial reform, the Portuguese did make considerable efforts to increase their control over Brazil, but the efforts of tiny Portugal to regain mastery of its sprawling American territory were less ambitious than those of Spain and provoked less colonial reaction. While the mining boom attracted a large migration of peninsular Portuguese to Brazil during this time, native-born Brazilians did not suffer the same imposition of an administrative and commercial elite newly arrived from Europe to replace the agents of local dominance.

International events of 1790–1810 affected Brazil differently from Spanish America, further strengthening the commercial hegemony of Great Britain over Portugal and its colony. Sensitive to the threat posed by France being in alliance with neighboring Spain, the Portuguese Crown still sought at all cost to maintain its lines of trans-Atlantic communication, which the British navy had the power to interrupt at will. The British naval blockade against Napoleonic Europe ultimately doomed Portuguese attempts to maintain neutrality in the conflict, and the decision to move the Portuguese court to Rio de Janeiro was not taken without significant pressure from Great Britain. João VI sailed out of Lisbon in late 1807 with a British naval escort in what amounted almost to an armed abduction. The result for Brazil was a sweeping commercial reorganization in which Great Britain received the status of most favored nation. Under the new treaty, British products paid lower tariffs than those of Portugal itself, and British merchants were exempted from the jurisdiction of ordinary Brazilian courts. Their disputes would be heard by a special tribunal, in a fashion reminiscent of European trading privileges in the Middle East.

This state of affairs naturally produced tensions, but the Portuguese monarchy had been so battered in the preceding two decades of European turmoil that it was unable to register the slightest resistance.

Undercut by this British commercial intrusion, the colonial compact binding Portugal and Brazil showed its fragility as the French occupation receded. In 1813, French power in the peninsula was crumbling, and the Portuguese court was free to return to Lisbon. Within the next two years, order had been restored throughout Europe, yet João VI showed no inclination to leave Rio de Janeiro. He had good reason to fear that the Brazilians would no longer submit to being ruled from Lisbon. In 1817, a republican uprising shook Pernambuco, in the sugar-growing region of the northeast Brazilian coast, and it was not easily suppressed. Finally, the 1820 liberal revolution in Portugal impelled the king to return to Europe, apparently advising his son Pedro to lead the independence movement himself when it became inevitable.

The trend toward independence, prepared by the dissemination of republican ideas in Brazil, accelerated after the liberal regime in Portugal decided to return Brazil to a colonial status. Pedro's efforts to avoid an open confrontation failed as Brazilian and Portuguese forces clashed in Bahia. When the liberal-dominated Portuguese assembly demanded Pedro's strict submission to its centralizing directives, the young prince trampled on the orders and declared Brazilian independence at Ipiranga on 7 September 1822. Portuguese recognition of Brazilian independence came under British prodding three years later.

Created with a minimum of violence and in harmony with the political climate of restorationist Europe, the Brazilian empire was often held up as a model for turbulent Spanish America. The survival of the monarchy under Pedro I appeared to explain the continued unity of Portuguese America, while the Spanish American republics became progressively more fragmented. Brazilian unity was not maintained without a struggle, however. In 1824, a republican rebellion erupted in Pernambuco, and the next year patriots in the Banda Oriental revolted against Brazilian occupation of that Spanish territory. (After defeating Artigas in 1819, the Portuguese had formally annexed the Banda Oriental, which temporarily became Brazil's new Cisplatine Province.) In Rio de Janeiro, Pedro I found it necessary to dissolve a rather defiant constituent assembly, preferring to author the Constitution of 1824 himself, with the advice of only a few trusted advisers. Pedro promised a liberal constitution, and the one delivered did establish a parliamentary system. Brazilian independence, accomplished with a minimum of social disruption, left power in the hands of substantially the same groups who had wielded it during the last years of Portuguese rule. Though Brazil escaped the level of civil disruption that characterized Spanish America in the coming decades, its early years of political independence were stormy nevertheless. In both areas, strife arose from the difficult search for a new internal equilibrium more compatible with the changed relationship between Latin America and the rest of the world.

CHAPTER III

THE EARLY

NATIONAL PERIOD

(1825–1850)

IN 1825, ONLY RUINS REMAINED of the former Spanish empire. Its trading networks had been undone, and the people most closely associated with it had suffered thorough persecution. The years of warfare had widened the circles of political power, and, in many places, they had put it within reach of new social groups. The people who had struggled for independence now looked ahead to a brighter future, but the legacy of colonialism was a heavy one, and the new order did not quickly emerge. These problems had parallels in the former Portuguese empire as well, though Brazil's transition from colony to nation had been less fraught with disruptions.

One explanation for the long hiatus of economic development in the aftermath of war centers on the impact of the wars themselves. The years of fighting had resulted in a militarization of Spanish American societies as both revolutionaries and royalists appealed to progressively larger sectors of the population and armed them for the fight. Especially in Venezuela, Mexico, and the Río de la Plata, the military mobilization of the masses had been preceded by only the sketchiest sort of political mobilization, completely incapable of providing effective discipline during the violent eruption of long-repressed racial and regional tensions. Patriot and royalist accounts offer mirror images of the bloody horrors committed by the other side. Each side excused the excesses committed by its own partisans as uncontrollable instances of mob justice.

The violence of the wars of independence had become more systematic and purposeful than such accounts suggest. Armies perpetually without supplies had been encouraged by their officers to extract what they required from local populations. Fifteen years of fighting had resulted in a proliferation of armed bands, each with its own esprit de corps. After the defeat of the royalists, such groups provided a power base for numerous officers drawn from the Creole elite. The arrogance of these officers became a topic of complaint from Caracas to Buenos Aires on occasions when their soldiers saber-whipped an "impertinent" priest, judge, or journalist. However infuriated by the arrogant officers, the civil authorities needed them to control the dissidents who abounded in the aftermath of war. Royalist guerrillas maintained a tenacious resistance in Pasto, a mountainous area of New Granada, despite, or perhaps because of, the violence committed by patriot bands there. The armies of Buenos Aires burned and looted in uncooperative Santa Fe, formerly aligned with Artigas against the port capital.

[margin note: violent disorganization following war]

Violence thus became an endemic fact of daily life in Spanish America. Nostalgic recollections of the colonial period often included descriptions of a countryside where travelers had no need to fear the attack of armed men. The wars of independence had made a return to that situation impossible. The only way to maintain public order was to keep the government forces better armed than the rebels and bandits.

Increasing militarization added to the economic burdens of the new states, and it contained the seeds of future political instability. The leaders of irregular armed forces could easily become independent of the governments that organized them. The armies of the young Spanish American republics arrived at independence with far too many commissioned officers for peacetime purposes, and in most cases, dismissing them was risky. In order to retain the loyalty of their overgrown armies, the new governments had to invest a major portion of their resources in military payrolls, but for that they needed more state revenues. Extracting those revenues required, in turn, the further use of force in what became a self-perpetuating cycle. The new republics that had sent their armies of independence beyond their borders—Argentina, Chile, and Gran Colombia—had yet another problem because they had created rural militias to maintain order at home during the armies' absence, and these groups, too, became armed power contenders in the period after independence. Militias of this kind, closely allied with the local interests of their areas, resisted the increasingly onerous demands of the regular army, but in order to do so, they required more arms themselves. As a result of this state of affairs, military expenditures accounted for more than half of the state budget in most of the new republics of Spanish America.

[margin note: increasing militarization ① burden econ. ② future instability]

[margin note: overgrown armies]

[margin note: half state budget on military]

At the outset, the militarization of society in the aftermath of independence presented opportunities for democratization by creating a much wider distribution of power than had characterized the late colonial period. However, the militarization of Spanish American so-

ciety quickly became a barrier to some of the democratizing changes it
had appeared initially to advance. In the first half of the nineteenth
century, the Spanish American republics were already gaining a reputation abroad as countries frequently occupied by their own armed
forces. Still, other democratizing tendencies presented a more encouraging picture, especially when viewed in the context of the late colonial social structures of only a few years earlier.

The decisive decline of slavery after independence is not the least
of these changes. Admittedly, the new republics shied away from
immediate abolition, preferring such halfway measures as the prohibition of the slave trade and the passage of laws granting free birth to
the children of enslaved women, but the erosion of the institution
occurred both steadily and rapidly. During the wars of independence
and during the civil strife that followed, the manumission of individual slaves became quite common. Such manumissions were directly
linked to the need for fighters, but the military recruitment of freed-
men could also be seen as a strategy for making sure that the black
population did its share of the dying. Even Simon Bolívar at one point
argued that manumission would help keep the white population from
being overwhelmed demographically. The argument held limited appeal for the cacao and coffee planters of Venezuela, who continued
their obstinate defense of slavery in the 1820s and beyond. As in the
sugar plantations of the Peruvian coast and the mines of New Granada,
however, the productivity of slavery declined markedly, indicating a
subtle but undeniable erosion of the institution from within. Without
the further importation of slaves, their replacement cost rose rapidly,
as much as tripling in Peru during the first decade after the decisive victory at Ayacucho. By the time of abolition (at mid-century in
most of Spanish America, the exceptions being Cuba and Puerto Rico,
which remained under the control of Spain), slavery had already lost
most of its former economic importance.

Admittedly, the emancipated slaves were not recognized as equals
by the white populations (or even by the population of mixed bloods,
for that matter), yet the caste system of the late colonial period had
lost its legal sanction and mestizos and mulattoes found fewer obstacles to their social mobility after independence. A good indicator of
the decay of caste distinctions in this middle range of the socioracial
hierarchy can be found in the racial categories used by census takers.
Even when the late colonial caste distinctions were maintained as
categories in the census enumerations of the postindependence era
(and this was not always the case), the number of individuals so

classified dropped drastically, showing that the distinctions had already blurred in practice.

The Indian communities of Mexico, Guatemala, and the Andean highlands survived comparatively untouched in the period after the wars of independence. Early republican governments generally left in place the colonial statutes whereby indigenous communities held a separate position within the rest of civil society. They did so not from any special desire to protect the Indian communities, whose corporate organization they theoretically disapproved, but rather because a sluggish market economy offered few profitable uses for land in this period. The internal market was particularly weak in the countries with large indigenous populations, who tended to supply most of their own needs, and agricultural export activities had been disrupted by the wars of independence. Great landowners, merchants, and urban lawyers had scant incentive to launch, as yet, the attack on Indian common lands that would come only in the second half of the century. As a result, the extensive landholdings of Indian villages remained, for the time being, in the hands of impoverished villagers who often lacked written title to their land.

Urban elites would later help to undermine the legal status of Indian communal landholdings, but in the years immediately following independence they were preoccupied with the defense of their own social position. The caste system and the de facto discrimination against Creoles of the late colonial period had helped urban elites to limit the upward mobility of mixed bloods and poor whites, but the years of fighting had increased that mobility among both royalists and revolutionaries. Agustín de Iturbide, briefly emperor of Mexico, had been born to a provincial Creole family in the last years of colonial rule. In Peru, another stronghold of the colonial aristocracy, the careers of the powerful mestizo leaders of the early national period (Andrés de Santa Cruz, Agustín Gamarra, and Ramón Castilla, for example) also exemplify this new mobility. The new rulers of Venezuela and the Río de la Plata represent a different threat to the urban elites of the late colonial period—the new rural power base created by the wars of independence. The force of numbers had become a more important variable in these militarized societies, and the greater numbers resided in the countryside, giving a distinct advantage to rural ruling groups in any conflict with the urban merchants, magistrates, and bureaucrats who had formerly wielded such disproportionate influence within the colonial regime.

There had occurred no profound change in the social order of the countryside itself, however, despite the incidence of seemingly radical episodes in places like the Banda Oriental. (José Artigas himself had approved of a requirement whereby the landless inhabitants of the Banda Oriental had to carry proof of employment in order not to be considered vagrants.) The mobilization of rural masses in the wars of independence had not been self-directed. In all cases, the leadership remained with members of the landowning class or their representatives, and that also applied to the rural militias after 1825. Landlords who had fled to the cities during the fighting now returned to claim their property, and their claims were generally honored. This reconstitution of the prewar order facilitated the revival of export production, an imperative that few were willing to question. It also brought personal advantage to many, such as the commanders of Venezuelan llaneros who eventually made themselves into the rural ruling class of an independent but conservative republic. The most important permutation in rural areas may have been an accelerated turnover in the ranks of rural landowners, especially in the areas most disrupted by the fighting of the war years.

As a group, rural landowners posed a challenge to the urban elites who had completely overshadowed them before the revolutions. Landed property had been less vulnerable to destruction and expropriation during the fighting. The armies that swept back and forth across the countryside were voracious consumers of crops and livestock, but after they passed, the land could easily bring forth more crops, and stocks of cattle and sheep recovered within a few years. Urban elites, on the other hand, suffered comparatively more lasting loss to their personal fortunes. In addition, urban elites had lost economic leverage in the decline of such institutions as convents, mining guilds, or commercial consulados. The once-haughty consulados, for example, had been reduced to embattled intermediaries between the merchants and the aggressive agents of state power. Finally, the military capacity of the landowners compounded their economic advantage, bringing political superiority over the urban elites.

The power and prestige of urban elites in the late colonial period had derived, in large part, from their positions within such largely urban institutions as the magistracy and the church. Indeed, the revolutionary participation of urban Creoles must frequently have been motivated by an ambition to wrest control of these institutions from their peninsular competitors. Paradoxically, the manner of the victory all but destroyed the prize, and urban elites loyal to the patriot cause inherited profoundly weakened institutions. The magistracy lost the domineering authority of colonial times, and after 1825, judges became mere agents of a central authority in which they no longer played a leading role.

Usually associated with the royalist cause during the revolutions, the church lost much of its power and prestige in the postindependence period. According to one leader of the Buenos Aires revolution, the church was duty-bound to lend its voice to the patriot cause or else reveal itself unworthy of enjoying liberty. This was no idle threat. The new republics banished uncooperative bishops and priests and replaced them with episcopal administrators more amenable to the purposes of the civil authorities. Some clergy participated enthusiastically in the subordination of the church to the new republican order and simultaneously improved their own standing by offering splendid donations—precious ornaments, convent slaves, or cattle from ecclesiastical estates—in tribute to the liberating armies. In the Río de la Plata, priests and friars deserted in droves to join the political and military activities of the revolution. The church fared much better in Mexico, Guatemala, New Granada, and Ecuador, thanks to the steadfast piety of the great majority of the people, but even there church-state relations were troubled by the refusal of Rome to recognize the new republics and by the insistence of the republican governments on their right to appoint clergy to fill vacancies.

The weakening of the magistracy and the church forced urban elites to seek a new place for themselves in the refashioned structures of social dominance. Access to political and administrative power was just as necessary to the accumulation of wealth in the new republics as it had been in colonial days. Political connections remained the principal route to landownership, and many formerly urban-based elite families acquired large extensions of property. The manipulation of trading privileges no longer offered the advantages of colonial times. On the other hand, the republican governments' chronic shortage of funds presented a different opportunity for the rich families of Spanish American cities. From Mexico City to Buenos Aires, moneylenders did a prosperous, albeit risky, business in short-term loans with high interest and outrageous collateral guarantees. Amid the political instability that characterized the times, a tottering government might mortgage anything—from its customs receipts to a public square—in a desperate bid to survive and to interest others in its survival.

Along with the impact of fifteen years of warfare, fifteen years of being fully open to the Atlantic economy had produced a transformation no less profound and enduring. The patriots had made freedom of trade part of their revolutionary program, while the royalists had been forced to adopt a similar policy in practice because of their dependence on a British alliance. The result was a fundamental alteration in the relationship between Spanish America and the rest of the world. The international context in which the change took place conditioned the outcome. During the first half of the nineteenth century (with the exception of the two feverish years preceding the London financial collapse of 1825), no European country made large capital investments in Spanish America. Although the political turmoil of the period is cited as the reason for this omission, a look at the European economies suggests an additional explanation. Precisely during the years in question, England and the other industrializing powers of Europe produced barely enough surplus capital to cover the requirements of the first age of railroad building in the European continent and the United States.

During the first generation of Spanish American independence, the industrial economies of Europe needed a market not for their capital but for the manufactured products of their own industries. Their main economic concern within Spanish American lands was the monopolization of trading circuits. Among the agricultural exports Spanish America could offer in return, only sugar received a priority on the European agenda. Spanish America's precious metals retained their luster, but even so, the mines did not attract sufficient outside capital to recover the levels of productivity of the late colonial period. Instead, Great Britain saturated Spanish American markets with manufactured imports as early as 1815. As other manufacturing countries, including the United States, began to enter the competition, the imagined promise of Spanish American markets sank ever deeper into red ink.

Those who lost most in these years were precisely those who had dominated the commercial system of the colonies. This group had first been weakened by the split between its Creole and its peninsular members. Hoping to benefit from the ruin of their peninsular rivals, Creole merchants found themselves even less able to resist the onslaught of the foreign traders who rushed in next. The foreigners—especially the British merchants—were less vulnerable to the extortions of the indigent republican governments. However, most important in the decline of the Creole merchants was the collapse of their former commercial networks. Their principal trade link with Cádiz had been cut by decades of war and revolution, and the new link with London (after 1820, with Liverpool) privileged above all their new British competitors. Meanwhile, British and North American shipping crowded the nascent Spanish American merchant marines out of the sea lanes.

The European commercial conquest pushed further, into the formerly internal trade circuits between different parts of Spanish America. From Tampico to Valparaíso, British merchants began to trade directly in secondary ports that had once dealt with the outside world through primary ports like Veracruz or Lima. In only a few years, the richest prizes in Spanish American trade passed into the hands of foreigners. In her trip to Mexico in the early 1840s, Fanny Calderón de la Barca found the most impressive dwellings of interior towns already belonging to British merchants. A generation later, British surnames abounded in the upper-class families of Buenos Aires and elsewhere. In many ways, the domination of Cádiz had simply been exchanged for the hegemony of Liverpool.

hegemony of Liverpool

There were important differences between the emissaries of Cádiz and those of London or Liverpool, however, and they made themselves felt strongly in the years between 1810 and 1815. Charged with finding outlets for their country's surplus industrial production, the British merchant-adventurers of this period raced aggressively into areas newly liberated from Spanish control, bringing with them a much higher volume of trade than had characterized the colonial system. At least initially, the refashioned trading network put a larger supply of money into circulation—something that the colonial merchants had been careful to avoid, since a general scarcity of currency gave them special advantages in their dealings with rural producers. Both changes constituted improvements for most Spanish Americans, but they sounded a death knell for the Creole traders, whose profits derived from strict limitations on the circulation of money and goods.

Creole monopolies collapse

Unfortunately, the new system quickly encountered limits of its own. A depression in Europe held down the prices of Spanish American exports while, as has been previously mentioned, the real capacity of the Spanish American market to absorb manufactures proved disappointing, especially given the entry of competitors into that market after 1815. The industrial economy of Great Britain required that its trading representatives handle a relatively steady volume of manufactured products, especially textiles, a circumstance that often burdened British merchants with excessive inventories. North American traders, on the other hand, were much less driven by the need to unload an industrial surplus. They typically arrived in smaller vessels and dealt in variable stocks selected according to the fluctuating exigencies of the Spanish American market. British commercial policy therefore became increasingly rigid with the passage of time.

Britain—excessive surpluses

US—smaller stocks to unload

Despite the rigidities of the emerging commercial system, its higher volume of imports constituted a major innovation. Most of the newly imported products were inexpensive goods for a mass market, often carefully tailored to suit local Spanish American tastes. Ponchos *mass-produced replicas outsell local artisinal products* [handwritten margin note]

woven in the mills of Manchester with designs imitating the looms of Pampas Indians easily undersold the local product in the Argentine hinterland. Crates of Mexican *sarapes* made in Glasgow crowded wharves alongside boxes of "Toledo" cutlery from Sheffield. Besides conquering existing markets, the early glut of manufactured imports shaped the expectations of new Spanish American consumers. A growing proportion of the total volume of European imports during this period consisted in ever-cheaper cotton fabrics for the widening market. One well-known consequence of this state of affairs was the slow and incomplete—but irrevocable—deterioration of artisan production, as in the Andean highlands, where the cotton cloth of New England gradually overwhelmed the sweatshops run with Indian labor.

unable to put limits on imports [handwritten margin note]

Another consequence of the permanently higher volume of importation was an enduring trade imbalance and a renewed drain on the money supply. The governments of the new republics were hardly able to put legal limits on the flood of importations, even when they recognized the benefits of doing so. Given the wide market for the imported goods of the period, such limits would have been vastly unpopular. Furthermore, the pressure of landowners eager to protect their export products forced governments to depend in most cases on import tariffs for the bulk of the states' revenues. Like their colonial counterparts, the new masters of the market wanted precious metals rather than agricultural products in trade for their manufactured imports. In the Río de la Plata, cut off from the mining areas of Bolivia that once supplied its silver, the consequence was a severe reduction of the money in circulation, and even Chile, which expanded its production of silver, suffered from a similar scarcity.

Little foreign investment [handwritten margin note]

Such was the emerging equilibrium of the Spanish American commercial system in the period after the wars of independence. The epoch of large foreign investments would not arrive until the second half of the nineteenth century. In the meantime, there must have been a modest, hidden flow of foreign investment as successful European merchants bought land, but this sort of investment was itself limited by the low profitability of the agricultural sector. The position of that sector had improved slightly, relative to the commercial sector, but not nearly to the degree that some had envisioned during the movements for independence. Instead, Spanish American producers had been integrated into a new international trading system that shared an important characteristic with the Spanish colonial system: it was controlled by Europeans for their own benefit. Again, the tutelage of Spain had been replaced by that of Great Britain.

Market control from Spain to Britain [handwritten margin note]

The British did not achieve their hegemony without overcoming

some serious competitors. Between 1815 and 1830, the main challenger was the United States. U.S. enterprises enjoyed a number of
early successes, and around 1825 British consular officials in Mexico,
Lima, and Buenos Aires were all sounding the alarm about the proliferation of Yankee traders. The U.S. presence was strengthened by
the ostensible political affinity among fellow American republics. Unfortunately for the U.S. interests, they tended to ally themselves with
the more progressive factions within Spanish American countries
against the more conservative forces allied with the British, and the
conservatives came out the winners almost everywhere. Soon the diplomatic representatives of the United States had the unpleasant duty
of reporting the courteous indifference of Spanish American officials,
who nevertheless rushed to ingratiate themselves with British diplomats. In economic terms, U.S. competition declined steadily as the
new commercial networks were consolidated, and the greater flexibility of the Yankee trading style became less of an advantage as the
steady fall in the prices of cotton textiles from Lancashire edged the
rougher New England product out of the Spanish American market.

After 1830, France became Britain's main rival in Spanish America. French commerce was more complementary than threatening to
British interests because France specialized in luxury consumer articles and in Mediterranean food products of the kind that Spain had
formerly supplied, but the mere fact that a great European power
maintained close ties in Spanish America presented a potential danger
in the eyes of British policymakers. Fortunately for the British, French
political claims, meant to affirm the country's influence, tended to
miscarry and eventually dissipated the perceived menace. An early
French intervention in Mexico did prove successful, but a simultaneous and more problematic involvement in the Río de la Plata obtained much smaller benefits. Both episodes served principally to
alienate the sympathies with which many Spanish Americans had
previously regarded France. Aggressive and unpredictable French policies were no match for the subtle, systematic imposition of British
hegemony.

Despite the occasionally alarmist reports of its diplomatic representatives, Great Britain's sway over Spanish America was never really
in doubt during this period. The British government used its undeniable political influence to defend the interests of its mercantile representatives (who were the object of growing unpopularity after 1815)
and consolidated its privileged situation by hurrying to recognize the
newly independent states and then securing in return highly advantageous treaties of friendship, commerce, and navigation. Their hege-

mony rested mostly on treaties, commercial superiority, and naval power, but it functioned so effectively because of the extremely restrained manner in which the British made use of their leverage. Without a lot of surplus capital to invest, the British preferred for the time being to restrict their activities to the mercantile sphere, while eschewing any deeper involvement in the local economies.

British economic dominance contrasted with former Spanish dominance in that it was accomplished without direct political control. The beneficiaries of this informal empire avoided the complication and expense of administering it. They bore no responsibility for arbitrating the violent clashes among various local interests. Instead, they left those dubious honors to the Spanish American elites and concentrated on their profit margins. They did, of course, have very well defined ideas about which policies were most advisable and displayed no inhibitions about vigorously advancing their point of view, but their goals were generally quite limited and always pursued with a keen eye to the diminishing returns of their efforts. Stubborn resistance usually brought a quick abandonment of British insistence, as their dismayed internal allies discovered in many an instance. This minimalist approach corresponded to the commercial inspirations of British policy, which originated more often among the country's merchant representatives in Spanish America than among the high policy-making circles of the Foreign Office. In general, such policies sought to maintain present advantages along with a reasonable degree of internal order. With exceptions that became increasingly rare as the century advanced, the status quo remained the cynosure of British policy.

This cautious conservatism, rather than a Machiavellian desire to divide and conquer, explains Britain's acceptance of the increasing political fragmentation of Spanish America in the 1820s and 1830s. Whenever the aggregation of fragmented states into larger political units appeared a real possibility, the British in fact supported it, as in the case of Bolívar's gestures at Pan-Hispanism or Santa Cruz's attempt at a Peruvian-Bolivian Confederation. It is true that Great Britain took the initiative in creating an independent buffer state in the Banda Oriental to end the fighting between Argentina and Brazil and true as well that the solution had very favorable implications for British commerce since it prevented Argentina from monopolizing control of the Río de la Plata, but the rapid restoration of peace to the region seems to be what most preoccupied the diplomats of Great Britain in this case, as in most others. A protracted struggle over questions of political organization was much more likely to damage

British interests than the maintenance of the smaller republics that had emerged spontaneously in the wake of the wars of independence. On the other hand, the highly advantageous British commercial accommodation in Brazil suggests that the dominant world power of the day had, at any rate, little reason to fear the power of large Spanish American republics.

The prudence of British policies in the region partly accounts for the abiding strength of that country's hegemony over Latin America long after its effective commercial monopoly had ended. The Argentine dictator Juan Manuel de Rosas, who prided himself on a nativist opposition to European aggressions, searched discretely for conciliatory solutions with the British while exhibiting a much more inflexible attitude toward the French. The French, he believed, would tire and withdraw, but even the most tenacious resistance seemed unlikely to erase the British presence in the Río de la Plata, nor was such an outcome desirable. The rulers of Brazil found themselves in a similar relationship with the British. British efforts to eliminate the slave trade between Africa and Brazil met stubborn antagonism from Brazilian elites. The conflict continued for decades and led at one point to the severing of diplomatic relations, but the idea of moving definitively out of the commercial orbit of Great Britain was never seriously entertained.

Only toward the middle of the nineteenth century did the United States begin to loom on the horizon as a contender for political supremacy in the Caribbean because of its triumph in the Mexican-American War and its tentative interest in annexing Cuba. The future influence of the United States received official recognition in the Clayton-Bulwer Treaty of 1850, an Anglo-American agreement regarding the future construction of an isthmian canal. The still-limited interests of the United States in northern Latin America were driven by the double engines of territorial expansionism (viewed by U.S. southerners as a way to strengthen the institution of slavery) and the need to find a quicker route between the eastern United States and the goldfields of California.

For the time being, however, the forays of an incipient U.S. expansionism in Mexico and Central America could not disrupt the new commercial equilibrium that had settled over the hemisphere. By the 1840s, the threat of a Spanish reconquest of its lost empire had disappeared completely, opening the door for a nostalgic reassessment of the placid virtues of a colonial existence. Among the changes brought by independence, the negative consequences stood out: the debasement of civil administration, a tendency to chronic upheaval, and heavy-handed governmental repression of an armed and politically mobilized populace, leaving insurgency as their only recourse. As civil war followed civil war, optimistic views of the future faded and reforming impulses slowed. Given this conservative mood and the unfavorable economic juncture in Europe, international trade stagnated. Between 1825 and 1850, the level of international trade in Spanish America as a whole rose only slightly.

Of course, there existed significant contrasts between different regions within Spanish America. Despite the disruptions of war in Venezuela and the Río de la Plata, the agricultural exportations of these areas soon surpassed the most prosperous years of colonial rule. Each had inherited from the colonial period an economy already oriented toward agricultural and livestock production for the trans-Atlantic market. The advantage of having such an orientation already in place outweighed the disadvantages of political turbulence. In Peru, Bolivia, and particularly Mexico, the economic picture was dismal by contrast. The mining industries of all three had suffered tremendous destruction during the wars of independence and could not return to prewar production levels without significant investment from overseas. In the absence of that investment, Mexico's mining output declined to half of that of the last decades of colonial rule. In New Granada and Chile, a rise in livestock production for export helped compensate for the decline of the silver mines. Chile also began to export copper worth more than its silver and gold combined in the mid-1820s (though silver exports recovered first place in the 1830s).

In a striking reversal, the former marginal areas of Spanish American colonization had surpassed the old core areas of the empire in economic vitality. In 1810, exports of the Río de la Plata had amounted to a mere fifth of the value of Mexican exports, but by mid-century the two areas exported products of comparable value. Though Platine exports no longer included silver from Potosí, livestock production for export had increased tenfold. The same pattern manifested itself in a less extreme form throughout Spanish America. Without production for export or capital for innovations, most of Central America had stagnated. In Honduras and Nicaragua, the American traveler John Lloyd Stevens met ranchers who owned extensions as vast as some European provinces but who were unable to transform their land and animals into capital wealth because of their isolation from the market. Meanwhile, the central valley of Costa Rica, one of the poorest parts of colonial Central America, had established a very profitable link to that market through the cultivation of coffee. Finally, Cuba, another of the marginal areas that had entered rapid economic growth on the eve of independence, ranked with Argentina and Venezuela as one of Spanish America's most dynamic exporters in the second quarter of the nineteenth century. The moment was quite favorable for Cuba because of the disruption of sugar production in the British Antilles (where slavery had recently been abolished) and because of the commercial liberalization allowed by Spain (desperate to retain the little that remained of its empire). Between 1815 and 1850, Cuban sugar exports surged roughly from 40,000 to 200,000 tons. The Atlantic coast of Spanish America, so secondary in the imperial scheme of things until the late eighteenth century, would lead the older highland and Pacific coast areas in economic growth during much of the nineteenth century.

The newly independent Brazilian empire shared in the dynamism of the Atlantic coast economies. To begin with, the disorganization of sugar production in the British Antilles stimulated Brazilian sugar exports as it did Cuban exports, bringing a temporary return of prosperity to the sugar-growing regions along the northeast coast of Brazil. In the far south, Brazilian territory witnessed an expansion of ranching analogous to developments in the nearby Río de la Plata. Economic vitality in the north and the south created a centrifugal tendency and strained the political dominance of Rio de Janeiro, and if the Brazilian empire remained intact in the 1820s and 1830s, it was not without considerable conflict. By the 1840s, however, the rise of the coffee economy in the lands around Rio de Janeiro helped restore political and economic equilibrium and ushered in a period of stability. The Brazilian adaptation to the new political and economic order became a model often compared to the Spanish American republics as a measure of their failure. Brazil adapted more successfully partly thanks to strong continuities between the Portuguese period and the independence period. The tutelage of Portugal had always rested more lightly on its colony than had Spain's on its colonies, and the exchange of Portuguese political hegemony for British economic hegemony had taken place gradually.

Still, Brazil's transition to the new order contained some difficult contradictions. The new prosperity of the sugar economy and the rise of coffee plantations put the Brazilian government at cross-purposes with Great Britain in the matter of the slave trade. Unlike the slave regime of the southern United States, the slave population of Brazil did not reproduce itself fast enough to compensate for its high death rate, and it steadily declined without the continuous importation of enslaved Africans. Thus, the Brazilian government came under intense pressure from the sugar planters to resist British efforts at abolition of the slave trade, and, even while agreeing in theory to ban the trade,

the Brazilians stubbornly protected it in practice. In some years during
the early nineteenth century, traders brought in record numbers of
slaves, partly because the determined British campaign against the
slave trade indicated that an inevitable crisis lay ahead. While tenaciously defending the slave trade, the Brazilian government gradually
gave ground in various other conflicts with the hegemonic power of
Great Britain. The 1827 treaty between the two countries confirmed
important concessions extracted by the British in 1810 during the
French occupation of Portugal: the complete opening of the Brazilian
market to goods imported from England (prohibiting any kind of protective tariff) and the retention of special courts for British residents in
Brazil. As a result, Brazil overshadowed all Spanish American countries as a market for British products. The value of British goods
imported into Brazil soon reached four times the value of British
imports to the Río de la Plata, producing a huge trade imbalance and an
inexorable drain on the money supply.

These financial difficulties were accompanied by a weakening of
centralized political power comparable to that which resulted from
the militarization of society in the Spanish American republics. In
Brazil, where the impact of the wars of independence had been minimal, Emperor Pedro I shared power with a General Assembly dominated by the landowning class and often at odds with his policies. The
underlying autocratic tendencies in this supposedly constitutional
monarchy soon surfaced, polarizing the political forces of Brazil between conservatives who supported the centralized control of the
monarch and liberals who favored decentralization and further limits
on the monarch's power. The conservatives tended to speak for urban
interests, especially bureaucrats and merchants in central Brazil, who
were closely associated with the former colonial order. (Many of them
were, in fact, Portuguese-born like the emperor himself—Brazilian
independence not having produced a mass exodus analogous to the
collective departure of peninsular Spaniards from Spanish America.)
The liberals, on the other hand, tended to identify with the landowners of the economically thriving north and south and were often
anti-Portuguese. To maintain his dominance over this group, Pedro I
relied on an army that included large numbers of Portuguese-born
officers and foreign mercenaries.

An ill-fated foreign adventure further contributed to Pedro I's troubles. As mentioned earlier, Portuguese forces had occupied the Banda
Oriental after the defeat of Artigas, formally annexing it as Brazil's
Cisplatine Province in 1820. The independence of Brazil shortly afterward did not change the situation, but an uprising of Uruguayan

patriots against the occupation began in 1825, and once the rebels gained momentum, the government of Buenos Aires joined them in a war against Brazil. Pedro I was in no mood to allow a humiliating defeat to further diminish his prestige, but those most likely to support his war effort were not his habitual backers among conservative bureaucrats and merchants but rather the predominantly liberal landowners of the far south, for whom the Cisplatine Province had offered rich opportunities to expand their properties. The war therefore further complicated political alignments within Brazil and ended, at any rate, in failure. Thoroughly beaten on land, Brazilian forces attempted to smother the enemy economically by blockading Buenos Aires before finally accepting the British proposal to recognize the independence of the Banda Oriental as a compromise and a buffer between the ambitions of Buenos Aires and Rio de Janeiro.

The war had created an exorbitant drain on the Brazilian treasury, and disastrous financial conditions within the country further undermined the power of the emperor. Willing to try anything in the crisis of war, Pedro I adopted the most criticized measure of his troubled reign, one strictly contrary to the economic doctrines of the time: the issue of paper currency. The resulting inflation provided a respite from the pressing problems of governmental penury and the lack of a sufficient medium of exchange in the economy as a whole, but the measure also created an almost chaotic situation in which banks of issue multiplied erratically, several debased metallic currencies competed with the paper currency, and counterfeiting ran rampant. As a result, the Brazilian *milréis* lost half its value against the British pound sterling in the first quarter century of independence. Landowners exporting to the international market actually profited from the inflation since they earned hard currency abroad and spent devalued currency at home. Urban groups (especially merchants) suffered, however, and salaried employees were hurt most of all. These town dwellers now added their voices to the chorus of political dissidence led by rural-based liberals, and the threat of seditious urban crowds provoked violent official repression. In 1831, Pedro I decided to turn his back on these problems. He abdicated his throne and returned to Portugal to defend his daughter's claim to the Portuguese crown, leaving his five-year-old male heir, Pedro II, to inherit the Brazilian throne when he came of age.

The regency that governed during the young emperor's minority nearly presided over the dissolution of the empire. Crippled by the departure of Pedro I, the conservative proponents of centralized power were unable to prevent the passage of constitutional amendments that strengthened the liberals. The Additional Act of 1834 conceded a large measure of autonomy to the provincial governments and began a de facto federalist experiment, releasing potent centrifugal forces within the Brazilian polity. By the end of 1835, major revolts raged in the Amazonian north and the cattle-ranching south, and they continued to multiply during the next five years. By 1840, the federalist experiment had become an acknowledged failure, the decentralizing reforms were being undone, and the chastened liberals in the central government henceforth made common cause with their former political foes to save the empire from fragmentation. The early accession of Pedro II to the throne, at the age of fifteen, marked a return to the predominance of the central government. The longest and most menacing of the provincial revolts, that of the cattle barons of Rio Grande do Sul, ended in 1845 when its leaders were lured back into the imperial fold, and a final revolt in the north flared and failed in 1848.

The long reign of Pedro II was characterized by internal peace and stability. The ideological rivalry between the liberals and conservatives, now formally constituted as parties, diminished thanks to the reigning consensus among the elites and the skillful intervention of the Crown in preventing either party from monopolizing power. Each party was built on local networks of kin and clientele that, when satisfied in their immediate interests, became largely indifferent to matters of larger policy. Power flowed from the top down, and the imperial army, strengthened by its role in suppressing the rebellions of the 1840s, functioned as the guarantor of internal peace. The reconciliation among formerly antagonistic political forces in Brazil had been possible also because the elite class found broad common ground in resisting British attempts to suppress the slave trade. Maintenance of the slave trade was believed essential for the well-being of both the sugar economy of the north and the coffee economy of the center. British policing of trans-Atlantic navigation drove the price of slaves up and offered opportunities to the merchants of Brazilian ports, happy to find at least one profitable business without British competition. Eventually, however, the rising cost of slaves caused a divergence of interests between the slave traders and the landowners, and the Brazilian government finally succumbed to British pressures by putting an effective end to the slave trade in 1851.

Its ability finally to end the slave trade indicates the political strength and stability attained by the Brazilian empire at the mid-nineteenth century. Imperial foreign policy was reinvigorated and acquired expansive force from the reconciliation between the central government and the formerly rebellious liberals of the empire's southernmost province of Rio Grande do Sul. In 1851, a Brazilian army reentered the international fray in the Río de la Plata, so long dominated by the Argentine dictator Juan Manuel de Rosas. In alliance with the internal adversaries of Rosas, the Rio Grandense cattle barons and regular imperial troops defeated Rosas and reestablished Brazilian hegemony over the Republic of Uruguay, where so many Rio Grandense ranchers owned property. For the next twenty years, the Brazilian empire was to play an active part in the affairs of its southern neighbors.

In economic terms, Brazilian progress had been relatively slow but steady. Export earnings had grown from a yearly average of about four million pounds sterling in the 1830s to almost five and a half million in the 1850s, but the trade deficit had also increased since the value of imports had risen slightly faster. Nor had the expansion of the economy kept pace with the growth of the population, which doubled from four to eight million in roughly the same time period. Nevertheless, there were enough economic advances to explain, in combination with the country's political stability, the undeniable prestige that the Brazilian empire enjoyed in nineteenth-century Spanish American eyes. During the first generation of postindependence commercial expansion, Rio de Janeiro had functioned as a distribution center for European imports to Buenos Aires and Valparaíso, and along with this larger volume of trade had come greater maturity of financial structures. Brazil thus acquired a stable banking system before any of its Spanish American neighbors. After 1851, Brazilian political intervention in the Río de la Plata went hand in hand with the extension of Brazilian banks into Uruguay and Argentina under the leadership of Irineu Evangelista de Souza, whose financial exploits merited him the title of baron, and later viscount, of Mauá from a grateful emperor. Like the triumph of Brazilian arms in Uruguay and Argentina, the financial conquests of Mauá were ephemeral, but at the time they appeared to confirm the superiority of the Brazilian path to independent statehood over the Spanish American path.

An often-cited sign of Spanish American failure was its division into more than a dozen republics while independent Brazil remained unified. Yet the political fragmentation of Spanish America flowed directly from the increasing subdivision of the Spanish colonial administration, which saw the creation of two new viceroyalties during the eighteenth century. The trend in the colonial administration of Brazil, on the other hand, was toward consolidation. By the end of the colonial period, all of Portuguese America had been brought together under the rule of a single viceroy in Rio de Janeiro. Given the concentration of Brazilian settlement along the Atlantic coast, such a solution was practicable for the Portuguese, whereas no single center could possibly have governed Spanish American territories that stretched from Florida and California to Peru and Argentina. The hard-fought wars of independence had confirmed the existing internal divisions of Spanish America and created a few new ones. It was the fighting for independence itself that had driven wedges between various parts of the former viceroyalty of the Río de la Plata. The wars of independence had resulted in the temporary unity of Gran Colombia but also planted the seeds of Venezuelan and Ecuadorian secession within a decade. Only in the United Provinces of Central America (which dissolved into its five constituent parts by 1841) did the process of fragmentation appear unrelated to the impact of the revolution itself.

Simon Bolívar had tried to maintain the unity of Spanish America by recognizing certain deeply ingrained traits of the old order. Bolívar's idealism had been tempered by his long career as war leader, and he had little use for the "Jacobin" ideologues of the new republics. Hostile to the principle of monarchy, he also pointed out that, in practical (and Machiavellian) terms, "no power is more difficult to maintain than that of a new prince." Bolívar advocated governments of an authoritarian cut that he believed were more suited to Spanish American traditions and realities. He recommended a limited franchise and a lifetime presidency to insure the predominance of the upper classes, providing stability to the political architecture of the new nations. However, Bolívar's conservative projects proved to be no more viable than what he called "the airy republics" of his more radical rivals.

In 1825, Bolívar's blueprint for an authoritarian republic became the basis of the Bolivian constitution. The next year the same blueprint was applied to Peru, where it replaced the more liberal document of 1823, and Bolívar took office as the first of Peru's lifetime presidents. From that point on, though, the Liberator's dreams for the postindependence political order met only disappointment. Within months of taking office in Peru, he had to return to Gran Colombia, which suddenly threatened to fly apart. Bolívar's old friend José Antonio Páez, the commander of Venezuelan llaneros, was unhappy with the rule of Gran Colombian president Francisco de Paula Santander. In placating Páez, however, Bolívar alienated Santander, and the breach between the two leaders quickly became unbridgeable. The opponents of Bolívar predominated in the framing of a new constitution, which Santander endorsed enthusiastically. Bolívar accused Santander of conspiring against him, while Santander progressively adopted the position of defender of the rule of law in the face of Bolivarian high-

handedness. The supporters of Bolívar substantiated these accusations
when they deposed Santander and placed all power in the hands of the
Liberator. Bolívar's suspicion of conspiracies also materialized in the
form of an attempt on his life that he barely escaped.

Meanwhile, the Bolivarian order had begun to collapse in the
south as well. The Gran Colombian army had remained stationed in
Peru and Bolivia after the battle of Ayacucho, to the displeasure of the
local population and of the troops themselves, who finally revolted
and put an end to the lifetime presidency of their nominal leader,
restoring the Peruvian constitution of 1823. The new president of
Peru, José de la Mar, a docile representative of the aristocracy of Lima,
had been a Spanish career officer and a royalist until 1821. The anti-
Bolivarian movement swept from Peru to Bolivia, ousting the Liberator's most-trusted lieutenant, Antonio José de Sucre, and abolishing
the constitution written by Bolívar for that country. War between Peru
and Gran Colombia followed, and all semblance of Bolivarian unity in
the Andes was lost forever when Venezuela and Ecuador seceded from
Gran Colombia. By that time, the disconsolate Bolívar had already
given up power and prepared to leave for Europe, comparing his efforts
to "plowing the sea." He died a few months later near the shores of the
Caribbean, apparently of tuberculosis.

Bolívar had inspired the most famous attempt to create a confederation of all the former colonies of Spain. This was the Congress of
American Republics, which met in 1826 in Panama, chosen as a central location easily reached by sea from any part of Spanish America.
Interestingly, the initiative was supported by British policymakers
who saw in it the potential to stabilize the unruly political situation of
the Spanish American republics. Not even the republican character of
the proposed league was an obstacle for Great Britain. Although theoretically proponents of constitutional monarchy, the British realized
that, in practice, efforts to create Spanish American monarchies were
apt to bring dynastic alliances with continental European powers.
Only Gran Colombia, Peru, Mexico, and Central America sent representatives to the congress, however. Neither Chile nor Argentina had
shown any eagerness to become part of a Spanish American organization dominated by Bolívar, and the Brazilian emperor had displayed
open hostility to the project (which he regarded as potentially a league
of Spanish American republics against monarchical Brazil).

The process of independence had changed Spanish America more
than Bolívar realized. He wanted to base his plans for the new order on
a practical evaluation of Spanish American realities. He was most
impressed by the weight of a prerevolutionary heritage that survived

into the new era, but he perhaps took insufficient account of some of the changes that had occurred. In seeking to establish the republican order primarily on the basis of urban elite participation, he built on an element greatly weakened during the revolutions and gave insufficient attention to the rural elite, whose military capacity had made it effectively dominant. Bolívar was hardly ignorant of the importance of military power, but he believed that its leading role would be ephemeral and that, in the end, the prerevolutionary social hierarchy was the only sound basis for political stability. Paradoxically, when he rode into Bogotá or Lima at the head of a conquering army, the urban elites on whom the Liberator had pinned his hopes naturally identified him with the ruralized military forces that had risen to challenge their social hegemony, and they worked against him precisely for that reason. Meanwhile, the military men became dissatisfied with the meager place reserved for them in the Bolivarian order, and they often made common cause with the urban elites to rid themselves of the erstwhile Liberator.

Elusive dreams of restoring key elements of the old order lasted longer in Mexico, where they effectively dominated the first political generation after independence. The nostalgia of the Mexican upper classes was understandable, given their prosperity during the last period of colonial rule, and their influence had remained powerful through the years of revolution and counterrevolution. Mexican conservatism became the haven of those who had observed the collapse of the imperial system with bitter resignation, while Mexican liberalism gathered together those who had hoped to better their social position as a result of independence.

As elsewhere in Spanish America, force of arms played a large role in the working out of new political arrangements, though in Mexico that force was concentrated in the regular army with its swollen officer corps inherited from the wars of independence. An army revolt ended the brief rule of the Creole emperor Iturbide after a matter of months. The leader of the revolt was the still relatively little known Gen. Antonio López de Santa Anna, followed by many former royalists like himself, unhappy with the indifference shown them by Iturbide (whose treasury did not enable much generosity). In the matter of Iturbide's overthrow, the former royalists could still make common cause with officers from the ranks of the former patriot insurgents, naturally unsympathetic to Iturbide's imperial airs. A constituent assembly then chose as the next leader of the country Gen. Guadalupe Victoria, a former patriot insurgent who tried to maintain a political equilibrium in spite of his own liberal inclinations.

The two parties destined to contend for supremacy through the middle of the nineteenth century began to define themselves during the constituent assembly. At this point they identified themselves by the names of the two Masonic lodges in which their respective networks of personal alliances were focused: the conservative Scottish Rite and the more liberal York Rite. The conservatives of the Scottish Rite enjoyed the support of the British minister in Mexico, while the liberals of the York Rite traced their Masonic lineage to a New York lodge, promoted by the consul of the United States.

Encouraged by their British tutor, the conservatives envisioned a new order in which Great Britain occupied a position analogous to the former position of Spain. Mexico received more British capital in this period than any other country of Spanish America, a circumstance that benefited the mining industry as well as the impoverished government of the new republic. Allied with their British creditors, the mine owners, the landowning aristocracy, and the remaining mercantile elite of Spanish extraction together formed a powerful bloc that wished the republican order to resemble the colonial one as much as possible. The restoration of health to the mining industry, according to the British minister, would produce the capital so badly needed to put the public finances in order and relieve the plague of high-interest, short-term moneylenders presently skimming off much of the country's modest wealth. Thanks to their British connection, the conservatives had to accept in return the permanently higher volume of manufactured imports from Great Britain. To boost exports and redress the resulting imbalance of trade, the British minister recommended an expansion of exports derived from tropical agriculture.

The outlook of Mexican conservatives was shaped by the changing social panorama of the country. They saw the emigration of the richest Spanish merchants after 1821 as a blow to the power of the upper classes. Those who rallied politically around the Scottish Rite also feared the new sense of initiative that the populace had acquired during the revolution. As a brake on that initiative, they courted the army and indulged its voracious appetite for public funds. Upper-class conservatives were less sympathetic to the continuing struggle of the urban middle classes to find a niche for themselves in the bureaucratic structures of the new Mexican state. The social climbing of middle-class politicians in provincial urban centers created an additional drain on the treasury. It also threatened to raise the specter of extreme federalism, an unpleasant prospect to the conservative masters of the existing centralized order. Their worst apprehensions were realized when the liberals seized on an issue even more popular and disruptive than federalism: the expulsion of all remaining peninsular Spaniards. Popular attitudes toward peninsular merchants can be gauged by the common belief that those who had already left took with them a hundred million pesos in ill-gotten gains. Admittedly, the Spaniards still in Mexico bore little resemblance to the richer sort who had already left. The remaining Spaniards were modest landowners and small-town store owners who hardly constituted a political menace. Nevertheless, these were precisely the Spaniards most in contact with the Mexican people, and, though not wealthy when compared to their departed compatriots, they were rich enough to replace them as objects of envy.

Agitation against the Spaniards enthused the Mexican people to a degree that few other political issues could—to the horror of the ruling groups, who had carefully kept the common people out of the political process since independence. As a result, the faction organized among the Masons of the Scottish Rite grew into a solid political alliance of all those who had something to lose in an alteration of the status quo. The conservative vision found its most lucid expression in the persuasive prose of the historian Lucas Alamán, who later painted the last years of the colonial period as a kind of lost golden age and the ensuing revolution as a catastrophe. Inspired by Alamán's nostalgic representations, having already endured a loss of prestige and having learned to tolerate the army as a permanent political player, and spurred by the liberals' populist appeal to anti-Spanish sentiment, the conservatives became increasingly intransigent. They appealed to the church as the only force capable of countering the influence of rabble-rousing liberals over the Indian and mestizo masses. The result was a Mexican conservatism generally ascendant during the next two decades, tenaciously opposed to advances in religious tolerance and much less enlightened than the late colonial reformism on which it supposedly modeled itself.

The new cohesion of the conservatives allowed them to impose their candidate as legal successor to the first president, but the army then intervened—as it had done in deposing Iturbide and would often do again—to designate who would rule Mexico. Again, too, the initiator of the army revolt was Antonio López de Santa Anna, and the candidate he favored was a fellow general and veteran of the wars of independence, Vicente Guerrero. Guerrero successfully defeated a rather feeble Spanish attempt to reconquer Mexico, then succumbed to the maneuverings of his own vice president, Anastasio Bustamante, who convinced the army to remove Guerrero in 1830. The liberal ex-president was then executed, to the surprise and horror of most Mexicans, who held an abiding respect for the heroes of the revolution. The conservatives were now strong enough to risk this popular displeasure, as long as they retained the loyalty of the army. This they failed to accomplish. In 1832 General Santa Anna initiated a new barracks revolt and made himself nominal president, almost immediately leaving the reins of government in the hands of a liberal-controlled congress and his vice president, Valentín Gómez Farías. The new government turned out to be too reformist for its creator's taste, however, and after it moved from anticlerical measures to attempts at limiting military privileges, Santa Anna reappeared to replace the liberal government with a conservative one. The conservatives learned this lesson well and thereafter placated the army by allowing it to consume more than half the national budget.

The reinstatement of the conservatives brought a renewal of centralism to replace the liberals' federalist emphasis, with grave consequences. Support for federalism was strong in several peripheral Mexican provinces, including Texas, where settlers from the United States revolted against the centralist policies of the conservative government in 1836. Santa Anna led an army north to suppress the Texan rebellion but was thoroughly defeated. Texas became independent as a result, but the Mexican government refused to recognize the fact despite the recommendation of Lucas Alamán, who believed that an independent Republic of Texas aligned diplomatically with Great Britain would protect Mexico from the expansionist tendencies of the United States. Within a couple of years, the defeated Santa Anna recouped his political prestige by leading Mexican troops against a French intervention. The French demanded indemnification for their citizens' losses in the recent Mexican civil war. Ultimately they got what they demanded, but not before one of their cannons took off Santa Anna's leg (which he then buried with full honors) and rehabilitated his reputation as a nationalist hero. The durable Santa Anna continued to exercise his influence over Mexican politics until the United States annexed Texas in 1845. Since the Mexican government still claimed Texas as its own, war ensued. The United States won an easy victory thanks, in part, to the continuing political division within Mexico. Decades of civil war had not prepared the Mexican army to face an enemy like the United States, and despite the heroic last stand of Mexican soldiers, the U.S. invasion culminated in the capture of Mexico City.

The conservatives had led Mexico to a humiliating defeat that exacerbated all of the accumulated resentments against their government, and the peace seemed even worse than the fighting when the victorious United States claimed half of Mexico's national territory as the spoils of war. Despite the disastrous defeat and the outbreak of Indian rebellions in the far north and far south, the conservatives held onto power in the early 1850s. Lucas Alamán searched the historical record for explanations of the current debacle and found them everywhere but within his own party. His proposal for a final solution to Mexico's problems lay in a return to monarchy. In the meantime, the conservatives again called on Santa Anna to put out the smouldering fires of incipient liberal rebellion. Santa Anna financed his holding action with the sale of further Mexican territory to the United States for ten million dollars. However, the coming liberal revolt had an intensity far greater than any previous ones. By 1855, the conservative alliance had been swept away by the forces of liberal reform.

The period of Mexican history protagonized by the enigmatic figure of Santa Anna is easier to narrate than to analyze. Santa Anna himself seems to have been motivated primarily by opportunism. More thoughtful men like Alamán and Gómez Farías, on the other hand, appeared to have been thoroughly committed to their conservative or liberal ideologies, each of which clashed with important aspects of Mexican reality and therefore could not be implemented without force of arms. As the popular mobilization of the revolutionary period faded and the social hierarchy was reaffirmed, the army became the only vehicle through which either party could gain power or, once in office, maintain order. Consequently, conservatives and liberals alike had no choice but to ally themselves with influential generals. Santa Anna gained influence early, by leading the overthrow of Iturbide, and the suppleness of his political principles made him the ideal military liaison for ideologues like Alamán and Gómez Farías. Santa Anna's high political contacts, in turn, increased his ascendancy within the army, making him an even more desirable ally for the next politician in power.

The greatest achievement of the conservatives during the period of their hegemony was simply holding onto power. In 1850, Mexico had still not recovered the economic prosperity of the last years of colonial rule. The government remained perpetually in debt, and the general shortage of capital in the postrevolutionary period severely crippled the recovery of Mexico's all-important mining industry. Mining required far larger amounts of investment than agriculture or ranching, and the capital-intensive quality of mining goes far to explain the slow recovery of the Mexican economy in the aftermath of the wars of independence. The fighting had occasioned widespread destruction of mining equipment and excavations, and the only hope of replacing them lay in investments from abroad. For this reason, the limited inflows of British capital played a crucial role despite their modest dimensions, and Mexican conservatives displayed a welcoming attitude toward outside influences. The Mexican conservatives' openness to neocolonial economic arrangements distinguished them among Spanish American conservatives since it conflicted with conservatism's characteristic mistrust of innovations. In sum Mexico's conservatives had no choice but to seek economic penetration to revive the country's mining industry, but they were ideologically ill-equipped to make a success of it, and the circumstances of the international economy of the period were against them as well.

Peru and Bolivia, the other great silver producers of the colonial period, encountered similar problems in the years before 1850. The diversity of elite interests made the creation of a stable political order in these Andean republics even more difficult than in Mexico. After the colonial administrative reorganization of the late eighteenth century, important tensions had divided Lima's commercial and bureaucratic elite from the merchants and miners of the Andean highlands. Differences no less profound separated highland hacendados (rich in land and Indian labor but poorly linked to the market economy) from the sugar planters of the coast. Though closely related to the commercial fortunes of Lima, the coastal plantations struggled to meet the high capital requirements of production based on irrigation and increasingly expensive slave labor. Meanwhile, the merchants of Lima faced new competition from others formerly under their sway in Guayaquil and Santiago, and the officers who led the fighting for independence, serving alternately in the armies of Peru and Bolivia, had their own demands to make.

The Indian peoples of the Andean highlands continued to live in a manner that hardly changed after independence. The agriculture of the highlands remained oriented primarily toward subsistence and also appeared impervious to the political and juridical implications of republicanism. Attempts to abolish Indian tribute and to privatize communal landholdings were abandoned, and indigenous communities managed to defend themselves fairly well in this period against hacendados, merchants, and prosperous mestizo farmers eager to carve up community property. Such communities could maintain their territorial integrity mostly because of the lethargy of the market economy during the early nineteenth century. The continuation of the tribute system may be traced to the same cause. So flaccid was Bolivia's external trade between 1835 and 1865, that almost 80 percent of government revenues came from the head tax paid by Indians.

Political instability was aggravated by the divisions (more pronounced in Peru and Bolivia than in Mexico) between Indians, mestizos, and whites. The first powerful *caudillo* to emerge from the wars of independence in Peru was the mestizo general Agustín Gamarra. Gamarra's wife, also of mixed blood, attracted the disdain of aristocratic society in Lima, but the two inspired an entirely different reaction among the mostly mestizo soldiers, whose loyalty was so important to the political balance of power. Eventually, Gamarra was replaced by another mestizo, Andrés de Santa Cruz, who made himself "Protector" of a Peruvian-Bolivian Confederation in 1836. Santa Cruz was an authoritarian executive with plans for reforming the confederation's civil administration, system of justice, and tax structure. For a brief moment, his seemed the model Spanish American government, receiving plaudits from the Vatican and various European powers. However, these faraway ovations did little to compensate for the implacable hostility of the Lima aristocrats, merchants, magistrates, and bureaucrats unsettled by the recent innovations of this overweening military upstart. Nor did Santa Cruz have strong support from the popular sectors, which had undergone less political mobilization here than in Mexico. Indeed, the creation of an ambitious Peruvian-Bolivian Confederation had resulted in higher taxes on the Indian masses in the short run and promised the elimination of community landholding sooner or later. After all, whether directed at the church or at Indian communities, the dissolution of collective ownership was a goal of most "progressive" governments of the period.

Without a strong constituency at the top or the bottom of the social hierarchy, the reformist Peruvian-Bolivian Confederation was destined to have a short life. The rise of Santa Cruz had inspired plotting among envious officers in his own army at a moment when their loyalty was much needed to carry out his ambitious plans. The unification of Peru and Bolivia had threatened the new state's neighbors to the south, particularly the mercantile interests of Valparaíso, who feared a reimposition of the commercial hegemony formerly exercised over them by Peru. The Chileans launched a military expedition against Santa Cruz in 1837. That expedition failed, but another in 1839 defeated the forces of Santa Cruz in Peru. The Chilean army had included many young Lima aristocrats who called for political "regeneration," by which they meant not having to share power with the rude, dark-skinned generals from the highlands, but the army had also included many of these same disaffected generals. To the dismay of the young Peruvian "regenerators," the Chileans thought it safer to leave Peru in the hands of the rude generals, and they chose Gamarra to head the government there after the breakup of the Peruvian-Bolivian Confederation.

Political stability continued to elude Peruvian elites until the middle of the nineteenth century. Gamarra's government lasted only until his army met defeat in Bolivia, where Santa Cruz held on for a bit longer than in Peru. The aristocracy of Lima then backed a satisfactorily white and aristocratic caudillo, Manuel Ignacio de Vivanco, whose eventual defeat spelled another postponement of their hopes to return themselves to power. The initiative now passed to another mestizo, Gen. Ramón Castilla, the son of an Indian mother and a low-ranking peninsular bureaucrat. Castilla was able to patch together a temporary reconciliation because the Peruvian economy finally had begun to respond to the stimulus of the international market. Large-scale exports of guano, the nitrate-rich accumulations of centuries of bird droppings on islands off the Peruvian coast, were relieving the penury of the Peruvian state. Gradually the government in Lima ceased to depend on Indian tribute collected in the highland areas controlled by provincial military commanders. The expanding export economy thus freed the national government from the tyranny of the army, soon making it possible for Lima's frustrated aristocracy to recapture, at long last, at least part of the political predominance it had lost in the wars of independence.

Bolivia did not experience a similar pattern of economic growth and consolidation of its national state until many years later. The 1840s saw a rapid succession of military leaders, the most significant of whom was Manuel Isidoro Belzú, the first Bolivian leader to appeal directly to lower-class urban mestizos and receive their support. Bolivia had no guano islands to grant independence of action to the national government. The government's desperate attempt to stretch the contents of its treasury by reducing the weight of its silver coins only compounded its difficulties. Merchants in neighboring Peru, Chile, and Argentina soon became leery of Bolivian money, and the land-locked country's exiguous external trade seemed in danger of ceasing altogether. Fortunately, exports of chinchona bark to make quinine provided at least some relief from this situation after mid-century. Since the export of the bark was a state monopoly, it especially bene-fited the government and the aristocrats of La Paz who received the official concession, but exports of chinchona were much too small to alter the essential contours of the Bolivian economy.

In sum, the postindependence development of Mexico, Peru, and Bolivia seemed especially disappointing in light of their former status as core areas of the Spanish colonial enterprise. The scarcity of invest-ment capital made the period a very difficult one for the mining industry so central to the economies of all three of these new re-publics. As a result, the bureaucratic and mercantile elites who had dominated there before 1810 found it difficult to recover their control after the disruptions of revolution. Without a revival of mining and trade, they lacked the resources necessary to gain ascendancy over the army and consolidate new structures of state power. The army, on the other hand, could do no better—at least in the cases where its power did not flow from internal forces. Frequently, the officers who led the armies of independence became peacetime commanders in regions far from their places of origin. It took time for them to form alliances with the local elites and begin to identify with their interests. Bolívar's officers from Gran Colombia, who played such important roles in postwar Peru and Bolivia, provide a striking example. In Mexico, too, the new political order was imposed on many rural areas by troops from other parts of the country. Afterward, the military newcomers allied themselves, helter-skelter, with one or another local group, pro-ducing confusing patterns of regional conflict analogous to Santa Anna's shifting alliances with liberals and conservatives at the na-tional level.

In the Spanish American countries whose revolutions were made from within, the postindependence conditions favored a quicker con-solidation of social and political power, though that outcome was by no means guaranteed. A look at the various fortunes of Ecuador, Co-lombia, and Venezuela, the three new republics resulting from the breakup of Gran Colombia in 1830, will illustrate this point.

Ecuador's situation was similar to that of Peru or Bolivia in that liberation had been accomplished by an invading patriot army from Colombia and Venezuela. Many of the military leaders of the new Ecuadorian republic were the Venezuelan associates of Gen. Juan José Flores, the first president to take office in Quito, though born on the shores of the Caribbean. The Venezuelans quickly began to carve out landed domains for themselves in the highlands around Quito. As president, Flores faced the difficult task of arbitrating between the Andean landlords, with their debt-bound Indian laborers, and the mer-cantile and plantation-owning elites of the coastal plains around Gua-yaquil. A Guayaquil aristocrat, Vicente Rocafuerte, soon challenged the dominance of Flores and his highland allies in a civil war that threatened to break the tiny nation in two. Neither the prosperous elites of the coast nor the Venezuelan officers who held sway in the highlands desired such an outcome. In the event of a split, Guayaquil would inevitably be annexed to Peru and subordinated commercially to Lima, while Quito would be dominated by Colombia. In 1834, Flores and Rocafuerte agreed to share power and alternate in the presidency.

The economically more dynamic coast infused the ruling coalition with a generally progressive spirit. During his presidency and afterward, Rocafuerte pushed for administrative innovations that made Ecuador at least superficially one of the more successful republics of the moment. Success was fleeting, however. The modernization of the country scarcely touched the isolated Andean highlands, and the entrenched conservatism of the area's hacendados often put them at cross-purposes with the commercial, cacao-exporting elites of the coast. As the Venezuelan officers integrated themselves increasingly with the landowning class of the highlands and identified with their outlook, they took a more aggressive attitude toward the coastal elites. The military lost any remaining function as independent arbitrator, and civil strife returned in the 1840s.

In contrast to the cases already examined, Colombia had undergone a revolutionary process originating, in large measure, within its borders, and the country's regional complexity prevented the radical dichotomy of coast versus highlands. The liberal administration of Francisco de Paula Santander, Bolívar's former vice president, coexisted in the 1830s with the steadily growing influence of Gen. Tomás Cipriano de Mosquera, also a follower of Bolívar and, at least for the time being, a conservative. Liberal desires to subordinate ecclesiastical to civil authority made the church a political issue that bolstered the conservatives. As conservative influence became hegemonic in the 1840s, the church was an active collaborator, experimenting cautiously with an expanded system of religious primary education and even making some gestures in the direction of secondary and higher education.

The conservatives were strongest in the old royalist stronghold of Pasto (near the Ecuadorian border) and in the region around Medellín, known already for traditionalism and religious piety but not yet for the economic energy that characterized it in the twentieth century. The liberals, on the other hand, controlled the Caribbean coast, where plantation agriculture had once thrived but now declined along with its associated commercial interests. Bogotá, the capital city, constituted another node of liberal power. There a large number of low-paid minor bureaucrats, unhappy with the conservative government, combined forces with fashionable young men eager to imbibe the new political currents of European liberalism and with artisans who had still other complaints against the conservatives. Although it may appear paradoxical, the conservatives had fostered policies of free trade inimical to the artisans' livelihood. The artisans had a double importance because of their influence among poor day laborers in this politically volatile urban population.

Though strongly polarized, then, the Colombian political scene lacked the ideological clarity of Mexican struggles in this period, and it displayed impressive stability when compared with either Mexico or the Andean republics. The conservative rule of the 1840s was not, in fact, profoundly different from what the liberals might have done. The conservatives encouraged the steam navigation of the Magdalena River, still the primary path connecting Bogotá to the outside world, and made initial efforts in the direction of railroad construction as well. The liberals might reproach them with the sluggish progress of these efforts, but future developments would show that the timid conservative attitude toward progress did not deserve the full blame for the slow pace of change.

In many ways, Colombia presented a political model for other Spanish American republics in the first decade after the wars of independence. What was the secret of this relative but indubitable success? The smaller role of the army comes immediately to mind. Colombia had effectively exported much of its potentially troublesome officer corps to Ecuador, Peru, and Bolivia during the wars of independence. In addition, the fragmented geography of Colombia resulted in a large number of fairly isolated regional elites who were mostly indifferent to the conduct of national policy as long as their local predominance and interests remained untouched. These local upper classes tended to form paternalistic bonds with their social subordinates within each region, an especially important fact in explaining post-independence political stability in an area where the mestizo country people had taken an active part in the revolutionary mobilization of 1810–25. The fierce civil wars that broke out later in the century owed their mass character to the high level of political mobilization that distinguished Colombia from its Andean neighbors to the south.

Venezuela, the neighbor to the east, faced similar challenges in the creation of a stable political order in the period after the wars of independence. Venezuela was perhaps the part of Spanish America most devastated during those wars, and the irregular patriot armies of the countryside that emerged triumphant—the mestizos of the llanos, the mulattoes of the eastern coast—faced daunting challenges of reconstruction. Although the cacao-planting aristocracy of the highlands around Caracas had been ruined, the rough military men who replaced them as rulers under the enduring sway of Gen. José Antonio Páez reconstructed the country along lines not unlike those of the prerevolutionary order. The opportunities of exporting to a much-expanded trans-Atlantic market were quickly realized in the coastal area, where coffee replaced cacao as the principal crop. By 1836, the level of exportation surpassed that of the years just before the revolution, and the general upward trend continued during the 1830s. This early recovery of export production allowed the first governments of independent Venezuela a fair degree of success, but the prosperity did not last.

In the 1840s, the market price for Venezuelan exports became less favorable, and the conservative political order began to exhibit fault lines. In the first place, the return to a social order of colonial cut had resulted in strong tensions. Large-scale merchants captured an exorbitant portion of the profits of exported coffee grown, for the most part, by medium-sized producers. Squeezed by the deteriorating market, the merchants passed the pressure on to the landowners who, in turn, attempted to impose labor regimes of a sort uncongenial to the rural masses who had made the revolution against Spain. In the coffee-growing coastal highlands, these efforts implied the reenslavement of people who had received sweeping grants of freedom during the revolution; in the llanos, they resulted in restrictive laws designed to force roving cowboys to tie themselves to a particular ranch. In addition, the social mobility promised by the revolution applied mostly to certain exceptional cases, like that of Páez himself, who rose from ranch foreman to become president of the country. Most veterans of the revolution encountered difficulties in taking possession of the lands that had been promised them in reward for their services. Those who received lands often had to sell them. Páez himself bought up many of his soldiers' plots at a highly favorable price. Since the lands distributed to patriot veterans often had been confiscated from royalists, other recipients eventually lost their land grants due to the legalism of a conservative government that chose to annul those confiscations after independence was achieved.

Gradually, some great landed families of the highlands around Caracas recovered their economic strength and organized a liberal political opposition to the generals who had ruled the country since the 1820s. A talented liberal journalist, Antonio Leocadio Guzmán, made the liberal cause popular as well among the lower and middle classes of the capital city. In contrast to the pattern of other Spanish American republics, however, Venezuelan liberalism was not primarily urban. It evoked a powerful response in the countryside among the disgruntled veterans of the revolution. Chafing under the reimposed rigidities of a colonial-style labor regime, rural people tended to regard the mercantile aristocracy as their enemies, and the opposition of these restless ex-soldiers was even more menacing to the government than that of the crowds of Caracas. By mid-century, dark clouds loomed on the political horizon of the Venezuelan republic.

At least initially, prospects seemed brighter for Central America, which escaped a destructive battle between revolutionaries and royalists by joining the Mexican empire of Iturbide in 1821. At the end of Iturbide's brief reign, the Central American provinces withdrew from the union with Mexico (except for the province of Chiapas, which has remained part of Mexico ever since) and declared their own independence. Unfortunately, the United Provinces of Central America were to have a short and tumultuous existence characterized by the violent struggles between liberals and conservatives. The stronghold of the conservatives was Guatemala, with the former colonial capital at Guatemala City—a land of isolated Indian communities oriented primarily toward subsistence agriculture, dominated by a small Creole minority of seigneurial landowners. The center of liberalism was El Salvador, a small but densely populated area that produced most of Central America's exports, the most important export being indigo dye for the European textile industry. Led by their caudillo, Francisco Morazán, the liberals proposed moving the Central American capital to San Salvador and tried to impose a number of other ecclesiastical and legal reforms unwelcome to the conservatives.

In 1837, a powerful conservative reaction began in Guatemala and eventually overwhelmed the liberals and shattered their dreams of a united Central America. The leader of this movement, which drew on widespread Indian discontent with the liberal innovations, was a mestizo of humble origins, Gen. Rafael Carrera. Carrera formed a conservative alliance that included aristocratic families of the old order, the church, and, through him, the mestizos and Indians of the Guatemalan countryside. The strength of this alliance allowed him to become lifetime president of Guatemala and to exercise hegemony over all of Central America until his death in 1865. The period of conservative hegemony witnessed the permanent fragmentation of the United Provinces of Central America into the five republics of Guatemala, El Salvador, Honduras, Nicaragua, and Costa Rica. (Panama had been part of New Granada since colonial times.) Except in Costa Rica, where the cultivation and exportation of coffee got an early start, little social or economic change occurred during the quarter century of Carrera's

rule. In some ways, however, the slow pace of change favored the
Indian majority of Guatemala, who willingly formed the military
force that kept Carrera in power. Out of all the postrevolutionary
experiences of Spanish America, Rafael Carrera presented perhaps
the most extreme example of the common people brought to power by
the militarization of society an example unusual, too, because Carrera's improvised militia did not derive from earlier colonial or revolutionary military traditions.

Paraguay attracted the curiosity of European observers as an extreme case of reaction against liberalism. In 1812, almost immediately
after the revolutionary process began in the Río de la Plata, José Gaspar
Rodríguez de Francia imposed an iron dictatorship that isolated Paraguay almost completely from its turbulent neighbors. Francia was an
ascetic and enigmatic ruler, the son of a Portuguese merchant and a
graduate of the University of Córdoba, where he had become a doctor
of law and theology. The isolation that he chose for Paraguay extended
to the economic as well as the political realm. During Francia's long
rule, which lasted until 1840, Paraguay's limited contacts with the
outside world came mostly through a few Brazilian merchants who
received individual permission to trade. Francia drew on the support of
Paraguay's mestizo majority against the small aristocracy, who saw
their export production of tobacco and yerba mate disappear almost
entirely during his rule. The mass of rural Paraguayans, on the other
hand, suffered little from the lack of imported goods and tended to
benefit, as in the case of Guatemala, from an economy centered on the
production of food for local consumption.

In defense of his closed system, Francia could easily point to the
devastation that a more open economic and political system had produced in the other areas of the Río de la Plata. By the time of the final
defeat of the royalists at Ayacucho, the revolutionary government of
the Río de la Plata had already dissolved, ushering in a long and painful
search for stability that lasted more than a generation. Both the "unitarian" central government of the Buenos Aires revolution and the
confederation once led by José Artigas lay in shambles by 1820. The
Portuguese had concluded their conquest of the Banda Oriental and
converted the former "Protector of Free Peoples" into a fugitive no
longer commanding the respect of his former allies in the other provinces of his erstwhile confederation. Artigas sought refuge in Paraguay,
where Francia kept him safely sequestered for the rest of his life. As
the remaining confederated provinces fought among themselves, the
province of Buenos Aires temporarily gave up its old ambition of
ruling the rest of the former viceroyalty of the Río de la Plata and

became simply one of a group of loosely associated provinces unconnected to any central governing institutions.

As a province by and for itself, Buenos Aires was indubitably the
most powerful and affluent in the Río de la Plata. Its port controlled
the overseas trade of the entire region and, with it, the all-important
customs revenues. No longer did these revenues have to flow into
administrative institutions or military campaigns that reached far
beyond the limits of the province of Buenos Aires. Without such
entanglements, the government of Buenos Aires could devote its attention to internal improvements. Its new orientation received the
support of a landowning class that had added to its ranks a number of
wealthy families recently displaced from mercantile endeavors by
British competition. The ranchers of Buenos Aires enjoyed peace and
prosperity while the surrounding plains regions languished in civil
war. As a result, the leaders of Buenos Aires showed little interest in
unification projects initiated by other provinces during this period.

Instead, they used the opportunity of the moment to embark on
"the happy experiment of Buenos Aires," an impressive project of
parliamentary government and liberal reform improvised by the intellectual elite of the province. The chief architect of the Buenos Aires
experiment was Bernardino Rivadavia, the son of a rich peninsular
merchant and a veteran participant in the revolutionary process, just
returned from a diplomatic mission to Europe. As chief government
minister during the early 1820s, Rivadavia oversaw the reduction of
the officer corps that caused such a drain on the treasury, the lowering
of tariffs to encourage trade and increase revenues, and the gradual
repayment of the public debt. The government of Rivadavia organized
public credit and created a bank to force down high interest rates. In
ecclesiastical matters, it showed sympathy toward the principle of
freedom of worship for Protestants and closed a number of convents.
However, the experiment of Buenos Aires could advance only by leaving aside two major difficulties that had to be resolved sooner or later.
One was the problematic relationship of Buenos Aires to its sister
provinces; the second was the continued occupation of one of them,
the Banda Oriental, by Brazil.

The two problems came together when a constitutional convention (proposed by Buenos Aires with the goal of reuniting the provinces of the Río de la Plata) coincided with a revolt against the Brazilian occupation of the Banda Oriental. Educated urban elites from
many provinces were eager to use the constitutional convention to
strengthen their position against caudillos in their home provinces.
The resulting interprovincial alliance offered the representatives of

Buenos Aires a way to compensate for the internal division in their own party. At just this time, the patriot army of the Banda Oriental won important victories against the Brazilian forces occupying that province and petitioned for admission to the newly created United Provinces of the Río de la Plata. Espousing the cause of the Banda Oriental clearly implied war with the Brazilian empire, something the government of Buenos Aires wished at all cost to avoid. The patriotic cause of the Banda Oriental was popular with the majority of the city of Buenos Aires, however, and certain officers of the former revolutionary army of Buenos Aires had taken up the issue. Political expediency moved the government of Buenos Aires to lead the United Provinces into the war.

Declared in late 1825, the war with Brazil erased many of the improvements that had occurred in Buenos Aires since 1820 and helped precipitate the breakup of the United Provinces. Once again, the maintenance of the army drained the treasury, and military officers regained lost influence within the government. A Brazilian blockade of the Río de la Plata disrupted commerce, and wartime inflation of an inconvertible paper currency ravaged the economy (just as was then occurring in Brazil). Despite the convincing Argentine victory at Ituzaingó in 1827, Pedro I stubbornly refused to admit defeat, and the war soon became unpopular in the United Provinces. The wealthy of Buenos Aires demonstrated increasing dissatisfaction with the interprovincial alliance that controlled the congress, led by Rivadavia, who had been chosen as the first president of the new republic. Rivadavia soon angered them further by putting the province of Buenos Aires under the direct control of the national government. His government alienated many of his supporters in the interior provinces, as well, with its support of a centralist constitution. During its short life, the central government had already accumulated considerable ill will in the interior provinces because of an unpopular treaty with Great Britain (imposing religious freedom) and thanks to a conflict between British mining companies associated separately with groups in Buenos Aires and with others in the interior.

Revolts in the interior provinces began the breakup of Rivadavia's project of state building in spite of the success of a British-mediated end to the war with Brazil in 1828. By the time of the peace treaty, Rivadavia had already resigned and another power struggle had begun between his political heirs (known as Unitarians) and those who wanted greater autonomy for the provinces (the Federalists). Soon after the end of the war, the Unitarians overthrew and executed the Federalist governor of Buenos Aires, Manuel Dorrego. The execution of Dorrego galvanized the Federalist landowners, already resentful of the burdens placed on them by Unitarian governments, to revolt and, within six months, cause the collapse of their enemies' last government in Buenos Aires. The leader of the Federalist uprising was a prosperous rancher, Juan Manuel de Rosas, who had organized an effective rural militia to defend his southern frontier region of the province against marauding Indians.

Rosas dominated the Río de la Plata for a quarter century, but first he had to defeat the Unitarians of the interior provinces and extend his hegemony over other provincial caudillos like himself. The most important Unitarian resistance was led by Gen. José María Paz of the province of Córdoba, while the most formidable rival Federalist caudillo was Facundo Quiroga of La Rioja, immortalized in Domingo Faustino Sarmiento's famous polemical biography, *Facundo, or Civilization and Barbarism* (1845). Fortunately for Rosas, these two also fought among themselves. Paz defeated Quiroga, driving him into the Rosas camp, and was himself captured by Rosas in 1831. As a result, the caudillo of Buenos Aires emerged as the dominant figure in a loose confederation of provinces governed by military strongmen like Quiroga.

The influence of Rosas derived partly from the relative importance of the province of Buenos Aires, but it also flowed from the strength of the political arrangements he created there. Rosas was the only Federalist chief to assimilate the lessons of the recent turmoil and create a style of rule adapted to the new conditions of political life. He correctly recognized that the mobilization of large portions of the population in antagonistic factions had become irreversible and that political stability depended on the total victory of one party over the others. Until then, the parties in conflict had lacked internal cohesion. Although strong enough to disrupt the rule of their adversaries, none had shown itself able to maintain order once in power. Rosas set out to build a disciplined organization capable of doing just that. Intensive use of mass propaganda played a key role, ranging from relatively sophisticated journalistic debate to an enforcement of public political conformity in which people, churches, and even horses were required to display the insignias of Federalism. The violence of Federalist mobs terrorized the educated elite into reluctant collaboration.

These tactics succeeded in Buenos Aires, where Rosas became governor in 1829. On the other hand, popular mobilization did not work as well in the interior provinces that had not undergone such intense politicization during the revolution. The other Federalist caudillos resisted party discipline, but they feared Rosas and accepted his hegemony to avoid conflict with Buenos Aires. While the creation of a powerful Federalist party made Rosas preeminent in Argentina, it also limited his freedom of action by obliging him to satisfy the extremism he had fostered. Having presented the Federalist cause as a kind of holy crusade against the iniquitous Unitarians (a label with which he branded many unconnected with the party of Rivadavia), Rosas had little choice but to wage permanent war on his enemies, many of whom had crossed the Río de la Plata to establish themselves in nearby Montevideo.

The turbulent early years of the independent Uruguayan republic *Uruguay* brought a series of international complications. During the 1830s, Uruguayans gravitated into the camps of two military caudillos: Gen. Juan Antonio Lavalleja, who had led the uprising against Brazilian occupation in 1825, and Gen. Fructuoso Rivera, who had collaborated with the Brazilian government during the occupation but quickly joined the patriot revolt. Lavalleja was better identified with the country's traditional landowning class, while Rivera (though himself a larger landowner than his rival) had great prestige among the landless people of the countryside, whom he had long captained, and a following as well among many in Montevideo who, like him, had reached a modus vivendi with the Brazilians during the 1820s. Rivera became the country's first president, an office that he exercised with utter indifference to the principles of financial management (and in spite of Lavalleja's attempts to overthrow him) until 1835, when he relinquished it to a member of the Montevidean elite, Manuel Oribe. Long oppressed by the military caudillos of the interior, the capitaline elite sought allies outside Uruguay, just as they had in the time of Artigas. Oribe put aside earlier Unitarian sympathies and found his allies in the Federalist Argentina of Rosas, while Rivera turned toward Brazil *Rivera + Argentine Unit. exiles v. Oribe and support of Rosas* and toward the enemies of the Argentine dictator—Unitarian exiles and French diplomats in Montevideo. When Rivera revolted and captured Montevideo, Oribe took refuge in Buenos Aires. At first suspicious of Oribe's past Unitarian connections, Rosas soon embraced the cause of restoring the legitimate president of Uruguay. The lines were drawn for the "Guerra Grande" that shook Argentina and Uruguay for *Guerra Grande* more than a decade and involved, at various moments, French, British, and Brazilian intervention.

Rosas outmaneuvered several serious challenges in the first years of the conflict. In an attempt to advance certain claims made against the Rosas government by French citizens, the French had blockaded Buenos Aires since 1837, bringing hardship and dissatisfaction in the provinces most closely linked to the Atlantic economy. Meanwhile, disruptions created by the war of the Peruvian-Bolivian Confederation stimulated anti-Rosas sentiments in the Argentine northwest. The resulting rebellions included one in the south of Buenos Aires province, the dictator's home territory. Though Rosas defeated this rebellion, a thousand of its participants emigrated to swell the ranks of the anti-Rosas alliance with France. Tenacious resistance against the external threat and ruthless repression of internal enemies allowed Rosas to weather the storm and sign a treaty with the French government. The dictator of Buenos Aires made concessions on almost every point under dispute, but he had some reason to claim victory after withstanding the onslaught of a major European power. By this time, a Federalist army had marched through the northwest to the borders of Chile and Bolivia, giving Buenos Aires a degree of control over Argentine territory exercised by no other government since the end of colonial rule. To complete the picture, the allies of Rosas had gained control of the whole Uruguayan republic except for the capital at Montevideo, now besieged by land and sea.

In the long run, however, the forces arrayed against Rosas were too many and too powerful. The merchants of Montevideo were able to secure the support of the British navy, more than a match for the naval squadron of Buenos Aires attempting to blockade the besieged port, and the French provided subsidies to maintain the anti-Rosas government of Montevideo. In 1845, Buenos Aires once again suffered a blockade itself, and a British commercial and naval expedition penetrated the Paraná River, a route to the interior that Rosas had struggled to keep closed. Although the European powers seem to have decided by 1850 that such interventions were counterproductive to their commercial interests, a new anti-Rosas alliance finally overwhelmed the dictator of Buenos Aires within two years. The principal members of the new alliance were the Brazilian empire, which had finally consolidated its own internal stability, and Justo José de Urquiza, caudillo of Entre Ríos, the most formidable internal rival of Rosas. After raising the siege of Montevideo, this powerful coalition crossed into Argentina and defeated the army of Rosas at Monte Caseros, a decisive battle that involved nearly fifty thousand combatants. Rosas fled to England, where he remained in quiet exile for the rest of his life.

Despite the turmoil of the Rosas years, Argentina prospered. The most favored area was, of course, the province of Buenos Aires, which had to supply soldiers for the Rosista armies but largely escaped destructive fighting on its own soil. Other riverine provinces with access to the Atlantic economy also thrived in these years, especially Urquiza's Entre Ríos, where a compact and wealthy landowning class began to see itself as a serious rival to the elite of Buenos Aires. The ranchers of Entre Ríos were eager to eliminate the middlemen of Buenos Aires and to engage in international trade directly from their ports on the Paraná and Uruguay rivers. Their push for freedom of navigation on those rivers helped bring about the alliance between Urquiza and the Brazilian empire, which wanted access to its western territories upriver. After 1840, the interior provinces of Argentina also entered a period of economic growth under the rough but effective discipline of Federalist governments. The provincial legislatures of San Juan, La Rioja, and Tucumán contained recently exiled opponents of Rosas who had returned to become discretely accommodated, if not sincerely reconciled, to his rule. The dictator's remaining critics in exile recognized the prosperity of their home provinces but presented it as exceptional. "San Juan," wrote Sarmiento, "is more fortunate than other provinces." Another famous exile, the political writer Juan Bautista Alberdi, wrote that his home province, Tucumán, "experienced exceptional tolerance." Although they were loath to admit it, the urban elites whose political project had failed in 1825–30 later found multiple advantages under the regime of Rosas.

The economic growth of Federalist Argentina paled beside that of Chile under a conservative government that had become, by the 1830s and 1840s, the most successful government of early independent Spanish America. However, Chile's stability emerged only after an extremely agitated decade in the 1820s that had given few indications of the future. Bernardo O'Higgins, the chief leader of Chilean independence, had tried initially to impose a progressive government that drew inspiration from the period of late colonial reform. He soon clashed violently with landowners over modification of inheritance laws, with the church over tolerance of Protestantism, and with the urban lower classes over limitations on the exuberance of popular celebrations. Frustrated, O'Higgins stepped aside, leaving the way open for liberal and federalist experiments that also failed. It was only then that minister Diego Portales laid the foundations of the stable conservative order.

Portales was a businessman of modest background who had done well as a merchant in Valparaíso. He entered political life as a representative of a group of moneylenders whose influence derived especially from the public penury that Chilean governments shared with other Spanish American governments of the immediate postindependence period. During the turbulent 1820s, Portales put together an alliance among commercial and landed interests nostalgic for more tranquil times, and he managed to secure the support of the discontented urban poor in addition. The presidency of the conservative Gen. Joaquín Prieto, beginning in 1831, marked the rise of Portales to power as the most important government minister. Portales promoted a rigidly authoritarian political program emphasizing law and order, codified in the new Constitution of 1833. Despite the assassination of Portales in 1837, the Chilean government went on to acquire a depersonalized institutional stability that made it the envy of Spanish American intellectuals, especially those fleeing from Rosas. Young Argentine political refugees like Domingo Faustino Sarmiento and Juan Bautista Alberdi, who found the newspapers, universities, and even occasionally the magistracy of conservative Chile open to them, became assiduous publicists of the Portalian order.

Their idealized descriptions of Chile in the 1830s and 1840s should be qualified, but they do reflect real achievements. Republican institutions quickly acquired a strength unheard of elsewhere in Spanish America, and, particularly during the presidency of Manuel Montt (1841–51), the government relaxed some of its original authoritarian tendencies in spite of powerful resistance from the most conservative groups. The gradual liberalization of the regime accompanied the general evolution of Chilean society and economy toward more liberal forms. Beginning in the 1830s, the expansion of mining in the area north of Santiago created a new group of wealthy entrepreneurs to rival the traditional landed aristocracy of the central valley, establishing new patterns of consumption in elite circles. Because of their increasing orientation toward export agriculture, even the landowners of the central valley became increasingly subject to cosmopolitan influences. Already under Portales, the dominant role of British merchants in the port of Valparaíso outweighed conservative resistance and brought the toleration of Protestantism.

The liberalization of Chilean society and economy under the conservative regime designed by Diego Portales eventually produced important contradictions. Expanded educational opportunities encouraged social mobility and gave a political voice to groups subordinated or marginalized by the Portalian order. By the middle of the nineteenth century, the conservative regime in Chile (as in Colombia and Venezuela) had to contend with widespread discontent fostered, to a degree, by its success and stability. New economic sectors, most notably the mining interests of the north, wished to acquire a share of political power commensurate with their considerable economic leverage, and they were not in a mood to be denied.

Popular gathering and elite salon, circa 1840, Chile

Creole inhabitants of the
countryside, circa 1840,
Uruguay

East sanctuary entrance,
Cathedral, Mexico City

Oxcart in Oaxaca, Mexico

Grocery store,
Guayaquil, Ecuador.
*California Museum
of Photography*

Sorting coffee, Nicaragua.
*California Museum
of Photography*

CHAPTER IV

EMERGENCE OF

THE NEOCOLONIAL

ORDER (1850–1880)

VERY SLOWLY AFTER 1850, Latin America began to harvest the fruits of political independence. Mexico, Peru, and Bolivia—countries with economies centered on silver mining—had been the least successful in the first generation of independence, while burgeoning agricultural exporters like Argentina, Chile, and Venezuela had benefited more. Beginning in the third quarter of the nineteenth century, sweeping and profound economic change came to Latin America as a whole, primarily because of developments originating in the powerful industrializing nations of Europe. The growth of these metropolitan economies finally provided the investment capital and the markets needed to expand and diversify Latin American export production. As a result, Latin American economies began to develop in the manner so long desired by the region's ruling classes.

Latin America's economic awakening occurred as a unified phenomenon, at least in part, because the discovery of gold in California and Australia drew the energies of the Atlantic economy into the Pacific basin. This development greatly enlarged the area effectively integrated into the world market and insured that the Atlantic and Pacific coasts of Latin America would participate equally in the resulting commercial opportunities. Transformations in transportation technology facilitated the creation of the larger integrated market. By the 1840s, steam-powered vessels no longer constituted a novelty in coastal and river trade. Suddenly, the formerly isolated Pacific coast of Latin America lay on a busy trade route, with corresponding advantages for the development of export production in Chile and Peru. Along with some portable export products, fortune hunters crossed the Andes from Mendoza, Argentina, on their way to California, where they found entire neighborhoods inhabited primarily by Chileans. The frenzy of consumption typical of successful prospectors stimulated Chilean wheat cultivation, resulting in increased con-

[margin notes:] Euro industrial power = L.A. investment capital

gold rush = Pacific coast expansion

struction in the country's capital city, Santiago. All along the new
route connecting the Atlantic and Pacific coasts of North America,
port cities profited from the sudden surge of goods and passengers in
transit.

Panama, always a shortcut between the oceans, was suddenly
flooded with prospectors on their way to California. By 1855, ambitious engineers had constructed a railroad across the isthmus to
encourage and profit from this movement of people. Hacked through
dense tropical forest and over mountainous terrain, the new railway
ran not far from the route used since the seventeenth century by
travelers between Spain and Peru. The transisthmian railroad, among
the first in Latin America, had been constructed at enormous expense,
and, not surprisingly, its owners were New York capitalists.

The tone of life in Latin America's port capitals responded to the
increased ease of communications with Europe almost immediately.
In the late 1850s, a traveler to Buenos Aires could still describe streets
choked with horses waiting for their owners around the stock exchange. However, streets were being paved and new theaters constructed as urban upper and middle classes recovered a level of prosperity lost to them since the early years of the wars of independence. A
series of technological advances contributed to the transformation of
the urban scene during the 1850s. Gas lighting replaced evil-smelling
street lamps fueled by oil or animal fat in Rio de Janeiro, followed by
Buenos Aires, Valparaíso, and Lima. A British packet steamer short-
ened communications between Portsmouth and the Río de la Plata to a
reliable thirty days (though slower-sailing vessels would carry the
brunt of trade for a few more decades). Improved navigation encouraged Italian opera companies to add Latin American cities to their
circuits, and the more ready availability of European products and
fashions afforded urban dwellers many opportunities for conspicuous
consumption. In Mexico, foreign observers noted that aristocratic
ladies adopted the latest European dress styles only to complicate each
with a profusion of costly adornments. Urban and suburban architecture underwent a similar transformation. Chalets in a dubiously "Norman" style sprang up in the outskirts of Buenos Aires, while nearby
Santa Fe boasted the construction of a house described as Chinese (but
termed "rather more Hindu" by one astonished chronicler). In Chile,
the mansions of Santiago's leading families no longer surrounded a
patio in the traditional manner. Instead, they featured impressive
central staircases and salons with decorated ceilings. The fancy wood
and marble for such construction was often imported.

These superficial signs of progress were accompanied by more gradual and profound changes in the countryside. In almost all parts of Latin America, the middle of the nineteenth century witnessed a quickening erosion of Indian community landholding, accompanied in some areas by a new assault on ecclesiastical lands as well. The process often coincided with an expansion of the cultivation of export products for the world market, but Indian and ecclesiastical landholding was threatened as well in regions where export production did not increase. Therefore, the primary motor of the process would appear to be a new aggressiveness of upwardly mobile groups: provincial landowners (not belonging to the capitaline oligarchies), small-town merchants (many of them mestizos), and even ambitious Indians (who had enriched themselves through social or political predominance within the same corporate communities that they now helped erode). If the growth of the urban domestic market motivated the early stages of the assault on village and church lands, however, increased access to the world market gradually intensified the process.

The increased availability of credit and the expanding market for Latin American exports together enabled formerly weak national governments to consolidate their power. Much of the investment capital that flowed from Europe to Latin America at mid-century went to reinforce national treasuries. Increasing customs receipts collected on export products did the same. As a result, Latin American governments became less dependent on traditional sources of funding. In Peru, European credit combined with tariffs on the exportation of guano to free Lima from dependence on Indian tribute collected in the highland provinces. In Argentina, European credits allowed Buenos Aires to pay for the military expenses of subduing the rebellious provinces and prosecuting the Paraguayan War, definitively affirming the dominance of the central government.

Foreign loans, of course, brought their own sort of dependence. Increasingly, these were long-term loans traded as bonds on European stock markets (especially the London market). They represented a vision of the Latin American future in which constant economic growth would allow the borrowing governments to grow their way out of debt. In the short term, the easy availability of European investment capital allowed the indebted governments to pay the interest on what they owed with new loans, but expanding credit opportunities could not be relied on over the long term. The commercial crisis of 1873 illustrated the problem when the availability of capital contracted sharply, creating severe disruptions. The relatively favorable prices of Latin American export products maintained the viability of the system until 1890. Thereafter, a gradual deterioration of the terms of trade brought increasingly grave consequences during the periodic crises. By that time, however, Latin American governments had come to rely on credit to meet some of their ordinary expenses.

The new flow of foreign investment created a situation analogous to the division of labor between Creoles and peninsular Spaniards in the eighteenth century. Commercialization and interoceanic transport were handled by foreigners—now generally from Britain or France rather than Spain—while the local ruling class reserved primary activities for itself. Gradually, foreign capital also penetrated the primary sector, especially extractive enterprises such as mining or guano exportation. Infrastructural elements like railroads were frequently foreign-controlled as well. Through land speculation, foreign capital even flowed into the agricultural sector occasionally, but for the most part, that sector remained in the hands of the local landowners.

Why did foreigners control the new economic system, as they had the old? Aware of how prejudicial this division of labor was to become, Latin American historians have lingered understandably, if anecdotally, on extreme cases like that of guano exportation from Peru, expressing indignation at how the ruling classes of their countries welcomed foreign investment. A parasitic official corruption easily thrived in such situations, sapping the vitality of the economy with excessive distribution of patronage, as those in power shared the wealth with friends, followers, and family. More importantly, however, the landowning classes of Latin American countries generally benefited from this division of labor. Agriculture simply became more profitable when foreign merchants provided easy commercialization for coffee, wheat, or hides, and the resulting rise in land values made many landowners wealthier quite effortlessly. Thus, the economic rationality of Latin American landowners actively encouraged an arrangement dominated, in most ways, by foreign capital.

The relationship between Latin America and Europe after about 1870 is generally described as neocolonial. From this perspective, the middle years of the nineteenth century saw the gradual arrangement of a new colonial compact, one orienting Latin America toward the industrializing centers of the European economy in a manner that some local elites had desired since the time of independence. Essentially, Latin America became a producer of primary products for European markets, while Europe traded its manufactures in return. These manufactures still principally consisted of textiles and other consumer goods, but gradually the more durable products of European metallurgical industry took an important place on importation lists.

Imported machinery ran on imported coal (a fuel Latin America largely lacked) and required imported replacement parts.

The almost universal adoption of free-trade policies—only partially accepted earlier—facilitated Latin America's new function in the international economy. Liberal ideas of free trade enjoyed exceptional prestige among the rulers of Latin America at this time, providing an ideological justification for the creation of a neocolonial order that ultimately served Europe far better than Latin America. Some Latin American elites may simply have been dazzled by free-trade ideology, but many espoused it for very practical reasons. Indubitably, untrammeled trading practices accelerated the economic transformations then under way, and the majority of the region's political actors agreed on the desirability of those changes. Political conflicts of various kinds were frequent during the third quarter of the nineteenth century, but rarely did they alter the fundamental elite consensus in favor of "progress."

The landowning class, for its part, had ample reason to participate in this consensus. Not only did landowners profit from new markets and from the valorization of their property, they also had enough political influence to protect themselves against the less favorable aspects of the new system. For example, the standard economic ideology included an emphasis on strong currencies based on gold or silver, but that was often ignored in practice by Latin American governments. Issues of paper money helped them weather the periodic financial crises and often worked to the benefit of export producers, who paid their domestic expenses in inflated paper while earning hard currency abroad. Much of the trade in imported European goods was conducted in credit accounts calculated in paper money, forcing the importers to absorb the devalorization that occurred before payment. Argentine mortgages contracted in paper currency occasionally even entered European financial markets. Overall, monetary policy constitutes one of the few matters in which Latin American ruling classes resisted the orthodox logic of the economic system controlled by Europeans.

Urban lower and middle classes had acquired habits of consumption that only European industry could satisfy. They also suffered particularly from the brutal economic oscillations of the period. Cycles of boom and bust affected the urban dwellers more than rural people, who still did not live totally within a market economy. Despite their occasional difficulties, however, many urban interests owed their very existence to opportunities created by the new system. Larger government budgets had raised the salaries and greatly increased the number of public employees. Their spending power had, in turn, permitted an expansion of small and middling retail businesses and had even stimulated some incipient manufacturing oriented toward the local market. Urban protests against the periodic hardships consequently focused on particular grievances and almost never challenged the broad outlines of the new system.

The real victims of the neocolonial compact were the ordinary people of the Latin American countryside. Villages whose common landholdings had survived until the middle of the nineteenth century now began to lose them, but there did not yet exist a rural labor market capable of absorbing the displaced villagers. An adequate wage system would not function until the countryside had become more fully integrated into a market economy, an eventuality that still lay years in the future. In the meantime, rural people often became laborers on the estate of some large landowner who offered them a garden plot in return for their labor in cultivating his crops. These plots remained comparatively large in the Andean highland areas of dense indigenous population, while in Mexico and, a bit later, in Guatemala, haciendas began to dominate the landscape.

The gradual creation of a rural proletariat brought scant benefits to the displaced villagers of these countries. Usually short of capital with which to pay wages, landowners preferred any alternative to remunerating their workers in cash. Wageworkers struck them not only as too expensive but also as too independent. Laborers who earned money might be tempted one day to pocket their wages and leave. A common solution was debt peonage, whereby landowners advanced credit to their laborers, binding them legally to remain until the debt was paid. In many cases, landowners had inherited from the colonial corregidores the privilege of setting the prices of goods more or less arbitrarily. Accounts could also be manipulated easily by the creditors in their own favor. Add to this the landowners' influence with local civil and military authorities, and the result was an effective system of labor discipline that advanced hand in hand with the expansion of export agriculture. Here one finds an explanation of the supposed laziness of Latin American rural workers, often cited in this period by foreign observers and by representatives of the local upper classes alike. Frustrated landowners wanted a work force with the docility of a traditional peasantry and the efficiency of a modern proletariat. Given their access to state-sanctioned coercion, nineteenth-century landlords usually got the docility they demanded but without the efficiency they desired. Of course, there were exceptions and variations in rural labor relations. In Chile, some rural workers gained autonomy from the landowners by paying rent for use of a plot of land and cultivating it successfully themselves. Similarly, immigrant renters in the riverine provinces of the Río de la Plata achieved an uncommonly high standard of living.

Immigration entered the rural labor equation increasingly after 1850. Since the time of independence, plans to attract immigrants had figured in many proposals for the social and economic transformation of Latin America, and the striking example of immigration into the United States heightened interest as the century progressed. In all parts of Latin America, the integration of foreigners into the upper levels of urban society increased with the growth of the neocolonial system. Only southern Brazil, Argentina, and Uruguay received truly large-scale immigration, however, and it did not reach major proportions even there until the last quarter of the century. Furthermore, many immigrants did not escape the exploitative labor regimes suffered by rural workers in general. Chinese coolies were brought to Cuba and Panama to take the place of slaves, and they were frequently treated like slaves. Although juridically free, Chinese laborers were "sold" by the importers (who had paid their passage from China) to landowners or public works companies involved in construction projects. Analogous arrangements were sometimes made in the Río de la Plata by the importers of Basque and Galician laborers between 1850 and 1870. Portuguese and, especially, Italian immigrants who came to Brazil later in the century still suffered, albeit less intensely, from the legal obligation to repay with their labor the cost of traveling to South America.

Rapid population growth constituted another force for change in Latin America after 1850. Despite the wars of independence and the turmoil that followed, and despite the disruptions accompanying the expansion of agrarian capitalism in the countryside, the region showed a high rate of natural fertility throughout the nineteenth century and particularly after mid-century. The demographic information we possess can be considered reliable only in its rough outlines, but taken together, contemporaneous estimates and enumerations present a persuasive picture of overwhelming growth. By 1875, both Brazil (10 million) and Argentina (1.8 million) had approximately tripled in population since the beginning of the century. Chile (2 million), Peru (2.6 million), Colombia (2.9 million), and Venezuela (1.8 million) had all roughly doubled, while Bolivia's population had increased by 70 percent and Mexico's by 50 percent.

Most significant as indicators of the accelerating transformation

of Latin America after 1850 were the measures of its thriving export
trade. By 1880, the value of exports from Argentina as a whole had
expanded by a factor of ten, and exportation from the stock-raising and
agricultural riverine provinces was fifty times greater than at the turn
of the century. Chile's exports had increased by a factor of fifty as well.
Once again, the formerly marginal areas of the Spanish empire in
America had shown the most rapid growth. Still, export expansion
was a notable trait all over the region. Brazil's exports had climbed to
ten times their late colonial levels; Colombia's and Venezuela's had
risen to seven times what they had been then; and Peru's and Ecuador's
were up by factors of five and three, respectively. Again, the old centers
of the colonial mining economy had lagged behind. Bolivia's exports
had increased by a comparatively unimpressive 75 percent, and Mexico's by a mere 20 percent since the turn of the nineteenth century.
Precious metal now accounted for a very small portion of the exportation of formerly important producers like Colombia (16 percent),
Chile (2 percent), or Brazil (where it had disappeared from the export
list altogether).

Latin America's export growth in the second half of the nineteenth
century was founded largely on agriculture. Coffee, one of the most
important new boom crops, entered large-scale cultivation in Brazil,
Colombia, Venezuela, and Central America. Sugar, the oldest boom
crop of all, expanded more moderately in Mexico, Peru, and the Antilles. Other export products were of more-localized importance: wool in
the Río de la Plata, guano in Peru, copper in Chile. None of these
products (including copper) required large quantities of capital to begin production, but large-scale exportation of them demanded the
construction of more expensive infrastructural elements such as railroads and telegraphs. In 1878, Argentina already had 2,200 kilometers
of railroad track and over 7,000 kilometers of telegraph line, Brazil had
almost as much of both, and smaller Chile had 1,500 kilometers of
railroad track and 4,000 kilometers of telegraph line. The construction
of modern communications systems advanced at very unequal rates in
the different Latin American countries, however. Mexico had half
again more telegraph line than Argentina but less than a third as much
railroad track. Neither Colombia nor Venezuela had much more than
100 kilometers of railroad track at this time. Moreover, in many places
railroads mainly linked agricultural producing areas with ports to
facilitate exportation, doing little to create a national rail network to
connect different parts of the country. Brazil and Peru provide particularly clear examples of this pattern.

The foreign capital that went to build railroads often received government guarantees of a certain return on the investment. Such guaranteed minimum profits, on capital very generously calculated in most cases, were seldom achieved in the normal conduct of business, so that Latin American governments paid out subsidies to foreign concessionaires year after year, often in the hope that economic expansion created by the new railroads would eventually cover the cost of subsidies. Generally, the investment in railroad construction did not yield a very high return, and, for that reason, some Latin American governments (including Chile, Peru, and Argentina) participated more directly in the construction of this vital element of infrastructure. From the perspective of European capitalists, railroad construction in Latin America assured a future market for their coal and steel. With profits guaranteed by public concession, they had little to lose in the endeavor. British companies dominated this field of investment like so many others.

debt from infrastructure

Latin America's entry into the world market could not be totally monopolized by the British, but they maintained a predominant role despite the competition of other European countries. Great Britain was not the principal buyer of important new products like "mild" coffees from the Caribbean or wool from Argentina, for example. However, the appearance of alternative European markets for Latin American exports did not automatically imperil British hegemony over Latin American imports. Argentina might sell principally to France, Belgium, and Spain, but it still bought mostly from Great Britain. As earlier in the century, Britain's main European rival in the region was France. French industry grew rapidly in this period, and the expanding urban markets of Latin America offered excellent openings for some of France's traditional export products: fine textiles and high-quality consumer goods like wine. Between 1848 and 1860, French exports to Latin America quadrupled in value. Once again, however, an overly grandiose French policy in the region, exemplified by Maximilian's ephemeral reign in Mexico, proved counterproductive.

Britain - largest importer in L.A.

many exports to rest of Europe

Where imperial France envisioned itself constructing a "Latin" and Catholic bulwark against the aggressive "Anglo" and Protestant imperialism of the United States (which, in turn, envisioned itself annexing the whole continent down to Panama), British imperialism was content to operate through local private interests kept firmly in its economic orbit. The great virtue of this policy was its quiet prudence, and it worked marvelously most of the time. Britain's hesitancy to engage in direct political manipulations also saved it from potentially damaging blunders. For example, British diplomats initially favored Rosas-style authoritarianism over the liberal governments theoretically more favorable to the interests of Great Britain. The subtle qualities of British hegemony prevented it from becoming a matter of public debate in Latin American countries. Occasionally, a disgruntled politician might attempt to make an issue of British domination, but the public tended to remain indifferent, attributing the complaints to private resentment. Only after the international financial collapse of 1929, when the neocolonial order disintegrated, did most Argentines or Brazilians discover that they had been victims of British imperialism.

British success was founded on an indirect hegemony that eschewed confrontation and operated through economic pressure. British banking and financial structures established in the 1860s enjoyed an undisputed predominance thereafter. London banks operated almost exclusively as the intermediaries of monetary exchange between Latin America and Europe, and most Latin American governments used London bankers as their financial agents. British control of credit exerted a subtle but powerful influence over perpetually credit-hungry governments, without need for angry rhetoric or threatening shows of force. Latin American leaders gained considerable prestige at home if they won praise in the pages of the London *Economist* or received a warm reception during a visit to the city's financial district. The British emphasis on "progress" and lack of overtly political objectives generally avoided conflict and appealed to a broader spectrum of Latin American public opinion than the traditionalist and authoritarian values championed by France.

In many ways, though, the Latin American political scene remained highly conflictive during the initial phase of the neocolonial order. The appearance of great potential wealth in new areas itself brought conflict, as in the case of the War of the Pacific (1879–83), fought over the nitrate fields in the border region between Peru and Chile. In addition, old internal conflicts became internationalized, as when the cycle of Argentine and Uruguayan civil wars developed into the largest Latin American conflagration of the century: the Paraguayan War (or the War of the Triple Alliance, 1864–70), pitting Argentina, Uruguay, and Brazil against Paraguay. Also, Mexico's long struggle between liberals and conservatives eventually drew European intervention when France sent an army to support the temporary empire of Maximilian. Other foreign interventions of the period include Spain's bellicose naval operations of 1864–65, which aggravated political tensions in Chile and provoked a change of government in Peru.

Internally, relations between church and state became increas-

ingly conflictive in many Latin American countries as a result of the
triumph of liberalism. Independence had brought a period of isolation
from Rome earlier in the century, and as ties with the Vatican were
reestablished, the Latin American church took on an intransigent conservatism quite different from the enlightened ecclesiastical attitudes
of the eighteenth and early nineteenth centuries. This "ultramon-
tane" orientation emphasized papal authority and put the church
squarely at loggerheads with the increasingly liberal attitudes of dominant Latin American elites. At first, ultramontanism awakened little
interest in a Latin American church steeped in traditions of state
control and close cooperation between political and ecclesiastical authorities. However, the church had emerged greatly weakened from
the period of independence and its aftermath, and large numbers
of priests began to arrive from Europe to rebuild it, bringing ultra-
montane attitudes with them. Soon, even quite mildly reformist governments (as well as others that were not reformist at all but simply operated on the traditional assumption of church subordination
to state authority) clashed with the newly zealous and combative
church, producing an atmosphere charged with the rhetoric of holy
war.

The ramifications of the conflict varied greatly in different Latin
American countries, occasionally becoming violent. Ecclesiastical
ability to wage holy war depended on the influence of the church
among the common people, and levels of popular piety had always
differed from one part of Latin America to another. In Mexico, a
traditional center of church power, the conflict became sharp and
bloody, eventually bringing foreign involvement because of the connections of local conservatives to European political and financial
forces through the Mexican clergy. Elsewhere, church-state conflict
expressed itself in skirmishes limited mostly to the upper and middle
classes, often around the issue of Free Masonry. Earlier in the century,
Masonic lodges had included not only liberal Catholics but also traditional ones, like Gen. Manuel Oribe, the Uruguayan ally of Rosas.
After 1850, however, Latin American bishops followed the Vatican's
lead in defining Free Masonry as antithetical to Catholicism, to the
dismay of many moderate Masons and Catholics alike—and to the
fury of governments unaccustomed to the church's defiant attitude.

The new confrontational style of Catholic militancy resulted especially from an infusion of clergy from Spain, where a bitter struggle
between church and state had raged for decades. Spanish priests who
had fled liberalism in Europe were determined to combat it in Latin
America. Their fanatical tenacity found a perfect complement in the

generally reactionary spirit of a church that felt itself embattled by the
progressive materialism of the age. Other European exiles from anticlerical persecution exhibited a similar belligerency. Ecuador's Prus-
sian bishop, Pedro Schumacher, perfectly embodied the mood of this
sector of the Latin American church in the late nineteenth century
when he discovered, to his delight, that his Ecuadorian flock still
reacted wonderfully to the threat of excommunication and began to
excommunicate right and left in hopes of stemming the liberal tide.
(The Creole archbishop of Quito, on the other hand, reacted more
calmly, confident that his church would survive and outlast the triumph of liberalism.)

The conservative militancy of the late nineteenth-century church
collided directly with anticlerical tendencies still mounting within
Latin American society. In Mexico, Colombia, and Guatemala, the
upper and middle classes coveted the church's vast wealth in land.
Intense opposition to the various religious orders corresponded neatly
to their lion's share of ecclesiastical property. Expropriation of these
lands was an irreversible process. Thus, when pro-Catholic conservatives later regained power in Colombia, they paid an indemnity to the
orders that had lost their land during the liberal reforms of mid-
century, but they did not question the title deeds held by the new
owners of the confiscated property. Hostility to the traditional pre-
rogatives of the church became an important force at this time even in
regions where the colonial church had much less wealth or where it
had lost that wealth during the fight for independence. By gradually
abandoning Catholic assumptions about society in favor of secular
ones, Creole elites confirmed the clergy's fear of the godless spirit of
the age. This new ideological independence did not automatically
make them angry anticlericals, but it did focus their respect for the
church primarily on its expedience as a form of social control.

Increasingly, the church became the militant arm of pious groups
rather than the institutional embodiment of a religious faith shared
by an entire society. Defectors from the formerly universal religion
remained a small minority, but an influential one, overrepresented
among the intellectual elites close to the levers of power. To combat
secular influences, the clergy set about mobilizing the faithful and, in
the process, discovered the limits of their own influence in Latin
American society. For hundreds of years, the Catholic church had been
the colonial institution with the greatest and most spontaneous resonance among the common people, but the sway of the church had been
weakened by the revolutionary tumult of independence. If the re-
ligiosity of the Mexican, Colombian, and Guatemalan masses could

not be questioned, neither could the ability of the Liberal party to gain an enthusiastic following among them, despite the most vehement ecclesiastical condemnations of liberalism. Catholicism had lost the unquestionable official sanction that had characterized its place in Latin American society for centuries. The breach in religious unity among the ruling classes opened the way for new expressions of ambiguity and defiance from below.

Deprived of its former position as exclusive spiritual and moral arbiter, the church was unable to maintain its opposition to governing elites for very long. Ecclesiastical authority had always rested partly on its solidarity with the power of the state, and when local priests proclaimed the end of that solidarity, they undermined their own influence. This explains the relative brevity of Catholic resistance to the establishment of the new order. In their attempt to repel the advances of nineteenth-century liberalism, the militant clergy had discovered how tightly Latin American elites still grasped the reins of power. All over the region, the masters of the new system of export growth retained nearly exclusive control of politics until 1880 or beyond. (If they shared power at all, it was with the military rather than the church.) Within a few decades, the church had adapted itself to the change and learned to cultivate its still considerable, if no longer dominant, influence over the ruling class. In most ways, the church reassumed within the new order the same sort of legitimating role it had exercised before.

The triumph of liberalism encountered resistance within the ruling class as well. The advent of the new secular creed usually implied generational conflict, as enthusiastic young politicians displaced representatives of the old order, few of whom accepted their retirement gracefully. Moreover, the program of liberal reform generally gained its earliest adherents among marginalized sectors of the urban elite, people with an education and a respectable social background who had not prospered in the sluggish economy of the early nineteenth century. Such individuals found the economic promise of liberalism particularly attractive. Often, these upper-class reformers appealed to members of the urban lower and middle classes to support their ambitions. All over Latin America, these groups clashed with narrow oligarchies motivated more by personal than by class interest. In the long run, however, the economic advantages of liberalism were everywhere irresistible for the upper class. Sometimes determined reformers emerged victorious after bitter struggles, while in the less conflictive cases, the groups in power experienced political conversions and led the way themselves. In one way or another, the determined resistance to liberal

reform evaporated from Mexico to Argentina as the tremendous potential for export growth was repeatedly demonstrated.

Such were the broad outlines of the triumph of liberalism and the
creation of neocolonial economic structures in nineteenth-century
Latin America, but the details varied greatly from one country to
another. In some nations, the process occurred quickly and with little
disruption. In others, it was long delayed. Two stages mark the transition to neocolonialism in the individual country sketches that follow:
first, the dominant groups finally accepted the establishment of the
new order; and second, they coopted it for their own benefit. This
second stage usually involved the gradual abandonment of political
reform in favor of an exclusive concentration on economic modernization, often with an authoritarian cast.

Mexico experienced the clearest and also the stormiest transition
of all. It began with the liberal revolt of 1854, which saw the rise to
national prominence of Benito Juárez, a Zapotec Indian from the state
of Oaxaca. Befriended by an Italian merchant who paid for his law
studies and whose daughter he eventually married, Juárez had become
governor of the state of Oaxaca before joining forces with Gen. Juan
Alvarez, a veteran insurgent and follower of Father José María Morelos
during the wars of independence. In 1854, the two liberals rose in
opposition to yet another presidency of Antonio López de Santa Anna,
that perennial representative of the alliance between high-ranking
army officers and conservative politicians. The moment seemed ripe
for a liberal takeover. Conservative leader Lucas Alamán had died the
year before, and many young men of elite Mexico City families now
showed intellectual sympathy for liberalism. Santa Anna abandoned
the crumbling conservative government without a fight.

The liberals placed Alvarez in the presidency and set about implementing their program, which became famous in Mexican history as
"the Reform." The main target of the Reform was the Catholic church
and its vast wealth in the country. One important measure, the Juárez
Law, removed the ecclesiastical *fuero*, a set of special legal privileges
enjoyed by the clergy since colonial times. Another measure, the
Lerdo Law, prohibited community ownership of buildings and land, a
measure aimed at religious communities though it was later applied to
indigenous communities as well. When the conservatives reacted violently, a more conciliatory liberal general, Ignacio Comonfort, replaced
Alvarez in the presidency, but the conservatives refused to be placated.
Their forces overthrew Comonfort and captured Mexico City, beginning a bloody three years' war in which both sides armed Indians and
mestizos. The liberals' destruction of churches and convents strength-

ened conservative calls to defend the Catholic faith. Undaunted, the liberals wrote a constitution embodying the principles of the Reform and chose Juárez as their figurehead in 1857. When the forces of Juárez consolidated their hold on Veracruz and the U.S. border area, they controlled the country's customs revenues and enjoyed superior communications with the outside world. In 1861, the liberals retook Mexico City, though conservative resistance persisted in many provinces.

Their backs to the wall, the conservatives played their trump card, encouraging European intervention against the Juárez government. While in power, the conservatives had accumulated large debts with French and Swiss banking houses, and British and Spanish merchants had suffered large losses as both sides requisitioned money and goods to supply their armies during the three years of civil war. Now these European powers demanded that the liberals settle these debts and indemnities, which Juárez claimed the government of his devastated country had no money to pay. In 1862 a combined British, French, and Spanish force occupied the port of Veracruz to extract payment by force from Mexican customs receipts. The British and Spanish soon withdrew, leaving the French to pursue a larger and riskier venture: the establishment of hegemony over Mexico through an alliance with Mexican conservatives. Early setbacks only steeled French determination, and in 1863 the capital city of Mexico once again changed hands as the government of Juárez retreated northward and Mexican clergy gave French troops a delirious welcome.

Once in power, the French and their conservative allies crowned their triumph by creating a Mexican throne and bringing a European prince to occupy it. Maximilian, Mexico's new emperor, was a member of the Austrian house of Hapsburg. He appears to have believed sincerely in the plebiscite arranged by the conservatives to legitimate his rule in Mexico. The conservatives had long dreamed of just such a solution to their country's chronic instability and dangerous flirtations with liberalism. Now they were quickly disappointed by the emperor's refusal to roll back the Reform against the stiff resistance of the new owners of confiscated church property. Many of the new owners were French, noted the disillusioned conservatives, but Mexican landowners, and especially merchants, from the national and state capitals constituted another part of this powerful vested interest. The issue drove a wedge into conservative ranks, narrowing the party's appeal. Upper-class Mexican families left out of the division of spoils became disenchanted with Maximilian's empire, especially when French troops proved unable to pacify the country despite their many victories. By 1866, the end of the U.S. Civil War and the outbreak of a new conflict in Europe led to the withdrawal of French forces from Mexico. Maximilian stayed behind to lead a futile resistance against the revived liberal onslaught, only to be captured and executed by order of Juárez in 1867.

The Reform had triumphed, but its prize was a Mexico in ruins. The defeat of the army of foreign intervention had been achieved only through the creation of another army itself too large and powerful for the good of the country. The army that had defeated the French and their allies was composed of regional caudillos with tremendous influence over their soldiers, making it particularly dangerous to the constitutional government. To make matters worse, discontent ran high because Juárez had demobilized the majority of this force without offering the customary bonus to troops mustering out. Instead, he reduced government spending in all areas except primary education, which he greatly increased. This farsighted measure did little to address the immediate crisis, aggravated by continuing economic ills. A surge in Mexican cotton production during the U.S. Civil War had evaporated when former Confederate states recommenced exports afterward. Once again, Mexico had to rely on its silver for foreign exchange, but the twenty-five million pesos exported in the early 1870s still did not surpass the figures of the last years of colonial rule.

Dissatisfaction within the military put an untimely end to the civil administrations of the Reform. In 1871, a three-way presidential election left Juárez in office without a convincing mandate. One of the other candidates was a hero of the fighting against the French and, like Juárez, a Oaxacan: Gen. Porfirio Díaz. Unhappy with the results of the election, Díaz tried unsuccessfully to raise a revolt, then fled into exile. The next year, however, the dying Juárez turned over the presidency to Sebastián Lerdo de Tejada, like himself, a veteran architect of the Reform. Díaz again raised the cry of rebellion against Lerdo, this time successfully. The banner carried by Porfirio Díaz in the 1870s, "Effective Suffrage and No Reelection," was almost identical to that later used against his long dictatorship in 1910.

The triumph of Díaz began the second stage of the process leading from liberal political reform to authoritarian modernization. At first, the new president swore fidelity to the principles of the Reform and accused Juárez and Lerdo of betraying them. He particularly criticized the policy of friendship with the United States pursued by both men. Despite his (possibly sincere) protestations of loyalty to the Reform, however, the rule of Díaz moved away from the emphasis on law and political liberalism that had characterized the administration of Juárez. Whereas Juárez had admired the ideas of Juan Germán Roscio, a

Venezuelan political thinker who justified the Spanish American revolutions in terms of natural law, Díaz and the men around him admired
newer, positivist social theories. Positivism, which became influential
in much of Latin America in the late nineteenth century, concentrated
on material and economic progress rather than on abstract first principles. The partisans of Díaz distinguished his "honest tyranny" from
Santa Anna's capricious and self-serving rule because the former had
developmentalist goals. The Reform had accomplished juridical "advances" like the abolition of community landholding in favor of modern private property. Now, the government of Díaz proposed to trans-
late those legal advances into economic modernization by insuring
political stability, constructing communications infrastructure, and
disciplining the labor force. Powerful groups inside and outside Mexico soon lost their initial wariness of Díaz and embraced his gospel of
orderly progress.

In the Río de la Plata, the fall of Rosas did not leave the road open
immediately for the triumph of liberalism in the way that many of the
young reformers like Domingo Faustino Sarmiento had hoped. Uruguay's uneasy bipartisan arrangements of the 1850s failed to resolve
that country's political divide, made deep and bitter during the decade-
long Guerra Grande. The former Uruguayan allies of Rosas, the Blanco
party, gained strength as the decade progressed. In addition, a rural/
urban split cut across the line between Blancos and Colorados as each
party developed a "doctoral" urban faction led by lawyers who talked
about political "fusion" versus a caudillo-led rural faction, willing, at
most, to make temporary pacts with the other side. Urban interests
represented the oligarchy of the capital, Montevideo, the country's
only real city. Further complicating matters, the Brazilian empire
remained a major player in Uruguayan affairs. In order to win Brazilian
aid in the victorious campaign against Rosas, the Montevidean government had signed an exorbitantly generous treaty with Brazil in
1851, and the imperial government meddled boldly in Uruguayan politics to guarantee the treaty's provisions. Ranchers from Rio Grande do
Sul, the Brazilian province bordering Uruguay on the north, had made
themselves owners of huge landholdings in the small republic, and
Brazil's famous capitalist and banker, the baron of Mauá, utterly dominated the financial life of Montevideo.

In Argentina, the advance of liberalism was even more conflicted.
The regional caudillo of Entre Ríos, Gen. Justo José de Urquiza, a
central figure of the anti-Rosas alliance, had occupied Buenos Aires
after the defeat of Rosas. At first, many of the fallen dictator's former
supporters made an easy transition of allegiance to the new caudillo,

himself a Federalist not unlike Rosas. Urquiza dissolved the legislature of Buenos Aires and assumed direct rule of the conquered province. Within a few months, however, liberal émigrés returning from exile in Montevideo allied themselves with others resentful of Urquiza's rule and led a successful rebellion against Urquiza and his occupying army. Triumphant in Buenos Aires, the liberals then sought to extend their revolution to the rest of Argentina, where the urban oligarchies in provincial capitals were eager to escape the hegemony of rural caudillos. However, resistance within the province of Buenos Aires undercut this attempt to spread the liberal reform. Years of military conscription had weighed heavily on the countryside of Buenos Aires, which would have to supply most of the soldiers for another round of wars. Refusing to join the liberal crusade, the rural garrisons of Buenos Aires instead revolted against the government of the port capital.

Fortunately for the liberal government of Buenos Aires, the city's commercial prosperity allowed it to placate the rebels with money, but for the time being, the reformers had to postpone their ambition of making Buenos Aires the capital of a united Argentina. As the rest of the country became confederated under Urquiza, the independent State of Buenos Aires went its own way for a decade. During that time, zealous liberal publicists succeeded in fostering the local pride of the city's populace and in identifying it with the concept of progressive liberalism. Sky blue (formerly the color of the liberal Unitarians) replaced Federalist red in the city's patriotic displays. The countryside of Buenos Aires, on the other hand, remained cool to the gospel of liberalism. Powerful landowners accepted the separation of Buenos Aires simply because they feared inclusion in a united Argentina they could not control. The common inhabitants of the pampa of Buenos Aires displayed their own hostility to liberal innovations, but their preferences counted less politically than in earlier years. Two decades of authoritarian rule had consolidated state control over the rural population.

While the independent State of Buenos Aires profited from the rising prices of its export products on the international market and the port city modernized rapidly, Urquiza presided over an Argentine confederation with a strongly presidentialist constitution also designed to encourage European investment and immigration. The welcoming attitude of Urquiza's confederation toward European capital and trade was partly an attempt to attract outside cooperation in the conflict with Buenos Aires. Loudly proclaiming the principle of free navigation on the tributaries of the Río de la Plata, the confederation initially secured the support of England, France, and Brazil, all of which had long argued for that policy. In fact, the government of Buenos Aires no longer opposed the free-navigation policies. It would appear that in backing Urquiza the Europeans and Brazilians acted on their belief that the traditional caudillo of Entre Ríos was likely to outlast the liberal ideologues of Buenos Aires. If so, they miscalculated completely. Urquiza did not live up to his authoritarian reputation and instead renounced traditional strong-arm tactics, trying sincerely to adapt to a new political style. On the other hand, the liberal leaders of Buenos Aires showed themselves capable of political expedients that belied their monotonous protestations of faith in strict constitutionalism. Foreign diplomats also may have misjudged the balance of power between Buenos Aires and the confederation. Despite the opening of the tributaries of the Río de la Plata to free navigation, Buenos Aires remained insolently rich and the confederation unexpectedly poor.

Meanwhile, having renounced the advantages of his old methods, Urquiza proved unable to master the new ones, and his ministers precipitated a clash between the Argentine confederation and the State of Buenos Aires with the hopes of furthering their own political ambitions. At the battle of Cepeda in 1859, Urquiza's forces defeated those of Buenos Aires. The proud port city and its rich hinterland lost their political independence but consoled themselves with the preservation of key economic advantages and with the retirement of their old enemy Urquiza from the presidency in 1860. Little more than a year passed, however, before Buenos Aires rebelled, and the government of the confederation had to turn once more to its war leader, Urquiza. The caudillo's aid was decidedly halfhearted. At the decisive battle of Pavón, he withdrew when the confederation still had some chance of saving the day, leaving the forces of Buenos Aires to control the field and, as a result, the future of Argentina.

The provincial governments of the rest of the country quickly adapted themselves to the triumph of Buenos Aires, but several steps remained to consolidate the liberal revolution in the Río de la Plata. Urquiza, for his part, accepted a limited role as ruler of Entre Ríos (along with the neighboring province of Corrientes), leaving the presidency of the new united Argentina to Bartolomé Mitre, the Buenos Aires liberal who had commanded the victorious army at Pavón. More problematical was the situation of Uruguay, under the control of the conservative Blanco party at this time. Argentine liberals like Mitre had strong ties of friendship with the other Uruguayan party, the Colorados, and after the election of Mitre in 1862, the Colorado Gen. Venancio Flores was able to use Argentine territory to organize his

"Liberating Crusade" against the Blanco government. Flores also received aid from Brazil, where influential Liberals from the southernmost state of Rio Grande do Sul had their own axes to grind with the Blancos. The hostility of the Argentine and Brazilian governments led the Blancos to ally themselves with the government of Paraguay, at the time a major military power in the Río de la Plata. The stage was set for the most terrible war ever fought in South America.

Paraguayan leaders had long sought an involvement in the Río de la Plata commensurate with the country's economic and military power. During the first half of the nineteenth century, a state monopoly on exports of tobacco and yerba mate, along with extensive state participation in cattle ranching, had put considerable resources in the hands of Paraguay's authoritarian rulers. President-for-life Carlos Antonio López, who took over from the ascetic dictator Francia in 1840, had a real interest in technical innovation. He acquired a fleet of steam-powered riverboats to maintain the landlocked nation's communications with the outside world. His son and successor, Francisco Solano López, had larger and more bellicose ambitions. Long-standing disputes with Brazil (over boundaries) and Argentina (over navigation of the Paraná River) naturally aligned Paraguay with Uruguay against the two larger nations. When a Brazilian force invaded Uruguay to support the Colorado insurgency led by Venancio Flores against the Blanco government, López declared war on Brazil in solidarity with the embattled Blancos. In order to come to grips with the main force of the Brazilian army, the Paraguayans requested permission to cross the narrow strip of depopulated Argentine territory separating Paraguay from Rio Grande do Sul. Denied permission, they invaded the Argentine province of Corrientes, bringing Argentina into the war against them as well.

Events went against the two smaller countries from the beginning. The Blanco resistance crumbled rapidly, and contrary to the Paraguayans' expectations, Urquiza did not support them. As a result, Paraguay was left alone to face Brazil, Argentina, and by 1865, a hostile Uruguayan government now controlled by the Colorados—all gathered in a "Triple Alliance" against López. In a secret treaty, Brazil and Argentina planned to punish the Paraguayans after the war by dividing between them lands that they had long disputed with Paraguay, totaling more than half the country's territory. However, the actual conquest proved more difficult than this premature division of the spoils. For five years, the Paraguayans resisted the onslaught of the Triple Alliance with a tenacity and courage that astonished the world and decimated the adult male population of the country.

Brazil and Argentina were less formidable adversaries than one
might assume from their territorial extension. The political unity of
Argentina remained precarious. The nimble maneuvering of Mitre had
neutralized Urquiza but failed to avoid first a mutiny of troops from
Urquiza's Entre Ríos and then a widespread Federalist uprising in
the interior provinces in the wake of discouraging setbacks for the
Argentine war effort. Brazilian leaders experienced difficulties that,
though not so severe as those confronted by the Argentine government, strained the resources and organizational ability of their sprawling empire. The rather plodding style of the allied command further
protracted the conflict, as the Paraguayans were pushed back from the
bits of Brazil and Argentina they had initially occupied and from their
stronghold at Humaitá (blocking the ascent of the Paraguay River), and
then driven up the Paraguay River toward Asunción, their capital city.
Even the fall of Asunción did not bring an end to the war. The Paraguayans did not surrender until the death of López, who had retreated
with the last of his army to make a last stand in the remote northern
part of the country.

In the aftermath of the fighting, Paraguay lay in ruins, but quarrels
among the victors limited the consequences of the defeat, at least in
regard to the territorial claims of Argentina. In the creation of a postwar government for Paraguay, Argentina supported Paraguayan exiles
who had opposed the government of López, while Brazil supported
generals who had led the Paraguayan armies during the war and who
managed to retain power afterward. Having satisfied its own territorial
ambitions, Brazil helped the new Paraguayan government to resist the
Argentine claims and, in that way, managed to exert a predominant
diplomatic influence over postwar Paraguay. In economic terms, however, Paraguay necessarily gravitated toward Argentina. The Paraná
River, a tributary of the Río de la Plata, was still Paraguay's only viable
commercial link with the overseas market, and Argentina consumed a
large portion of the landlocked country's export products. Meanwhile,
Paraguayan landowners bought up former state property that the new
government happily auctioned to the highest bidder, strengthening
liberal economic patterns.

The shattering war had disrupted, then refashioned, the delicate
internal political balance of Argentina, obliging it to raise and maintain an army of tens of thousands, an army repeatedly decimated by
casualties and disease. While Mitre was directing the army's operations in Paraguay, his party had fallen apart in Buenos Aires. When the
Federalist revolt in the interior provinces had threatened the country's
fragile unity, the army had put down the uprising and made itself the

arbiter of the political order, throwing its weight against Mitre's preferred candidate for president in 1868. The new president was Domingo Faustino Sarmiento, who governed with the help of the army
until the assassination of Urquiza finally brought to an end Federalist
hopes of recovering power through confrontation with the liberals.
Undeterred, the former Federalists joined the political status quo and,
working from within, managed to take over province after province.
Sarmiento's successor, Nicolás Avellaneda, had yet to face an armed
challenge from the provincial leaders of Buenos Aires when advocates
of a strong national government proposed to separate the capital city
from the province of Buenos Aires, making it an independent federal
district. In many ways, Argentine national unity remained more an
aspiration than a fact until the end of the 1870s.

The decade of the 1880s marked the consolidation of the liberal
order in Argentina. In the first year of the decade, Gen. Julio Roca
became president after leading a successful and highly popular campaign against southern Indian nations, adding a huge expanse of land
to the effective national territory. Roca used his considerable political
skill to build a solid alliance of provincial politicians willing to collaborate to control the central government. During the 1850s, an ideological rival of Sarmiento's, Juan Bautista Alberdi, had charted the course
on which his country was finally about to embark. Alberdi had recommended an authoritarian government to insure order and to guarantee
the conditions necessary for economic progress. Believing that Urquiza was the leader most likely to provide that order, Alberdi had
aligned himself with the ill-fated confederation against Buenos Aires.
In the intervening years, the internal balance of power and the creation
of representative institutions had monopolized the political agenda,
but Roca's strong government of the 1880s shifted to an emphasis on
economic transformations. Much as in Mexico, triumphant liberalism
quickly evolved into authoritarian developmentalism in the last quarter of the nineteenth century.

The political system created by Roca in Argentina preserved more
liberal features than did the Porfirian system in Mexico, however.
Although the Argentine government perfected a system of electoral
fraud that allowed voting to be administered from above, it respected
the principle of a single term for presidents and observed certain
constitutional guarantees such as freedom of the press. These forms
cloaked a powerfully disciplined new political order that Roca directed
with consummate skill. Figures of the old order had to adapt themselves or be swept away. Sarmiento refused to conform and consequently disappeared from the national scene. Mitre more prudently

accepted the role assigned to him as patriarchal symbol of Argentine nationality, becoming the venerated figurehead of an impotent opposition that Roca cultivated for the sake of appearances.

The period between the fall of Rosas and the rise of Roca had witnessed tremendous social and economic transformations, despite the periodic financial crises of these years. In the province of Buenos Aires, railroad construction had quadrupled land values and quintupled the value of exports. In the province of Santa Fe, along the west bank of the Paraná River, where tenacious Indian tribes had fought white settlers until quite recently, European immigrants (especially Italians) had bought or rented small parcels of land to plant wheat. This new agricultural boom caused the rapid growth of Rosario, the river port of the wheat-growing region. The city of Buenos Aires swelled from a hundred thousand inhabitants in 1850 to half a million in 1880. In the capital city, as in the wheat lands, more than half of the people were immigrants. Merchants and landlords reaped the fattest profits of all, but the sheer volume of economic expansion permitted the growth of the urban middle class and, to some degree, the formation of a rural middle class as well. The impact of this expansion on the provinces of the Argentine interior was less favorable. The railroads made the interior provinces consumers in the international market at a time when most of them lacked the ability to produce competitively in that market. Only the province of Tucumán developed a modern economy during this period. Tucumán sugar production benefited mostly the local aristocracy, which used its influence in the national government to gain tariff protection and bank credit.

Despite the financial oscillations of the times, Argentina seemed to have entered a long period of prosperity. Short-term ups and downs resulted in indubitable political tensions, but such conflicts tended to subside as quickly as they arose. The general consensus concerning the country's economic vigor was broad enough to undergird and stabilize the politics of the neocolonial order in Argentina. The national state reaped only limited benefits from this state of affairs, however. Export-oriented ranchers and farmers, importers and middle-class consumers of imported goods—all demonstrated decided hostility to property taxes and tariffs. They preferred that the government borrow or print more paper money to supply its budgetary requirements. The military and police costs of maintaining public order put further pressure on the available state resources. Within these limitations, the state spent its money on education and public works. Sarmiento, "the teacher president," and his successors gave the country's public schools notable and sustained support. Those who bragged that

Argentina had more teachers than soldiers may have exaggerated, but the assertion contained a significant kernel of truth.

As president, General Roca was not hesitant to present himself as the leader of a national project essentially economic in character, but national involvement in major infrastructural improvements was intermittent. The country's first railroad was the property of the provincial government of Buenos Aires. British capital eventually controlled most of the railroads there and in the booming province of Santa Fe but not so in the interior provinces. When the financial crisis of 1873 interrupted the flow of foreign investment, the government stepped in to continue the construction of the country's railways. Local capital participated alongside foreign investment in the construction of the rapidly growing capital city and in such rural improvements as the costly introduction of wire fencing and pedigreed breeds of cattle and sheep. Roca's "Conquest of the Desert" made another twenty thousand square leagues of Indian lands available to the landowning class in 1880.

On the other side of the Río de la Plata, Uruguay underwent a comparable transformation in a shorter time. During the middle years of the nineteenth century, the small republic had continued to suffer a chronic political instability that ravaged the countryside and multiplied conflicts among holders of competing land claims. The long and bitter Guerra Grande of the 1840s had renewed Brazilian incursions along the country's northern border in the 1850s, and the Brazilian-supported "Crusade" of the Colorado Gen. Venancio Flores in the 1860s had limited expensive innovations in agricultural and livestock production. While Uruguayan political life spun violently around its old polarities (Blancos versus Colorados, caudillos versus "doctores"), potential investors, wary of the government's inability to guarantee the security of their investments in rural areas, preferred to apply their capital elsewhere. In the early 1870s, the "doctores" generally replaced the caudillos, but their endless lawyerly debates on fine points of political liberalism did nothing to impose order in the countryside.

In the wake of the international financial crisis of 1873, a new sort of government came to power in Uruguay. Col. Lorenzo Latorre, not a rural caudillo but a career army officer, imposed the country's first true military dictatorship. In less than a decade, Latorre's authoritarian government accomplished in Uruguay what Rosas had begun and Roca had finished in Argentina. The Uruguayan military imposed ruthless order in the countryside with the support of the landowning class, now organized in the Rural Association to promote its collective interests. Strengthened public and private police forces controlled the landless rural population and obliged them to accept the erection of wire fences that permanently isolated them from informal access to the land, forcing them into wage labor for their survival. In Montevideo, the military government gained the support of the port city's influential merchants, and some of its reforms were decidedly urban and liberal in inspiration. Latorre's regime initiated the ambitious expansion of public schools directed by José Pedro Varela, despite the opposition of the church and the indifference of the country's educated elite, who, at heart, rather enjoyed their monopoly on the printed word. Meanwhile, Uruguay's exports of hides and wool rose steeply, and the population of Montevideo reached 100,000 (of a total national population of half a million, 30 percent of which was foreign-born).

Soon, though, the stability and prosperity fostered by Latorre's dictatorship called attention to the absence of political liberties in the country. Losing support within the army as well as the political elite by the late 1870s, Latorre first attempted severe measures against the opposition, then departed for exile in Argentina in 1880, leaving behind an Uruguay very different from the one in which he seized control four years earlier. The dictatorship appeared to have prepared this land of formerly indomitable liberty to accept the new progressive authoritarianism.

In Mexico, Argentina, and Uruguay, armed dissidence had been a constant of political life, and though these countries' constitutional liberal reformers of mid-century had won respect throughout Latin America, the progressive creed had been imposed only through more or less authoritarian and military means. Similar outcomes might be expected in countries where the reforming impulse had been less profound and preexisting authoritarian tendencies therefore encountered less resistance. This was the case in Venezuela and most of Central America, as well as in Ecuador.

Venezuela's transition to authoritarian progressivism occurred when a collapse of coffee prices undermined the country's conservative hegemony. José Tadeo Monagas, elected president in 1846, chose as his vice president a popular opposition journalist, Antonio Leocadio Guzmán. Monagas had been elected with the support of the old Venezuelan caudillo José Antonio Páez, but the popularity of the reformist cause allowed him to throw off the tutelage of Páez, who rebelled briefly and then fled to the United States. Unfortunately, the reform movement led by Monagas functioned as a vehicle for large-scale political corruption. After satisfying the personal ambitions of elite youths of Caracas, a brother of the first Monagas succeeded him in the presidency, and the Monagas regime set about creating a family dy-

Monagas family dynasty

nasty. Twelve years of rule by the family concluded only in 1858 when dissatisfied liberals and conservatives combined to topple them. The struggle between liberals (identified by the color yellow) and conservatives (by the color blue) then recommenced. Adopting the banner of federalism, the liberals gained the upper hand, and, in 1861, old General Páez returned to lead the conservative resistance. At this point, Antonio Guzmán Blanco, son of the first Monagas vice president, emerged somewhat unexpectedly as the leading figure among the liberals.

Antonio Guzmán Blanco

Like his father, Guzmán Blanco became a spokesperson for popular discontent, in this case, for the rural masses whose angry protest fueled the federalist revolution. The rhetoric of Guzmán Blanco combined intransigent liberalism with a constant hostility to rich ranchers, sugar planters, Caracas coffee merchants, and financiers. He blamed the wealthy local representatives of mysterious market forces for the social devastation brought by the present moment of economic change. After the defeat of Páez and the conservatives, however, Guzmán Blanco restocked the country's military hierarchy with trusted officers and proceeded to rule substantially in the interest of the economic elites whom he had formerly excoriated. The new regime presided over increasing foreign commercial penetration and export growth in Venezuela. It promoted the development of the country's transportation infrastructure, the reform and codification of its law, and the organization of its system of elementary education. It oversaw the institution of civil marriage, the suppression of religious orders, and the removal of cemeteries from church control. If Guzmán Blanco's progressivism was indubitable, his authoritarianism was no less so. He brooked no opposition in his federalist Venezuela and adorned many of the country's public squares with colossal statues of himself. During his frequent trips to Europe (where he recruited more investment for Venezuela), angry crowds sometimes pulled these statues down, only to see them returned to their pedestals on Guzmán Blanco's return. In 1889, however, the statues were toppled permanently. Venezuela's progressive authoritarianism functioned so smoothly that it could continue quite well in the hands of the mediocre interim president whom the now-superfluous Guzmán Blanco had elected to govern temporarily in his absence.

After the fall of Guzmán Blanco, political power in Venezuela devolved into the hands of a military quite different from the people's army that originally brought the federalists to power. Instead of popular mobilization, it was the national treasury that provided the resources needed to maintain military rule. An officer corps recruited among the upper classes of Venezuela's less affluent and more backward regions controlled the army and disciplined the Venezuelan masses to obedience and silence. The situation was disrupted only by periodic feuds between regional cliques within the officer corps. Lawyers from Caracas occasionally served as figureheads for the military regime, but the country's urban upper class had for the most part accepted their separation from direct political control. Regardless of whoever appeared to rule at one moment or another, the social and political order proceeded firmly along the lines set by the unfaithful heirs of the federalist revolution.

In Guatemala, the alliance between mestizo caudillo Rafael Carrera and the country's landowning aristocracy, established before the mid-nineteenth century, continued until Carrera's death in 1865. The Guatemalan economy had long been oriented inward, its exportation of cochineal being the only exception, but it now began to change slowly. Expansion of coffee production became the chief motor of economic transformation, rising to 92 percent of the country's exports by 1880. With the rise of coffee came the triumph of liberalism in national politics. The liberals found their champion in another mestizo general, Justo Rufino Barrios, who took power in 1873. Barrios quickly launched a set of reforms that included state promotion of primary education and the confiscation of churches. He also attempted, but failed, to reconstruct the Central American union of bygone years.

The general prosperity that coffee brought to the Guatemalan upper classes explains their tolerance of Barrios's authoritarian style. Some of Guatemala's numerous Indian communities, on the other hand, were adversely affected by the rise of coffee. Production of the new export crop expanded above all in sparsely populated middle altitudes of the country's Pacific slope. In that region, the liberal government sought to create a class of middling landowners, many of them *ladinos* (mestizos and Hispanicized Indians). In higher-altitude areas suited to coffee, larger landowners (most of them white) adopted the profitable new crop as well. Both groups needed the labor that only the indigenous communities could provide. In order to assure them that labor, the liberal government reinstituted the colonial institution of forced-labor drafts under the new name of *mandamiento*. This resurrected version of the old system obligated Indian communities to supply a fixed number of seasonal workers, which government administrators distributed among the coffee planters.

At his death in 1885, Barrios left a complex legacy. The economic principles of Guatemalan liberalism and its vigorous program of secularization had received the unanimous endorsement of the propertied classes, who accepted, in turn, their marginalization from the direct exercise of political power. The military ruled, and urban elites were reduced to staffing a decorous, but essentially impotent, institutional facade. The rural masses had been pushed from their communities onto the coffee plantations by the naked force of the liberal state. However, as earlier with cochineal, they also turned the export system to their own needs, using the additional income derived from their work on the coffee plantations to support the rapid population growth taking place within their indigenous communities. The coffee economy also had a mixed impact on landowners. Some of them lacked the financial resources necessary to weather the market's abrupt cycles of boom and bust, and many lost their lands as a result. Those who accumulated such properties were the merchants and financiers of the coffee trade, often German immigrants. As a result, the best coffee lands in the country had passed into German hands by the early twentieth century.

The other countries of Central America evolved in a substantially similar manner. For several reasons, however, the emergence of the neocolonialism in most of Central America lacked the stark extremes that characterized Guatemala. Elsewhere, conservative ascendancy had been less marked, the closed seigneurial economy less dominant, and the opposition between a white aristocracy and Indian masses less clearly defined. In addition, the rise of new export activities took place more slowly in indigo-producing El Salvador and cattle-producing Honduras and Nicaragua. During the second half of the nineteenth century, struggles between liberals and conservatives in all of these countries eventually resulted in military regimes (loosely connected with one of the traditional parties through some influential leader), but the progressivism of these authoritarian governments was often more theoretical than effective because of the slow pace of economic change. Costa Rica constituted an exception to this pattern. In this country of only half a million inhabitants, a class of middle-sized landowners prospered with the introduction of coffee and managed to resist the concentration of political power in a dictatorship. In contrast to its neighbors, Costa Rica reduced its armed forces to a minimum. It could boast more truthfully than Argentina of having more teachers than soldiers. The fundamental characteristics of Costa Rica's "exemplary democracy" lasted through the middle of the twentieth century. El Salvador also appeared for a time to resist the tide of progressive dictatorship, but the impact of the coffee economy on that overpopulated former stronghold of Central American liberalism finally pushed it down the political path taken by most of its neighbors.

The strategic importance of the Central American isthmus began to affect the course of the region's political development at mid-century. Great Britain and the United States, both of which aspired to control an interoceanic canal, frequently backed different sides in the complicated internal politics of Central American countries. A hypothetical canal route through Lake Nicaragua made that country a particular object of diplomatic contention. In the 1850s, a North American adventurer by the name of William Walker led an army (financed by Cornelius Vanderbilt) in a temporarily successful bid to take over Nicaragua—much to the alarm of Great Britain (which alleged its own somewhat questionable dominion over the sparsely populated Mosquito Coast of the country). However, these transitory meddlings were mere shadows of the sustained twentieth-century interventions that would make Central America a region only nominally independent of the United States.

[margin note: 1850. temporary occupation of Nicaragua by U.S.]

The small Andean republic of Ecuador presents an unusual variant of neocolonial development in Latin America: a progressive dictatorship rooted not in the military but in the Catholic church, an institution attacked by reformers almost everywhere else. The architect of this original solution was the son of a peninsular merchant, Gabriel García Moreno. Born in Guayaquil, García Moreno shared the liberal attitude prevalent in his coastal birthplace during the first part of his political career, but after his marriage to a wealthy heiress from Quito, he identified himself increasingly with the conservative aristocracy of the highlands. He fought against Juan José Flores when that former president tried forcibly to retake power with Spanish support in 1846, then against the liberal military regimes that followed in the 1840s and 1850s. In 1859–60, García Moreno's nimble political maneuverings (he first supported, then opposed, Peruvian claims in a border conflict) allowed him to consolidate his control over Quito and then over all of Ecuador. The triumphant dictator hoped to secure his rule by incorporating Ecuador into the French empire, but he was disappointed to find the French more interested in Mexico and built his dictatorship instead on the support of the highland aristocracy, then on the power of a police state, and always on the approval of the Catholic church.

[margin note: Ecuador; G. García Moreno]

García Moreno ruled for a decade and a half under the twin signs of intransigent Catholicism and coercive force, dedicated to "civilizing" the Indian and mestizo populations whom he scorned. French priests directed educational institutions at all levels (gradually replacing Ecuadorian clergy in the country's religious life), while the army acquired modern arms and training. Although strongly conservative in

[margin note: Catholic civilizing projects]

its dedication to the church, the regime's greatest project was a progressive one: the construction of a railroad from Guayaquil to Quito, ending the long economic isolation of the highlands. Though widely hated, García Moreno displayed an honesty in his management of public funds and a modesty in his personal life that even his enemies begrudgingly recognized. In addition, a year of study in Paris had provided the dictator with an understanding of the rudiments of nineteenth-century science that unsophisticated Quito regarded with awe.

García Moreno's authoritarian project gradually faltered after the dictator's assassination in 1875. Inspired by the protests of journalist Juan Montalvo, the liberal opposition had never disappeared, but it could not quickly replace the conservatives in power. The regime constructed by García Moreno continued to dominate Ecuador for twenty years after his death. In the long term, however, the political alignments of the country remained unaltered. The commercial and plantation elite of the coast still constituted the prime movers of progressive change, not accompanied in Quito except by a noisy but marginal opposition to the predominantly conservative highland oligarchy. García Moreno's subordination of the military to civil authority had canceled the army's former role as mediator between the coast and the highlands and had left the conservatives of Quito to reassume their former predominance at the national level. They exercised power less despotically than had the dictator, but they had none of his renovating impulses. The continuation of García Moreno's reformism would be left to the liberals.

In other Latin American countries, the emergence of the neocolonial order occurred without the imposition of a military dictatorship. Frequently, liberal progressivism became the new creed of oligarchies that broadened themselves socially even as they consolidated their political power. Such was the case in Colombia, where authoritarian tendencies developed only late in the century, and in Chile, where the oligarchy rapidly overthrew an incipient dictatorship. In Peru, the emergence of neocolonialism provided the opportunity for the old aristocracy of Lima to recapture a preeminent position by directing urban discontent against the military. Brazilian oligarchies, finally, shared political power with the army without in any way accepting military dominance.

Colombian reformers, enthused by Europe's liberal revolutions of 1848, set to work the following year when the conservative president Tomás Cipriano de Mosquera was succeeded by a liberal, José Hilario López. With the full support of the influential Mosquera, whose political alignment now began to shift, the liberal government abolished slavery, imposed free-trade policies, expelled the Jesuits, declared religious liberty, and introduced federalism. Before long, however, the liberals divided into radicals (called Gólgotas) and moderates (Draconianos) and fought among themselves. The Gólgotas held sway on the country's Caribbean coast, while the Draconianos, inveighing against the current free-trade policies, gained popularity among the populace of Bogotá. After a brief Draconiano dictatorship, the Gólgotas gained the upper hand. In 1861, they installed the former-conservative Mosquera as president and instituted a very lax form of federalism. As Colombia entered its phase of export growth based on tobacco and then coffee cultivation, the country's internal order became increasingly insecure. Provincial governments struggled against one another and were shaken by violent conflicts at the local level.

Liberal president Rafael Núñez, a Gólgota ideologue elected in 1880, curbed these centrifugal forces with a project he called "the Regeneration." In order to achieve economic progress, he called for liberal and federalist Colombia to renounce its liberalism and its federalism. Believing that the earlier reforms had proved a very costly and disorderly experiment, Núñez restored the Catholic church to a dominant position in public education and increased the powers of the central presidency. Rather than a return to conservatism, however, Núñez presented the Regeneration as a step beyond the traditional conservative and liberal ideologies: a progressivism built on practical interests, not abstract ideals. His former liberal allies were furious at the apostasy of their leader, but the defection of Núñez and his followers decisively shifted the balance of power away from liberalism. Institutionalized by a concordat with the Vatican in 1883 and by the Constitution of 1886, the Regeneration endured because the mercantile and landowning classes of Colombia strongly approved of it. Under its aegis, they consolidated their influence at the national level, where Núñez remained directly or indirectly in control until his death in 1894.

Peru, Bolivia, and Chile underwent processes of development that were profoundly divergent yet intimately intertwined. The Peruvian government organized by Gen. Ramón Castilla in 1845 initiated a period of economic transformation based on guano. This natural fertilizer, found principally on the desert islands near the coast of Peru, was exported to Europe by British commercial houses that paid duties to the Peruvian treasury. By 1847, government income had attained large proportions, permitting the consolidation of the country's internal obligations and the cancellation of its external debt. Lima saw its first railroad in 1850 and its first public gas lighting soon thereafter. The new Civil Code of 1852 favored the abolition of the Indian communities' common lands, their protection against the rapacity of large landowners and merchants. These years also witnessed the immigration into Peru of Chinese laborers to work in the sugar and cotton fields of the Peruvian coast. In the midst of these rapid changes, Castilla was able to impose as his successor another general, José Rufino Echenique, to preside over the continued prosperity. Castilla soon repented of his choice, however. Accusing Echenique of having permitted widespread corruption, the ex-president led a successful uprising against him. During the fighting, Castilla abolished black slavery and Indian tribute. Both measures aimed to facilitate the recruitment of soldiers for Castilla's army, but they also reflected great transformations afoot in mid-nineteenth-century Peru. The plantation economy of the coast no longer depended on slave labor, and the government treasury could finally dispense with the Indian head tax.

The corruption of Echenique's government had been only one manifestation of a more general process: the diffusion of guano wealth from public into private hands. This diffusion of wealth continued through a second mechanism as rich and influential residents of Lima acquired old government bonds at a fraction of their face value and profited enormously when the newly prosperous government redeemed them in full. The process entered a third stage when, by 1860, Peruvian consignees in Lima began to export guano directly to Europe, where a variety of foreign merchant houses handled the distribution. This arrangement, highly profitable for the Peruvian consignees, recalled the position of those Lima moneylenders in the colonial silver-mining complex who had kept the mine owners permanently on the edge of insolvency. The consignees of the guano trade operated in a similar manner with the public debt, keeping the government financially besieged, then coming to the rescue with further short-term loans at exorbitant rates. Thus did some of the old aristocratic families of Lima recover their former grandeur, and new fortunes arose as well, but those who did not participate in the giddy conquest of Peru's guano windfall—the bankrupt losers and the urban poor—looked on with growing ill humor.

In 1862, Castilla again left the presidency to a chosen successor, but civil war soon broke out, this time complicated by a conflict with Spain. Using as its pretext a minor incident involving Spanish sailors in Callao, a Spanish flotilla demanded reparations and began to menace belligerently the Peruvian coast. The disconcerting Spanish actions produced an ephemeral national unity within Peru and an equally ephemeral international alliance with Chile, Bolivia, and Ecuador, who joined with Peru to resist what they feared might be a Spanish attempt at reconquest. After a devastating bombardment of Valparaíso and a less destructive attack on Callao, the Spanish vessels withdrew without waiting for the reparations they had demanded. The absence of an outside threat and the outbreak of Indian rebellions then returned Peru to a state of civil war.

In 1868, the victors of a "conservative revolution" began a new stage of Peru's neocolonial development. The young finance minister, Nicolás de Piérola, eliminated the multiple concessions formerly accorded for the exportation of guano and instead granted a monopoly to the French commercial house of Dreyfus. A major loan negotiated in Europe by Dreyfus immediately delivered the Peruvian government from the state of financial crisis in which the former consignees had so long held it. Aside from opening the flow of foreign capital, Piérola's initiative inaugurated a period of railroad construction in which the leading figure was Henry Meiggs, a North American entrepreneur who had already made and lost one fortune before arriving in Peru. This new wave of easy money also led to another increase in political corruption, amid the outspoken moral outrage of the former consignees. The critics of the government closed ranks around Manuel Pardo, scion of an aristocratic Lima family, whose Civilista party first dominated the political scene of the capital and then made him president in 1872.

The Civilista government launched a moralizing drive (virtually indistinguishable from political revenge) against the perpetrators and the beneficiaries of the preceding government's policies. It also tried to deal seriously with the impact of the financial crisis of 1873 on the Peruvian economy, which had become quite dependent on outside credit and trade. The country's straitened circumstances did not favor the consolidation of civilismo, however, and in the next election, Pardo was obliged to accept the candidacy of Gen. Mariano Ignacio Prado, whose limited affection for his Civilista sponsors became increasingly clear after his inauguration as president. Manuel Pardo's assassination in 1878 further diminished his party's strength.

As the guano prosperity faded, glimmers of a new hope of mineral wealth appeared, only to be obscured by a mushrooming financial crisis. In Peru's far south, the desert lands around the town of Iquique contained exportable nitrates much in demand in Europe, but their exploitation had been leased to private companies, and the Peruvian government threatened in desperation to cancel the leases in order to renegotiate them to greater advantage. Peru's impoverished treasury

had by then begun to issue paper currency and was eventually obliged
to authorize private currency issues by Henry Meiggs. Moreover, the
government had become embroiled in lawsuits with its chief European agent, the house of Dreyfus, as each accused the other of default-
ing on its contractual obligations. Meanwhile, Lima had become a
modern city (outgrowing its colonial walls, which were leveled in
this period by initiatives of Meiggs), and its urban economy depended
on the conspicuous consumption of the rich and on the salaries of
middle-class public employees—all undermined by the crisis. Eventually, an improvement in the international economy might have
alleviated this crisis, made particularly acute by the characteristics of
Peruvian modernization in the 1870s. Instead, Peru's woes were deepened and prolonged by the outbreak of the War of the Pacific in 1879.

For years, Chile had coveted the nitrate lands of Bolivia and even
the adjoining mining areas of southern Peru. Chilean entrepreneurs
frequently operated on the Bolivian side of the border, and Chilean
workers supplied much of the labor for the nitrate fields of both
countries. The Peruvian government feared that the Chileans might
take Bolivia's nitrate fields and offer Peru's nitrate fields to the Bolivians as a compensation. Such an agreement would prove attractive to
Bolivia, they believed, because the Peruvian lands in question included the Pacific ports currently used by Bolivian overseas trade.
These considerations led Peru to make common cause with Bolivia
against Chile during the ensuing war.

The Peruvian defeat caused a collapse of immense proportions in
the country's economic development, which, it should be remembered, now went well beyond guano and nitrate exportation. Although
ephemeral and corrupt, the thirty-year boom had brought the recovery
of irrigated commercial agriculture in coastal Peru. In 1878, sugar and
nitrate had been of equal value among Peruvian exports to Great
Britain, at over a million pounds sterling each. Another development
of the period, the expansion of the railroad network (particularly the
beginnings of a line to link Lima and Cerro de Pasco), had laid the
groundwork for a future recovery of mining.

Bolivia lost its Pacific coast altogether as a result of the war, and yet
the immediate impact of defeat was relatively less there because the
brief nitrate boom had not made fundamental changes in the country's
sluggish economy. Only much later did the lack of an outlet to the sea
come to be seen as a chief determinant of the landlocked nation's continuing economic backwardness and isolation. During the period in
question, Bolivia's central problem was not the difficulty of communications with the international market but the continuing scarcity of

surplus production to sell there. Silver mining, the historic strength of the Bolivian economy, had not emerged from its long depression, and quinine exportation had proved to be a poor replacement.

The Bolivian political scene had remained stormy since mid-century. In 1855, the populist Gen. Manuel Isidoro Belzú was succeeded by two civilian presidents initially more to the liking of the upper classes. The second of these, José María Linares, greatly improved the possibilities of Bolivia's international trade by reestablishing the value of its debased currency. In addition, Linares reduced the size of the army's swollen officer corps and successfully combated rampant administrative corruption. Both achievements vastly improved the situation of the national treasury, but they also brought the disapproval of upper-class Bolivians accustomed to business as usual and already irritated by the president's authoritarian style. Linares was followed by a string of military presidents.

The second of these, Mariano Melgarejo, took power in 1864 with the support of members of the urban oligarchy eager for a larger share of political power, a more valuable commodity now that the exportation of nitrates had begun on the coast. British and Chilean firms sought nitrate concessions that promised to be quite lucrative for both the concessionaires and the Bolivian officials involved. Under Melgarejo, the Bolivian government deeded away considerable fragments of the national territory to Chile and Brazil and began the privatization and sale of land formerly belonging to Indian communities, all of which offered further possibilities for profitable corruption.

In 1870, Melgarejo was overthrown and for a moment it appeared that the urban oligarchy might recover the initiative from the army. Instead, after a quick succession of short-term presidents there arose another plebeian dictator, Hilarión Daza, the illegitimate son of an Italian acrobat. Daza, whose humble origins and turbulent youth made him a figure of fun for the disgruntled aristocracy, was the general destined to lead Bolivia into the War of the Pacific. Taking power in 1876, he tried to alleviate the constant penury of the Bolivian treasury by limiting and, in some cases, canceling the concessions of companies exploiting the country's nitrate fields. Some of the companies involved had been formed in Bolivia, but their capital was, for the most part, British. In an attempt to resist Daza's abridgment of their privileges, the companies now declared themselves Chilean enterprises and invoked the protection of an 1866 treaty between La Paz and Santiago providing for the joint exploitation of the nitrate fields. Chilean willingness to press these companies' claims triggered the war, and foreign investors openly supported Chile in the conflict, but

Santiago acted in its own interest as well. As we will see, the conquest of the mineral wealth of these coastal deserts brought great advantages to the victors.

In sum, Peru's urban oligarchy (centered in Lima) recaptured social dominance from the mestizo army officers of the highlands during the third quarter of the nineteenth century, while Bolivia's urban oligarchy was unable to do the same. In Peru, the temporary prosperity brought by guano and then nitrates had filled state coffers and enabled impoverished aristocrats to recover some of their lost status. Lima's blue bloods regained significant influence over the national government through their moral hegemony, applied selectively against policies unfavorable to their interests, and through their social ascendancy over the country's urban middle and popular sectors. By contrast, Bolivia's urban elites had experienced no such recovery. The still-stagnant Bolivian economy left them relatively weak in the face of a rude mestizo officer corps whom the white aristocrats regarded with undisguised disdain. They could criticize the unbridled corruption of the military governments, but without a more dynamic economy, the administrative and fiscal reforms promoted by the urban oligarchies produced few results and many enemies. For the time being, Bolivia's urban elites had to content themselves (as decorative legislators and diplomats) with the trappings of civil authority and with the benefits brought by their acquiescence and cooperation (during the privatization of Indian community lands, for example).

The evolution of Chile had quite different contours, beginning with the role played by the army. Victory in the earlier war against the Peruvian-Bolivian Confederation (1836–41) had given the Chilean armed forces an early prestige without equal among the other Latin American republics, but Chile's conservative governments of the period had managed to limit the internal political role of the armed forces. Individual generals served as president during the first twenty years of conservative hegemony without contributing to the dominance of military institutions. The officer corps was quick to appreciate the advantages of the army's being primarily an expression of nationalism and only secondarily (and very discreetly) the guarantor of internal order, and benevolent observers took this as another symptom of Chilean exceptionality, a sign that its experience was more European than Latin American.

The central contradiction of this experience was its simultaneous social traditionalism and openness to the world market. Already before mid-century, the expansion of mining had introduced new elements into a society long dominated by the landowners of Chile's

central valley. After 1848, international economic conditions accelerated the process of change, causing further stress to the traditional
supports of the conservative order through the rapid modernization of
Santiago and through an ideological challenge to the church. Such was
the stability of the institutional order that it attempted to absorb,
rather than resist, these challenges. The result was a kind of conservative progressivism that retained a traditional, authoritarian style but
promoted economic and cultural modernization. Chile's conservative
progressivism found its leading figure in Manuel Montt, a government
minister of modest social background who began to dominate the
national scene in the 1840s.

    Although Montt satisfied neither the extreme conservatives nor
the true liberals, his middle position found enough support to elect
him president in 1851. Projects carried out by his administration
included the creation of a national bank and the expansion of the
railway network linking the central valley to the port of Valparaíso.
Montt also oversaw legal reforms such as the abolition of entailment
and obligatory tithes, provoking further opposition from extreme conservatives. This antagonism from the right, exacerbated by a conflict
between the Montt administration and the church, did not preclude
increasing hostility from liberals, who continued to suffer the consequences of the president's authoritarianism. Montt was automatically
reelected at the end of his first five-year term, as his predecessors had
been, but the question of succession after his second term became
conflictive enough to produce a brief civil war in which liberals and
conservatives joined against the government. Finally, the government
accepted a candidate chosen from among its own ranks but particularly pleasing to the liberals. Thus began the transition from conservative to liberal hegemony, a transition that culminated in 1871 with the
inauguration of Federico Errázuriz Zañartu, the first declared liberal to
become president of Chile.

    In the 1870s, the principles so long maintained by the liberal
opposition were finally implemented. Chilean public education advanced with the creation of a system of secondary institutions and the
expansion of the university, and, though cautious in its assault on the
social position of the church, the liberal government proclaimed freedom of worship. Possibly the most significant liberal initiatives led to
the attenuation or dispersion of state authority. A less active approach
to governing replaced the energetic conservative rule that had imposed
order in the second quarter of the century. After 1871, presidents could
no longer be reelected and were forced to seek the support of various political groups in a panorama made more complex by the overt

divisions between liberals and conservatives. Liberalization did not
necessarily mean democratization, however. If the country's export-
oriented economic growth had created greater diversity of interests
and attitudes among the upper class, it had also strengthened that
class vis-à-vis others. The dissemination of political power engineered
by the liberals was strictly limited to the social and economic elite.
Furthermore, liberalization was made possible only by an unusual
harmony among older and newer elements within the Chilean upper
class, who had shared both the benefits of the country's opening to the
international market and the exhilarating experience of the War of the
Pacific. In the eyes of its neighbors, Chile became a Latin American
Prussia, respected and feared, a model of successful oligarchical politics without comparison in the region, replacing the old favorite of
outside observers, Brazil.

The Brazilian empire had lost some of its luster as the nineteenth
century progressed. Its vaunted political equilibrium (somewhat exaggerated by those who earlier had held it up as an example to Spanish
America) threatened to deteriorate rapidly in the late 1860s as the
country became locked in the unexpectedly difficult Paraguayan War.
During the war, the conservative commander of Brazilian forces in the
field, the duke of Caxias, quarreled with the liberal cabinet, bringing a
political crisis when the emperor dissolved the cabinet and put the
government in conservative hands. The disaffected liberals then renewed earlier demands for reform. Along with their traditional em-
phases on federalism, parliamentarianism, and limitation of the emperor's powers, some liberals initiated attacks on the institution of
monarchy itself.

A large number of army officers joined the critics of the imperial
system after the Paraguayan War and the retirement of Caxias. The
younger generation of officers who emerged from the war had fewer
attachments to the monarchy. In Paraguay, they had forged a new
confidence and esprit de corps, and they displayed, on the one hand, a
growing impatience with the monarch's inattentiveness to their demands and, on the other, an increasing mistrust of the country's traditional ruling groups. Many younger officers had discovered in the
positivism of Auguste Comte a perfect ideological justification for
their attitudes. Comte vindicated their rejection of a narrow political
elite close to the throne (army officers tended to come from the poorer
outlying regions of the empire) and buttressed their criticism of that
elite's rhetorical and legalistic political culture (the officers preferred
applied sciences and engineering). Positivism also provided a blueprint
for the progressive authoritarianism that suited their temperament, an

authoritarianism tempered more than in Spanish America by human-
itarian goals, especially the abolition of slavery. Military support for
the creation of a republic spread throughout Brazil as the movement
became identified with the interests of the officer corps. In 1885, the
officers closed ranks behind one of their number who was threatened
with punishment for publishing an article critical of the minister of
war, leading to open confrontation with the monarchy.

By the last quarter of the nineteenth century, Brazil's monarchical
institutions had also lost the firm support of the church. The split
occurred after several priests appeared publicly in Masonic ceremo-
nies in 1871 and a number of bishops came forward to declare Catholicism totally incompatible with Free Masonry, despite the fact that
some members of the imperial government were Masons. The government announced that the bishops had exceeded their powers, demanding that they retract their pronouncements and imprisoning the bishops who refused to do so. As much as a defense of Masonry, the clash
represented a continuation of the old contest between Portuguese
regalism and Catholic ultramontanism. At this time, however, the
Crown encountered an indocile clergy, quick to declare itself per-
secuted by secular authority and eager for confrontation. In 1875, the
monarchy desisted from its efforts to bend the church hierarchy to the
royal will and lifted its sanctions without wringing any concessions
from its clerical adversaries. The government's defeat was especially
significant because its policy had the explicit support of Pedro II.

The Crown was losing support from the church, the army, and the
liberals just as Brazil entered a period of rapid social and economic
change. Between 1870 and 1885 the country's export structure displayed a decisive shift. At the top of the list of export products in 1870
were sugar, of perennial importance, and cotton, which had expanded
during the U.S. Civil War to occupy the market share left vacant by
blockaded southern plantations. Fifteen years later, both products had
been surpassed by coffee, representing nearly two-thirds of Brazilian
exports, while sugar accounted for scarcely more than a tenth and
cotton no longer constituted a major product at all. As a result, Brazil's
economic center of gravity shifted away from the northeastern region,
where sugar and cotton had been primarily cultivated, and moved into
the center-south around Rio de Janeiro. Despite the difficult readjustments, the growth of coffee barely compensated for the decline of
sugar and cotton, and the total value of exportations remained substantially unchanged. In addition, the international financial crisis of
1873 had grave consequences in Brazil. The Brazilian financial structure was technically more advanced than that of the Spanish Ameri-

1873 financial crisis bankrupts Brazil (handwritten margin note)

can countries, but its foundations were shaky, and during the Paraguayan War Brazil's external debt had increased significantly. As a result, the crisis in European capital markets spread rapidly to Brazil, causing the collapse of the bank of the baron of Mauá, who dominated Brazilian financial life during the third quarter of the nineteenth century, and revealing a total lack of autonomy in the country's financial life.

In this ominous climate, the weakened imperial regime had to deal financially with the most burdensome legacy of all, the institution of slavery. The importance of servile labor had been declining steadily since mid-century when the slave trade from Africa had finally ended, because Brazilian slave owners had always depended on continuing importations to replenish their work force. In 1871, the law of free birth, whereby the children of slaves were no longer born into slavery themselves, accelerated the decay of the institution. From 2.5 million slaves in 1850, the number declined to one million in 1874. From the point of view of Brazilian planters, the erosion of slavery appeared as one aspect of a general deterioration of the country's export agriculture, and they held the imperial government responsible. The emperor himself favored emancipation, but fearing the possible consequences, he long hesitated to install a government that shared his views. Therefore, despite widespread support for abolition in Brazil, conservative cabinets refused to countenance the idea of general emancipation. An important sticking point was the slave owners' demand for the payment of indemnities in the event of abolition. The imperial treasury was in no position to make such outlays, and the planters who had already made the difficult transition to a free labor force ardently opposed such a subsidy for their laggard competitors. When emancipation finally occurred without indemnities in 1888, the planters who still depended on an enslaved work force considered themselves betrayed by the monarchy.

1888 - emancipation that provokes the end of the monarchy (handwritten margin note)

The moment for the creation of the first Brazilian republic had arrived. Support for the monarchy was at a low ebb within Brazil's traditional parties, and the new Republican party had sunk roots in São Paulo, the province at the forefront of the latest wave of coffee cultivation. Ever more popular within the military, republicanism gained an exceptionally important convert in Manuel Deodoro da Fonseca, a top member of the army hierarchy. In November 1889, Fonseca led a military coup that toppled the Brazilian empire almost without resistance.

Like several Spanish American regimes of the period, the Brazilian republic combined military influence with that of the landowning oligarchy. Their spirit was manifest in the positivist motto—"Order and Progress"—that they inscribed on the new Brazilian flag. The economic foundations of the republic proved more vigorous than might have been expected, given the languid economic evolution of the imperial regime's last two decades. The elites of the coffee region, among the chief beneficiaries of the institutional change, successfully replaced slave labor with European immigrants. In the long term, the quickening growth of the Brazilian population (which leapt from ten to fourteen million between 1872 and 1888) assured them of an abundant, inexpensive labor supply. Unburdened at last of its peculiar institution, Brazil entered the period of feverish growth and devastating crises that typified neocolonial Latin American economies.

In the Antilles, the emergence of the neocolonial order occurred most rapidly in Cuba, where the steady expansion of the sugar economy brought sweeping and complex transformations. Before discussing the Cuban case, however, we should turn to the significantly different experience of Puerto Rico and the Dominican Republic.

Neither of these two former Caribbean colonies of Spain kept pace with Cuba during the third quarter of the nineteenth century. In Puerto Rico, sugar production expanded at a much slower rate and with social consequences more limited than those observed in Cuba. Coffee cultivation in the island's central highlands was more important than the sugar production of the coastal plain. As for the Dominican Republic, its economy had changed little in the course of the nineteenth century. Occupied by Haitian forces until 1844, the Dominican Republic had become independent in an uprising led by the Creole elite of Santo Domingo. In order to retain their social dominance in the country, the elite engineered a return to Spanish rule in 1861–65, then lost power. The mulatto presidents who ruled the Dominican Republic after this temporary recolonization accepted the broad outlines of the status quo, though army officers of humble origin joined the ranks of the privileged class and thereby partially transformed it, as had occurred in other parts of Spanish America.

Cuba, on the other hand, underwent explosive economic growth. From fifty thousand tons of sugar exported in 1820, Cuban production quadrupled by 1850 and then more than tripled again by 1870, at all times representing at least three-quarters of the island's export earnings. The sheer growth in the volume of production allowed the Cuban sugar industry to overcome both its relatively rudimentary technology and the slow decline in the price of sugar on the international market. The chief bottleneck in the island's sugar economy was labor. The importation of an enslaved work force became more difficult (and therefore more expensive) as the British government tried to cut off the slave trade from Africa, but the Spanish authorities discreetly fostered a continuation of the illegal traffic. They also entertained alternative solutions such as the importation of Mayans captured during the Caste Wars of Yucatán or the promotion of Chinese immigration as in Peru. In addition, the Cuban sugar industry faced tariff barriers erected around the U.S. market in defense of Louisiana sugar producers, and access to the U.S. market became increasingly important as beet sugar gradually displaced cane sugar in Europe. During the 1850s, many on the island viewed annexation to the United States as a way to solve the problems of labor and market, but this idea lost its appeal with the end of slavery in the southern United States.

Meanwhile, Cuba moved toward its long-delayed independence from Spain. After 1850, Spanish support for the illegal slave trade began to waver, to the discomfiture of the island's sugar-producing elite. Cuban tobacco growers, for their part, resented the large profits taken by Spanish middlemen. As the imperial authorities depended increasingly for support on Spaniards resident in Cuba, the friction between Creoles and peninsulars mounted to levels surpassing the situation in other parts of Spanish America half a century earlier. Provoked by the high-handed behavior of a militarized colonial regime, Cuban Creoles launched a ten-year war for independence in 1868. The insurgent coalition was weakened by internal contradictions evident, for example, in its attitude toward the institution of slavery. Unlike early nineteenth-century revolutionaries in South America, the Cuban leaders did not dare to emancipate even the slaves who bore arms in the insurgent ranks.

In 1875, Spain was able to appease some of the rebels by granting the island political autonomy under Spanish sovereignty and allowing the Cubans some legislative representation in the imperial government. Radical elements led by the black general Antonio Maceo carried on the fight for three more years, demanding independence and the abolition of slavery. At Maceo's defeat in 1878, many of the island's Creole and peninsular fortunes had been destroyed, and the field lay open to large-scale North American investment in both sugar production and commercialization.

The entrance of foreign capital was facilitated by a drop in sugar prices that obliged the Cuban industry to modernize its technology in order to survive. As a result, the first large and highly capitalized sugar mills called *centrales* were built in these years. The centrales refined the sugar grown on their own large landholdings and also that of the surrounding small and middle-sized cane growers. Because they depended on the refining capacity of the centrales, even fairly large cane growers with considerable land and large numbers of workers became tied to the large mills by contractual commitments and debts.

Cuba thus experienced a new type of foreign participation in the economy. Unlike British capital, which generally limited itself to the commercialization and transportation of export products, U.S. capital flowed directly into productive enterprises: the sugar mills and plantations themselves. In this fashion, the colony that had yet to escape direct political domination from Spain was already coming under a different kind of domination from the United States. In the new Cuban economy taking shape after the Ten Years' War, more than one Spanish American country could glimpse the outlines of its own future.

CHAPTER V

MATURITY OF

THE NEOCOLONIAL

ORDER (1880–1930)

THE ADVANCE OF A primary export economy in most of Latin America signaled the consolidation of the neocolonial order in the final quarter of the nineteenth century. After about 1880, Latin American economies grew more rapidly than ever before, but they also experienced crises of increasing intensity, revealing the limits and presaging the eventual collapse of the new colonial compact so recently established. In the first quarter of the twentieth century, the primary export economies of the region underwent explosive growth that, in some cases, left behind little more than a trail of social devastation comparable to the aftermath of a natural catastrophe. In part, this economic turbulence resulted from the jarring transformations under way in the industrializing economies to which Latin America had bound itself in the new colonial compact.

From the moment of its consolidation, the neocolonial compact began to evolve in favor of the new colonizing power, or metropolis. The original distribution of labor assigned primary production to the local ruling classes and commercialization to the metropolis, but foreign interests soon became involved in primary activities, like mining, that required especially high levels of capital input. Even in cases where the distribution of labor remained unchanged, transformations in technology, in financial structures, or in the functioning of the international market generally drew the foreign partners deeper into Latin American economies. Railroads, sugar mills, grain storage silos, and refrigerated meat-packing plants often became foreign enclaves, and, in extreme cases, penetration of dependent Latin American economies brought outside ownership of the land itself. In Guatemala, German merchants gradually took control of the best coffee plantations. North American capital pursued this sort of expansion throughout the Caribbean basin, most notably in Cuba (where it moved from sugar commercialization and processing to sugar cultivation) but also

in Haiti, the Dominican Republic, and Central America. While coffee
cultivation expanded in the Central American highlands, the lowlands saw the establishment of a "banana empire" ruled directly from
Boston. In such cases, local elites had lost their share in the partnership, and the neocolonial compact had become simple economic
hegemony. These extreme examples signal a general weakening of
Latin American landowners in their dealings with the agents of the
metropolitan economies.

coffee & bananas

In countries with more vigorous national economies, landowners
usually retained more control in the face of mounting external pressures, but national prosperity presented them with formidable internal rivals: burgeoning urban middle classes and (less frequently) organized labor in the more modern sectors of the economy. These groups
demanded their share of political influence. If Mexico underwent a
revolution for that reason, the oligarchies of Argentina, Uruguay,
and Chile preferred to extend suffrage rights without breaking institutional continuity. The resulting processes of democratization
weathered the abrupt economic fluctuations of this period of feverish
growth, but both democratizing systems and unreconstructed oligarchical systems tended to break down in the crisis of the 1930s, which
marked the end of the neocolonial period as a whole.

The end was foreshadowed during the first part of the twentieth
century by an internal weakening of the new colonial compact and
also by competition between metropolitan powers. Beginning with
Cuba, one Latin American country after another slipped out of the
exclusive orbit of Great Britain and gravitated economically toward
rising international powers like the United States. As a variety of
creditors struggled for primacy in the region, Latin America added to
its old pattern of commercial dependency an increasingly restrictive
financial dependency. The United States emerged dominant despite
repeated challenges from its European adversaries, and by the first
years of the twentieth century, it began to act as the new metropolis of
the Caribbean basin, accompanying its financial penetration with
direct political and military intervention. For extended periods, the
U.S. forces exercised functions that ranged from the collection of
customs duties and internal policing to the outright exercise of governance in countries that still retained nominal independence.

shift to influence of U.S.

The transition from European to North American tutelage in the
Caribbean area was consummated in the Venezuelan conflict of 1902.
The incident arose after powerful British, German, and Italian creditors angrily demanded repayment of loans made to the Venezuelan
government and various of its citizens. In order to attenuate the ten-

sions between them, the creditors presented a common front against their insolvent South American debtors—much as Great Britain and France had done half a century earlier in the Río de la Plata—and together they blockaded Venezuelan ports. U.S. president Theodore Roosevelt believed that those responsible for the financial affairs of Latin America needed such a lesson, and he gave prior approval to the plan, but Latin American public opinion reacted violently to this revival of an earlier style of gunboat diplomacy. The North American public, for its part, expressed concern at the reappearance of European power in a part of the world it had quickly begun to consider reserved for U.S. influence. The results of the confrontation were, on the one hand, Argentina's announcement of the Drago Doctrine, condemning the use of military force to collect international debts, and, on the other, the announcement of the Roosevelt Corollary to the Monroe Doctrine in U.S. foreign policy. The Roosevelt Corollary reserved unilaterally to the United States the right to use force to insure the collection of debts involving Latin American countries and foreign creditors. In this manner, the United States assumed the role of policing the international financial relations of the mature neocolonial order in Latin America, and the events of the next thirty years demonstrated the seriousness of its intent.

The Roosevelt Corollary was not, however, the only innovation in U.S. relations with Latin America. Occasionally, U.S. interventions of the period aimed to reform Latin American governments with a political puritanism applied erratically in some cases, forgotten in others, and usually met in Latin America with a mixture of skepticism and indignation. (Actions such as Woodrow Wilson's moralizing intervention against Mexican president Victoriano Huerta in 1914, furthermore, often harmed more than helped the cause they meant to support.) Moral justifications of military intervention appeared pure hypocrisy to most Latin Americans, who failed to recognize the sincerity with which such justifications were accepted by the North American public. Progressive North Americans saw the self-indulgent style of Latin American elites in politics and finance as an example of the same wickedness that they combated, without total success, at home. Inattentive to this subtle counterpoint between two cultural traditions, Latin Americans well understood that high-flown principles were sustained steadfastly by U.S. policymakers when in accord with clear material advantages for U.S. interests, and they also observed that, in some cases, U.S. interests were pursued through methods repugnant even by less puritanical Latin American standards.

Because of this perceived hypocrisy, U.S. hegemony in Latin

America rankled more than had British hegemony. The British had declined to identify their imperialism in Latin America as an act of charity or an obligation toward "lesser breeds," nor had they justified it, as did the French, by any grand ideological campaign. British sway had extracted material advantages from Latin American populations without obliging them to listen respectfully to the kind of exhortations and reprimands that characterized the U.S. approach. The pedagogical vocation of the new metropolis was partly cultural, but it also responded to the fluid international economic system of the time. The United States promoted an image of hemispheric relations that, once accepted by Latin American countries, tended to make a rupture of those relations unthinkable.

This ideological dimension explains the tenacity of U.S. efforts to institutionalize inter-American relations, beginning in the 1880s and culminating after World War II in the Organization of American States. The process of institutionalization, so gradual and initially so vague regarding the commitments undertaken by member states, was able to incorporate even portions of Latin America far from the zone of U.S. military and economic power and undisguisedly hostile to it. During the first half of the twentieth century, the creation of inter-American organizations seemed to offer a multilateral alternative to direct U.S. expansionism and a restraint against that country's frequent military interventions. As a model of hemispheric relations, Pan-Americanism found most support among U.S. policymakers in moments when direct tutelage had been frustrated and momentarily abandoned, but the appearance of shared interests and equality among member countries was a fiction that ultimately strengthened the hegemony of the United States by disguising the real relations of power in the hemisphere.

The desire for economic expansion in Latin America was the chief inspiration for U.S. Pan-American initiatives at their inception. First promoted by Republican secretary of state James G. Blaine in the late 1880s, U.S. proposals for a tariff union and a Pan-American railway can be best understood as replies to other imperialist projects of the day, such as the Berlin-Baghdad or Cairo–Cape Town railways. U.S. influence in Latin America was still concentrated in the Caribbean region, however, and even there European competitors had not been swept completely out of the picture. In addition, the United States encountered a rather more intractable preexisting international order in its imperial bailiwick. Whatever their political and economic insufficiencies, the sovereignty of Latin American countries was well established, complicating any project of imperial expansion in the region.

U.S. Pan-American projects met open and effective resistance organized by Argentina, whose rapid economic growth in this period had
linked it closely to Great Britain. In the Pan-American Congress of
1889–90, Roque Sáenz Peña, a member of the Argentine delegation,
became a spokesperson for others who feared the advance of U.S.
hegemony in Latin America and wished to maintain their relationships with European powers. These delegates rejected the U.S. "America for the Americans" formula, proposing instead, "America for Hu-
manity." At any rate, the objection did not prevent Argentina from
participating in the International Office of American Republics, set up
by the congress to collect and disseminate economic information.

This organization grew and developed during successive meetings
of member states. At the Mexico City meeting of 1901–2, it acquired a
governing body made up of Latin American ambassadors to the United
States and chaired by the U.S. secretary of state. At the Buenos Aires
meeting of 1910, it became the Pan-American Union. Even as the Pan-
American movement underwent this progressive elaboration in the
years before World War I, Latin American countries sought a more
effective restraint to U.S. power in other international organizations
such as the World Court at The Hague, where they hoped that the
participating European powers would provide a more effective balance
to the United States. The collapse of the concert of Europe between
1911 and 1914 undercut this alternative, however, and it also under-
scored the virtues of isolating the Western Hemisphere from the international conflicts of Europe. British naval power, which had performed
that service in the past, might now plausibly be replaced by that of the
United States operating within a stronger Pan-American framework.

Attempts to construct such a framework dominated the next
meeting at Santiago, Chile, in 1923, where Uruguay proposed the
"internationalization of the Monroe Doctrine," a multilateral guarantee of the independence and territorial integrity of all American states.
The United States, subject to rising isolationist sentiments during
these years, refused to support the proposal and thus confirmed Latin
American suspicions regarding the unilateral nature of U.S. policies.
Matters came to a head at the Havana meeting of 1928. Bitter and
widespread Latin American criticism of the self-arrogated U.S. "right
to intervene" and of protectionist U.S. tariff policies convinced policymakers in Washington, D.C., to seek a different approach in the coming years.

During the first quarter of the twentieth century, U.S. policymakers had wished to limit the Pan-American movement to narrow
economic purposes, while Latin American delegates to the successive

meetings had wanted to create a more comprehensive regional organization. This changed in the late 1920s and 1930s. Latin America became more dependent economically on the United States as large U.S. investments in the region were followed by an international economic crisis that destroyed the European-centered system of the past. The United States, for its part, began to value the support of a stronger Pan-American organization when rising international tensions began to augur the coming of another world war. It was only after the end of the neocolonial period that U.S. inter-American initiatives finally recovered the importance that Blaine had intended when he called the first Pan-American Congress in 1889. Overall, Pan-Americanism occupied only a marginal role in inter-American relations during the period under consideration in this chapter. The main thrust of U.S. policy in neocolonial Latin America can best be understood as a unilateral pursuit of strategic and economic interests.

Strategic interests clearly motivated U.S. expansion into the Caribbean and Central America, the location of a vital communications route linking the east and west coasts of the United States since the middle of the nineteenth century. The extension of direct political hegemony in the Caribbean began in 1898 with the Spanish-American War. An amazingly easy victory over the decrepit forces of Spanish colonialism suddenly provided the United States with its own collection of overseas possessions (including Puerto Rico), required the new metropolis to gain experience in colonial administration, and tended to encourage further expansionist adventures. Latin American public opinion displayed a well-founded ambivalence regarding U.S. actions in Cuba, whose second bid for independence had sparked the confrontation between the United States and Spain. Although the former Spanish colony became nominally independent as a result of the war, the United States exerted a level of control that obviously compromised the sovereignty of the new island nation. Latin American public opinion became even more alarmed by the separation of Colombia's Panamanian province to become an "independent" client of the United States.

Panama had been the object of U.S. and European interest since the middle of the nineteenth century. The railroad built across the isthmus as a shortcut route to California during the gold rush years had become less profitable since the completion of transcontinental railroads within the United States, but the possibility of constructing an interoceanic canal maintained the attraction of the isthmus. The French builder of the Suez Canal, Ferdinand de Lesseps, led the attempt to build such a canal between 1878 and 1889 with a concession from the Colombian government, but the project proved much more expensive than expected, and, after ten years of work, de Lesseps's company collapsed spectacularly amid political and financial scandals that rocked all of France. The disappointed creditors of de Lesseps combined the existing excavations, the remaining machinery, and the Colombian concession to form the New Panama Canal Company, which they hoped to sell at a price that would recoup some of their losses. They found no buyer until after the Spanish-American War, when the United States prepared to take the next step in its path of imperial expansion in the Caribbean basin.

In 1903, U.S. and Colombian negotiators agreed to transfer the New Panama Canal Company's concession to the United States along with a lease to a strip of territory ten miles wide from ocean to ocean, but the Colombian congress refused to ratify the treaty. On 3 November, an uprising led by officials of the New Panama Canal Company proclaimed Panamanian independence, and U.S. naval vessels appeared offshore to prevent a deployment of Colombian military forces to put down the rebellion. The U.S. State Department recognized the new government on 6 November and signed a canal treaty with it less than two weeks later in New York City. Representing Panama was Philippe Bunau-Varilla, formerly chief engineer of the New Panama Canal Company, now Panamanian diplomatic representative in Washington, D.C. Bunau-Varilla conceded in perpetuity to the United States the strip of territory across the isthmus in return for an annual subsidy to be paid by the United States along with guarantees of Panamanian independence.

The creation of a U.S. client state in Panama elicited widespread but ineffectual reactions in Latin America and elsewhere. Critics in the United States argued that, however important the immediate advantages gained by the maneuver, more was lost by sacrificing the respected norms of international behavior. U.S. president Theodore Roosevelt, on the other hand, proudly trumpeted the success of his Panamanian policy. Roosevelt believed that the United States should not vacillate in using its "Big Stick" to discipline the unruly republics of Latin America. As the emerging Pan-American organizations contributed to the fiction of a community of equal sovereign states, the United States pursued a parallel policy more in accordance with the imperialist fashion of the times, which called for political "realism."

The realistic limits of U.S. power were geographically narrower than those of its Pan-American policy and tended to coincide with U.S. strategic and economic interests in the Caribbean basin. According to Roosevelt, only in this area was the development of Latin

American countries so laggard as to necessitate direct U.S. tutelage. In contrast, countries like Argentina, Brazil, and Chile had shown themselves capable of exercising their sovereign rights responsibly, and therefore, according to Roosevelt, they had nothing to fear from the United States. The leadership of these southern countries proved responsive to this line of reasoning. Putting aside conflicts that had divided them prior to the twentieth century, Argentina, Brazil, and Chile formed an informal alliance (called by their initials, ABC) with a sphere of diplomatic action that widened gradually until, in 1914, the ABC countries even attempted to mediate between the United States and Mexico. These efforts were not badly received by U.S. president Woodrow Wilson, whose approach to inter-American relations differed noticeably from Roosevelt's. However, the coming of World War I disrupted the international system into which the ABC powers had sought to integrate themselves, and after the war, as Latin American governments became absorbed in their own internal sociopolitical conflicts, the ABC diplomatic initiatives were gradually forgotten.

During the 1920s, North American economic influence advanced rapidly beyond its earlier Caribbean focus. The extension of new commercial ties occurred more rapidly on the Pacific than on the Atlantic coast of South America. In the third decade of the twentieth century, Argentina continued to seek economic advisers in Great Britain, while Peru and Chile had already begun to receive periodic visits from North American economic missions. The end of the railroad age (though some small Latin American countries still had no railways) signaled the loss of one of Great Britain's most important avenues of commercial and financial penetration. The United States was the chief beneficiary of the automotive age that in the 1920s began to open up new markets without the level of capital investment required for the construction of railroads. North American investment flowed into a greater variety of activities than had British investment. Along with mining and other extractive enterprises oriented to the U.S. market, North American capital invigorated production destined for local markets and thus further broadened U.S. economic influence in Latin American life. Although not accompanied by the military and political intervention characteristic of U.S. policy in the Caribbean basin, North American economic expansion provoked resistance in South America as well. The economic hegemony of the United States was penetrating many activities that the local ruling classes had previously reserved for themselves, and U.S. tariff barriers continued to frustrate South American producers in many cases.

The economic powers of Europe beat a cautious retreat in the face

of the North American advance. Great Britain had always refused to
launch grand political designs in Latin America, but it continued to
engage in a skillful rear-guard action in defense of particular interests.
Germany, a rising power in the Caribbean basin until 1914, did not
recover from its wartime defeat during the 1920s. France, a country
that once aspired to dominate vast areas of Latin America, supplied
very limited investment capital after the war and became definitively
a second-rate power in the region.

The clarity of North American ascendancy and the absence of an
effective European counterpoise encouraged Latin American intellectuals to turn to their Spanish heritage as an inspiration for cultural and
political unity. Serenely oblivious to twentieth-century realities, the
Nicaraguan poet Rubén Darío occasionally paused in his renovation of
Spanish-language poetry to represent all Latin America. Darío de-
fiantly invoked the supposed spiritual superiority of traditional Catholicism against a Protestant Anglo-America personified in Theodore
Roosevelt. In *Ariel* (1900), the Uruguayan José Enrique Rodó expressed
analogous ideas in terms less linked to Christian tradition. His alle-
gorical essay opposes the ethereal idealism of Latin America, symbolized by the spritely figure of Shakespeare's Ariel, to the gross materialism of Anglo-America, represented by the figure of Caliban. It is
symptomatic of the epoch that such literary figures should have invited Spanish American elites, confronted by a new imperialism more
aggressive than Great Britain's and by rising tensions within Latin
American societies, to explore their Hispano-Catholic heritage. In the
early twentieth century, the unhappy consequences of some recent
economic innovations contributed to the nostalgic mood of the ruling
classes.

This backward-looking Hispanophilia was one aspect of an increasingly sincere reconciliation with the original metropolis. Potentially a source of opposition to U.S. domination, turn-of-the-century
Hispanophilia never created an effective international alignment. The
Spanish-American War had provided Spain with an object lesson concerning the limits of its international power, and after 1898 Spanish
leaders had no wish to use the affections of their former colonies as a
springboard for further confrontations with the United States. Nevertheless, Hispanic traditionalism presented an obstacle to the cultural hegemony of the new metropolis. In extending its economic and
political control over Spanish America in the twentieth century, the
United States encountered resistance from traditionalists on the right
as well as from revolutionaries on the left. The traditionalist mood did
not prevent neocolonial economic penetration, but it did keep the new

metropolis from achieving a degree of influence over elite thought and culture comparable to that exercised by England and France during the middle years of the nineteenth century. Only the polarizing forces of the cold war would transform that conservative opposition into fervent support for the United States.

The new traditionalism found little echo outside elite circles, with the exception of Mexico (where the masses defended the Catholic faith against revolutionary assaults). The middle and popular classes were growing impatient with the oligarchical political order that characterized the first phase of neocolonialism in Latin America. The 1890s saw the creation of urban labor movements in Buenos Aires, Mexico City, and Santiago de Chile. During the same decade, the Argentine Radical party, the Peruvian Democratic party, and the Uruguayan Colorado party all adopted antioligarchical political lines (though often under the leadership of individuals themselves descended from the oligarchy), but in order to rally support against the oligarchies, some of these parties adopted platforms that could hardly be called progressive. Both Argentine Radicals and Peruvian Democrats were closer to traditional Catholicism than were their frequently anticlerical oligarchical rivals. Such parties menaced the political hegemony of Latin American oligarchies without proposing any important innovations in the social and economic policies of their opponents.

Truly radical opposition movements developed more slowly. During the first decades of the twentieth century, large-scale political mobilization of the working classes occurred only in the Mexican Revolution. For the most part, working-class radicalism was limited to small groups of urban laborers in the modernized sectors of the economy. As a result, the numerical strength of opposition movements among the popular classes often lagged behind the membership of the middle-class opposition, and, because of the small and relatively privileged nature of these early labor organizations, their leadership easily drifted into alliances with the larger middle-class opposition. Both groups directed their vituperation against the privileged classes at the top of the social hierarchy rather than against the neocolonial order as a whole.

The political struggle against oligarchical privilege in the early twentieth century thus brought together groups ranging from conservative Catholics to revolutionary socialists, sometimes even in the same organizations. In spite of the ideological diversity of these antioligarchical political movements, their behavior was fairly consistent on the occasions when they were able to win control of the government. First, they strove to augment the power of their constituent groups in the political system. Second, they attempted to defend the interests of those groups through early forays into the realm of social legislation. They did not, however, introduce any significant changes in the larger economic and societal structures associated with export growth in Latin America. Overall, the ideological aspirations of the antioligarchical movements were ambitious but imprecise, while their actions were moderate and practical.

The distance between ideology and practice can also be observed in one of the antioligarchical movement's most characteristic aspects, the process of university reform that began in Argentina and spread through Latin America soon after World War I. Inspired by the Mexican and the Russian revolutions, Latin American students demanded that university faculties (recruited most frequently from among the oligarchy) share some of their power with the students (often of more modest, but rarely working-class, social origin). This early twentieth-century reform movement led to a permanent politicization of the student body at Latin American universities, providing spokespersons for the popular classes still hesitant to speak for themselves. Many future reformers and revolutionaries, from Víctor Raúl Haya de la Torre to Fidel Castro, began their political careers as student leaders, as did other future leaders across the political spectrum.

The ideological eclecticism of the university reform movement reflects the hopeful but disoriented spirit of Latin America in the 1920s. Between World War I and the devastating depression that began in 1929, the former European centers of the world order, regarded in Latin America as models of civilization, were entering a profound political and economic crisis. As a result, the United States was able to extend over parts of Latin America (now well beyond the Caribbean basin) its hegemonic influence, showing itself more inclined than the British to exercise political and military power. A second result of the European crisis was an end to the monopoly on political legitimacy attached to the ideology of constitutional liberalism since the time of independence. Communism and, within a few years, fascism (or, more precisely, an authoritarian statism loosely based on the Italian model) now vied with constitutional, liberal solutions that seemed ill-adapted to Latin American realities.

The period of ideological ferment found its most articulate and mature expression in the work of Peruvian thinker José Carlos Mariátegui. Drawing on an idiosyncratic Marxism as much informed by Sorel as by Lenin, Mariátegui succeeded better than any of his contemporaries at placing the Latin American issues of his day in a coherent interpretive framework. It is revealing, however, that the political impact of Mariátegui's thought was not felt until decades after his death. The ideological renewal of the 1920s introduced political motifs of lasting importance (anti-imperialism, Marxism, and student militancy), but it failed to animate any mass movement of the time. Revolutionary socialism, the most radically innovative political current, circulated only weakly in Latin America, where the collapse of the old order responded less to the affirmation of new forces than to the exhaustion of old ones.

By the 1920s, the successes and failures of the region's export economies had combined to produce social realities that no longer fit the political forms inherited from prewar days. The oligarchical republics and progressive dictatorships had been erected on narrow social bases, and Latin American states now needed more popular support in order to assure their stability. Argentina and Uruguay created a broader social base through democratization within a liberal-constitutional mold; Peru and Chile, within an authoritarian framework; and Mexico, with a social revolution. However, the political formulas of the 1920s did not take hold as vigorously as those they replaced. Afflicted by the uncertainties so characteristic of the postwar period internationally, Latin American countries also experienced a slowing of social and economic progress. In 1930, when the effects of the global depression had settled over the region, the more economically developed and institutionally stable Latin American countries, those that had considered themselves bright exceptions to general patterns of authoritarianism, began increasingly to resemble their less fortunate neighbors.

The crisis of the 1930s came as a rude anticlimax to half a century of economic expansion composed of discrete local cycles of boom and bust (many of which had reached the end of their prosperity well before 1930). Each of these component cycles of economic expansion and contraction responded to particular stimuli within the international economy. The production of food products—wheat, beef, bananas, and coffee, for example—varied with the buying power of the working classes of Europe and the United States. Expansion in other areas reflected technical or industrial advances: the case of Andean copper and tin and of Yucatán's henequen boom. Still other cycles (such as the ephemeral Amazon rubber boom and, more permanently, oil exploration and drilling) were related to the diffusion of the internal combustion engine and the automobile.

One of the most important of Latin America's agricultural cycles, beginning generally in the last third of the nineteenth century, was the expansion of coffee cultivation in tropical highland areas of middle altitude in Brazil, Colombia, Venezuela, Central America, and Mexico. Established Caribbean coffee growers were ill-able to compete with this new wave of production. By the first years of the twentieth century, Brazilian coffee exports accounted for 70 percent of the world supply. Coffee provided the impetus for the impressive economic development of the southern Brazilian state of São Paulo, whose capital city, formerly dominated by its law school, grew from 65,000 inhabitants in 1890 to 350,000 in 1905, becoming a bustling commercial center. Brazilian coffee growing was characterized by an advancing line of cultivation that exhausted the fertility of new lands within a few years. At the time of the coffee boom in São Paulo, formerly productive lands in the Paraíba Valley of Rio de Janeiro had already been passed over by the hollow coffee frontier. Left behind was an eroded landscape good for little more than pasture—the price exacted by an agricultural economy in which land abounded but labor and capital remained scarce. In their search for a labor force to replace the emancipated slaves, Brazilian coffee planters encouraged European immigration, but the arrival of almost two million (mainly Italian) immigrants by 1914 was not enough to prevent the continuation of patterns of cultivation that devoured the land.

In Spanish America the expansion of coffee cultivation was steadier and less dramatic. Nowhere did potential coffee lands appear as limitless as in Brazil, but few areas of Spanish America experienced the labor shortage that plagued Brazilian coffee planters. An exceptionally high rate of natural increase among the mestizo population provided workers for coffee cultivation in El Salvador and Colombia, while Guatemalan growers drafted Indians formerly isolated from the national market. Spanish American coffee regions differed, however, in the pattern of land tenure that accompanied the expansion of coffee. Middle-sized properties administered directly by the owners produced most of the coffee in Colombia and were common as well in Venezuela and El Salvador, but large plantations dominated production in Guatemala and Mexico. Both patterns contrasted with the standard arrangement in São Paulo, where sprawling coffee estates were farmed by large numbers of *colonos* under a system that combined wage-earning with sharecropping.

The commercialization of coffee became quite a lucrative business, presenting multiple opportunities for speculation. As coffee production developed at differing rates in widely separated areas, large variations in supply compounded normal seasonal fluctuations, making the coffee market extremely dynamic. By the turn of the century, a period of overproduction—with crises in 1896, 1906, and 1913—led to rapidly falling prices for coffee producers. The middlemen of the coffee trade used their financial resources to hold some of this production off the retail market, keeping consumer prices relatively higher. As a result, coffee traders and transporters reaped huge profits, as did their business partners in metropolitan financial institutions.

Perhaps because of their greater political experience, Brazilian coffee planters were more successful than their Spanish American counterparts in defending themselves against the threat of overproduction. They did so not by limiting their harvests but by controlling excess production themselves in an official valorization program adopted in 1906. The program financed the purchase of excess production to be stockpiled and released gradually when the international market was able to absorb it. The operation prevented a sharp drop in prices to the Brazilian producers, but the stabilized price was disappointingly low. Those who benefited most from the valorization program were the bankers who financed it, the majority of them German. Large stocks remained after the crisis of 1906 had passed, including considerable reserves stored in Germany at the outbreak of World War I.

Despite its limitations, the program was deemed a success in Brazil, and it also benefited Spanish American producers by artificially limiting the world supply of coffee, but the feat could not be repeated indefinitely. In 1924, the Brazilian government began a much more ambitious stabilization plan. Whereas the 1906 program had attempted to remedy a temporary glut on the world market, the 1924 plan proposed to deal with long-term and constantly increasing overproduction. The instrument was the Coffee Institute, charged with purchasing Brazil's entire crop and administering its commercialization. The Coffee Institute managed to maintain the profits of producers only by accumulating ever-larger stockpiles of coffee beans, and, encouraged by the favorable price, Brazilian coffee planters continued to harvest an ever-larger excess. Meanwhile, Brazil's Spanish American competitors took advantage of the price supports to increase their own sales and profits at Brazilian expense.

The Brazilian coffee valorization experiment was indicative of future trends in Latin American economic development. A powerful group of landowners had embarked on a program of direct market manipulation, thereby abandoning, without formally renouncing, their supposed faith in economic liberalism. The precociousness of Brazilian coffee growers in taking this step may be explained by their exceptional level of control over the Brazilian republic and by their extreme dependence on a single crop. For the moment, no alternatives to coffee cultivation seemed sufficient to save this powerful class from ruin. Coffee planters were willing to go to extremes in protecting a source of wealth to which they saw no viable alternative.

In the temperate climate regions of southern South America, export production developed more smoothly. After about 1880, exportation of wool, beef, and grain from Argentina outpaced coffee exportation from Brazil. In 1898, the total value of exports from the two countries amounted to twenty-five million pounds sterling each, but Argentina was exporting ten times that much by 1928. Argentine grain cultivation, begun on a large scale in the 1870s, was a chief factor in this growth, particularly after the financial crisis of 1890. Amid falling international prices and wavering foreign investments, Argentina redirected its economy by expanding the amount of land planted in corn and wheat. The provinces of Santa Fe and Córdoba, limited to rudimentary ranching in earlier years, now attracted a large number of European immigrants and became the scene of intense commercial agriculture. Although the flow of immigration paused as a result of the disruptions of 1890, many earlier immigrants had collected in the cities without finding employment and could now be lured into agricultural labor as tenants and, due to the scarcity of cash, as sharecroppers.

Even more clearly than in the case of Brazilian coffee, commercial middlemen with overseas financial connections dominated the exportation of Argentine cereals. The landowners of the cereal regions of Córdoba and Santa Fe were much less powerful than their coffee-planting counterparts in Brazil—less powerful, too, than their livestock-raising counterparts in the province of Buenos Aires. The old landlords of the cereal region had been joined by newer ones, many of immigrant origin, who bought property as a result of successful commercial activities and who lacked close connections to the national centers of political decision making. Agriculture demanded a larger work force, and large commercial firms controlled international grain markets to a greater degree than other commodities' markets. After the turn of the century, Argentine cereal exportation was dominated by a marketing oligopoly that forced landowners of the cereal-producing region to sacrifice a part of their profits and make concessions to renters and sharecroppers in order to maintain the rhythm of production in moments of unfavorable market conditions.

Commercial middlemen never gained the same degree of ascendancy over Argentine livestock production, centered in the province of Buenos Aires. The landowning class of Buenos Aires had jealously maintained its links to national political power despite the federaliza-

tion of its port capital in 1880, when the provincial capital was transferred to the city of La Plata. After 1895, the province of Buenos Aires
took the lead over Santa Fe in the process of export expansion, and by
1914 Buenos Aires had become the largest exporter of cereals as well as
livestock products. The increase in grain cultivation in the province of
Buenos Aires was the work of families who rented land without ever
acquiring title to it, while property ownership remained firmly in the
hands of the landowning class from before the cereal boom. Also
during these years, livestock production was transformed by a drop in
international demand for wool and by the construction of refrigerated
meat-packing plants. By the last decades of the nineteenth century,
trans-Atlantic shipments of frozen beef became possible; in the first
decade of the twentieth century, more perishable chilled beef could be
successfully exported. Instead of raising longhorn cattle for hides and
jerked beef, the ranchers of Buenos Aires turned to selective breeding
of imported pedigreed cattle, which satisfied the more-exacting requirements of the European market.

The transformation of livestock production in Buenos Aires could
not have occurred without substantial capital investment. Landowners paid to erect fences and import fancy European breeds, but most of
the needed capital came from the state and from foreign investors. The
primarily British-owned railroad network became denser—from 2,500
miles of track in 1880 to 33,000 miles in 1914. The ports of Buenos
Aires and La Plata—Ensenada were dredged and renovated in large and
very expensive government projects. Construction of a canal system
helped drain the large swampy area in the central part of the province
of Buenos Aires. Finally, the refrigerated meat-packing plants, except
for some of the earliest and smallest ones, also belonged to foreign
capital, primarily British before 1905 and afterward British and North
American capital in competition. This competition guaranteed favorable prices to ranchers until the time of World War I. The war itself
encouraged the livestock industry on the pampa with even higher
prices, but at its conclusion the ascendancy of North American capital in transportation and commercialization activities began to work
against the ranchers of Buenos Aires, forcing prices down.

Across the Río de la Plata in Uruguay, the neocolonial order
evolved in a manner analogous to the Argentine experience, though
with permutations less extreme and on a smaller scale. Grain cultivation did not expand in Uruguay to the same degree as in Argentina, but
Uruguayan ranchers engaged in selective breeding of their livestock,
made more intensive use of their land, and began to produce frozen and
chilled beef for the European market, just as their counterparts had

done in the province of Buenos Aires. The value of Uruguayan exports—based overwhelmingly on livestock—rose from six million pounds sterling in the first years of the century to twenty-seven million after World War I. As in Argentina, Uruguay's landowning class resisted the process of democratization that characterized urban politics in the period. In their dealings with foreign middlemen and transporters, however, these landowners gradually lost the battle for economic control, just as their Argentine counterparts had.

The cultivation of Argentine cereal and Brazilian coffee created highly unstable rural societies in which the power and prosperity of the landowners could be maintained only at the cost of chronic insecurity for agricultural laborers. The Italian immigrants so important in the production of both cereal and coffee (in Santa Fe, Italian farm workers outnumbered native Argentines four to one in 1914) very frequently gave up and returned to Italy. During the first decade of the twentieth century, some Italian workers migrated seasonally back and forth across the Atlantic to harvest Argentine corn and wheat. Of course, this system would never have arisen unless the migrating workers found some advantage in it. The situation of rural workers was probably best early in the period, deteriorating gradually as land became harder to acquire and local supplies of labor became more abundant. At any rate, the need to attract European laborers necessitated initial concessions that the ruling classes in other parts of Latin America never had to make, and therefore, despite their manifest defects, the agricultural export economies of Uruguay, Argentina, and central Brazil can be counted among the relative successes of neo-colonial development in Latin America.

Economies organized around mining or around the cultivation of sugarcane limited the social benefits of export development more narrowly, creating economic enclaves better linked to the metropolis than to the surrounding national market. In some cases, these links drew entire countries into a pattern of economic dependency far stricter than had formerly been the case.

In sugar-producing areas of Puerto Rico, Cuba, and Peru, large industrial sugar mills rapidly accumulated acreage and, through their control of processing facilities, extended their effective sway well beyond the properties they owned. The system reached its logical conclusion in Puerto Rico and Cuba, where the private rail lines of the sugar mills—most owned by U.S. capital—assured them access to the crops of surrounding areas. Tied to specific mills by the rail lines, local sugar growers lost all control of the marketing of their crops. The sugar economy of Puerto Rico took on particular starkness because of the abrupt manner of its implantation in the years after the U.S. take-over of the island, when U.S. firms operating large mills transformed a landscape not formerly dominated by sugarcane cultivation. The much older Peruvian sugar industry (which had thrived before the commercial reforms of the late eighteenth century and the labor short-ages of the early nineteenth century) also expanded in the neocolonial period, rivaling the value of nitrate exports by the 1880s. An infusion of British and North American capital allowed the industry to expand along the northern coast of Peru in the early twentieth century, but not without a concentration of landholding by large companies parallel to what was occurring in other sugar-producing zones.

Overall, the weak price of sugar on the international sugar market accelerated the process of concentration by giving a competitive ad-vantage to larger producers. The flagging international market had long presented problems for Latin American sugar growers. Edged out of the continental European market by the production of beet sugar, limited in the British market by competition from the West Indies, Latin American sugar found its principal outlet in the United States. However, U.S. protectionist legislation insured that an increasing vol-ume of importation would be accompanied by steady price reductions. Consequently, the expansion of sugar production left an unhappy legacy, affecting Cuba and Puerto Rico in particular.

Other tropical crops also gained new importance in neocolonial *henequen*
Latin America, but none had as extensive an impact as sugar. Exports of henequen fiber underwent an enormous boom in the period, ac-counting for 15 percent of the value of Mexican exports by 1898, but cultivation of henequen was restricted to one primary producing area, the arid northwest of Yucatán. The establishment of banana planta- *bananas*
tions in the late nineteenth century affected a much wider area—humid lowlands around the Caribbean and along the Pacific coast of Ecuador—with even more direct participation by U.S. companies. At the beginning of the twentieth century, a number of these merged to form the United Fruit Company, a banana empire with operations and *UFCo.*
large landholdings in Guatemala, Honduras, Nicaragua, Costa Rica, Panama, Colombia, and Venezuela. The company found some of these tropical lowlands quite sparsely populated and began to induce the migration of prospective workers into their plantation zones. The ethnic makeup of Costa Rica changed as blacks of mostly West Indian origin settled on the coast, juxtaposing a new element to the white population of the country's central valley. Bananas became the chief export of several Central American countries, and the essential mar-ket for all of them was the United States. Of the bananas exported

from Nicaragua in 1918, for example, more than 90 percent went to U.S. ports. The banana trade thrived as consumption of the fruit increased in the United States.

The Amazonian rubber boom began at the same time as the banana boom and likewise affected thinly populated tropical lowlands, but in contrast to bananas, which were to enjoy an enduring economic importance in the area of their cultivation, rubber provides one of the most extreme examples of ephemeral, speculative prosperity. Most of the laborers, called *seringueiros* in Portuguese, were refugees from the drought-ridden Brazilian northeast who migrated into Amazonia in search of work. Their job was to draw the sap periodically from rubber trees growing naturally in the tropical forest. At the time, settlements by people of European or mixed blood existed only along the banks of the major rivers—transportation arteries—of the Amazon basin. The activities of the seringueiros resulted in an extension of Brazilian territorial ambitions in the upper reaches of Amazonia, leading to the purchase of rubber-rich Acre from Bolivia in 1902. Rubber accounted for a fifth of Brazilian export earnings by the end of the nineteenth century, a quarter by 1910. The profits of rubber exportation, derived from lands without owners, could not be absorbed by any landowning class, and the seringueiros themselves kept little of the wealth they produced. Attracted by cash advances from local merchants, the seringueiros were bound to collect rubber in order to pay off their initial debt under conditions of payment that favored a perpetual renewal of their indebtedness. Within Amazonia, only the merchants profited from the rubber boom, but their profits were sufficient to create lasting architectural monuments to rubber in the city of Manaus. This city of 100,000 inhabitants, flanked by the great river on one side and the tropical forest on the other, boasted luxury hotels and a splendid opera house visited by touring companies from Italy.

Amazonian areas of Colombia, Ecuador, Peru, and Venezuela also participated in the rubber boom, and their pattern of exploitation was even more primitive and destructive. Lacking accessible manpower reserves like those in the arid Brazilian northeast, rubber exporters in the Spanish American fringe of Amazonia relied on even more drastic means to recruit and discipline their workers, many of whom were unacculturated Indians suddenly swept into the maelstrom of a twentieth-century tropical export boom. In the drive to secure quick profits, the wave of rubber extraction in this portion of the Amazon basin destroyed both the forest giants that supplied the latex and the forest people who abandoned their neolithic way of life under the double stimulus of alcohol and terror. Rubber exportation in equatorial America thus created horrors analogous to those occurring at the same time in equatorial Africa.

Neither the ostentatious fortunes of the rubber exporters nor the social and ecological ravages of the process of extraction lasted for many years. By the time of World War I, the mad rush for rubber was ending in Latin America because of competition from Malaysia and the Dutch East Indies, where rubber trees were cultivated on plantations, allowing for a more abundant and less expensive product. U.S. interests failed in their attempt to cultivate Amazonian rubber trees in a similar manner, and Amazonian rubber production faded gradually into insignificance, its ghostly boomtowns swallowed up once more by the tropical forest.

after WWI, bust of rubber boom

A revival of mining production also characterized neocolonial Latin American economies, and the first new boom affected one of the most traditional export commodities: silver. From Bolivia to Mexico, the late nineteenth century finally surpassed—and substantially so—the levels of production typical of the best years of the colonial period thanks to advances in mining and transportation technology. New equipment made old mines newly profitable, while improved transport facilities lowered the cost of sending the product to market, but both necessitated major capital investment. In Mexico and Peru, the capital requirements of the new technology led to control of production by British and North American companies. Bolivian production, on the other hand, was financed by the country's own "silver lords" (backed, in any case, by Anglo-Chilean financiers), who also oversaw the regularization of Bolivian political life in the last decades of the nineteenth century. The renaissance of silver was vigorous indeed. At 7.5 million pounds sterling, silver amounted to 60 percent of the value of Mexican exports in 1898, almost double the eighteenth-century record. Bolivia's silver exports reached 1.5 million pounds sterling, and Peru's, 1 million at about the same time. However, the silver revival of the late nineteenth century was not destined to continue into the first decade of the twentieth, when the value of the metal declined because of the progressive demonetization of silver in the world's major currencies. In 1910, Mexican silver production barely maintained the level of a decade earlier, while Bolivian and Peruvian production fell off. By 1920, silver no longer dominated the export structure of any Latin American country. "Baser" metals with increasing industrial uses—like copper for electrical wiring and tin for canning—now took the lead.

silver

Copper mining boomed in the Andean region during the first decades of the twentieth century. The extraction of this metal was far

copper and tin

from new there, and earlier it had undergone a modest expansion in
Chile, but there had been nothing on the scale represented by the
Cerro de Pasco Copper Corporation, a U.S. company that began operations in Peru at this time. Located above twelve thousand feet in the
Andes, the Cerro de Pasco mines necessitated an audacious feat of
engineering: a railway that zigzagged down the steep Pacific slope to
reach the port of Callao. At the top stood an ultramodern industrial
complex surrounded by the primitive huts of the highland Indians
who worked the mines. Chilean copper production advanced even
more rapidly in the early twentieth century, also progressively dominated by U.S. capital.

nitrate

Nitrate extraction, so closely linked to the late nineteenth-century War of the Pacific, continued to overshadow copper among Chilean exports until 1930. The activity of the nitrate fields caused substantial towns like Iquique and Antofagasta to spring up in the coastal
desert, requiring supplies of food and even water to be brought in from
afar. The decline of Chilean nitrate production began as a result of
World War I, which separated Chile from its best markets in central
Europe. Cut off from their supplies of Chilean nitrates, the blockaded
German consumers invented a synthetic fertilizer that afterward competed strongly with the natural article. As a result, the Chilean nitrate
industry stagnated in the 1920s and collapsed completely in the following decade.

oil

Oil drilling became important in Latin America a bit later. Scattered exploratory wells were sunk all over the continent in the early
years of the twentieth century, but they gradually concentrated in a
few major centers of petroleum production. In the 1920s, Mexico had
taken a clear lead, followed (at a distance) by Venezuela, Colombia,
and Peru. In contrast to the Mexican economy as a whole, petroleum
exports expanded steadily during these revolutionary years, overtak-
ing silver at the top of Mexico's export list. The foreign oil companies involved—British and, especially, North American—created a
communications and transportation network that managed to survive
the reigning disorder. The situation was quite opposite in Venezuela,
where the dictator Juan Vicente Gómez imposed an authoritarian
order highly conducive to foreign investment. The basin of Venezuela's Lake Maracaibo was soon festooned with oil-drilling rigs, while
offshore, on the Dutch island of Curaçao, the Royal Dutch Shell Company installed refineries for Venezuelan petroleum. (Standard Oil and
other U.S. companies operating in Venezuela preferred to ship their oil
to the United States for refining.) After a deceptively promising start,
the petroleum industry lagged behind in Colombia and Peru. In Argen-

tina, where major international companies shared the process of oil exploration with an official state corporation, the industry also grew slowly.

The agricultural and mining booms of the mature neocolonial period frequently created monopolies (or, at least, oligopolies) and resulted in companies whose capitalization surpassed that of many Latin American national treasuries. That kind of economic power could be translated into internal political power in various ways, ranging from direct financial leverage to collusion and corruption. In moments of crisis, companies might offer large sums to modify government policy in their favor. More routinely, foreign companies won influence within the local ruling classes by recruiting lawyers and advisers chosen for their political connections rather than for their technical competence. Powerful foreign interests possessed numerous indirect paths of control that are difficult to trace but widely believed to be important in the internal politics of the period. Less mysterious was the international influence of foreign capital that identified itself with a metropolitan power. The War of the Pacific, in which British, French, and North American investors used their national affiliations in favor of their private interests, provides a case in point. A more typical form of influence was the zeal with which French diplomatic personnel in the Río de la Plata promoted importations of French fencing wire during the transformation of rural production on the pampa.

The impact of powerful economic enterprises in neocolonial Latin America went far beyond the relatively limited portions of society directly reorganized by the new export booms. More than one national state depended on the fiscal contributions of export interests to balance its budget, to satisfy the acquisitive desires of its armed forces, or to meet the demands of its newly politicized masses. In spite of the large sums remitted abroad as profits to foreign shareholders, the earnings of export production provided the hard currency needed to buy the imported goods to which some Latin American consumers—mostly urban dwellers—had become accustomed. Mexico City's population tripled between 1895 and 1910, reaching a million inhabitants if the surrounding suburbs are counted. Buenos Aires, with a population of 1,700,000 in 1918, had experienced similar growth, as had Havana, Lima, Santiago, Bogotá, and Montevideo. After 1900, it became increasingly difficult to maintain the level of importation that these urban populations craved.

The international market had favored exporters of primary products during much of the nineteenth century, but as more primary exporting areas around the world entered that market in the early twentieth century, competition among them stiffened and the terms of trade underwent a crucial shift, now favoring the exporters of manufactured products. The United States, as the world's new leading industrial power, was far less dependent on foreign imports than had been Great Britain. Latin American countries generally strove to compensate for the worsening terms of trade by exporting more rather than by limiting production in an effort to drive up prices. To the previously discussed Brazilian coffee valorization project, one might add Chile's and Cuba's schemes to withhold nitrate and sugar exports, but such tactics were highly exceptional and never effective for long.

During the half century leading up to the international financial crisis of 1929, the production of primary exports like petroleum, bananas, and rubber defined the contours of Latin America's national economies without fully transforming their national societies. In rural areas, large segments of these national societies continued to live in a manner oriented more toward subsistence than toward participation in the international market. The advances of the market affected them mostly by putting pressure on their resources. In Mexico, the expansion of commercial haciendas on lands formerly farmed by peasant communities contributed to a revolutionary explosion of a scope and duration unparalleled in twentieth-century Latin America. The violent but localized and ephemeral uprisings of Andean peasants responded to similar causes. Rural social tensions also had political impacts in the cereal region of Argentina and the mining districts of Chile—two areas particularly affected by the process of economic change. For the most part, however, it was in the cities that social turmoil animated political conflict in these years.

The political evolution of most Latin American nations during the mature phase of neocolonialism remained within the familiar limits of oligarchical or military rule. The important exceptions were Mexico and the Southern Cone. In the three Southern Cone countries of Chile, Argentina, and Uruguay, peaceful democratization made important strides, including the triumph of broad-based political parties. Mexico, to which we turn first, took a different course after ending the long rule of Porfirio Díaz in 1910.

During the last decades of the nineteenth century, "Porfirian" rule had become the very epitome of Latin American progressive dictatorships. Díaz had begun, at least in theory, as heir of Mexico's mid-century liberal "Reform," but he concentrated on simply restoring order to the ravaged countryside after long years of civil war. Díaz presided over the creation of the country's railroad network, the recovery of its silver mines, and the prosperity of agricultural export production. The most talented ideologue of his regime, Justo Sierra, presented Díaz's Mexico as the synthesis of its Indian and Spanish antecedents—the mestizo country finally come into its own—while most leaders of the regime had a more European vision of Mexico that constituted both a congenial fiction about the present and a project for the future. On important state occasions, the police force herded people of Indian appearance away from the central district of the capital city so that foreign visitors would not get the "wrong idea" about the country. Although this attitude toward indigenous Mexicans was hardly novel, it had a new and explicitly racist justification. Gradually, the progressive dictatorship had mended its fences with the supporters of the earlier conservative hegemony, becoming a government of landowners and a friend of the church. This social conservatism went hand in hand with economic progressivism, as the expansion of railroads speeded the dissolution of communal landholdings and their reconcentration in the hands of large landowners. The conquest of a few warlike Indian tribes that had remained unsubjugated until the late nineteenth century added yet more new territory to the bounty of Porfirian landowners.

By the end of the century, Díaz could be described as an "honest tyrant" putting his disinterested power at the service of progress. The authoritarian tendencies of his government had emerged early in his long rule. In 1880, he had acted in accordance with his original slogan ("No reelection") and stepped down to allow a four-year term by a chosen successor, but in 1884 Díaz assumed the presidency again, this time to stay until 1911. He built a pervasive political machine to rule Mexico and gradually purged it of independent-minded politicians. Late in his rule, Díaz sometimes referred to his parliament as his "herd of horses." The gradual solidification of the dictator's permanent tenure gave him time enough to overcome the scattered resistance to it. His lavish generosity in dealing with potential adversaries was effective in winning them over, if costly to the Mexican national treasury, and it obviated other measures that might have marred the Porfirian regime's excellent reputation in Europe and the United States.

For the 1910 centennial of the movement for Mexican independence, the Díaz government had planned a stirring tribute to its own apparently unshakable permanence, but the issue of who would succeed the aging dictator intervened to spoil the performance. Díaz seems to have precipitated events himself when he remarked to a North American interviewer in 1908 that Mexico was ready for a return to political pluralism. The response surely occurred much faster than he might have wished. Believing that Díaz had personally called them into existence, the first opposition groups almost immediately sought the blessing of the dictator. Francisco Madero, a northern landowner and eventual leader of the opposition, at first hoped to accompany the inevitable don Porfirio as an opposition vice president (since Mexican presidential and vice presidential candidates did not form a unified ticket) but was soon forced to challenge Díaz directly. The challenger's campaign slogans ("Effective suffrage" and "No reelection") were strongly reminiscent of those used by Díaz himself in the early years, but the opposition had no chance to win the ensuing election. The Porfirian electoral machine functioned perfectly, delivering millions of votes to Díaz and only a little over a hundred to his upstart challenger.

Thrown into jail and then exiled, Madero adopted a new rhetoric that marked the transition from reform to revolution. The Plan of San Luis Potosí, which became the program of the Maderista revolution, demanded the return of lands illegally taken from peasant communities. The plan was to rectify abuses rather than to change the juridical underpinnings of the country's system of land tenure, but it allowed the Maderista movement to make common cause with a group of agrarian rebels led by Emiliano Zapata in the south-central state of Morelos. Zapata's followers had suffered the progressive loss of their village lands to the encroaching sugar plantations, and they eagerly supported Madero's banner of land reform.

The most important base of the challenge to Díaz lay, however, in northern Mexico, a region that had grown much faster than the rest of the country during recent decades. Northerners had different grievances from those of the Zapatistas. The region's new social and economic importance contrasted with its marginal place in the political arrangements of Porfirian rule, an aggravation to the northern ruling class. In addition, many northerners—from mine workers to ranchers—felt the deleterious consequences of their tight regional links to the powerful neighboring economy of the United States. Until 1907, those links had been advantageous, but the U.S. economy's subsequent slump had hit northern Mexico hard.

The Díaz regime collapsed within a matter of months, and the former dictator fled into exile. In a sense, the victory had been too easy, leaving Madero to become president without any real test of his heterogeneous and rapidly assembled constituency. That constituency was further diversified after the triumph of the Maderista revolution by the sudden conversion of many former Díaz supporters, and clashes among Madero's diverse followers began immediately. Madero was soon opposed by his erstwhile supporters, the Zapatistas, on the one hand, and by a nephew of Porfirio Díaz, on the other. In both conflicts the new president relied on a former Porfirian military leader, Gen. Victoriano Huerta, to defend his regime. Madero's confidence in Huerta proved fatal in 1913 when Huerta reached a temporary agreement (inspired by the U.S. minister in Mexico City) with the nephew of the former dictator and had Madero arrested. The deposed president was then murdered while under arrest.

The reaction to Madero's murder gathered strength only gradually, but it swelled into a revolutionary tide that eventually shook Mexican society in a manner comparable only to the wars of independence a hundred years earlier. The resistance to Huerta was strongest in the north. In Sonora, the state government refused to recognize the presidency of Huerta. Pancho Villa, the chief of Maderista forces in the neighboring state of Chihuahua, used his natural talent as a war leader and his experience as a marginal member of society to build the revolution's most powerful fighting force. Meanwhile, Venustiano Carranza, a former (Porfirista) governor and (Maderista) senator from the northern state of Coahuila, announced his plan for a Constitutionalist revolution. Carranza's goals were limited to the restoration of the constitutional order, but his political respectability allowed him to become the nominal leader and unifier of the anti-Huerta coalition.

At this point, the United States again intervened in Mexican events, this time because President Woodrow Wilson took a dim view of the Huerta government (which U.S. diplomacy had helped to install) and refused to recognize it. When Huerta stubbornly declined to abandon his unconstitutional presidency, Wilson tried unsuccessfully to win the backing of Carranza's forces. Finally, an incident between Mexican and U.S. troops involved in guarding the oil installations of Tampico provided Wilson with a rationale for military action, and in early 1914 he ordered the occupation of the country's chief port of Veracruz, to the outrage of Constitutionalists and Huertista forces alike. The occupation did not have the immediate effect of toppling Huerta. Instead, it gave rise to a ponderous diplomatic process in which Argentina, Brazil, and Chile tried to mediate. As the months passed, however, Huerta was weakened by the continued sequestration of the customs receipts from Veracruz, and he finally gave up the presidency and fled, leaving the Constitutionalists to occupy Mexico City a few weeks later.

The loose coalition of anti-Huerta forces had lost its common enemy, and strains soon became evident. Pancho Villa's legendary Division of the North and Emiliano Zapata's rebellious peasants of

Morelos had contributed importantly to the defeat of Huerta. After their victory, neither Villa nor Zapata was disposed to take orders from Carranza, whose role as Constitutionalist leader had been largely symbolic up to that point. An open split came in November 1914, when Carranza left Mexico City to set up his headquarters in Veracruz, where he could control the most important source of government funds. The loyalty of his supporters from the northwestern state of Sonora now became crucial to Carranza's efforts to win the revolution for the Constitutionalists. The Sonorans were headed by Alvaro Obregón, whose past held few clues to the role he would play in leading Mexico out of its revolutionary bloodbath.

Obregón prevailed upon Carranza to include in the Constitutionalist program such socially conscious measures as an agrarian reform and the right to organize and strike, and he also became the best general among the Constitutionalists. Villa and Zapata had abandoned Mexico City after the departure of Carranza because the inhabitants of the capital proved notably disinclined to support their rustic conquerors. These two former allies of Carranza now constituted the main obstacle to a Constitutionalist triumph. Villa, the more formidable militarily, was the first to be defeated. At the decisive battle of Celaya in 1915, Obregón used tactics then being developed on the battlefields of World War I to smash Villa's forces, allowing the Constitutionalists to regain momentum. The Zapatistas could hold on to their home ground in Morelos, but they could not operate effectively outside of it, so the Constitutionalists set about consolidating their control of the rest of Mexico.

The 1917 constitution lay the cornerstone in the process of institutionalizing the revolution. Some aspects of the new document, particularly its anticlericalism, recall the liberal constitution of 1857, but very significant new motifs had been added as well. Article 27, for example, reclaimed all mineral rights in the subsoil for the national government and set Mexico on a course toward land reform. Article 123 required the state to protect the rights of labor and recognized the legal existence of unions. The nationalist and socially progressive elements of the new revolutionary order owed more to Obregón than to Carranza, who tried to shut the Sonoran leader out of the presidential succession in 1920. Obregón became president only after a revolt within the Constitutionalist ranks drove Carranza out of the capital. During his flight from Mexico City, the former figurehead of the anti-Huerta coalition was murdered as Madero had been. Zapata, too, had been murdered shortly before Carranza, and Villa followed not long afterward. Mexico had lost a million inhabitants during ten years of fighting and economic devastation.

The peasant demands for land reform were achieved in Zapata's Morelos, but they quickly bogged down elsewhere. Peasant organizations became docile clienteles of the new power structure, and large landowners from before the revolution were often able to retain much of their best land. The Sonorans showed little enthusiasm for the restoration of *ejidos*, community lands eroded by mid-nineteenth-century reforms and the subsequent expansion of agrarian capitalism. Instead, they preferred to issue titles to individual beneficiaries of the government's land-distribution program, and many of these titles went to swell the fortunes of revolutionary leaders and their personal followers.

The Sonoran Dynasty begun by Obregón and continued in 1924 by his successor, Plutarco Elías Calles, inherited a constellation of political forces in which the gains of Mexico's poor majority were at best partial. As for organized labor, its legitimacy had been recognized, but the existing unions—soon riddled with corruption—represented only a small fraction of Mexico's miners and industrial workers. The limited agrarian and labor reforms provided the revolutionary government with a base of support, but that base grew very slowly because of the leadership's own ideological ambiguities and its desire to overcome the penury that had resulted from a decade of fighting. Efforts to stimulate the export sector imposed strict limitations on the process of social transformation that some revolutionaries had envisioned. It also implied a return to the economic formulas of the Porfirian period and a new modus vivendi with the continuing hegemonic power of the United States. The efforts of Obregón and (especially) Calles eventually led to closer Mexican-U.S. relations than had been maintained by the Díaz regime, especially after a 1927 decision of the Mexican Supreme Court that denied retroactive claims against foreign companies based on article 27 of the constitution.

In Mexican cities, neither the opponents nor supporters of the postrevolutionary order were willing to push forward at the cost of further violence, making rural areas the chief venues of conflict in the 1920s. Although the same socioeconomic elites who had been arrayed in earlier days against Mexican liberalism now resisted the revolutionaries' projects of social engineering, they essentially accepted the triumph of new ruling groups and sought to establish ties with them. On the other hand, the urban middle classes (among the staunchest supporters of nineteenth-century liberal reforms) lacked enthusiasm for the northerners who had quickly devoted themselves to a widespread and ostentatious corruption after emerging victorious. As the possibilities for enrichment in the new order absorbed the attention of urban dwellers, a clear clash of social forces continued in the countryside. Some of the beneficiaries of the agrarian reform had inherited, along with pieces of prerevolutionary haciendas, the conflict between hacendados and neighboring villagers. The land struggle was exacerbated by the anticlerical measures that Calles was determined to impose throughout the national territory. This phase of the struggle pitted conservative peasants against the *agrarista* beneficiaries of the government's land reform program and against rural schoolteachers who had become missionaries of the revolutionary creed. In a broad arc stretching from north-central to western Mexico, the *Cristeros* rose up to defend the Catholic faith in 1926, and the bloody fighting was stemmed only after Calles reached an agreement with the Vatican.

The question of Calles's successor seemed for a time to augur a return to the personalism that had characterized the regime of Porfirio Díaz. In 1928, the principle of no reelection was revoked to allow Obregón to have a second presidential term, but a Cristero assassinated Obregón shortly thereafter. Calles embarked instead on a process of political institutionalization, founding the National Revolutionary party to gather all the disparate political forces identified with the new order. Within the framework of the party, military and regional caudillos all over Mexico recognized Calles as first among equals, the country's dominant caudillo, while the presidency passed to a series of lackluster figureheads.

The revolutionary regime consolidated itself in this traditional manner—not so different from that of Porfirian Mexico—without renouncing its socialist banners and radical slogans. A bevy of superb mural painters offered the Mexican masses (and the international art world) an epic image of Mexican history with the revolution as its culmination, but in the late 1920s only the recently reawakened struggle with the church imparted a truly revolutionary quality to the political order. Not until the 1930s would the international economic crisis revivify the revolutionary process by bringing into play the labor unions and other mass organizations that stood (however lacking in autonomy vis-à-vis the state) as reminders of what had changed irreversibly during ten years of fighting.

In the far south of Latin America, democratization took a less violent course, as we can observe in the cases of Uruguay, Argentina, and Chile. Uruguay entered the era of democratic mass politics as a result of developments within one of its traditional elite parties: the

Colorado party. Half a century earlier, the Colorados had fought the Uruguayan allies of Rosas and had defended Montevideo during its long siege of the 1840s. After 1851, the distinction between the Colorados and their Blanco adversaries had softened as urban members of each party joined forces to escape the domination of rural caudillos. Partisan distinctions blurred further during the military dictatorship of the 1870s and 1880s, though elements associated with the Colorado party retained the upper hand. Uruguay had changed much during the period of military rule. The population of Montevideo had risen rapidly, and the countryside had been subjected to an iron hand that favored the interests of large landowners and facilitated the modernization of ranching. At the return to civilian rule in the 1890s, the Colorado wing of the urban oligarchy reassumed direct control of the government, and partisan politics recommenced. Within a few years, renewed challenges from Blanco caudillos in the countryside led to an 1897 pact whereby the Colorado government ceded control of certain local areas to the Blancos. Once again, a rival Blanco power had risen up in the backlands to challenge the Colorado oligarchy of Montevideo.

New influences within the Colorado party now came to the fore, led by José Batlle y Ordóñez. This son of the traditional Montevidean elite put together a political alliance with a broad base in the capital city and in a limited portion of the Uruguayan countryside lately transformed by the introduction of family-scale farming. Becoming president in 1903, Batlle initiated the final contest of strength between the modernizing south of Uruguay and the economically static north (a Blanco stronghold), the bloody but definitive civil war of 1904. After winning the war, Batlle pushed ahead with a series of reforms destined to remake the Uruguayan state in the twentieth century. Batlle encouraged a level of state participation in the economy unique at the time in Latin America. In the area of trade policy, official regulation of commerce and nationalization of insurance complemented Batlle's systematically protectionist tariff legislation. After 1920, the Batllista state's promotion of highway construction sought to undermine the transportation monopoly of British-owned railroads.

Batlle deliberately avoided disruptive reforms in the ranching districts that produced the country's wealth and made possible his experiments in social engineering. The reform impulse moved from political democracy to social democracy during Batlle's second term (1911–15), during which the government took a benevolent attitude toward the advance of unionization and introduced an official retirement and pension system, but in the Uruguayan countryside large landowners continued to reign supreme over their workers. Uruguay remained more divided than it appeared, and Batlle tried to legitimate that division and defuse its dangers by offering the opposition party a share of executive power. The results were the beginning of Uruguay's series of experiments with collective presidencies, on the one hand, and a split in Batlle's own party, on the other. The split came during the constituent convention of 1916, which created a Council of Government to take on administrative powers formerly exercised by the president and also institutionalized Batlle's growing anticlericalism.

In fifteen years, Batllista Uruguay had vanquished the country's last Blanco insurgency and created a welfare state, but its political innovations rested on fragile foundations. Batlle's personal hegemony had survived the split in the governing party only because the opposition was equally divided. Furthermore, despite its programmatic emphasis and its mass base, Batlle's new political force rallied above all around the person of its leader. The man who had definitively bested the country's caudillos on horseback was himself a caudillo of a different stripe, so much so, in fact, that after Batlle's death the problem of succession (conceived in almost dynastic terms) became a cause of renewed political instability. Then, too, the Batllista agenda depended on economic prosperity to finance its reforms without disturbing the large landowners of the interior, where most of the country's wealth was produced. Batlle's reforms flowered especially in the first and third decades of the century, flush times during which Batlle's own optimistic confidence became something of an Uruguayan national characteristic—so different from the permanent anguish of a country divided against itself in the nineteenth century. Harder times and gradual disappointment lay ahead, but in the meantime Uruguay offered the brightest example of political democratization and social modernization in Latin America. The Argentine and Chilean achievements of the period pale by comparison.

In Argentina, as in its smaller neighbor across the Río de la Plata, the march toward democracy was closely associated with the figure of a civil caudillo and dependent on a high level of economic prosperity. The starting point of the process of democratization was the regime created in 1880 by Gen. Julio Roca. Argentina changed more in the following decade than in all its previous history, thanks to a flood of immigration (mostly Italian) and a parallel inundation of foreign capital (principally British).

The political configurations of Roquista Argentina centered on an alliance between the landowners of the riverine provinces (especially Buenos Aires and Santa Fe) and foreign commercial interests, but the upper classes of the less-modernized interior provinces were sometimes able to secure their own portion of the general prosperity through participation in politics. The urban workers and agricultural laborers of the riverine provinces—lesser beneficiaries of the process of modernization—lost political influence as their ranks were increasingly filled by immigrants, while the lower classes of the interior, for their part, remained excluded from the economic, as well as the political, benefits of the regime. The country's leaders claimed to have replaced political conflict with technical expertise and nonpartisan administration.

British capital became so routine an element of administrative life that municipal and provincial governments vied with the national state for funds in the London stock exchange. The Roca regime initially tried to put limits on the financial conquests of foreign investment, but it soon abandoned the attempt. As local capital went primarily into land speculation (the most profitable investment of all), outside funds became essential to the normal functioning of government. In order to maintain the feverish rhythm of economic growth, Roca's brother-in-law Miguel Juárez Celman, who succeeded him as president in 1886, had to allow private banks to issue paper money, leading to rampant inflation. A severe financial crisis precipitated a political crisis in 1890.

The civil-military revolution of 1890 quickly collapsed, but its repercussions were unexpectedly wide. Juárez Celman resigned, leaving his office to Vice President Carlos Pellegrini, who enjoyed an especially strong reputation in European financial circles. Some of the rebels of 1890 refused to be mollified by the resignation of the president and formed a party of determined opposition to the conservative order, the Unión Cívica Radical. The Radical platform of constitutional integrity and electoral honesty was hardly revolutionary, yet the conservative regime showed itself unwilling to risk open and untrammeled elections, and the Radicals launched further "revolutions" in 1893 and 1904. Neither brought a military victory to the Radical cause, but the sustained opposition gradually undercut the stability of the conservative order. After 1904, General Roca's personal influence waned, unbinding the loose alliance of provincial groups that had held Roquista Argentina together. In 1912, President Roque Sáenz Peña, the last heir of the old order, finally inaugurated an era of effective universal suffrage, practiced before that time in name only. In the next election, a Radical veteran of twenty-five years of conspiratorial opposition became president of Argentina.

Hipólito Yrigoyen's 1916 victory drew on wide middle-class backing in the riverine provinces (including the rural middle class of the cereal-growing zone), on the support of urban popular sectors in the same region, and on the endorsement of disgruntled elite elements in the interior provinces. This unwieldy coalition obviously did not lend itself to a program of sweeping changes. As president, Yrigoyen devoted his modest administrative talents to restaffing the bureaucracy with his own followers and creating, in the process, an invincible electoral machine. If the victorious Radicals showed little interest in social or economic innovation, they did try to overcome the old pattern of confrontation between the government and the labor unions of Argentina's major cities. Despite the general moderation of the labor movement in Argentina, the previous conservative regime had viewed it as extremely dangerous. Yrigoyen's Radicals encouraged the most unthreatening elements within organized labor, especially those who, because they were not associated with the Socialist party, could become silent partners of the Radicals' electoral machine. As for rural matters, the government of Yrigoyen passed the first laws benefiting agricultural renters like those of the cereal zone, whose Agrarian Federation received discreet but decisive official support. Despite the extremist rhetoric of certain student leaders, the government offered similarly discreet support to the university reform movement, which it hoped would end the academic predominance of certain members of the conservative aristocracy. Taken together, all of these measures were intended to undermine conservative influence and augment that of the government's constituency within the existing social order.

Revolutionary challenges to that order were met with rigor by the Radicals, who denied the existence of grave social problems altogether. Hundreds of workers died in the Tragic Week of 1919, when the government allowed conservative volunteer groups to help the army crush a labor uprising. Similar brutality was applied in 1921, even more unnecessarily, against striking rural workers in Patagonia. Yrigoyen's alternating encouragement and repression of the forces of change always obeyed a pragmatic political purpose. In order to strengthen his party's hand against the oligarchy, Yrigoyen applied all of his considerable skill at political maneuvering while somehow preserving his lofty (if slightly hollow) moral conscience. As in the case of Batllismo in Uruguay, the meaning of Radicalism was hardly separable from the person of its leader. Hipólito Yrigoyen achieved a vast popularity incomparable in Argentine politics and all the more striking in a man who, in contrast to the country's oratorical traditions, almost never personally addressed the public.

In 1922, Yrigoyen was succeeded by a man of his own choosing, Marcelo Torcuato de Alvear, a cosmopolitan aristocrat who had adorned the salons of Paris in the dying days of the Belle Epoque. Unable to succeed himself, the crafty president had selected someone he obviously judged incapable of disputing his continued leadership behind the scenes. By 1924, though, Yrigoyen and Alvear had parted ways, beginning a prolonged power struggle within the Radical ranks. In 1928, Yrigoyen showed that he retained control of the party's electoral machinery when he returned to the presidency with a majority unprecedented in the history of the country. However, the Radicals had now alienated most of their former supporters among the country's upper and upper-middle classes, a politically dangerous situation even at the high point of Argentine prosperity.

In 1928, the country's export earnings reached 200,000,000 pounds sterling in gold, twice the total of 1913, but in the next year the first shock waves of the global financial crisis began to devastate Argentina's economic structures, always so open to the international environment. The country's Radical governments had never altered the tax structure, which relied most heavily on imports (to the benefit of landowners) and as the crisis drastically reduced importation and the economy crumbled, the government's revenues plummeted and its currency lost its backing in gold. Meanwhile, Yrigoyen's attention remained on partisan politics. He was now intent on finally capturing the senate, a conservative stronghold throughout the period of Radical ascendancy, but he never carried out this last conquest. Instead, the elections of early 1930 revealed that Yrigoyen's support, while still a majority, had dropped sharply, inspiring the army to depose him later that year.

When compared with the Uruguayan experience, the trajectory of Radicalism in Argentina suggests a more complex equilibrium between old and new. The Radicals introduced fewer innovations and showed greater respect for the social and economic order that they inherited from the conservatives. The exuberant prosperity of the period was perceived as the culmination of a process of economic growth begun by the political adversaries of Radicalism, a circumstance that undercut the hegemonic pretensions of the Radical vision. Thus, as Batllismo was becoming something of a consensual national ideology when viewed from the streets of Montevideo during the 1920s, the dominant mood in Buenos Aires was a bemused ambivalence. In both cases, the attempt to democratize the political system and effect a moderate redistribution of income without upheaval had depended on the steady export expansion that came to a sudden end in 1930.

Chile

In Chile, upheaval had accompanied political transformations in spite of the country's neocolonial prosperity. The triumph of liberalism in 1871, coming after more than a quarter century of conservative hegemony, reflected the changes that had come about because of the mining and commercial booms of mid-century. In 1883, Chilean victory in the War of the Pacific had altered the balance of power in South America, conferring great prestige on the liberal victors, both within the country and internationally. Exports like wheat and cattle hides—produced on the lands of the country's traditional elites—steadily lost importance, while nitrate and copper mining continued their expansion. As a result of the war, liberal president Domingo Santa María obtained large territorial gains from Chile's defeated opponents (Bolivia and Peru) and used the revenues of the country's nitrate exports to multiply the functions of the state and its programs of public works. He also implemented measures long on the liberal agenda, such as removal of ecclesiastical control over marriage registration and public cemeteries. No longer united in opposition to conservative hegemony, progressive Chilean elites divided into three parties (National, Radical, and Liberal) during the controversy over who was to succeed Santa María, though all three groups finally accepted the president's own choice of his successor.

José Manuel Balmaceda, the official candidate, no doubt owed his electoral victory to the government's abundant resources, and he continued to spend them in the sort of innovative programs that Santa María had initiated. The prosperity of the 1880s was not limitless, however, and the expansion of presidential power ended with the exhaustion of the plentiful revenues that had fueled it. Balmaceda eventually had to seek foreign loans to maintain the rhythm of public spending, and the international financial crisis of 1890 thus brought a political crisis at home. Balmaceda precipitated a conflict with the openly hostile congress when, in early 1891, he promulgated his budget without congressional approval. The result was civil war between the president's supporters and those of the majority forces in congress, who rallied the navy and part of the army and quickly took control of the northern mining areas that produced so much of the government's revenues. After gathering their forces in the north for a few months, the rebels invaded central Chile, won a couple of bloody battles, and managed to capture Santiago, while the defeated president preferred suicide to capture or exile.

political fragmentation

The overthrow of Balmaceda marked a resurgence of oligarchical power in Chile and the end of vigorous executive initiatives for a number of years as political parties became increasingly fragmented.

The political paralysis of the period after 1891 seemed to be interrupted only when social ferment led to episodes of popular agitation followed by violent repression in Santiago, Valparaíso, and the northern mining region. The gradual widening of the suffrage had a limited impact because of systemic electoral corruption. To have a chance of victory, candidates required large sums of money to grease the gears of the electoral machine. As in England before 1832, political parties wanted candidates who were able to finance their victories out of their personal fortunes. Two loose electoral coalitions dominated the political scene: the liberal Union and the liberal-conservative Alliance.

With the presidential election of 1920, Chilean politics took on a more conflictive ideological content. Arturo Alessandri, a defender of labor organizers in the nitrate fields, ran for election as the liberal Union candidate in that year amid a climate of rising social discontent, denouncing the Chilean ruling class as a "gilded mob" and inviting his followers to besiege the sumptuous residences of the oligarchy. Alessandri won the election by a narrow margin, but his triumph had broad consequences, particularly the political mobilization of the working class (which strongly supported the president) and the advance of labor organization (including the creation of a Communist party). The congressional elections of 1924 became a plebiscite on Alessandri, one that the popular president won easily, though not without applying the resources of the state to his political advantage during the campaign. Still, the long history of congressional factionalism and indiscipline seemed to prevent effective legislation. In an attempt to break the legislative deadlock, Alessandri left the country in the hands of a military junta, but when the junta began to favor the liberal-conservative Alliance, another group of officers deposed it and recalled Alessandri. The January Revolution of 1925 created the conditions for more decisive political change, and a new constitution was approved within the year. The Constitution of 1925 finally separated church and state, and it also enshrined a number of principles—such as government responsibility in the areas of public health and worker protection—that many called socialistic. The new order gave the national executive an advantage over the legislative branch, but it also affirmed the army's role as arbiter between the two.

The officer who had led the dominant military faction in the January Revolution, Col. Carlos Ibáñez, became Alessandri's defense minister and seemed his most likely successor. Ibáñez did not immediately become the next president when Alessandri resigned after the ratification of the new constitution, but he did not have long to wait. Elected president in 1927, Ibáñez launched a vigorous program of

Ibáñez

construction (highways, port facilities, and school buildings), public health, and educational reform. His rule became increasingly dictatorial, but as long as the country's export-driven prosperity (and access to foreign credit) lasted, he maintained the support of his intimidated congress while attending as well to the aspirations of the masses. In 1929, the international financial collapse undermined his popularity, bringing harsher government repression, popular unrest in Santiago, and the fall of Ibáñez in 1931. Chile suffered a national economic disaster as the demand for Chilean exports withered and the value of its peso plummeted.

The military's role as arbiter between the country's political elite and the forces of democratization distinguishes the Chilean case from those of Uruguay and Argentina; however, no less than Batlle or Yrigoyen, the renovators of Chile's political system had depended on the general prosperity and the government revenues accompanying neocolonial export growth in order to carry out their reforms. Although much was accomplished in all three countries, much was lost after 1929. In the rest of Spanish America, the circle of participation widened more slowly and sporadically and had less impact than in the three nations of the Southern Cone. Peru and Ecuador, to which we now turn, still struggled with the division between modernizing coastal regions and the Indian highlands that, in many ways, had never been effectively incorporated into the nation.

Perú

Peru's defeat in the 1879–83 war with Chile brought a temporary return to military caudillismo in the defeated nation, but the same war made opposition leader Nicolás de Piérola a popular hero. In 1895, Piérola overthrew the military government in a bloody civil war, with strong support from the populace of Lima, and became president. Once in office, Piérola introduced measures not calculated to maintain his popularity with those who had put him there. His monetary reform, for example, helped regularize Peru's economic life by putting the country on the gold standard, but it impoverished the working class while especially favoring import/export merchants. Piérola began to create an administrative structure to guide the recovery of commercial

*Piérola-
uneven
economic
progress*

agriculture on the coast and livestock raising and mining in the highlands, and he reformed the system of taxation by putting it partly in private hands. Such measures encouraged the recovery of the Peruvian economy from the blows dealt it by the war, but the new prosperity flowed primarily to old beneficiaries: first to the Lima aristocracy, then to the landowners of the highlands and the urban middle and popular sectors and (in quite limited measure) to the rural laborers who participated in the agricultural revival of the coast. The Indian masses of the highlands remained on the margin of the national economy, except when they migrated to the coastal plantations. The governments that followed Piérola's continued the impulse toward uneven economic progress. Somehow, this singular civil caudillo retained his popularity among lower-class true believers, and he never established close relations with the oligarchy whose economic interests his government had favored.

Between 1919 and 1930, Peru entered a progressive dictatorship more attentive to the welfare of the masses but equally disinclined to let them guide their own destiny. Augusto B. Leguía had been minister of finance and constitutional president before becoming head of an authoritarian state that he termed the "Patria Nueva." Leguía's dictatorship reduced the political influence of the Lima oligarchy, whose internal rivalries he exploited deftly. Under his rule, an avalanche of U.S. loans and investments gave strong impetus to the process of economic expansion and the rhythm of public works. Clearly, there was also much that was not new in the Patria Nueva. Even the government's mobilization of popular support ended, for the most part, in the outskirts of Lima, though Leguía realized the potential power of the Indian masses and made attempts to tap it. Some measures, like his adoption of the Indian title "Viracocha," were merely symbolic gestures, but others were more effective. For example, influenced by "Indianist" intellectuals during the early part of his rule, Leguía granted legal recognition of Indian corporate communities. In some ways, however, government sponsorship only increased the vulnerability of Indian communities by making them more dependent on a central bureaucracy over which they had no control. Perhaps the most substantial highland initiative of Leguía's government was the program of highway construction that linked Indian communities to a national transportation network, but construction of these roads was often carried out by forced labor recruited in highland communities, a strategy unlikely to win the affection of their inhabitants.

After 1923, Leguía's dictatorship took a more decidedly conservative course and acquired new adversaries on the left. The president's official consecration of Peru to the Sacred Heart of Jesus provoked a student protest that made one of its leaders nationally famous. Víctor Raúl Haya de la Torre, destined to become Peru's most durable political figure of the twentieth century, had begun his career by supporting a workers' movement in 1919. Exiled because of his leadership of the student protest against Leguía, Haya de la Torre maintained contact with his political allies in Peru while Leguía sought at all cost to keep them from extending their influence among the urban populace and rural masses. Consequently, the government took a hard line against organized labor in Lima and the coastal plantation areas and even against José Carlos Mariátegui (the political theorist whose intellectual audacities Leguía had long tolerated) after Mariátegui was found to be involved in unionization schemes.

The government's alarm may have been excessive. As long as the general prosperity of the 1920s lasted, the Patria Nueva had little to fear from its enemies. Although the Peruvian oligarchy was more powerful than that of Uruguay, Argentina, or Chile, the popular challenge from below was notably weaker and, above all, more heterogeneous. As elsewhere, however, the end of the economic boom was also the end of a political epoch. The army, which had taken a quite limited role in Peruvian politics since 1895, returned to center stage in 1930, when Col. Luis Miguel Sánchez Cerro, a tenacious organizer of military conspiracies against Leguía, was able finally to overthrow him, and the Patria Nueva collapsed almost without resistance.

Ecuador's modern political origins date from an 1895 civil war that marked the triumph of Liberal caudillo Eloy Alfaro. The liberal victory initiated a new stage in the perennial political contest between the highland capital, Quito, and coastal Guayaquil, center of the country's export economy throughout the nineteenth century and Alfaro's political base. Defeating the conservative landowning families of Quito, Alfaro immediately sponsored a new constitution (followed by a second one a decade later) to transform Ecuador into a secular state. In 1908, the government inaugurated the long-awaited rail line between Quito and Guayaquil, an event that marked, in liberal eyes, the birth of a new Ecuador more closely linked to the outside world. Unfortunately, the development of a closer relationship with the international market depended on more than transportation, and the liberal vision remained illusory until the highlands found a profitable export product for the new railroad to carry. The liberal government also failed to transform the social relations of the highlands, where a landowning aristocracy continued to hold sway over rural Indians. The final weakness of Ecuadorian liberalism derived from its own internal divisions. Alfaro's impatient authoritarianism and his populist tendencies clashed with the more circumspect style of the party notables, and the caudillo did not begin his second term in 1906 without encountering substantial resistance among liberals as well as conservatives. After his second presidency, Alfaro was lynched in Quito by a mestizo mob that continued to look on the liberals as intruders from the coast.

In death Alfaro became the leading symbol of the liberal cause, and middle-class liberal families placed his bust in corners formerly devoted to the images of saints, even as the leadership of the party passed securely back into the hands of Alfaro's erstwhile detractors among the coastal oligarchy. Membership in the dominant group broadened only to include a few upper-class professionals somehow associated with international commerce, whether on the coast or in the high-lands. For the time being, Ecuador's indigenous peoples intervened in elite politics only occasionally, and then usually in support of the conservative resistance to liberal innovations. Ecuadorian liberalism became increasingly fragmented and, in 1925, finally succumbed to a military coup. The military transferred the government to another progressive dictator, a medical doctor named Isidro Ayora, who set about reorganizing the financial and administrative structures of the state. Ayora's approach was energetic and heterodox but ultimately inefficacious. When the international crisis of 1930 raised social and political tensions throughout Latin America, his government was swept away like so many others.

In the rest of Latin America, the mature neocolonial period brought fewer alterations to the existing political patterns. Although there were many differences among them, most countries continued to alternate between military and oligarchical rule, undergoing little of the democratization process that advanced, to varying degrees, in the countries already discussed. Military dictatorships often occurred when transformations in patterns of export production—repeated market crises or the introduction of novel export activities—weak-ened the economic dominance of traditional oligarchies. Especially in areas close to the United States, outside capital helped undercut exist-ing political arrangements. This was frequently the case in the Carib-bean and Central America, areas characterized by military authoritar-ian solutions and repeated U.S. intervention.

Cuba's late break with Spain, arriving seventy-five years after inde- *Cuba* pendence in most of the hemisphere, created exceptional conditions initially, but the politics of the island moved ever closer to general Latin American patterns during the early twentieth century. At the outset, those who had led the fight against Spain congregated in the Liberal party, while those who had made common cause with the Spanish joined the Conservative party. The United States, simulta-neously a liberating and a conquering power in Cuba, feared the former protagonists of independence as much for their virtues as for their defects, and it used its influence to avoid an outright liberal triumph. The 1900 constitution, written by a liberal-dominated assembly, insti-tuted universal male suffrage against U.S. wishes, but it bowed to U.S. pressure in guaranteeing minority representation in the Cuban legislature. The first president of the newly independent country, Tomás Estrada Palma, was elected by a bipartisan coalition, though he inclined increasingly toward the conservatives. Eventually, it was the liberals who made first recourse to the Platt Amendment, a provision (attached to the Cuban constitution due to the pressure of the United States) conferring the right of U.S. intervention in Cuba to protect individual and property rights. As a result, the U.S. government placed Cuba under a military administration in 1906. In 1908 the occupying power announced a "fraud-proof" new electoral law and left the Cuban government in the hands of the liberals, who had won the subsequent election.

The next president, Mario García Menocal, was a conservative whose second term coincided with the fabulously high price of sugar on the international market during World War I. The Cuban political class participated enthusiastically in the "Dance of the Millions" and in the resulting opportunities for lucrative corruption. The United States chose to ignore Menocal's increasing authoritarianism because of his support for the U.S. line in international affairs and allowed him to impose his chosen successor, Alfredo Zayas, in 1921. Zayas had to confront the economic crisis that followed the collapse of artificially high wartime sugar prices, and he appealed to the U.S. government for advice. As a result, a U.S. bank extended a new loan to the Cuban government, and North American companies acquired still more of the Cuban sugar lands they had been accumulating for decades.

The election of 1924 was won by a liberal, Gerardo Machado, who had formerly directed the Havana branch office of General Electric. The slump in sugar prices continued, but the easy availability of international investment capital in the late 1920s allowed Machado to embark on an ambitious program of works that included a central highway and numerous public health projects. Meanwhile, the corruption characteristic of earlier years remained unabated, and the international sugar market narrowed further due to protectionism in the United States. An attempt by the Cuban government to force sugar prices up by buying and warehousing part of their crop to hold it off the market, as the Brazilians had done with coffee, failed to alter the price substantially. As the economic crisis deepened after 1928, it was accompanied by a political crisis. Machado's rule became openly dictatorial, provoking considerable resistance. University students, in particular, began to adopt violent means of political agitation that the government was unable to subdue despite the brutality of its attempts to do so. Further opposition came from both organized labor and the representatives of Cuba's landowning classes. In 1933, the new administration of Franklin Roosevelt lent its weight to the anti-Machado forces, and within a few months a military revolt overthrew the dictator.

The fall of Machado closed the first chapter in the political history of an independent Cuba. From this point on, the country's economic and political dependence on the United States became universally recognized. In his highly influential 1927 study, *Sugar and the Population of the Antilles*, Cuban author Ramiro Guerra y Sánchez predicted that the largest Caribbean island would go the way of its smaller cousins in the West Indies. Cuba's future seemed especially bleak as the informal colony of a metropolitan power that had its own sugar-producing areas at home. The island's relationship with the hegemonic giant of the north would become the central political issue of the next period of Cuban history.

Puerto Rico felt the consequences of U.S. hegemony most acutely of all. The peace treaty that ended the Spanish-American War made Puerto Rico a U.S. possession and brought the island firmly into the economic orbit of its new metropolis. The resulting configuration of capital, tariffs, and markets led to the triumph of sugar over coffee in the Puerto Rican export economy. The population grew rapidly, thanks, in part, to the sanitation projects carried out by the North American administration. The island's new rulers also tried to combat illiteracy by means of a school system that used English rather than Spanish as its principal language. Puerto Ricans reacted to the imposition of U.S. colonialism with a variety of proposals ranging from independence, to an intermediate "autonomy," to statehood. For the time being, however, only the upper and middle classes of the island showed much interest in these proposals, and their outcome depended to a high degree on the disposition of the United States. Although U.S. administrations could effectively repress active dissidence, they could not insure the success of their cultural and educational policies. Despite the transformations imposed on the island after 1898, the Puerto Rican people firmly resisted complete acculturation.

In Nicaragua, an alternative interoceanic canal route attracted the vigorous exercise of U.S. hegemony. In 1907 U.S. pressure helped topple the Liberal dictator José Santos Zelaya, and after 1912 the marine guard of the U.S. legation in Nicaragua supported the presidency of a conservative who authorized the United States to construct a canal in return for three million dollars to be used in the repayment of the country's international debts. When the marines were withdrawn in 1924, fighting between liberals and conservatives resumed, and the marines quickly returned to shore up a new conservative president against the armed opposition. That opposition was led by Gen. Augusto César Sandino, who became famous for his ability to thwart both the U.S. and the Nicaraguan government forces arrayed against him. The tenacious resistance of Sandino's guerrillas convinced the United States to accept a liberal president in 1928, but North American hegemony proved adaptable. Within a short time, Sandino was murdered and the national guard—organized and armed by the United States to fight the guerrillas—emerged as the dominant power in Nicaragua. Its commander, Gen. Anastasio Somoza, founded a dynasty destined to last, in close association with the United States, for half a century.

The Dominican Republic also experienced direct North American intervention beginning in 1916. U.S. troops were originally invited in to help preserve internal order, but when Dominican president Francisco Henríquez y Carvajal refused to put the country's treasury, customs receipts, and army under direct U.S. supervision, the occupying forces took control of the country's customhouses and laid economic siege to a Dominican government that they themselves had installed. Unable to gain the compliance of that government, U.S. forces concluded by replacing it with a direct military administration that lasted until 1922. Here, too, the legacy of North American occupation was the creation of a powerful national guard that dominated the country after the departure of the marines. With the support of the National Guard, another durable dictator, Gen. Rafael Leónidas Trujillo, became president of the Dominican Republic in 1930.

The rest of Central America experienced subtler forms of hegemonic influence. In most cases, U.S. policy favored the political stability provided by authoritarian regimes. Such regimes were also a natural outgrowth of the social and economic development of the isthmus during the mature neocolonial period. In Guatemala, the dictatorship of Manuel Estrada Cabrera from 1898 to 1920 was the earliest to develop. The rulers who replaced the dictator during the 1920s had barely begun to attenuate the political legacy of Estrada Cabrera's tyranny when another strong man, Gen. Jorge Ubico, began his own long rule in 1930. The oligarchical system of El Salvador and the political instability of Honduras in the first decades of the century had given way to respective military dictatorships in those two countries as well by the early 1930s. Only Costa Rica, whose government continued in the hands of the coffee-growing rural middle class, moved in the direction of democracy at this time. An attempt at dictatorship interrupted the government's institutional continuity in the second decade of the century, but the ultimate outcome—dissolution of the army—only increased the contrast between Costa Rica and its Central American neighbors.

Farther south, authoritarianism remained solidly rooted in neo- *Venezuela*
colonial Venezuela. In 1899, the rise of Gen. Cipriano Castro inaugurated a regional power shift as military officers from the western
highlands of Venezuela (comprising the northern tip of the Andean
chain) took up positions of power that they did not relinquish, as a
group, for half a century. Applauded by the Caracas elite with the stagy
enthusiasm it reserved for successive waves of conquerors from the
interior, Castro continued the cult of progress and the secularizing
bent of the authoritarian regimes that had preceded him. However,
perhaps because of his isolated Andean origins, this dictator lacked an
appreciation of the importance of Venezuela's links with Europe, and
he drifted into a confrontation with Great Britain, Germany, and Italy,
the damaging consequences of which were minimized only by late
U.S. mediation. Next he entered a conflict with the Netherlands concerning Venezuelan exiles who had taken refuge on the Dutch island
possession of Curaçao. During the ensuing Dutch naval blockade, an
ailing Castro left Venezuela to seek a European cure. His vice president, Gen. Juan Vicente Gómez, then made peace with Castro's international enemies and took over the government permanently in 1909.
The regime of Gómez, who ruled until his death in 1935, offers something of an "ideal type" of early twentieth-century Latin American
dictatorship. It lacked nothing: ferocious repression of dissidents, iron
discipline of labor, ingratiating deference to foreign powers and investors, and an obsession with "progress" in the form of public works.
Gómez even preserved constitutional forms by periodically allowing
the presidential office to be occupied by a closely supervised minion.

During the rule of Gómez, Venezuela became a major oil producer, the annual production of a million barrels in 1920 becoming
150,000,000 by the time of his death. Oil changed Venezuela in ways
quite familiar to the observer of Latin American export booms. The
resulting prosperity had its greatest impact in expanding urban professional and service sectors and public employment. Meanwhile,
the economy's primary sector (especially agricultural production) declined in importance on all fronts except for petroleum production,
which absorbed relatively little of the available labor force. The rise of
oil production changed Venezuela enough to loosen the grip of aging
officers from the Andean region who had exercised power since the
days of Cipriano Castro, and the region's ascendancy in national politics ended amid an outburst of savage popular jubilation when Gómez
died in 1935.

We conclude our survey of neocolonial Latin America with a look at the countries that remained under firm oligarchical rule during this period: Brazil, Colombia, Paraguay, and Bolivia. In contrast to the Caribbean and Central American countries, where traditional oligarchies were significantly weakened (Cuba's, for example, almost disappeared), leading in most cases to long periods of military rule, the countries with stronger oligarchies in the early twentieth century were better able to maintain republican forms, though without coming any closer to democratic substance.

Brazil

Brazil's rural oligarchies, entrenched in the state governments of the republic formed in 1889, together determined the course of national politics until 1930. The Republican parties of the various states drew their power from local bosses called *coronéis*, often landowners and always representatives of the oligarchy, who herded their rustic clientele to the polls to elect the federal deputies who would then provide patronage from the federal government. The army, which had helped to install the oligarchic republic originally, retained a significant gravitation in politics, most notably during the terms of the first two presidents, Deodoro da Fonseca and Floriano Peixoto, both of whom were military men. However, the landowning oligarchy recovered direct power when Prudente de Morais, a coffee planter from São Paulo, became president in 1894, to be followed four years later by another Paulista oligarch and, four years later, by yet another. In 1906, a coalition representing other state oligarchies managed to install a president from outside São Paulo, this time from the state of Minas Gerais.

The election of 1910 was the first to be contested in a way that involved some elements of wider participation. The opposition candidate was Rui Barbosa, a Bahian who had taken a part in the overthrow of the monarchy only to be excluded from the inner circles of power shortly thereafter. The official candidate, another high-ranking army officer, was Hermes da Fonseca, nephew of the first military president. Despite the excitement generated by the opposition campaign, the government's electoral machine delivered the inexorable victory to the official candidate. After 1910 political tensions increased gradually with the repeated frustrations of opposition candidates at the oligarchical government's ability to control the outcome of elections. In the early 1920s, a new source of opposition arose. Junior military officers, collectively called *tenentes* because so many of them held the rank of lieutenant, rebelled against oligarchical domination. The rebellions were suppressed, but the participants—among them, Luís Carlos Prestes, the future leader of the Brazilian Communist party—

continued to play an important role in the military and in Brazilian politics for more than a decade.

In 1926 another Paulista, Washington Luís Pereira de Souza, became president in the usual manner, and he attempted to impose Julio Prestes, also from São Paulo, as his successor. The Paulistas' attempt to monopolize the presidency had, at this point, alienated their former partners in Minas Gerais. The result was a new opposition party called the Liberal Alliance, in which Minas Gerais joined with smaller northern and southern states to resist the dominance of São Paulo. The presidential candidate of the Liberal Alliance was Getúlio Vargas, governor of Rio Grande do Sul and right-hand man of Antônio Augusto Borges de Medeiros, veteran governor of the state and one of the most powerful electors of the oligarchical republic. When the Paulista won the election, the Liberal Alliance rebelled, and, after two weeks of half-hearted resistance, the military asked the president to step down and replaced him provisionally with Getúlio Vargas.

The revolution of 1930, like all the preceding power shifts of the oligarchical republic, had been caused by an internal rift among members of Brazil's political establishment rather than by a challenge from outside it, and nothing in the manner of Vargas's rise necessarily promised to widen the circle of political participation. Even at its zenith, however, Brazil's oligarchical republic, weakened by an excessive federalism that kept the central government in penury and by the negative consequences of the country's almost exclusive dependence on the exportation of coffee, had never enjoyed the relative solidity of that of Argentina and had arrived at the revolution of 1930 significantly weakened. Vargas was acute enough to realize the bankruptcy of the system he had inherited, and he guessed correctly at the new possibilities existing at his accession to power, but the road to change remained hedged by limitations. As long as Brazil's rural population remained under the sway of the landowning class, a widening of the suffrage would only augment the power of the rural oligarchy by increasing the number of votes under its control. With the onset of the international economic crisis in 1930, Vargas's challenge was to privilege those sectors disposed to find a solution to the impasse of the national economy, giving them more influence than they had wielded in the oligarchical republic but also more than they would have derived from the effective universal suffrage. Under these circumstances, the road to broad-based politics in Brazil would differ from the one traveled earlier in neighboring Argentina or Uruguay.

Of the Spanish American countries, Colombia displayed the greatest continuity of oligarchical solutions in this period, under the aegis of conservatism. The conservative ascendancy had begun in the 1880s, when president Rafael Núñez—a former radical liberal—launched the country's "Regeneration," and it endured for almost half a century despite the bloody and disruptive internal dispute known in Colombian history as the "War of a Thousand Days" (1899–1903), in which regional elites once again demonstrated their ability to mobilize mass followings in partisan disputes. That calamity, followed immediately by the U.S.-supported secession of the Colombian province of Panama, caused the elite some momentary doubts about the continued validity of the country's political traditions, so refined and at the same time so bellicose. Gen. Rafael Reyes, a conservative proponent of reconciliation between the country's two parties who became president in 1904, attempted to remodel Colombian politics along the lines of Porfirian Mexico. Reyes had the support of the liberal caudillo Rafael Uribe Uribe in his efforts to professionalize the army, an essential aspect of the Porfirian model, but he provoked the opposition of university students of both parties, who demonstrated against his efforts to retain the presidency in 1909. It was not the first time—nor the last—that Colombians of both parties came together to save their political institutions from the authoritarian temptations of the leadership. Reyes resigned, opening a twenty-year period of peace between conservatives (who retained firm control of the presidency) and liberals (who no longer suffered partisan harassment and were allowed to occupy positions of modest political influence). The predominance of a party that sought above all to be the political expression of Catholicism well suited the collective temper of the elite in this period of slow social and economic change.

The rate of socioeconomic change quickened during the 1920s. In 1921, a treaty with the United States healed the rupture opened between Colombia and the United States by the secession of Panama, and Colombian borrowers avidly entered New York financial markets formerly closed to them because of that dispute. Especially after 1926 under the presidency of Miguel Abadía Méndez, the government's fiscal policy stimulated economic expansion through an ambitious plan of public works supported by U.S. credits and investments, much as Peru and Chile were doing on a larger scale at the same time. This process of economic expansion was fueled by the advances of coffee exports in the international market, where Colombian coffee enjoyed the indirect benefits of Brazil's valorization program. The social impact, however, was ambiguous. Salaries rose, and the popular sectors were able to purchase more manufactured and imported products. At the same time, the demand for basic foodstuffs grew, and the supply became less certain because agricultural resources were being diverted increasingly into export production. Destabilization of living costs for the masses, coupled with the reservations of dissident conservatives about the excessive activism of their own administration, prepared the way for a political change with the onset of the international economic crisis.

As the 1930 election approached, the archbishop of Bogotá, who customarily had a decisive voice in the presidential succession, failed to prevent the emergence of two rival conservative candidates. Seeing an opportunity to escape their long political marginalization, the liberals nominated the Colombian ambassador to Washington, D.C., Enrique Olaya Herrera. Olaya's utter moderation attracted the support of several important conservatives, and his image as a candidate of national unity, above the petty partisan concerns, carried the election. The peaceful transfer of the presidency to a member of the Liberal party was hailed as a sign of the consolidation of Colombia's republican institutions, but it did not signal a broader distribution of political power. Although the liberals appeared increasingly sensitive to the aspirations of new social sectors, the Liberal party remained just as elite-dominated as the Conservative party. In 1930, Colombian national politics continued to center on alliances and rivalries among the upper-class groups that controlled various parts of a country still notable for its rural predominance, its regional fragmentation, the resulting multiplicity of its urban centers, and, above all, the extremely uneven manner in which its various regions were linked to the international market. These characteristics, which had gravitated so long and so powerfully in Colombian political history, were nevertheless fading slowly. The days of the oligarchical republic were numbered even in Colombia.

In Paraguay, rule by a landowning oligarchy had begun only after the country's defeat in the 1864–70 war against Brazil and Argentina. Postwar Paraguay's economy became more oriented toward the international market by the late nineteenth century, exporting hides to Europe and tobacco and yerba mate to the Río de la Plata. In addition, timber and tannic acid from the Chaco region of Paraguay were exported by British and Argentine companies with their own ports and fluvial transport system. The government had passed into the hands of high-ranking officers, war veterans who had learned to cooperate closely with their former adversaries, the Brazilians. The most important of these officers was Gen. Bernardino Caballero, founder of the Colorado party that governed Paraguay during the last third of the nineteenth century. The twentieth century saw the rebellion and triumph of the opposing Liberal party, but neither the Colorados nor the liberals could afford, when in power, to risk extending full political rights to the opposition. Each party was built on the patronage networks of its elite leadership, without a popular base beyond their respective clienteles. The liberals presented a cautiously modernizing and antimilitarist program, but the party's ascendancy owed more to its support in Argentina than to its appeal among the Paraguayan people. The liberals suspended political rights and imposed martial law just as frequently as had the Colorados before them.

Bolivia

Bolivia's oligarchical republic, perhaps the quintessential example of such a republic in this period, emerged in the wake of the neocolonial mining revival, within a few years after the end of the War of the Pacific in 1883. The Bolivian oligarchy of the late nineteenth century was headed by the owners of large silver-mining operations (made possible by loans and investments from the victorious Chileans) who proclaimed themselves conservatives. A transition to liberal rule had begun by the turn of the century as silver declined once more, to be replaced by tin as the country's most profitable export product. The owners of tin mines (like the wealthiest, Simón Patiño, a mestizo born in the mining zone) tended initially not to occupy the high government offices vacated by their silver-rich predecessors. Instead, those offices went first to the military leaders who had drawn on popular dissatisfaction to overthrow the conservatives in 1900. The liberal revolution received support from Indian communities besieged by assaults on their collective landholdings and from the city of La Paz, Bolivia's largest urban center, which chafed under its political subordination to the city of Sucre. Once in power, the liberal officers satisfied the aspirations of La Paz and crushed their former supporters in the Indian communities, becoming themselves the enthusiastic promoters and principal beneficiaries of the liquidation of community lands. Gradually, the military rulers were replaced by liberal businesspeople and landowners who shared their exclusive concern for the one-fifth of the Bolivian population who spoke Spanish and participated in the international market. The relative stability of Bolivia's oligarchical republic depended on the marginalization of most of its people.

Tin acquired increasing importance to the country's oligarchical project as the twentieth century advanced. The large Bolivian-controlled companies that dominated the extraction and exportation of tin became closely integrated with foreign financial institutions and were even able to control the refining operations based outside of Bolivia. Inside the country, the tin companies extended their power directly over tens of thousands of Indian miners who, for the time being, accepted it submissively. Docility to the interests of tin also characterized the urban elites who administered the country's republican institutions. For the time being, Bolivian politics escaped the frightening confrontations and military predominance typical of the mid-nineteenth century, but the veil of constitutional rule masked the realities of power only thinly. In few parts of Latin America was the tyranny of export production more complete.

If Venezuela seemed the model of military dictatorships in neocolonial Latin America, Bolivia provided the epitome of oligarchical republics; however, these were extreme, rather than typical, examples. Most regimes presented more complex political configurations that are less easily schematized. Whatever the contrasts between dictatorships and oligarchies, both were representative of major trends in this period of increasing influence from abroad. Export growth had led to a redistribution of political power under the paramount influence of outside forces whose chief concern was not the democratization of Latin American political life. Progressive incorporation into a global economy had also made Latin America more vulnerable to systemic crises originating outside the region. The greatest of these crises, the international financial collapse that began in 1929, irremediably weakened the neocolonial arrangement in the years ahead.

CHAPTER VI

Progress in

a Stormy World

(1930–1945)

THE WORLDWIDE CRISIS that erupted in 1929 had a rapid and devastating impact on Latin America. The clearest indication of it was the collapse, in most countries, of existing political arrangements. Although the intensity of the crisis made itself felt immediately, most Latin Americans did not then realize its long-term implications for the political and economic formulas that had characterized the mature neocolonial order. The return to normalcy was, in fact, not "just around the corner," and it would be necessary to find significantly new solutions to the unfamiliar problems of the years ahead.

At the time, the economic catastrophe of the 1930s seemed strictly the result of an accident that took place in the centers of international finance, but in retrospect one can identify signs of exhaustion appearing within Latin American primary-export economies themselves during the 1920s. In some cases, like that of sugar, a previously booming export business had lost virtually all its former vigor. Others had climbed to unprecedented levels of prosperity but had lost the steady upward trend of the past in ever more erratic oscillations—the case of Argentina's wheat, wool, and beef. Still other export products, like Chilean nitrates and Brazilian coffee, had come to depend on large state subsidies to maintain their viability.

Even as the export roots of Latin American economies weakened in the 1920s, new branches had been developing. Industrialization advanced significantly in the larger countries as export earnings and foreign borrowing stimulated internal demand and nascent industries began to attract outside capital. The resulting imbalance—a weakening export base coupled with an increasing tendency to expand beyond it—could not be maintained without steady investments and loans from the world's new financial headquarters on Wall Street. This flow of capital maintained a superficial well-being in countries like Cuba, Peru, Chile, and Brazil, whose economies had, in reality, been fatally undermined, and in healthier economies it led to patterns of consumption that could not be sustained with internal resources.

The economic crisis that began in 1929 radically redefined the context in which Latin American economies operated, as the volume of international trade contracted by half in three years. The disintegration of the international financial system cut off the flow of credits and investments that had kept more than one Latin American economy afloat during the previous decade. However, the unprecedented magnitude and breadth of the breakdown actually mitigated its ill effects in Latin America by spreading them internationally. The stigma of chronic indebtedness and the threat of insolvency became as common in Europe as in Latin America, with the result that the masters of international finance began to view such problems more sympathetically. Even had they not been inclined to be tolerant, Latin America's creditors were now less willing and less able to impose sanctions. The most obvious punishment for tardy repayment of loans, suspension of further credit, lost meaning after all hope of new loans had disappeared. In fact, the central industrialized economies needed Latin America more when the near-collapse of internal demand inspired a feverish search for external markets.

Latin American economies had problems enough without the pressing need to repay old debts. The disappearance of further foreign loans and investments quickly aggravated the financial imbalances created in the preceding decade, while dwindling export markets led to an even more ominous deterioration of the region's balance of trade. The volume of international trade was declining enough to place the very notion of a world market in question, and entire national economies could be dragged down by the collapse of their external markets. European countries tried to protect themselves by establishing bilateral reciprocal trade agreements. When the pound sterling became inconvertible in 1931, this pattern extended throughout its far-flung economic sphere. Only the United States was strong enough to continue to withstand the violent shifts of the international market, but it did so by adopting protectionist measures that accelerated the further contraction of world trade.

National states were now the only economic entities rugged enough to navigate in such high seas, but measures to palliate the disaster had to go well beyond state management of international trade, and Latin American states began to exercise functions and adopt techniques unimaginable only a few years before. The level of imports sustained even by fairly successful adaptation to the new context was only a small fraction of former levels. Rationing of scarce resources

was the only way to mitigate potential conflicts and maximize benefits to the national economy as a whole—by channeling importation
in such a way as to stimulate employment, for example. In order to
achieve this effect, Latin American governments varied monetary exchange rates for different products or even controlled outflows of
hard currency by granting or withholding permission for individual
transactions.

The drastically reduced level of importation occurred partly because of the general breakdown of international commerce but also because of a decisive shift in the terms of trade. Although prices declined
across the board, the drop was less for manufactures than for the
products of mining or, especially, agriculture. The crisis had brought a
spasmodic contraction of factory production, but the reduction of
mining production was slower, and some agricultural producers actually increased output in a desperate effort to counteract their declining
earnings. For countries that had specialized in the exportation of primary products, this change in the market erased the comparative
advantage that had made those exports attractive in the past, and it
invited a shift of resources to the manufacturing sector. The opportunity to substitute local manufactures for imported ones was not
immediately realized, however. The immediate effect of the crisis was
the collapse of the internal market for the consumer goods that could
no longer be imported. Without a revival of internal demand, there
could be no import-substitution industrialization.

Latin American governments turned first to the task of preventing
further overproduction in their primary-export sectors. This task inspired new patterns of state intervention in the economy as national
governments set prices, assigned maximum production levels, and
even arranged for surplus production to be destroyed (sometimes without prior indemnities for the producers). In the larger South American
countries, the new functions led to a further elaboration of bureaucratic structures, such as regulating bodies to coordinate the production of each major export commodity and central banks to handle
international commercial and monetary arrangements. Although the
smaller, more rudimentary states underwent less bureaucratic elaboration, they too exercised such functions when necessary. The mul-
tiplication of state functions signaled a total abandonment of the
laissez-faire principles that had guided neocolonial economic policy.
Awareness of the emergency was so widespread that, though bitter
controversy might erupt over the specific measures taken in the state's
exercise of its new functions, none disputed the expansion of state
power per se. Powerful economic interests within each Latin Ameri-

can country now accepted direct state regulation with equanimity and even admitted that impoverished national governments could no longer afford the kind of price supports that had been the preferred instruments of economic policy before the crisis. The reaction of Brazilian planters to the state's economic policies in the 1920s and 1930s will illustrate the point. In the 1920s, the coffee planters had taken advantage of state subsidies to continue overproducing, and their indignation knew no limits when the state ran out of money; in contrast, by the 1930s the planters accepted the need to limit production, and they showed themselves appropriately grateful for the government's efforts to place their coffee on the international market at prices once regarded as insulting.

The international economic crisis of the 1930s spread its effects evenly over all of Latin America at the outset (the significant exception being Venezuela, where oil production experienced only minor setbacks), but some countries—the larger ones—recovered much more quickly than others. Large countries like Mexico, Brazil, and Argentina (along with middle-sized ones like Peru, Colombia, and Chile) had internal markets of sufficient size to support industrialization, while smaller countries (like those of Central America) were simply unable to absorb the sustained production of local factories. The critical variable was the size of the market, not population alone. Thus, Uruguay's small population enjoyed an exceptionally high standard of living that constituted a sufficient market for nascent industries, while Ecuador's heavily indigenous population did not. After 1935, then, some Latin American countries not only recovered from the worst effects of the international crisis but also diversified their economic structures. The long-term results varied, but in 1937 the industrializing countries of Latin America constituted bright spots in the still generally dark world picture. Argentina, in particular, received the plaudits of John Maynard Keynes, who attributed the country's success to policies like those he espoused.

Latin America's import-substitution industrialization of the 1930s was inherently limited, however. Following a common pattern, it began with consumer products—processed food and beverages, textiles, and a few chemical and pharmaceutical products with modest technological requirements—and extended next to the light electrical industry, frequently employing the excess capacity of factories that had been established before 1929 with foreign credit or investment. Very rarely did domestic production supplant imports altogether, even in the mentioned light industries, and new industrial plants were constructed only slowly. The industrialized countries were more eager to provide light manufactures than capital goods (since exportation of the former would stimulate their own depressed industries and exportation of the latter would strengthen their competitors), and Latin American governments themselves placed a higher priority on rehabilitation of their export sectors than on industrialization. Over the course of the decade, the gradual recovery of traditional exports stimulated the recovery of the import trade as well and, therefore, undermined the push for import substitution.

Unfortunately, this process of partial industrialization further accentuated the regional inequalities that had appeared during the earlier period of export expansion. Industrial growth was most likely to occur in areas that brought together skilled workers, future managers, and potential consumers. Where did such a combination exist outside of the urban areas that had prospered at the nexus of national and international trade and that often had administrative importance as well? Consequently, the same parts of Latin American countries that had most benefited from neocolonial arrangements became the industrializing centers of the somewhat more self-contained national economies that emerged during the 1930s.

World War II introduced another radical change in the international context. Between September 1939 and December 1941, Latin American economies lost access to markets in continental Europe and East Asia and confronted a progressive contraction of the shipping available for their overseas commerce. This new challenge was destined to accelerate the expansion of state intervention in economic affairs that had begun as a result of the depression. The entry of the United States into the conflict solidified a new system of international trade administered from Washington, D.C., and London in the interest of the Allied war effort. The resulting arrangement included a tight rationing of maritime transport and strict control of trade in certain goods considered to be of strategic importance. The effect was to revive external demand for Latin American exports, but in a way that affected volume more than prices because of the rigid monopoly imposed by the Allies to avoid competitive pricing. Latin American imports, on the other hand, did not undergo a complementary revival. The scarcity of shipping and the reorientation of production to war materials in the industrialized countries left consumer demand increasingly unsatisfied. Those that barely produced supplies of food sufficient to feed their populations (and there were a number of these, from Mexico to Chile) suffered with particular intensity.

World War II also boosted the process of import-substitution industrialization more than had the economic crisis of the 1930s. The reactivation of export production augmented domestic employment and income (as well as accumulating monetary reserves in the form of payments held by the United States and Great Britain until after the war). The rise in buying power, coupled with the enforced limitation of imports, provided a powerful stimulus to local factories, which entered a period of dizzying growth that lasted for the duration of the war. The industries of the larger Latin American countries were able not only to dominate their domestic markets but also to initiate exportation of manufactured goods. Brazilian industrial production soon reached markets in Spanish America and Africa. Some countries organized their own merchant marine fleets using the vessels of Axis countries that had been caught in Latin American ports and requisitioned at the outbreak of the war. In peacetime, such fleets would not have been able to compete with those of the great maritime powers in volume, price, or quality of service, so that, here again, the special circumstances of the wartime environment aided Latin American economic development.

On the negative side, the industrial growth of the period only aggravated the problems that had accompanied the process in Latin America since its inception. The regional unevenness of the development became more marked with each successive advance of industrialization. The infrastructure necessary to sustain the expansion of manufacturing remained insufficient. Technical shortcomings in the industries themselves inevitably multiplied because of the difficulty in acquiring needed tools and machinery from suppliers at war. For the time being, the absence of competitive imports permitted Latin American manufacturers to disregard the higher cost that resulted from their sometimes primitive technology, but these weaknesses could no longer be ignored once the special conditions that fostered industrial growth during the war vanished.

At the end of the world conflict, then, virtually all of Latin America's national economies (except for a handful of the smallest) had fully recovered from the depression and grown in size and complexity, but they had also become more imbalanced than before. The imbalances could be detected without the need of subtle analysis by people who lived in cities that had suddenly outgrown their public services. Electric power had to be rationed ever more severely in Latin America after the city lights of Europe had been relit. Many of the new workers lived in sprawling shantytowns without electricity or running water, the most obvious outward sign of a process of industrialization that had outrun the concomitant process of urbanization. The high cost of housing and the scarcity of public services also affected the urban

middle classes that had thrived with the rapid industrial expansion of
the war years but now found it difficult to maintain their new standard
of living.

In 1945, it was generally recognized that Latin America had
reached a crossroads, that the accumulation of old and new problems
called for nothing less than a complete economic restructuring. The
moment seemed ripe for the region to escape the peripheral role that it
had played in the international economy during the colonial and neocolonial periods. Latin America had been spared the worst effects of
the crisis of the 1930s, and the subsequent rechanneling of resources
into industrialization had given an unprecedented direction to the
region's economic growth. For the first time in their history, Latin
American countries had become creditors, rather than debtors, to
Europe and the United States. Recalling the general prosperity that
had followed World War I, Latin Americans had high hopes for economic development in the years ahead. But this optimistic postwar
panorama was made more ambiguous by political factors, notably the
final breakdown and disappearance of the neocolonial order in international affairs and its replacement by a new constellation of forces.

The Eurocentric world to which Latin America had belonged since
before the time of independence had been altered by the clear ascendancy of the United States, victorious militarily and economically,
and by the wartime devastation of Europe. Given the magnitude of
these changes, the relationship between Latin America and the United
States was certain to be redefined. The redefinition had begun, admittedly, in the 1920s, when the world's financial center—temporarily
flush with investment capital—had moved from London to New York.
In general, however, U.S. hostility to bilateral trade agreements reduced the advantages that it might have reaped as potentially the
largest foreign market for Latin American producers during the decade
before 1929, while increasing U.S. protectionism after the onset of
the crisis provoked considerable resentment and further complicated
the reorientation of commercial relations in the hemisphere. Only the
stormy international scene of the late 1930s disposed the United
States and Latin America more favorably toward each other.

The better hemispheric relations institutionalized as the "Good
Neighbor Policy" by the administration of U.S. president Franklin
Roosevelt clearly responded to the international political stimulus of
the moment, but the roots of the policy reached back into the Hoover
administration, which had already contemplated renouncing a policy
of unilateral military intervention in Latin America. The result was a
renewed emphasis on strengthening and widening the functions of

Pan-American organizations to become the principal instruments of
U.S. policy in the hemisphere, without abandoning the leverage already gained through earlier applications of military force. Building
on experience gained in Cuba and the Philippines after the Spanish-
American War, the United States had equipped a number of the countries of the Caribbean basin with national guards that, in turn, often
installed stable, dictatorial regimes faithful to the interests of the
United States. Direct political pressure might still be applied in matters of sufficient importance—to assure the alignment of Latin American countries on the side of the United States in the coming conflict,
for example—but the renunciation of direct military intervention
clearly went beyond the dimension of rhetoric, as evidenced by the
fact that use of force was not seriously considered by the U.S. State
Department during the bitter dispute over the nationalization of Mexico's oil industry in the late 1930s.

The U.S. penchant for military intervention in Latin America had
long constituted the most obvious obstacle to the success of its Pan-
American initiatives, and the renunciation of force now combined
with the collapse of the international order centered on Europe to give
the hemispheric organization added luster in the eyes of Latin American public opinion. One aspect of that collapse was the withering of
the League of Nations, which many Latin Americans had viewed as a
preferable alternative to a Pan-Americanism dominated by the United
States. Instead, and despite lingering Latin American reservations, the
conflagration in Europe suggested the virtues of hemispheric solidarity, just as had occurred briefly during World War I. This attitude
was frequently shared even by Latin American leaders who found in
fascism the theoretical justification for their own dictatorial regimes
or the inspirational example of a certain kind of social change but who
desired nothing less than to join the dance of death that fascism was
about to unleash on the world. Despite their theoretical sympathies,
they offered their support to the creed of international peace that
Franklin Roosevelt promoted in the Pan-American conferences of the
1930s. The Spanish Civil War offered an object lesson in this regard. In
1939, after the victory in Spain of Gen. Francisco Franco with German
and Italian aid, an Argentine army officer reflected sadly on the devastation that the fighting had caused in Madrid. Although he was, at the
time, a fervent admirer of fascism, Maj. Juan Perón concluded that not
even the worthiest cause could justify such destruction.

The advantages of Pan-American cooperation thus outweighed
both a lingering mistrust of U.S. hegemonic pretensions and the attractions of right-wing political experiments. The last bastions of

[margin note:] U.S.-trained national guards who installed/maintain dictatorial regimes

[margin note:] Pan-American cooperation

early support for fascism gives way to Pan-Americanism

resistance to the hemispheric idea tended to occur instead in areas where connections with the former European metropolis—Great Britain—remained strongest, most notably in Argentina, which had resisted U.S. diplomatic hegemony since the first Pan-American Congress in 1889. Argentine reluctance to hew to the U.S. line thus responded more to its earlier international alignment than to the very real prestige of the Axis among Argentina's conservative politicians and army officers. By the 1930s, however, the inexorable decline of British influence led to the erosion of the antihegemonic line even in Argentina.

In the Pan-American Conference held in Montevideo in 1933, the Argentine initiative for a pact of mutual nonaggression and conciliation received the unexpected support of the U.S. secretary of state, Cordell Hull, who thereby managed to deflect hemispheric condemnation of his country's protectionist tariff legislation. The conference endorsed the idea of bilateral accords for the reciprocal liberalization of trade between the United States and individual Latin American countries. The main concern of the United States was forging a Pan-American organization capable of united action in the international political arena. U.S. initiative for a 1936 conference in Buenos Aires, including a visit by Roosevelt to the Argentine capital, led to a reaffirmation of the principle of nonintervention without accomplishing that larger goal. Nor was it fully accomplished two years later at another conference in Lima, where Argentina successfully blocked the U.S. proposal for the creation of a permanent inter-American advisory committee. The resulting Declaration of Lima instead recommended ongoing consultations among American states without making them obligatory.

At the outbreak of World War II, another Pan-American Conference (this one held in Panama) made a vast zone in the oceans of the Western Hemisphere off-limits to the wartime operations of the belligerent nations. The dubious legality of the declaration was matched in Latin America by an utter lack of will to implement it. Within three months of the declaration, the British and the Germans engaged in the major naval battle of Punta del Este within sight of the Uruguayan coast. Nevertheless, in Panama the Pan-American movement had adopted its first unanimous policy in the face of an international emergency and seemed on its way to becoming a league of neutral nations such as had existed, from time to time, in Europe.

L.A. not enforcing waters during WWII

Neutrality, of course, was not destined to last. As the Roosevelt administration moved toward entering the war against the Axis in 1940–41, it undertook the delicate task of bringing the Pan-American

movement along. At the Pan-American Conference of Havana, meeting in late 1940 under the shadow of German triumphs in Europe and
growing signs of U.S. support for an embattled Great Britain, the
representatives of most Latin American countries behaved with extreme caution, going no further than to announce their intentions to
act together to prevent the transfer among European powers of the
remaining colonial enclaves on the American continent. Their only
further concession to the U.S. agenda was an authorization for American states to act in emergency situations without previous recourse
to a time-consuming consultative process. The United States forged
ahead with its increasingly open involvement in the conflict without
further recourse to Pan-American mechanisms, leasing naval bases in
British possessions unilaterally and occupying Dutch Guayana jointly
with Brazil. Only in 1942, after it had formally joined the Allied cause,
did the U.S. government call another Pan-American Conference, this
time in Rio de Janeiro. There, because of Argentine and Chilean opposition to more drastic measures, the member nations limited themselves to recommending the severance of diplomatic relations with
Axis powers. Chile waited a year and Argentina waited two years
before doing so.

[handwritten margin note: L.A. cautious to enter war]

[handwritten margin note: only gradually severing diplomatic relations to Axis]

U.S. policy received more enthusiastic support in other parts of
Latin America, especially in Central America and the Caribbean,
where many nations issued declarations of war against the Axis as
early as November 1941. Mexico and Brazil entered the war in support
of the United States in May and August 1942, respectively. For Mexico, the war provided an opportunity to smooth over—without humiliating retractions—the rockiness that had characterized its relationship with the United States since Mexican nationalization of the oil
industry in the late 1930s. Brazil took advantage of the alliance to
increase its political and military power in Latin America. A few
months after the fall of France inspired Brazilian president Getúlio
Vargas to announce the obsolescence of liberal democracy, he joined a
chorus of Central American dictators in supporting the democratic
crusade led by the United States.

Brazilian enthusiasm for the war effort threw Argentine reticence
into sharper contrast. After much of Latin America had committed
itself to the war, the United States became less hesitant to make open
demands of the states that remained uncooperative. Argentina, ruled
by a military government after 1943, became the object of increasingly
severe pressures. In 1944, coupling the explicit threat of intervention
with denunciations of German infiltration in the Argentine consular
service, the U.S. government finally persuaded its reluctant ally to

break diplomatic relations with Germany and Japan. The reaction of
the Argentine army to this demonstration of weakness on the part of
its government led to an internal coup, provoking U.S.-imposed diplomatic quarantine. Argentina finally rejoined the hemispheric organization thanks to a Pan-American Conference in Mexico City that
encouraged the Argentine generals finally to declare war on Germany
in March 1945.

Argentina's return to the fold created formal unanimity for the
transformation that the Pan-American organization underwent in the
aftermath of the war. With the emergence of the United States as
the preeminent economic and military power in the postwar world, its
dominance among the American allies had become a foregone conclusion. Among the functions accorded the new regional organization was
the defense of the Western Hemisphere against any aggression originating outside it, but the attribution of this new responsibility was not
accompanied by the creation of mechanisms essential to the execution
of truly multilateral policies. Many of the participants in the Mexico
City conference probably failed to appreciate the implications of this
new initiative for the future of the Pan-American movement.

Latin America had escaped the worst effects of depression and war,
but the changes that had occurred outside the region would necessitate changes within it as well. In both economic and political terms,
the relationships established during the long century since independence now had to be redefined. An abiding faith in economic liberalism, among the most axiomatic principles of the defunct neocolonial
order, had been among the first casualties of the world crisis in a Latin
America attentive, as always, to the current wisdom of the more
advanced nations. The listlessness and drift of the international economy in the 1930s had been a persuasive inducement to skepticism,
and a return to liberal orthodoxy was not encouraged by the general
lack of postwar consensus regarding economic models.

The developed countries' slow and painful recovery from the economic collapse of the early 1930s included few laissez-faire success
stories to inspire Latin American imitators. Neither the spectacular
but fragile achievements of Hitler's Third Reich nor the slower and
more solid accomplishments of Roosevelt's New Deal suggested a
return to classical liberalism. The interest awakened by Soviet experiments with a command economy, even among circles resolutely opposed to the Russian Revolution, indicates how low the prestige of
liberal orthodoxy had fallen. Even those most committed to the capitalist system believed during the 1930s that radical restructuring
might be necessary to insure its survival.

Although it may seem excessive in retrospect, this disenchantment with liberal solutions, combined with the economic challenges
of the period, operated powerfully to provoke ideological ferment and
sharpen political conflicts. On the one hand, the economic crisis of the
1930s augmented the attractions of the revolutionary socialist vision
that had gained relatively few adherents in the previous decade; on the
other, it encouraged the propagation of other interventionist political
models, such as those associated with European fascism. As a result,
the period between 1930 and 1945—like the revolutionary and Napoleonic cycle of more than a century earlier—was characterized by
ideological conflict that complicated the contests of strength among
great powers. The European ideological consensus in which Latin
American elites had previously sought inspiration and guidance had
been replaced by cruelly confrontational polarities.

Latin America's political actors now acquired a much wider ideological repertory. Earlier innovations, such as late nineteenth-century
anarchism and early twentieth-century social democracy of Marxian
inspiration, had never acquired mass followings. Anarchism had nowhere become a really significant force. Social democracy had stalled
after early advances in Argentina and turned toward the revolutionary
Bolshevik model in Chile, whose Communist party—the most successful among those organized in Latin America during the 1920s—
still managed to occupy only a marginal place in that country's political spectrum. During the 1930s, in contrast, Communist parties were
organized throughout the hemisphere, taking a truly important political role in Brazil, Chile, and Cuba and becoming at least a force to be
reckoned with in a number of other countries from Argentina and
Uruguay to Colombia and Venezuela. The social disequilibrium created by the impact of the international economic crisis helped create
fertile conditions for these developments, as did the gradual sharpening of preexisting social conflicts. However, such internal tensions
could also have catastrophic consequences for nascent communist
movements. In El Salvador, for example, the early success of communist organizers in mobilizing peasant protest provoked a government
response (the Slaughter of 1932) drastic enough to nip the movement
in the bud. Overall, the greatest impulse to ideological pluralism
derived from the reigning insecurity concerning the future direction of
a world economically in ruins, since this circumstance gave socialist
models an appeal that reached well beyond their traditional working-
class constituencies.

Nowhere did Communist organizing have the political impact
achieved by more homegrown radical movements in Mexico (which

entered a second period of effervescence in the 1930s under the presidency of Lázaro Cárdenas) or, most notably, in Peru. Peru's Popular American Revolutionary Alliance (APRA) proved more successful than any other Latin American political movement of the time in presenting itself as an ideologically eclectic, revolutionary alternative to communism. APRA drew on the heritage of 1920s radicalism in which the movement's founder, Víctor Raúl Haya de la Torre, had participated first as a student agitator and then as an exile. Haya de la Torre envisioned a regime supported by the peasantry and working class united under the political tutelage of the middle class—an "anti-imperialist state" dedicated to redefining the unequal relationship between Latin America and its metropolis so as to create the conditions for capitalist development in Peru. These ideas became widely influential in Latin America after World War II. The influence of Aprismo often passes unnoticed, however, because APRA's terminology, coined in the interwar period, was not copied by postwar movements that adopted its outlook.

During the 1930s, the profoundly Latin American eclecticism so evident in the program of APRA also characterized ideological innovations on the right. Whether inspired by Catholic conservatism or European fascism, right-wing movements usually flowed more or less directly from preexisting currents, and only two new Latin American rightist movements fleetingly emerged as significant political forces during the period: Integralismo in Brazil and Sinarquismo in Mexico.

In sum, the ideological ferment of the period expressed itself as an exploration of multiple new perspectives. Direct opposition to the former political-ideological consensus was unlikely without any significant turnover in the composition of political elites. Political behavior changed a bit more than the personnel, but the greatest transformations occurred in the realm of ideological rationalizations and justifications of behavior. Far from clarifying the political expression of social conflicts, the world economic crisis produced increasingly tangled lines of ideological cleavage in Latin America, making the political impact of that crisis extremely difficult to analyze. Political actors themselves often seemed disoriented as they felt their way along with the aid of ideological guides in which they placed much less trust than formerly. Beyond the general failure of the political status quo, no single political pattern emerged, so political developments are most profitably examined within individual national contexts.

In Argentina, where substantial democratization had occurred during the heyday of the neocolonial order, the world economic crisis

of 1929 set the stage for the first successful military uprising since the
achievement of national unification in 1861. Seizing power in 1930,
the army briefly contemplated installing a corporativist regime of fascist inspiration before settling on the more oblique, and time-honored,
approach: a restoration of liberal institutions combined with electoral
fraud to neutralize the effects of universal suffrage. Under President
Agustín P. Justo (1932–38), a coalition of Conservatives, dissident Socialists, and anti-Yrigoyen Radicals pursued programs intended above
all to restore the health of the agricultural export economy and, secondarily, to foment industrialization. In the short term, the government attempted to palliate the effects of the economic crisis by promoting public works to provide employment. Many of these projects
involved infrastructural improvements, such as roads and grain eleva-
tors, that also augmented Argentina's economic competitiveness. Although handled with skill, the economic policies of this government
inevitably injured powerful interests. Among those that found little to
celebrate were livestock producers who believed that the interests of
their internal rivals—the fatteners—had been favored by the Roca-
Runciman Treaty, signed by representatives of Argentina and Great
Britain in 1933, which incorporated Argentina into the British trading
sphere.

The fiction of constitutional legitimacy became increasingly
transparent as time passed, and, though Justo exaggerated the danger
of an outright authoritarian takeover in order to keep the majority
opposition in line, such a takeover might well have occurred were it
not for the scant resistance encountered by his government during the
mid-1930s. Amid allegations of corruption, the Radicals in congress
and on the Buenos Aires city council lent their support to highly
controversial government contracting for transportation and other
public services. The increasingly moderate Socialists and the officially
proscribed Communists (whose activities were nevertheless tolerated)
concentrated their attention on the organized labor movement, which
had quickly revived after absorbing the double blows of economic
depression and government repression in the early 1930s. As the force
for political opposition lost fervor and vigor, the government cultivated the support of a Catholic traditionalist movement whose fascist
overtones intensified after the beginning of the Spanish Civil War in
1936.

In 1938, Justo passed the presidency to Roberto M. Ortiz, an anti-
Yrigoyen Radical, in hopes of placating the most powerful opposition
party, whose victory at the polls had been prevented the year before
only through an unprecedented orgy of electoral violence. Ortiz sur-

prised his predecessor and patron by going so far as to allow fair and open elections for the provincial government of Buenos Aires, leading to a transfer of that former stronghold of the regime into Radical hands. The democratic opening continued at the national level as the new government clarified its preference, within the context of formal neutrality, for the liberal democratic forces in the international conflict. The announcement of that preference met a cold reception among influential sectors of the conservative coalition, which still held substantial power and within which alarm over the president's penchant for electoral liberties was already widespread. The illness and death of President Ortiz soothed conservative anxieties by elevating to executive office the ultraconservative vice president, Ramón S. Castillo, whose commitment to the principle of controlled elections no one doubted. Indeed, Castillo's blatant authoritarianism and clear Axis sympathies were pronounced enough to produce unease within his own governing coalition. At that point, the U.S. declaration of war against Japan and Germany undermined the former Argentine consensus in favor of official neutrality in the war, and former president Justo came out strongly in favor of supporting the Allies. Until his death in 1943, Justo also seemed the leader most likely to orchestrate a return to open elections. The disappearance of General Justo's influence within the military allowed President Castillo to counteract prodemocratic currents until, in 1943, the increasing probability of an Allied victory dictated a prudent change of course in foreign policy. Castillo then designated a successor disposed to carry out the change.

The military leadership was less than thrilled by these plans, and its 1943 coup replaced Castillo instead with his minister of war, Gen. Pedro Pablo Ramírez. Ramírez could only watch with frustration as the fortunes of the Axis steadily declined and those of Argentina's great rival, Brazil, rose along with the Allied cause. Some within the government of Ramírez saw a reconciliation with the United States as the only way to counteract Brazilian ascendancy in South America, but their conditional overtures were rejected in Washington, D.C. This failure ultimately brought a confrontation with the United States that provoked, in turn, the final rupture of Argentine relations with Germany, leading to the fall of President Ramírez and to his replacement by Gen. Edelmiro J. Farrell in 1944. During the diplomatic isolation of that year, Argentina seemed to move internally toward a fascist-style dictatorship, but suddenly, in early 1945, Farrell prepared to call elections after declaring war on what remained of the Axis and negotiating Argentina's return to the Pan-American fold.

Behind the scenes, a group of neutralist army officers led by Col.

Juan Perón had taken an important role in the government of Farrell, and Perón's influence promised to continue after the return to constitutional rule thanks to the working-class support he had gained as secretary of welfare and labor during the war. Perón also hoped to dicker for the support of the existing political parties, but memories of his participation in the semifascist regime of only a few months before placed significant obstacles in the path of a smooth, negotiated transition. Perón faced further resistance from the foreign policy of the United States, aggressively expounded by the new U.S. ambassador Spruille Braden, who quickly became a leading spokesperson of the opposition after his arrival in Buenos Aires in 1945. On the eve of general elections (or possibly civil war), Argentina began to confront the thorny process of postwar political redefinition.

Uruguay's liberal-constitutional framework had collapsed in 1933, shortly after Argentina's, when the constitutional president, Gabriel Terra, put aside severe constitutional limitations and assumed dictatorial powers, alleging that the country's collective executive council lacked the efficiency demanded by the economic emergency. Terra's policies were particularly sensitive to the interests of the propertied class and received support from majority elements in Uruguay's Blanco party, as well as from various Colorado minority factions, his chief opponents being the political heirs of the great Colorado reformer, José Batlle y Ordóñez. In 1934, Terra imposed a new constitution with electoral laws designed to increase the leverage of his supporters within each party. During the second part of the decade, an improvement in economic conditions reinvigorated the opposition (still clearly in the majority among Uruguayan voters) and emboldened it to press for Terra's departure.

In 1938, Terra turned over the presidency to his brother-in-law, Gen. Alfredo Baldomir, whose unpopular government had to seek the support of the Batllistas as the international situation became ever stormier. The question of Uruguay's foreign policy during World War II was less difficult than Argentina's, since both parties were traditionally oriented toward one of the Allies (though the majority line within the Blanco party pushed strongly for Uruguayan neutrality in the conflict). The various factions of the Colorado party managed to unite behind a single candidate in 1942 and won a convincing victory in legislative elections, beginning the process of democratic restoration. The Batllismo that emerged from the authoritarian interlude had lost some of its reformist zeal, however, and it left intact the electoral laws instituted by Terra to dampen the volatility of the country's democracy. In spite of the country's increasing social diversity and strong labor movement, the stability of liberal constitutionalism in Uruguay was still based on the faithful support of the electorate for its traditional parties.

Chile and Peru, the reader will recall, had presented a markedly different political pattern in the early twentieth century. While Argentina and Uruguay had undergone a widening of political participation within a liberal-constitutional framework, Chile and Peru had broadened the narrow social base of oligarchical politics instead through the imposition of progressive dictatorships that sought support among formerly marginal elements of the population. Then the breakdown of the 1930s had swept away liberal constitutions and progressive dictators alike. In Chile, to which we turn first, the depression reached an intensity unparalleled among the major countries of Latin America, yet Chilean politics emerged from the crisis on a course of significant democratization within a constitutional framework. In Peru, on the other hand, the result was a long standoff between the forces of APRA, whose progress seemed impossible to detain in the context of free elections, and conservative forces equally determined to halt that progress.

Before 1930, Chile's export economy had been shored up by government subsidies paid for with foreign loans. The evaporation of international lending during the next decade brought a total collapse of this arrangement. Some export activities, nitrate extraction foremost among them, never recovered. Chilean currency lost value at a rate so vertiginous that the "easy money" policies introduced to stimulate the depressed economies of other countries became totally inapplicable. Without recourse to this measure to encourage recovery, the depression lingered unusually in Chile, and the prolonged hard times had particularly sharp consequences on political life.

In 1931, the overthrow of military president Carlos Ibáñez, who had pursued a popularly oriented policy of public works and maintained an authoritarian hold on the country in the waning boom years, led to a brief period of unity among the country's constitutional parties. When the new government showed itself incapable of taking the kind of measures called for by the national emergency, there followed another military takeover, this one led by a flamboyant self-styled socialist, Col. Marmaduke Grove. Chilean politics appeared to have become as agitated as the Chilean economy when Grove, too, was replaced within the year by Arturo Alessandri, who captured the presidency at the head of a center-right electoral coalition. Nevertheless, the election of 1932 also revealed the continuing appeal of Grove's brand of political radicalism among significant elements of the middle as well as the popular sectors. This current was institutionalized in 1933 by the formation of the Socialist party.

Alessandri adopted a rigidly conservative economic policy that did little to remedy Chile's economic woes. Meanwhile, the standard of living of the Chilean working class deteriorated in shocking contrast to the artificially high expectations formed under Ibáñez's populism. The natural result was a rising level of social and political confrontation that Alessandri, bent on dramatizing his new role as bulwark of order, did little to defuse. Widespread disenchantment with Alessandri allowed the Communist party to bring middle-class Radicals and working-class Socialists together behind a Popular Front candidate, Pedro Aguirre Cerda, a professor and landowner of moderate conservative views despite his leadership of the Radical right wing. The surprisingly enthusiastic response to Aguirre Cerda's presidential campaign transformed the candidate into a sincere and fervent defender of popular aspirations during his period in office, 1938–41, ending with his untimely death.

The fondness of Aguirre Cerda's memory has somewhat obscured the general failure of the Popular Front. In fact, the Popular Front never controlled the Chilean congress, and the participation of the right-leaning Radicals within it further limited its legislative effectiveness. A much greater impact of the Popular Front was its invigorating effect on the organized labor movement, but there again rivalry among various elements of the coalition undercut its effectiveness as Communists vied with Socialists to organize various sectors of the work force. The trouble grew worse after the German-Soviet Pact of August 1939, when the Communists muted their opposition to fascism, while the Socialists continued to regard antifascism as the chief source of solidarity among parties of the left. Nor did the labor organization drive associated with the Popular Front extend into the countryside, a circumstance indicative of the Popular Front's cautious approach to certain basic facts of Chilean life. The narrowness of the Popular Front's electoral victory made it impossible to challenge the dominance of large landowners in rural society, and thus Conservatives and Liberals were able to maintain in the countryside an electoral base sufficient to give them veto power over initiatives thought too audacious. The progressive coalition instead concentrated its attention on the urban middle class and the militant industrial working class. When the onset of World War II caused new economic problems and the devastating earthquake of 1939 placed further demands on the nation's limited resources, the Popular Front could hardly satisfy even its urban constituency.

Overall, in economic as in political matters, the Popular Front strengthened new players without displacing those already dominant. The country's industrial development in the period provides a case in point. The government created the Chilean Development Corporation (CORFO) to channel public credit preferentially into industrial enterprises, a policy that would be maintained by diverse governments down to 1973. The agricultural sector received little such credit, but it enjoyed the benefits of a domestic market protected by the devaluation of the Chilean currency. When unable to satisfy internal demand because of its technical backwardness, the agricultural sector required that the importation of competing products be strictly limited (a policy that could be rationalized also as a defense of the country's balance of trade). The efforts to maintain a balance between old and new were clearly explicable in terms of political limitations, but they blunted a more general and self-sustaining economic expansion.

The resulting modest industrial growth did little to bolster the fortunes of the Popular Front, which appeared to have exhausted its political possibilities by the time of the 1942 election called at the death of Aguirre Cerda. In that election, the country's traditional right supported another try for the presidency by Carlos Ibáñez, whose popularity had been restored by the hard times that had afflicted the country since the relative prosperity of his early administration. In foreign policy, Ibáñez stood for rigid neutrality vis-à-vis the belligerent powers then engaged in World War II. Opposing Ibáñez was the Radical candidate, Juan Antonio Ríos. Ríos also received the votes of the Communists (due to his support for the Allied cause, which now included the Soviet Union) and won the election. The Ríos victory seems to have been a cautious reaction by the Chilean electorate to the multiple uncertainties that another Ibáñez presidency would have implied. The essentially conservative Ríos government maintained good relations with the United States, and a welcome inflow of credit from the north gave new stimulus to Chilean industrialization.

At the death of Ríos in 1946, the presidency passed to a more conservative interim president. This change convinced the Communists to abandon the ruling coalition and rejoin the opposition parties of the left. The Socialists, on the other hand, accentuated their loyalty to the government in hopes that official favor would strengthen their hand against Communist rivals within the labor movement, which had continued to grow in political importance. After the turbulence of the years since 1920, the country seemed poised to enter the postwar period with a modestly enlarged cast of political players and a script emphasizing institutional continuity. In sum, Chilean politics re-

turned to the distinctive modus vivendi that permitted the incorporation of new social groups more slowly but less disruptively than
elsewhere—a national characteristic that even the most fervent revolutionaries were beginning to regard with patriotic pride.

Peru presented a far different picture. The Leguía dictatorship of
the 1920s had weakened the existing parties and ill-prepared the country's political system to incorporate large social groups formerly excluded from political participation. As these groups nevertheless demanded participation, two forces competed for their allegiance. The
first was APRA, the Popular American Revolutionary Alliance hastily
put together in the months following Leguía's fall and already mentioned here as an example of Latin American creativity in this period
of ideological ferment. The second was Col. Luis Miguel Sánchez
Cerro, a mestizo officer of humble origins who had led the uprising
against Leguía and whose great popularity offered Peru's traditional
political interests the only viable alternative to APRA. In the first important election of the 1930s, APRA emerged dominant in the northern region, the home of its principal leaders, but Sánchez Cerro combined elite and mass support in Lima. The southern highlands, where
political bosses maintained electoral control of the Indian masses,
tipped the balance in favor of Sánchez Cerro. APRA charged fraud and,
in 1932, began a revolt in the city of Trujillo, the center of its northern
stronghold. The revolt failed after capturing and executing a considerable number of officers from the local garrison. In vengeance, the army
slaughtered thousands of Apristas and issued an absolute veto against
APRA's participation in future governments.

Resolute military opposition to the proscribed but increasingly
popular APRA became a cardinal fact of Peruvian political life for
decades. The one barrier to APRA's ability to form an unquestionable
electoral majority, Sánchez Cerro, was assassinated by an Aprista sympathizer in 1933 and succeeded by another military president, Oscar
Raimundo Benavides. Although not allowed to participate in the presidential election of 1936, APRA threw its support to an independent
candidate. When that candidate won, the government annulled the
election, convinced that electoral democracy now necessarily imperiled the existing order. The terror of Peru's ruling groups had less to do
with APRA's specific proposals than with the awesome spectacle of
multitudinous Aprista demonstrations thunderously denouncing the
oligarchy. Highly visible individual acts of violence carried out against
individual members of the government further steeled the resolve of
the right. If there was something vaguely fascist about the Aprista
emphasis on disciplined obedience to the "Maximum Leader," the

government, too, renounced electoral politics as inherently dangerous and flirted with fascism, influenced by the international prominence of fascist regimes elsewhere and by the need for an antidote to APRA's "Indianist" ideology. While APRA found inspiration in the indigenous past, the right found it in the vanished glories of the Spanish empire. By the late 1930s, Peruvian political life thus centered on the direct confrontation between two implacably opposed forces.

The frozen civil war between APRA and its foes overshadowed the dictatorship's cautious reformism, which nevertheless had a gradual impact. Official efforts to broaden the country's labor legislation and provide more public works may have reflected sincere aspirations for social progress (in urban and coastal areas, at least) but were also undoubtedly aimed at undermining the appeal of APRA. Fixation on the Aprista threat encouraged the government to be more tolerant of the Communist party, a small and disciplined force that, despite making some modest headway in the southern highlands, seemed relatively much less menacing than the proscribed APRA. When presidential elections were held in 1939, the winner was a member of Peru's traditional "enlightened oligarchy," Manuel Prado, a prosperous banker. Prado's administration benefited from the stimulus of World War II on Peruvian mineral exports and industrialization.

In 1942, territorial gains in the short undeclared war against Ecuador added to Prado's prestige and created an unexpected climate of political consensus in the afterglow of victory. The Communists enthusiastically declared Prado to be "the Stalin of Peru," and even the Apristas seemed disposed to rebuild bridges. Both opposition parties were encouraged by the government's antifascist line in foreign policy and hoped that their concurrence on that point might confer internal legitimacy as well. As the end of the global conflict approached, the emerging postwar order seemed to require a process of democratization sensitive to changing social forces. In 1945, therefore, APRA formally reconstituted itself as the People's party and entered into a Democratic Front that managed to win the presidency for its candidate, José Luís Bustamante y Rivero, a jurist of moderate "social Christian" orientation. The results of the congressional elections showed that the Aprista People's party constituted the dominant force within the Democratic Front, giving that party decisive control of the Peruvian legislature. APRA's sudden triumph ended the brief era of good will, and the deep reservations harbored by the army and the traditional political leadership immediately resurfaced, auguring an untranquil future for Peru's democratic experiment in the postwar period.

In oligarchical republics like Ecuador of the 1920s, the impact of *Ecuador* depression and war in the period 1930–45 was no less than that experienced by the fragile democracies or progressive dictatorships already discussed. The coming of the global crisis hit the Ecuadorian economy especially hard. Cacao, the country's principal export, never recovered the modest prosperity of the years before 1929, nor would any other export product take its place until after World War II. Meanwhile, the collapse of the export economy failed to stimulate import-substitution industrialization in Ecuador because of the small size and weak integration of its national market. The new environment shifted the balance of power between the conservative oligarchy of the highlands and the coastal-based liberal oligarchy that dominated since the turn of the century.

The hard times of the 1930s rapidly eroded the liberals' political base as social conflicts sharpened in the export-oriented coastal zones. Communist organizers in the labor movement of Guayaquil had made significant headway since the end of the previous decade, and the city's growing lower class showed little inclination to rally behind the traditional liberal oligarchy in its confrontations with the conservatives. Instead, they turned to José María Velasco Ibarra, a leader of *Velasco Ibarra* Liberal extraction whose popular appeal enabled him to reach beyond the regional base of the coastal oligarchy and become the central figure of Ecuadorian political life for the next thirty years. Velasco Ibarra's willingness to give political expression to the country's social ferment catapulted him to power in 1930, but his eloquent denunciations of the status quo had made his followers attentive to national problems he could do little to remedy, and once in office he reacted to their insistent demands with authoritarian measures, only to discover that the army would not back him. This sequence of events, in which the popular leader was destined to play the protagonist more than once, concluded with Velasco Ibarra's removal by the military and the restoration of the liberal oligarchy in 1935. Defeat in the undeclared war with Peru had left the Ecuadorian military disenchanted with the government, which it accused of failing to provide adequate support for the war effort and of then accepting with undue equanimity a diplomatic confirmation of territorial losses. In 1944, the army declined to suppress an uprising led by dissident liberals, socialists, and communists and prepared itself to accept another attempt by Velasco Ibarra to overcome the oligarchical limits of Ecuadorian political life, encouraged by the democratizing climate of the postwar period.

In Colombia, where the liberal and conservative oligarchies had *Colombia* mobilized sizable popular followings for their nineteenth-century civil wars, that mode of conflict had fallen into disuse in the early twentieth century, and politics had become a more staid and rarified affair without mass participation. Before 1930, the liberals accepted a formal minority status that brought with it, in return for cooperation with the conservatives, access to a certain amount of political power. The coming of the depression then brought a split in conservative ranks and opened the way for a time of liberal ascendancy, confirmed by the election of Alfonso López Pumarejo in 1934. López Pumarejo, a successful banker and political organizer who had taken the initiative in challenging conservative hegemony, played on the circumstances of the depression to widen the liberal electoral base.

Presented to the public simultaneously as a vindication of traditional liberal principles, a shift to the left, and a Colombian version of Franklin Roosevelt's New Deal, the program of the López Pumarejo government set out to redraw the political map of the country to assure his party of future dominance. Burgeoning cities offered opportunities for liberal organizers to outflank rural party structures of patronage and clientele and build a new electoral majority by reaching out directly to the new urban masses. Both liberal and communist organizers promoted the urban labor movement with the approval of the president. Outside the cities, a rapidly growing population no longer found new agricultural lands available for settlement, and the liberal government announced measures that eased tensions in the countryside (and garnered further partisan advantage) while doing rather less than advertised to help the landless. Much to the irritation of the conservatives, the López Pumarejo government also managed to end the liberals' long feud with the Vatican by negotiating the separation of church and state in a manner highly favorable to ecclesiastical interests.

All this seemed too audacious to the traditional liberal leadership, alarmed over what it viewed as the dangerous growth of the party's left wing, led by Jorge Eliécer Gaitán, whose personal popularity and lack of party discipline it found particularly menacing. In 1938, Eduardo Santos, a liberal of the old school, was elected president, just as the economic circumstances that had favored the policies of López Pumarejo began to disappear. The immediate impact of World War II was to limit gains in urban standards of living and exacerbate social tensions. Liberals found it difficult to continue representing the political establishment while simultaneously mobilizing support in the lower and middle classes. The Liberal party retained sufficient unity to reelect López Pumarejo in 1942 under the banner of support for the Allied cause (toward which Colombian conservatives remained reticent or frankly hostile). The personal influence of López—manifest in large, supportive street demonstrations that helped him quell a military takeover in 1943—was not sufficient to prevent a split in the Liberal party during the electoral campaign of 1946, when the ever more popular Gaitán mounted a direct challenge to the traditional leadership.

The conservatives benefited from the division in their opponents' ranks just as the liberals had done in 1930 and recovered the presidency in the person of Mariano Ospina Pérez, a coffee grower of moderate views. However, the conservative victory in 1946 had narrower consequences than the liberal victory of 1930. Rather than broad opportunities to build political support, the conservatives faced a new and formidable challenge: a Liberal party rallying now behind its populist caudillo, Gaitán. The antioligarchical rhetoric of Gaitán threatened to make inroads even among the conservative masses. Thus, the Liberal party was to retain and consolidate its dominant position over the Conservative party as the oligarchical regime of the early twentieth century gave way to more broad-based politics. Despite the strains implied by this transition, few could foresee the tremendous upheaval that would convulse Colombia in the postwar period.

Brazil, with its vast and variegated social landscape, remained Latin America's largest oligarchical republic on the eve of depression and war, but the Brazilian status quo no longer had many committed supporters, even among those whom it had benefited for so long. The oligarchs themselves recognized that their narrow and loosely articulated political system could not deal with the difficult problems looming on the horizon. One of these, the decline of the Brazilian coffee export economy, had reached crisis proportions by 1927, and the economic crisis had close political parallels, since the state of São Paulo had been the center of both the coffee economy and the oligarchical republic since the turn of the century. The Revolution of 1930 was carried out by state oligarchies dissatisfied with the continued monopolization of power by São Paulo. Without ending the oligarchical republic in themselves, the events of 1930 opened the way for a restructuring of Brazilian political life.

The Liberal Alliance that came to power as a result of the revolution stood for a "purification" of the electoral system and the elimination of the pervasive rural clientelist structures so important to the oligarchical system, ideas that appealed to urban voters throughout Brazil. In this fashion, Brazilian reformers proposed broadening the social foundations of the state as the Radical party had done earlier in Argentina, but the step from theory to practice proved hazardous. The provisional president installed by the Liberal Alliance, Getúlio Vargas, seemed in no hurry to carry out the reforms, even after he had been invested with dictatorial powers. The prospects of effective electoral reform were, in fact, quite questionable as long as Brazilian society remained predominantly rural and the ties of economic dependence and social deference in the countryside remained strong. Nor did the revolutionaries of 1930 fully agree on the priority of this aspect of their program. Many (particularly the reformist military officers who had taken important places in the new regime) urged more audacious social and political transformations and believed that an emphasis on electoral representation would sidetrack fundamental changes.

The early Vargas regime thus displayed considerable ideological ambivalence, and its reformist impulses varied according to the orientation and vigor of its regional leadership. In São Paulo, the local representative of the regime precipitated a three-month civil war when the president's capricious authoritarianism alienated prospective urban supporters and his social reformism provoked the ire of the states' displaced oligarchs. The national army defeated the Paulista state militia, but the uprising finally convinced Vargas to call elections for a constituent assembly and begin the institutionalization of his regime. The resulting Constitution of 1934 gave the vote to women and created a number of seats to represent corporate groups in the Chamber of Deputies, but neither innovation really changed the dynamics of the representative system. As the more ambitious reformers had feared all along, the return to electoral politics only reinforced the national influence of rural areas dominated by conservative landowners.

Stymied by this impasse, Brazilians who dreamed of radical transformations and national integration fanned out across a political spectrum that reflected the diverse ideological currents of a world in crisis. Led by Luís Carlos Prestes, the most popular of the rebellious junior military officers who had attracted national attention in the 1920s, the Communist party became an important force for the first time in Brazilian politics. With the approval of the Third International, Prestes attempted to gather various forces on the left into an Alliance for National Liberation capable of carrying out an insurrection against Vargas. An uprising in 1935 was easily repressed, giving Vargas an excuse to impose a state of siege. Radical groups continued to organize on the right, however. The Integralist movement, launched by Plínio Salgado, a Paulista intellectual, attracted considerable support among the urban middle class. Though the Integralists proposed the Portuguese regime of Antônio de Oliveira Salazar as their explicit model, their tactics and rituals reflected a clearly fascist inspiration. Even the supporters of Vargas were divided by the ongoing process of political polarization. As the election of 1938 approached, the president could have little confidence in the future of his political project. Worse, the likely winners of the approaching election were left-leaning groups unpalatable to the army.

Vargas solved his dilemma by canceling the election and assuming dictatorial powers in November 1937. He imposed an Estado Novo, or New State, equipped with a centralist, and thoroughly authoritarian, constitution that he offered to submit to the electorate for its approval in a plebiscite. However, the promised plebiscite never took place. Instead, after suppressing an attempted Integralist putsch, Vargas eliminated all traces of partisan politics and introduced, for the first time in Latin America, mass propaganda and indoctrination of the style recently invented by European fascist states. Such tactics were not required to protect the regime from political enemies who, in reality, no longer posed a threat. Instead, they aimed to create a central state powerful enough to carry out integrating functions at which the oligarchical republic had so egregiously failed. This agenda attracted participants of various political hues. If the jurists and ideologues of the Estado Novo were overwhelmingly oriented to the right, its mid- and lower-level functionaries (recruited for the first time for their competence rather than their connections) included many sympathetic to the left.

The Estado Novo owed its stability, at least in part, to the renewed dynamism of the Brazilian economy and to the prevailing opinion, within the dominant class, that government action had been instrumental in bringing about the recovery. As throughout much of Latin America, the process of industrialization had gained momentum in Brazil after the mid-1930s, but the official measures most popular among the country's economic elites were those keeping open the foreign markets of Brazilian exports. Indeed, rather than a central initiative of the Estado Novo (as it is often portrayed), the promotion of industrialization may have been mostly an ad hoc response to particular economic conditions. The economic policies of the regime were accompanied by labor legislation, including the creation of government-controlled labor unions along the lines of those in Benito Mussolini's Italy. As with other innovations drawn from fascist models abroad, these labor policies seem to have been efforts to create a stabilizing framework for Brazilian society more than merely tactics to shore up the regime. Nor did social legislation lead to serious tensions between the Vargas regime and Brazilian industrialists. New labor regulations were not rigorously enforced and did not, at any rate, always conflict with the immediate needs of the industrialists themselves. Limits on the length of the work day, for example, were introduced at a moment when overproduction of textiles made such a measure convenient to owners and managers.

By joining the Allied camp fairly early in World War II, Vargas positioned Brazil to reap large economic benefits and, at the same time, put the Estado Novo on a path of planned obsolescence. Brazilian industries received greater wartime stimulus than did those of any Spanish American country. The strategic importance of Brazil convinced U.S. policymakers to subsidize the creation of a state-owned steel industry at Volta Redonda in the state of Rio de Janeiro despite their long-standing hostility to such enterprises. However, the fascist cut of certain elements of the Estado Novo put it painfully out of step with the international democratic crusade of which Brazil had become a putative part. Ever the flexible politician, Vargas announced plans to restore representative government at the end of the war. Immediately, the regime evinced an interest in building an electoral base. Beginning in 1942, the Ministry of Labor applied an unaccustomed zeal to its mediation of workers' grievances and to its enforcement of social legislation governing the workplace. As in Argentina, authoritarian rulers foresaw the need to prepare for a postwar order that promised to be quite different in spirit from that of the past decade, but no one really knew who would be the winners and who the losers in the resulting process of political reorganization. The past decade and a half had shown how rapidly politics and the state could change in Brazil.

The Mexican experience in the 1930s and 1940s presents a contrasting picture of continuity. After leaving office in 1928, Plutarco Elías Calles had continued his efforts at state consolidation as the real power behind several nominal presidencies. At the onset of the depression, Calles endorsed an official swing to the right, but the popular dissatisfaction with the economic results of this move brought an about-face by 1933. In response to the prevailing political winds, the "Supreme Chief" returned to a near-forgotten discourse on Mexico's socialist future and opened the way for the revolutionary party's left wing to assume leadership. His choice for president was Lázaro Cárdenas, a revolutionary veteran of the state of Michoacán, in whose personal loyalty Calles confided.

Although unopposed in the election, Cárdenas campaigned from one end of Mexico to the other in an effort to create an independent political following. Once in office, he cultivated alliances with regional caudillos who felt ill-served by Calles and even made discreet preparations to mend fences with the Catholic church. Cárdenas also worked to strengthen the left wing of the party and extend its influence, promoting the organization of unions closely connected with the state in a new federation of organized labor both broader in membership and more militant in its demands than its predecessor. Eventually, Calles decided that Cárdenas had gone too far, but when he began to protest openly against his wayward protégé he found that the reins of power had slipped from his fingers. In 1935, Cárdenas forced Calles out of Mexico and accelerated his program of political renovation. The next important step in that program was agrarian reform, a measure Cárdenas undertook partly to fulfill the promise of the revolution, partly to curb the influence of Vicente Lombardo Toledano, the powerful leader of organized labor. As a result of the distribution of twenty million hectares of land, community landholdings called *ejidos* (the Spanish term for village commons) replaced large privately owned haciendas as the dominant mode of land tenure in central and southern Mexico. Because the agrarian reform affected lands owned by foreigners as well as Mexican nationals, it created new tensions in the country's foreign relations.

By the late 1930s, these tensions came to a head in the conflict over oil. A labor dispute provided the spark that ignited the blaze when state support for the workers' grievances led foreign companies to suspend operations in protest. The Cárdenas administration moved boldly to requisition and then to nationalize the oil wells, provoking a rupture of diplomatic relations with Great Britain. The measure was received with a display of patriotic solidarity not seen in Mexico for decades, as the government's nationalization ceremony was announced throughout the country to the peal of church bells. An international boycott organized by the offended parties closed Mexican petroleum out of its habitual markets, and though Germany and Japan offered partial alternatives, the Mexican economy inevitably suffered.

Straitened circumstances precipitated an end to the Mexican Revolution's second wave of social reform, already slowing because of some of its own consequences. Although not as disruptive as some had predicted, the redistribution of land had increased the consumption of agricultural products in the countryside and therefore raised their prices in urban areas. This rise in prices joined a number of other inflationary pressures stemming from ambitious government programs— the upward movement of wages owing to unionization, for example, or the easy credit supplied by the state to promote industrialization and expand ejido production. Unionized workers and ejido dwellers were insulated against the inflation of the late 1930s, and industrialists actually benefited, but workers without unions and peasants without ejidos suffered, as did middle sectors generally. The impact of socioeconomic reform thus became an obstacle to the process of national unification that Cárdenas had aspired to promote.

The ideological radicalization of the Cárdenas years became another divisive influence. With the approach of another presidential election, groups alienated by the government's reformism flocked around the lackluster opposition candidacy of Gen. Juan Andreu Almazán. Sinarquismo, a Catholic movement with millenarian overtones, mounted a different challenge in rural areas. In the face of rising opposition, Cárdenas was forced to concede the failure of his efforts to rally national unity around a radicalized revolutionary creed. It seemed clear, in fact, that an official successor identified with that creed would be unlikely to win either a majority vote or the military backing necessary to insure an orderly transfer of power. Given his limited options, Cárdenas chose to nominate his minister of war, Gen. Manuel Ávila Camacho, a colorless candidate acceptable both to his recently reorganized Party of the Mexican Revolution and to the military and business interests whose defection the president had reason to fear. At the time, the revolutionary party remained under the control of leftist leaders who accepted the Ávila Camacho candidacy as a necessary hiatus in reform. Little did they imagine that his presidency, beginning in 1940, would mark a definitive change of course for Mexico.

The transfer of power from Cárdenas to Ávila Camacho ended the social and political momentum of the Mexican Revolution for at least half a century. Although the wartime scarcities of the early 1940s eroded the gains in the standard of living won by popular sectors in the previous decade, the spirit of antifascist solidarity prevented the left from pressing its case against a Mexican government aligned with the Allied cause. Perhaps the leaders of the popular organizations that had grown rapidly under the official aegis of the Cárdenas government now had doubts, too, about their ability to mobilize their memberships against the regime. The agrarian reform of the 1930s had a similarly unexpected denouement. The ejidos that now produced much of Mexico's food had no overarching organization independent of the state, and, by holding down the prices of agricultural products, the state used its control of peasant organizations effectively to subsidize industrial and urban growth. This tactic, adopted ostensibly to confront wartime exigencies, became a permanent feature of the Mexican economy, one that deprived ejido dwellers of the ability to save and reinvest profits, leading to a situation that one acute observer on the

Mexican left later called "permanent primitive accumulation" of industrial capital at the expense of the peasantry.

In this way, the Ávila Camacho government used Cardenista organizational structures to promote economic growth and diversification and to redistribute income away from the popular sectors whom the organizations had been designed originally to favor. Other Latin American regimes sought to defuse the destabilizing consequences of a similar process of redistribution in the early 1940s by repressing political mobilization. At the end of World War II, the international trend toward democratic opening spelled trouble for such regimes. The Mexican solution, on the other hand, had preserved—even augmented—the outward forms of popular mobilization, while draining away their spirit. As a result, Mexico did not face the political crisis threatening so much of Latin America in the postwar period. Once again, the interplay of continuities and transformations in the process set in motion by the 1910 revolution imparted to Mexican history a pattern of development without parallels in the rest of the hemisphere.

Central America and the Caribbean present economic and political patterns different from those of the larger and more developed countries in the years leading up to and including World War II. Because of their tiny national markets, the crisis of export production in these countries found no mitigating echo (except in Guatemala, and there only slightly) in a process of import-substitution industrialization. The hardships of depression and war therefore sharpened social conflict throughout the region, pushing the existing oligarchical systems in the direction of open dictatorship.

The case of El Salvador illustrates this pattern with starkest clarity. In late 1931, Col. Maximiliano Hernández Martínez overthrew a reformist president who had emerged surprisingly from within the oligarchy itself. When peasants revolted against the military government the following year, the army repressed them with killings so numerous that these events subsequently became known as the Slaughter of 1932. Thereafter, Hernández Martínez was able to govern a stunned country for a decade without further overt opposition, but during these years, the gradual revival of the export economy and the expansion of the coffee plantations exerted increasing pressure on the rural poor. As the end of World War II approached, threatening to undermine dictatorships all over the hemisphere, massive urban protests and a withdrawal of military support convinced Hernández Martínez to relinquish power in 1944.

Guatemala and Honduras present minor variations on the same theme. In the early 1930s, Guatemala returned to dictatorial rule after

[margin annotations: El Salvador coup; slaughter of reformist uprising; 10 yrs. unquestioned rule until 1944; Guatemala]

an oligarchical interlude of no more than a decade. Gen. Jorge Ubico, the new strongman, imposed his rule on a country brimming with potential social conflict. Guatemalan society had become more complex as cities grew and increasing numbers of Indian people adopted Spanish and defined themselves as *ladinos*. Both oligarchy and dictatorship had become more difficult in a country with substantial urbanized lower and middle classes. Nevertheless, Ubico maintained his control, partly by playing these social groups against each other until 1944, when the imminence of an Allied victory undercut his dictatorship as occurred with Hernández Martínez in El Salvador. In Honduras, Tiburcio Carías Andino, whose political capital had been inherited from the country's traditional Conservative party, took dictatorial powers in 1932. The relative abundance of land in relation to the Honduran population attenuated the pressures that the export economy placed on the rural populations of El Salvador and Guatemala, allowing Carías to hold onto power until 1948, slightly longer than his authoritarian neighbors.

Always the exception, Costa Rica did not succumb to dictatorship, but neither did it quickly shake off oligarchical control despite its high rate of literacy and more equitable social structure. Still, the country's enlightened patriarchs saw their dominance challenged in these years by the emergence of minority parties representing the coffee growers and popular sectors. Although neither of these opposition forces represented a real threat, they combined with the effects of the economic crisis and the heightened ideological tone of international affairs to convince Costa Rica's traditional elite to redefine their political identity. Their National Republican party, founded in the mid-1930s, was seemingly inspired by the example of the European right. However, in yet another example of the protean ideological transformations of these years, the National Republicans turned social reformist after 1940 and laid the foundations of the Costa Rican welfare state. They were aided in these efforts by the Communist party, based principally among the West Indians who had come to Costa Rica's Caribbean coast to work on the banana plantations of the United Fruit Company. Contrary to what had occurred in El Salvador, Guatemala, and Honduras, the revival of export growth during the war years had allowed Costa Rica to take considerable strides toward broadening the social base of its political life. The advent of the postwar era therefore did not bring with it the sort of regime change that characterized the juncture in so many Latin American countries.

As for Nicaragua, the importance of long-term U.S. intervention there overshadows all other influences in the period. By 1928, the

United States sought to extricate itself from Nicaraguan involvement without losing its ascendancy in the country, but U.S. policymakers were frustrated by the armed opposition of Augusto César Sandino. Sandino's forces fought under the banner of the traditional Liberal party, but they evoked nationalist themes reminiscent of the Mexican Revolution. The election of a liberal president in 1933 led to a withdrawal of U.S. Marines from Nicaragua and an end to Sandino's guerrilla war. Convinced that the new government did not represent a continuation of U.S. dominance, Sandino underestimated the degree to which the Nicaraguan National Guard—organized to support the occupation forces—constituted exactly that. In 1934, Anastasio Somoza, the commander of the national guard, had Sandino murdered and thus cleared the way for his own consolidation of power.

Somoza governed Nicaragua, personally or through a proxy, for the rest of his life, and control of the country subsequently passed to other members of his family. Never popular among his compatriots, Somoza retained power thanks to his devotion to U.S. foreign policy and his protection of the U.S. economic interests that found new opportunities in Nicaragua after so many years of internal strife. Somoza promoted some public works (mostly highway construction) and export growth (limited, until after World War II, to a modest expansion of coffee). Not born into Nicaragua's ruling class, the newly rich Somoza allied himself with the country's Liberal elite through marriage and economic patronage, and he manipulated elections so as to make his regime appear constitutional while carefully reserving real power for his political allies (increasingly synonymous with his business associates). In this manner, a regime with very shallow roots in Nicaraguan society successfully coopted one of the country's traditional political parties.

The case of the Dominican Republic shows strong parallels to developments in Somoza's Nicaragua. U.S. Marines had been withdrawn from the Dominican Republic in 1924, and the national guard organized by the occupying power had inherited control of the island nation from the withdrawing U.S. troops exactly as in Nicaragua several years later. The commander of the Dominican National Guard, Rafael Leónidas Trujillo, assumed direct political control in a 1930 coup. Rather than Nicaraguan-style competition between two well-established parties, the Dominican Republic had a history of political disorganization punctuated by the rule of strong personalist leaders. In some ways, Trujillo's rule repeated the modernizing despotism of the late nineteenth-century caudillo Ulises Heureaux, but with greater success. Trujillo made the official party and the state itself little more than expressions of his personal cult, renaming the country's capital city after himself and its second largest city after his mother. The dictator's totalitarian ambitions were unadorned by any particular ideology and included attempts to attract immigrants among Jews fleeing repression in Hitler's Germany as well as among republican refugees from Franco's Spain.

no ideological alignment

The Dominican Republic underwent a rapid economic transformation under Trujillo. After more than a century of political turmoil and economic stagnation, the country was finally incorporated into the Caribbean sugar boom, as large U.S. companies (and others controlled directly by Trujillo) initiated large-scale operations. Because of the lucrative opportunities presented by sugar, U.S. capital played a larger role here than in Nicaragua, and Dominican landowners had to share more of the fruits of dictatorship with their overweening senior partners than did their Nicaraguan counterparts. For its part, the government constructed basic transportation infrastructure and increased its spending on public health and education, providing further conduits for Trujillo's influence over Dominican society. Dominican economic expansion and its concomitants began to attract impoverished Haitians from the other side of the island by the mid-1930s, and Trujillo's slaughter of thousands of them in 1937 revealed the latent brutality that undergirded his regime.

slaughter of Haitians

Cuba, the largest nation of the Antilles, exhibited a more complex pattern of political development during the period. In 1933, the dictator Gerardo Machado had governed for almost a decade when widespread dissent within Cuba (protagonized especially by university students), a general strike, and outside pressure from the United States combined to topple him. At the exit of Machado, power devolved into the hands of a group led by university professor Ramón Grau San Martín, in whom the students of the University of Havana saw personified the conscience of the nation. The ascendancy of Grau San Martín was confirmed by the support of low-ranking army officers, led by Sgt. Fulgencio Batista, who seized control of the armed forces from the existing military hierarchy. Upper-class Cubans watched uneasily as the new regime began to take on revolutionary overtones, denouncing the inequalities of their country's relationship with the United States and announcing plans for radical social reforms. Alarmed, Franklin Roosevelt's personal envoy, Sumner Welles, recommended that the United States not recognize the new government and also threatened the closure of U.S. markets to Cuban sugar. In the face of U.S. hostility, Cuba's new military leaders themselves deposed Grau San Martín, found civilian figureheads less menacing to the status quo, and conse-

Cuba

quently won U.S. approval. Their leader Batista was to remain arbiter of Cuban politics for a generation, but his regime would eventually be undermined by its original sin, the overthrow of a government that, however briefly in 1933 and 1934, had seemed to incarnate perennial Cuban hopes for political redemption.

Batista's early years as the power behind the throne resulted in a mixed record. After an initial period of repression, strongly seconded by his allies in the traditional ruling class, Batista attempted to create for himself an independent political base through social programs administered by the army. Most of these concentrated on rural areas, and in many ways they anticipated the military "civic action" efforts launched throughout the hemisphere in the 1960s. Perceiving that the costs of this approach outweighed the political returns, however, Batista shifted his emphasis after 1937 (in a supposed alignment with the New Deal) to officially support the Communist party's unionization drives in urban, as well as rural, areas. The government's new line, exemplified in its open sympathy for the republican cause during the Spanish Civil War, culminated in the convocation of a constituent assembly controlled by Grau San Martín's Authentic Revolutionary party. Political democracy and social reform were the national goals set by the resulting Constitution of 1940, and Batista chose the moment of its promulgation to make himself titular head of state for the first time, with the backing of both the Communist party and the country's traditional parties (reduced, by this time, to mere shadows of their former selves).

Batista's durability depended, in part, on his ability to gain political advantage in rural areas from the new sugar importation policy of the United States, which replaced the older system of protective tariffs with a set of import quotas. Under the former system, Cuban exporters had steadily reduced their prices in order to remain competitive in the North American market, whereas the new arrangement assured them a fixed volume of sugar exports to the United States. Cuba's sugar industry thereby acquired an assured market, but one without prospects for future growth. As a result, U.S. investors rapidly lost interest in Cuban sugar production, and control of both cane-growing lands and sugar mills reverted increasingly to local ownership. Batista was able to direct this transformation so as to benefit and win the support of both the unionized cane cutters and mill workers and the farmers who (operating on vastly varying scales) supplied cane to the mills. After 1941, however, urban dwellers became restive as U.S. industrial production devoted its energies to the war effort. Reciprocal trade agreements, though the salvation of Cuban sugar, prevented the introduction of industrial production to develop the urban economy. Tourism (and other, subsequently notorious, service activities associated with it) did not become a major source of dollars until the postwar period. As urban standards of living declined, Batista lost popularity where it counted most politically. At the end of his presidential term in 1944, Batista had not succeeded in neutralizing the opposition, still led by Grau San Martín, and as the end of World War II approached, intense pressure from the United States finally obliged him to accept Grau San Martín's victory in the next election. As in so many other Latin American countries, the end of the global crisis marked, or seemed to mark, a clear political break.

The postwar watershed also affected other countries—such as Venezuela—whose atypical characteristics group them at the conclusion of our survey of the years 1930–45. Venezuela weathered the economic crisis of the 1930s on the uninterrupted wave of oil wealth that had accompanied, for over twenty-five years, the dictatorship of Juan Vicente Gómez. Gone were the local and regional caudillos whose uprisings periodically threatened the stability of the national state in the nineteenth century, but a new sort of dissidence had begun to express itself, most notably in the student protest of 1929. At the dictator's death six years later, his heirs tried to channel the spirit of ferment. They continued to use fraud and manipulation to determine electoral results but also gradually allowed more freedom of speech. The Communist party, savagely repressed by Gómez, began a successful campaign of union organizing with first the implicit, and then the explicit, approval of the government. More threatening to the government was the formation by dissident communists of another party, Democratic Action. In 1945, when it became evident that the military hierarchy created by Gómez decades ago had no intention of letting the presidency slip beyond its control, younger officers sympathetic to the opposition executed a successful coup, leaving power in the hands of a mixed junta of officers and civilians. The junta was led by the head of Democratic Action, Rómulo Betancourt, whom the young officers expected to replace the old military hierarchy and allow them to help supervise the process of modernization in the closely controlled manner typical of past generations of Venezuelan rulers. They were sorely mistaken. Instead, Betancourt embarked on the most ambitious of all Latin America's projects of democratic mobilization in the postwar years.

The history of Bolivia and Paraguay in the 1930–45 period was shaped, above all, by their experience in the Chaco War. The war began in 1932, when the Bolivian government decided to resolve the repeated

skirmishes taking place since 1928 along its disputed border with
Paraguay. An easy victory, hoped the Bolivians, would assure them not
only substantial territorial gains in the tropical plains of the Chaco but
also an outlet to the Atlantic through the international waterways of
the Río de la Plata system. The Paraguayans dealt Bolivian aspirations
a cruel disappointment, however, winning a string of victories that
brought them, in three years of fighting, to the eastern foothills of the
Andes. Protracted peace negotiations, begun in 1935, made permanent
a portion of the Paraguayan advances, leaving Bolivia much the worse
for its wartime adventure.

Bolivia loses territory

Within Paraguay, the chief outcome of the war was to strengthen
the political influence of the military. When it became evident that
the peace negotiations were not going to confirm all of the territorial
gains won during the war, a group of indignant junior officers overthrew the reigning liberal government and installed one of their own,
Col. Rafael Franco, in the presidency. The sources of inspiration of the
new regime, ranging from fascist Germany to the Soviet Union, be-
spoke the ideological eclecticism of Latin America in the 1930s, all in
the name of somehow accelerating Paraguay's lethargic march toward
socioeconomic progress. This regime proved short-lived when it failed
to win at the peace negotiations a result any more favorable to Paraguayan claims. In 1937, the Liberal party returned to power in the
person of the extremely popular war leader, Gen. José Félix Estigar-
ribia. The liberal restoration did not turn back the clock completely,
however. The Constitution of 1940 contained clear echoes of the
social concerns of the brief Franco government of a few years before. It
also created a corporativist Council of State and encouraged military,
rather than liberal-oligarchical, dominance in the country. At Esti-
garribia's death, his successor, Gen. Higinio Morínigo, further advanced military control by allying himself with the opposition Colorado party, whose leaders had been out of power for decades and had
more modest aspirations than their Liberal counterparts. The Colorados were willing to supply civilian personnel to legitimate what
remained essentially a military dictatorship, despite the foreseeably
limited prospects of such an arrangement in the international climate
of postwar democratization.

Paraguay military strengthened

Bolivia felt a sharper political impact from the war, and not merely
because it suffered defeat in the fighting. When Bolivian president
Daniel Salamanca had initiated the conflict, he had been hoping to
divert attention from the country's hopelessly deadlocked internal
politics and economic problems. The crisis of 1929 had revealed the
severe deterioration of Bolivia's position in the international tin mar-

ket, which had become marginal at best. As the depression reduced both prices and demand, the country's smaller tin producers failed, and the larger ones (particularly Simón Patiño, who also owned mines and processing plants abroad) insured their own survival by squeezing the salaries of their employees and generally reducing their contributions to the Bolivian state and economy. The oligarchical order built around the tin-mining industry was thus imperiled even before its wartime defeat, which further discredited the country's rulers in the eyes of the middle-class youths who served as junior officers in the expanded army.

A military takeover in 1936 raised the banner of "military socialism," initiating a feverish debate over socioeconomic reforms that, as in Paraguay, ran the gamut of ideological possibilities, and had its most tangible outcome in the nationalization of Bolivia's oil wells. The measure had been proposed by Gen. David Toro, a versatile veteran of Bolivian politics, who used it to legitimate his bid for revolutionary leadership, but Toro was soon replaced as president by Col. Germán Busch, a more authentic representative of the generation of officers who had come of age during the Chaco War. In 1938, the military government convoked a constitutional convention in which forces of the left far outweighed traditional political elements, but the resulting document was less innovative than suggested by the radical rhetoric of the convention. Through literacy requirements, it limited the electorate to the country's small, Hispanicized upper and middle classes. It addressed the social themes obligatory in twentieth-century constitutions, but without adapting them effectively to Bolivian conditions. President Busch rapidly lost interest in the reformist experiment and began to oscillate between progressive measures (like the promulgation of a labor law) and regressive ones—at one point suspending the new constitution. His suicide in 1939 opened the way for a comeback by traditionalist forces within the military, led by Gen. Enrique Peñaranda.

Up to that point, Bolivian events seemed to parallel what had occurred in Paraguay during these years, but the defeat and the economic crisis had weakened Bolivia's traditional leadership too much for it to reassert its control for long. In addition, Bolivia had a much more vigorous radical working-class movement. The Revolutionary Leftist Front, the electoral expression of the Communist party, got nearly 20 percent of the vote in the election won by Peñaranda, and the (Trotskyite) Revolutionary Workers' party exercised considerable influence in tin-mining areas. Finally, the National Revolutionary Movement (MNR) brought together an eclectic collection of radical

impulses from across the political spectrum. Thanks to the professional prestige and journalistic talent of its leadership, the MNR enjoyed wide (if diffuse) support in the middle class; on the other hand, it
lacked the communists' devoted core of party militants. World War II
brought hard times to the Bolivian economy, and the opposition accused the Peñaranda administration of making matters worse by refusing to impose monopoly pricing on Bolivian tin after Japanese conquests in Asia made the South American producer the Allies' only
source of the metal. The continued low price of tin led to intensified
exploitation of the miners and then to a tin strike, to which the regime
responded with violence in the 1942 massacre of Catavi. The next
year, the opposition responded with a military takeover and installed a
government including cabinet ministers from the MNR.

The new military regime had little chance of success. It supported
the organization of the Revolutionary Workers' party in the tin mines,
but the leaders of the armed forces refused to accept the communist
participation that would have improved their reputation with officials
in the United States who suspected them of sympathizing with Nazi
Germany. Instead, Bolivia's new military rulers had to demonstrate
their friendliness to the Allied cause by maintaining the low tin prices
of the previous government, a tactic that deprived them of the where-
withal to carry out their reform initiatives. Their hands were further
tied by the rigid anti-inflationary measures adopted by their finance
minister (and head of the MNR), Víctor Paz Estenssoro. Such straitened circumstances reduced the new government's revolutionary aspirations to symbolic gestures that revealed their insufficiency when the
(Communist) Party of the Revolutionary Left made an unexpectedly
strong showing in the elections for another constituent assembly. The
armed forces, which had already purged the cabinet of MNR members
at the insistence of the United States, countered the Communist gains
by ordering the assassination of several excessively popular organizers
and by persecuting their followers. These draconian methods combined with the deteriorating economic situation to make the military
government even less attractive to the country at large. Resistance
from traditional forces led, in turn, to a mass execution of some of the
best-known oligarchical leaders. The result was an alliance between
the oligarchy and the left, culminating, in July 1946, in a major strike
and a riot in La Paz, where the military president Gualberto Villarroel
died at the hands of the enraged populace. The MNR and the union
leadership associated with the fallen government had to accept the
stigma of defeat, while the victorious Communists prepared to direct
Bolivia's revolutionary impulses in the postwar period.

In all of Latin America, ruling groups, opposition parties, and emergent political forces expected to see the advent of a new era in the years following World War II. They expected the rules of the political game to be rewritten and the international context to be fundamentally reordered. They could not be sure that the turbulence of the period since 1929 had ended permanently, but they felt confident that their world would be decisively influenced by the return of peace.

Central Avenue,
north to Bay,
Rio de Janeiro, Brazil.
*California Museum
of Photography*

Railroad climbing
through the Andes, Argentina.
*California Museum
of Photography*

La Compañía,
Quito, Ecuador.
*California Museum
of Photography*

Upperclass Bolivian
woman.
*California Museum
of Photography*

Aftermath of the "Bogotazo" riot, 1948, Bogotá, Colombia. *AP/Wide World photos*

Demonstration supporting President Salvador Allende during 1973 coup, Santiago, Chile. *AP/Wide World photos*

Soldiers inspecting bodies of alleged guerillas, 1982, Nebaj, Guatemala.
Jean-Marie Simon © 1993

Women on market day at stalls, Pisac, Bolivia.
Jean-Marie Simon © 1993

CHAPTER VII

NEW DIRECTIONS

IN THE POSTWAR PERIOD

(1945–1960)

THE WORLD ORDER THAT BEGAN to emerge from the ruins of war was indeed new, but it also differed from what many had expected. Regarding economic matters especially, the postwar recovery happened more rapidly and painlessly than predicted, and within twenty-five years, the economies of the major developed countries had made achievements unthinkable in 1945. Latin America, on the other hand, encountered a number of major problems and frustrations that, though unsurprising in retrospect, had not been foreseen during the war years.

In 1945, Latin American leaders expected a continuation of the generally favorable direction their economies had taken during the war. Most promising in this regard was the reopening of international trade in Europe, a region that now desperately needed what Latin America could supply: food and raw materials for construction and industry. Experience in the aftermath of World War I convinced Latin American analysts that recovering European economies would be unable to absorb much of their own industrial production. They were confident that, as had occurred during the 1920s, European industries would seek an outlet for their manufactures in the peripheral areas of the world economy, providing a counterbalance for their importation of Latin American products and thus maintaining a healthy rhythm of trade. Given this shared confidence in the future, those who controlled the course of Latin America's economic development disagreed mainly over which opportunities to pursue, a choice complicated politically by the fact that each of the alternatives implied a different distribution of the resulting economic benefits within Latin American societies. The basic question, with many specific variations, was whether or not the industrializing thrust of the past fifteen years should remain a top priority.

The economic crisis of the 1930s and the conflict that followed had stimulated in many Latin American countries a process of rapid industrial expansion. Isolated by the collapse of international trade and then by wartime limitations, these industries had enjoyed de facto protection from outside competition and had therefore prospered in spite of their low level of technological development. Many believed that the moment had arrived to push the process forward, creating firmer foundations for further industrial growth. During the war, Latin American countries had accumulated considerable credit with their Allied trading partners, and that capital could now be used to supplement the profits that were expected to flow from the revival of primary exports to Europe.

This approach required a transfer of resources from the primary export to the industrial sector, thereby raising the main point of contention in the postwar debate. Export interests were quick to object that the surge of industrialization during 1930–45 had been a response to the exceptional circumstances of depression and war, that a return to more normal conditions would probably renew the comparative advantage of traditional export activities, and that, should this not prove to be the case, investment capital would then flow spontaneously into industry anyway. The earlier consensus that had encouraged sweeping transformations of official economic policy and rapid progress in industrialization now disappeared. The new dissensus had implications reaching far beyond technical considerations of economic management. In effect, at issue was the distribution of wealth and power in the future development of Latin American societies.

Each of the two basic alternatives had powerful champions. On the side of industrialization stood all those who had benefited from the progress made thus far, clearly a majority in the most economically advanced—and therefore politically influential—regions of Latin America. The other side counted not only the traditional Latin American defenders of export growth (weaker than in the past but still quite accustomed to being heard) but also powerful international interests for whom the principles of comparative advantage and free trade seemed the keys to restoring the vigor of the global economy. These latter interests were vigorously promoted by the United States, whose economic hegemony over Latin America had been confirmed by the war. European countries, themselves dependent on economic support from the United States, had no choice but to concur in what became the new orthodoxy in U.S. thinking on Latin American development.

After 1945, then, industrialization became one of two alternative courses of development, and its promoters needed wide support in order to counteract the influence of those who preferred a return to the older model of export growth. To create a political understanding with workers, the advocates of further industrialization moderated the exploitation of the labor force. To gain the adhesion of the urban popular sectors, they favored maintaining real income levels and broadening urban employment opportunities beyond what the factories themselves could provide. To expand their electoral coalition, they directed state agencies into a variety of social welfare functions. Thus, the progress of industrialization in the postwar period was predicated on a daunting list of political preconditions that tended to consume the energies of its promoters to the detriment of narrower, more technical needs. At the end of the war, all analysts had agreed on the urgency of technological improvement in Latin American industries that had enjoyed de facto protection from outside competition during the preceding decade and a half, but difficult obstacles lay in the path to higher productivity. Besides the modernization of the industrial plant itself, urgent infrastructural projects (ranging from road construction to energy generation) and long-postponed general needs such as housing and communications demanded huge outlays of resources simultaneously.

Unfortunately, these demands converged just as the favorable economic prospects glimpsed by many Latin American countries in 1945 suddenly seemed to vanish. The reconstruction of Europe, for example, did indeed raise the demand for Latin America's primary exports, as had been foreseen, but it also absorbed the lion's share of the capital goods on the world market. The credit accumulated in Latin America during the war could therefore not be put to the best use. As British and U.S. industrial goods were channeled to the devastated countries of Europe and their prices quickly rose, Latin American countries turned their available hard currency to nationalizing foreign-owned public services, repatriating the public debt, and importing manufactures not destined preferentially for European reconstruction. Gradually and without explicitly making the decision to do so, the industrializing countries of Latin America abandoned the priority of technical modernization so central to their economic plans at the war's conclusion.

By the late 1940s, they found themselves struggling to assure the survival of their still-inefficient industrial producers by manipulating tariff schedules and monetary exchange rates so as to favor the industrial sector domestically. In addition, by maintaining a high exchange rate vis-à-vis foreign currencies (to make imports generally less expensive), Latin American governments defended the interests of urban consumers at the expense of primary exporters, whose internal costs rose in relation to their foreign earnings. At the same time, adjustments of the duties to be paid on particular categories of imports protected local industries and facilitated the importation of necessary capital goods. As we have already observed in the case of Mexico, national economic policy forced agricultural producers to subsidize the costs of urbanization and industrialization, but in few cases did landowning interests bear the burden as patiently as the Mexican *ejidatarios*, to say nothing of the international companies whose mines, transportation networks, and commercial arrangements also suffered from official dispositions unfavorable to the primary-export sector. Given the strength of the forces pushing for industrialization, the protests of resentful export interests found little resonance in the first decade after 1945. (One exception is the drastic devaluation of Peruvian currency undertaken by the military dictatorship that replaced that country's elected government in 1948.) Most Latin American exporters held down or even reduced their production.

By the middle of the 1950s the postwar export boom had ended, imperiling both the general economic model that had been adopted by Latin American governments and the political alignments that kept them in power. Two signs—rising inflation and a declining balance of trade—augured particularly ill. Inflation initially provided hard-pressed administrators a way to compensate for their declining revenues and disguise their manipulations of the faltering economic system. In the absence of measures designed to counteract it, however, inflation tended to accelerate. A devaluation of Latin American currencies on the international market then became necessary in order to prevent further deterioration of the balance of trade. Continued inflation cushioned the impact of devaluation on wage earners and consumers, but eventually it made further devaluations necessary, and so the cycle became self-perpetuating. As this train of events repeated itself, the hopeful mood of 1945 was replaced by general apprehension.

A parallel transformation occurred in the attitudes of those who had set out to analyze the economic mechanisms of Latin American development, create a collective consciousness of the problems that confronted the region, and act as spokespersons for regional interests in international forums. Chief among these were the members of the Economic Commission for Latin America (ECLA), organized by the Argentine economist Raúl Prebisch under the auspices of the United Nations. As chief administrator of Argentina's Central Bank during the 1930s, Prebisch said he had implemented Keynesian policies without knowing it, but in the 1950s he proclaimed that approach irrelevant to the Latin American situation. Keynesian remedies worked for mature, industrial economies, argued Prebisch, but not for economies that encountered mounting obstacles in their struggle for industrial development. Addressing the economic dilemmas of Latin America required an analysis of these obstacles, and Prebisch's analysis focused on the peripheral position of Latin America within a world economy dominated by an ever more powerful industrial core. ECLA analysts pointed out that the terms of trade (the price imbalance between manufactured goods produced in the core and primary goods exported by Latin America) had tilted steadily, over many years, in favor of the industrialized countries. They observed that the industrial labor force of the core countries had been able to secure better salaries, raising the cost of manufactures, while low-paid workers in the peripheral countries saw their position undercut by rapid population growth. Central control over international finance and transportation systems put Latin American countries at a further disadvantage in their efforts to attain more favorable terms of trade.

ECLA proposed, not a frontal assault on the asymmetries of a system much too well established to be vulnerable to that tactic, but rather an escape from existing patterns through a broader and more intense concentration on industrialization in Latin America itself. Only by eschewing the fatal attractions of the doctrine of comparative advantage and striving to create complex, "mature" economies like those of the industrial countries could Latin Americans equalize their trade relationship with the United States and Europe. How could this feat be accomplished? Prebisch posed the question without being able to answer it, but his persuasive formulation of the issue became hugely influential at this crucial postwar juncture, and the lack of a pat answer facilitated political appropriations of his analysis in ways remote from his original intentions. In effect, when "developmentalist" political forces in Latin America adopted the language of the ECLA analysis, they most often did it to justify strategies of industrialization that Prebisch himself considered insufficient.

Developmentalists promoted the expansion of basic industries such as steel (established in Brazil during World War II, just after the war in Argentina, and considerably earlier in Mexico), and, even more, others to manufacture durable consumer goods, especially automobiles. Their approach is well exemplified by this last industry, which they sought to expand by encouraging European and U.S. companies to set up national affiliates in Latin America. Other new industries included some that produced capital goods, like tractors and railroad stock, and many others catering to the demands of middle-class consumers, particularly electrical appliances. These developmentalist

policies began to satisfy demands that had gone unattended during the
war years and became more acute as middle-class Latin Americans
observed from afar the soaring living standards of postwar consumer
societies in the central countries of the world economy. As an overall
economic strategy, developmentalism returned dynamism to industrializing initiatives that seemed, a few years earlier, to have run out of
steam, and, by attracting new flows of foreign investment, it relieved
the pressure on a primary sector that could no longer bear the burden
of indirectly subsidizing economic diversification.

Until this time, foreign investment had played a limited role in
Latin American industrialization. Metropolitan economies had possessed little capital to invest abroad during the depression, and in the
early 1940s their energies were absorbed by World War II. After the war,
when Latin America's declining international balance of payments led
governments in the region to limit the remission of profits to foreign
corporations, that circumstance tended to discourage further outside
investment. The fact that some foreign companies did set up shop
during this period, especially in the largest Latin American countries—Mexico, Brazil, and Argentina—but also in some middle-sized
ones like Peru and Chile, is explained by the relatively small investment required (much less consequential from the point of view
of these corporations than from the perspective of their economic impact in the host countries) and by the multiple advantages of operating
in a closed market where new industries could dictate their own
terms. The brunt of their investment took the form of capital goods—
much of it used machinery that had already become obsolete at home
(whether because newer equipment produced more efficiently or because it better satisfied the consumers' taste for novelty in a more
competitive market). Once established in Latin America, foreign firms
drew on domestic capital and enjoyed the benefits of ingenious credit
arrangements, such as advanced payment for goods to be delivered at a
later date, and they were able to sell their products at prices much
higher than in their countries of origin.

This style of foreign investment obviously did not imply an opening of Latin American economies to the full play of market forces.
After all, industries that still compared unfavorably in productivity
with foreign competitors had little hope of success without continued
strict control of imports, and concerns with Latin America's unfavorable balance of payments caused governments in the region to limit
the exportation of large sums of money. When foreign corporations
demanded the right to dispose more freely of their profits, the outcome
was a system authorizing foreign companies to repatriate a contrac-

tually stipulated percentage of their earnings within a strict framework of currency exchange controls. Such compromises permitted the successful grafting of this new branch of industrialization—composed of subsidiaries of European and U.S. firms—onto the main trunk of Latin American industrialization. The industrial sector thereby expanded, gained some prospects of renewed dynamism, and, more importantly, underwent a significant internal differentiation that imparted to the new surge of industrialization a social impact quite distinct from what had gone before.

The wave of industrial expansion that began in the 1950s was much less labor-intensive, hiring fewer, but better-trained and better-paid, workers and generally producing things of the sort that only relatively well-off people could buy, a pattern that contrasted sharply with industries of the previous wave of industrialization and proved inherently limiting. The textile, chemical, and pharmaceutical industries established in the 1930s and 1940s had concentrated on unsophisticated and inexpensive products accessible to society as a whole and, most importantly, to the popular sectors that constituted the true mass market. The first electrical appliances manufactured in Latin America were also aimed at this market. In Argentina, the automotive industry began in much the same way, introducing motor scooters as an alternative to collapsing mass transit systems even before producing its first cars in 1950. Due to their orientation toward the lower end of the market, the older import-substitution industries had a self-interest in maintaining wage levels throughout the work force. The newer industries, on the other hand, cared less about the buying power of the majority who were unlikely to acquire big-ticket items like automobiles, while the older industries became increasingly unable to pay satisfactory wages as their prosperity continued to fade. Therefore, Latin American industrialization in the second half of the twentieth century increasingly served those at the top of the social pyramid, and only the largest countries of the region had national markets whose upper ends could absorb large quantities of durable consumer goods. Brazil, Mexico, and Argentina (in descending order of success, and with not inconsiderable difficulty in the case of Argentina) were able to take this step in the 1950s. Middle-sized countries like Chile and Peru made isolated attempts without transforming their economies in the same way.

While the altered course of industrialization had several decisive long-term consequences for Latin American development, the most obvious immediate impact was a further deterioration of the balance of trade. The industries of the earlier period had reduced importations of expensive finished goods and replaced them with less expensive raw materials, but the new industries did not have this import-substituting function. The sorts of products they manufactured had not been imported in any quantity for decades, so that importation of the raw materials and machinery necessary to produce them only worsened existing trade imbalances. The developmentalists argued that, despite this drawback, the new industries constituted an essential step toward full economic diversification and therefore represented the definitive, long-range solution to unequal trade. In the meantime, however, more foreign loans and investments would be required to prevent the process of development from stagnating. Foreign capital had, indeed, become increasingly available as the fully industrialized countries recovered from the effects of depression and war, but it came with strings attached. Lenders and investors objected to the controls on currency exchange rates exercised by Latin American governments and pressed for their termination. Tariff barriers on imported goods could still offer protection to domestic industries, but the removal of currency exchange controls helped undermine the social and political alignments that had provided a measure of stability to the postwar scene.

Even had the developmentalist strategies succeeded better than they generally did, existing political alignments would have been threatened as new social groups entered the political arena and a surge of inflation added further complications to economic policy-making. Inflation was having quite an uneven impact on, and driving apart, the various components of the political coalition that had backed industrialization in Latin American countries. At a more fundamental level, Latin American population growth (which had picked up speed in the 1920s and made itself felt in a more limited way before World War II) now imparted to the process of social transformation a dynamism unlikely to be contained by the shrewdest economic manipulation and inevitably of political consequence. When the pressure of rural population on the land reached a critical point in El Salvador and Colombia, observers of other regions began to fear a similar, impending destabilization. Clearly, the configuration of forces in industrializing urban areas could no longer dominate the political agenda as they had since the 1930s.

Rising social tension in the countryside inevitably pushed the topic of land reform toward center stage in Latin American politics during the second half of the twentieth century. The proponents of industrialization themselves contributed to raising the profile of agrarian issues by identifying rural backwardness—both technical and social—as the chief drag on the development of national economies. Turning attention away from the insufficiencies of the industries per se, developmentalists began to argue that the low productivity of agriculture and the low living standards of the rural poor stymied further advances of industrialization by excessively narrowing the market for manufactured goods. Agrarian reform figured importantly in the revolutionary programs of both Guatemala and Bolivia in the 1950s, and by the end of the decade, it had become a standard feature of reform proposals throughout the hemisphere.

Meanwhile, Latin American cities demanded no less attention as burgeoning population growth, combined with the archaic social hierarchies of the countryside that generated currents of internal migration, accelerated urbanization. In retrospect, the urban expansion of the period before 1945 appeared as merely the first taste of a process that showed no signs of abating in the postwar period. Swelling squatter neighborhoods posed problems that further industrial growth alone could not solve. As the social composition of Latin America's urban masses diversified, so did their political objectives, and it became increasingly difficult to gather them into the kind of alignment that had worked in the past. The developmentalists now had to compete with challengers on both the left and the right who appealed to new urban dwellers unable to find factory employment and sorely in need of housing and basic services. By the close of the 1950s, many had lost the hope that Latin America could simply develop its way out of the profound social ills then accumulating in both cities and countryside, and they began to redefine the terms of political conflict accordingly. That process of redefinition was encouraged by the direction of international relations, where the ephemeral concord among the victorious Allies had long since faded into the cold war.

Dominant for decades in the hemisphere, the United States had suddenly become the hegemonic military and economic power of the postwar world, a status accepted by both its defeated enemies and its victorious allies, with the exception of the Soviet Union, which established itself as the second pole in a new bipolar system of international politics in the 1950s. The Soviet Union had been so weakened by the destruction of the war that it could not provide an equal counterpoise to U.S. military and economic influence, least of all in the Western Hemisphere, but the cold war was a battle between ideologies as well, and on the ideological plane the forces of communism appeared more robust. The Soviet Union had showed itself willing to impose social and political transformations from without when spontaneous revolutionary impulses were lacking, and western European fears of this combination of persuasive ideology and traditional Russian expansionism facilitated the reorganization of the world's chief industrialized countries into a system dominated by the United States. After securing control of the center of the global economy, the new hegemonic power prepared itself for the cold war by extending its political and military sway over much of the rest of the world through a series of regional treaty organizations.

A U.S.-dominated Organization of American States (OAS) had been among the first of these to emerge, with the groundwork laid at the Pan-American Conference held in Mexico City just before the end of World War II and with a military component added at a 1947 meeting in Rio de Janeiro. The Rio treaty committed the signers jointly to repel any aggression from outside the hemisphere and also to oppose any internal threats of foreign inspiration. The descriptions of such internal threats were carefully phrased to cover the possibility of local revolutionary movements—a considerable novelty for an international treaty alliance. The Peronist government of Argentina carried on that country's traditional role as opposition leader within inter-American forums, arguing that unanimity, rather than a simple majority, should be required to approve the initiatives discussed in the treaty. The compromise solution was to require a two-thirds majority and to make collective initiatives that involved military action nonbinding on the members. Few at the time foresaw the likelihood that such collective security provisions would be activated, because the gains made by Latin American Communist parties during the depression and the subsequent U.S.-Soviet alliance were being reversed by 1947. If Latin America gave the United States no cause for alarm in the late 1940s, however, other world regions did. In the last year of the decade, determined Communist insurgents triumphed in China, and the Soviet Union exploded its first atomic device, events that worked a dismaying change in the tenor of the world conflict as perceived in Washington, D.C. Within a few months, the world hegemony established with such ease by U.S. power in the aftermath of World War II seemed suddenly to have evaporated, and the disappointed architects of world domination began to view the United States as a fortress under siege.

This mentality does much to explain the U.S. reaction to the perils it soon discovered in the reformist government of Guatemalan president Jacobo Arbenz. At an OAS meeting in Caracas in 1954, the United States denounced the political direction taken by Guatemala, alleging that it tended to shatter hemispheric solidarity in favor of the free world. The resulting Declaration of Caracas classed Communist activities as an outside intervention in American affairs and stated that the establishment of a Communist government in any American state would constitute a direct threat and would automatically trigger a consultative meeting of the OAS to adopt appropriate measures. Mexico and Argentina abstained from endorsing the declaration, and only Guatemala voted against it. Enthusiastically in some cases and resignedly in others, the remaining republics thus endorsed the criteria that now guided the Latin American policy of the United States, though they did not commit themselves to military action. Viewed from the outside, U.S. fears of communism seemed quite exaggerated, and some observers remarked that U.S. hegemony over Central America had always been explained as necessary to counteract (first British, then Mexican) designs from without.

Since the OAS declined to engage in a joint military venture and a unilateral U.S. intervention seemed too costly in political terms, the United States opted to sponsor disaffected Guatemalan army officers whom it helped to arm and organize secretly in Honduras. Their easy victory over the Arbenz government suggested that the menace had been quite exaggerated and marked the return of a practice that U.S. policymakers had forsworn twenty years earlier. The Guatemalan intervention of 1954 reaffirmed U.S. hegemony in Latin America. For millions of Latin Americans, and not simply those who sympathized with the Soviet Union, the Guatemalan episode represented the continuation of a long story of rapacious aggression, as told in *The Fable of the Shark and the Sardines* (1956) by Juan José Arévalo, who had initiated the country's social reforms in the 1940s.

At the end of the period 1945–60, another crisis of the Pan-American system drew larger resonance from the progressive breakdown of postwar international polarities. The reconstruction of Europe was complete, and Charles de Gaulle had shown that the North Atlantic Treaty Organization (NATO) could be something more than an institutionalization of U.S. military tutelage. Dwight D. Eisenhower's official visit to India, a country that had become an important member of the nonaligned movement, seemed to indicate that nonalignment no longer precluded friendship with the United States. The socialist world had weathered serious troubles following the death of Stalin and, though its reputation had been somewhat tarnished by Soviet repression of the Hungarian uprising, continued a rhythm of economic growth more rapid than that of western Europe. Under the leadership of Nikita Khrushchev, who optimistically predicted paradisiacal abundance with the imminent transition from socialism to communism, the Soviet Union abandoned its earlier caution and audaciously explored the possibilities of the new international context, particularly those created by the process of decolonization in Africa and Asia, the Communist-led Vietnamese rebellion against French colonialism being only the most dramatic example of these new opportunities. The United States, for its part, also recognized that the challenges presented by the underdeveloped world required methods more subtle than those employed in previous cold war confrontations, and, for that reason, the U.S. government vetoed a British, French, and Israeli military response to the Egyptian nationalization of the Suez Canal. However, the new flexibility applied only to areas not already under U.S. control, and most emphatically not to Latin America, where the hegemonic zeal of the United States gained new intensity just when the 1959 Cuban Revolution arrived to put an end to its "Pax Monroviana" (in the apt expression of Richard Morse). The Cuban Revolution profoundly reshaped the relations between the United States and Latin America by making tangible a revolutionary alternative that previously had seemed an almost mythical object of dread or yearning.

As we consider the history of individual Latin American countries from 1945 to 1960, it will become evident that the immediate postwar years constitute an unusually well-defined period, marked by high hopes for industrialization in the larger nations and by the high prestige of liberal democracy everywhere. Before the Cuban Revolution, socialism in the hemisphere seemed not to compete with liberalism for primacy but rather to complement it by requiring ascendant representative governments to incorporate into their goals a concern with social reform. The international climate so favorable to liberal constitutionalism swept away a number of authoritarian or oligarchical regimes, but in Brazil and Argentina, formerly authoritarian regimes managed to survive the transition. The result was a phenomenon that later students of Latin American politics have called populism.

Brazilian president Getúlio Vargas had ruled in an authoritarian manner for more than half a decade when he sponsored the postwar restoration of democracy by temporarily absenting himself from office in 1945. Before stepping down, Vargas prepared the way for his return by strengthening his ties to unions and to the working class generally. Their pro-Vargas loyalties then provided a bulwark against rising anti-Vargas sentiments among the urban middle sectors. The *queremistas* (so-called because they *wanted* Vargas) acquired surprising allies among Communists who had long suffered at Vargas's hands but had gradually become reconciled after he joined the international crusade against fascism. At the end of World War II, the Communists prepared to expand their political base after a decade of proscription. Aghast at the ease with which the protean dictator seemed about to weather the postwar political transition, those who had suffered under Vargas convinced the army (concerned with democratic appearances and with the approval of the U.S. ambassador) to remove him from office, leaving the chief justice of the Brazilian Supreme Court to assure the impartiality of the ensuing presidential elections. The leadership of the army was confident that its influence in the government would be perpetuated by the heir apparent, Marshal Eurico Gaspar Dutra.

Dutra easily won the election with the votes of two new pro-Vargas parties, the Social Democratic party (PDS) and the Brazilian Labor party (PTB), which gathered the durable leader's followings among traditional political clienteles and new working-class sectors, respectively. The first congress of the new republic was controlled by the representatives of traditional political clienteles, a logical outcome in a country still predominantly rural, but by providing for the direct election of the president by popular majority, the Constitution of 1946 changed the dynamics of Brazilian politics. In a direct election for president, more politicized and progressive urban voters would have a decisive voice, setting the stage for future conflicts between the legislative and executive branches.

Vargas remained very much on the scene as head of the PTB and senator from his home state of Rio Grande do Sul. As Dutra became increasingly conservative over the course of his term, Vargas was able to position himself to Dutra's left in the presidential election of 1950. His campaign, endorsed by the Communist party (made illegal again by Dutra in 1948), raised great hopes for social change and culminated in a wide margin of victory when large numbers of PDS voters abandoned their party's candidate out of personal loyalty to Vargas. However, Vargas encountered huge difficulties in his new term as constitutional president. He had no way to remedy the basic cause of the disaffection that had returned him to power. The country's model of industrialization, having reached the end of its import-substituting stage, was being maintained after the war only by currency manipulations that put a heavy drag on the export sector. Vargas's inability to solve Brazil's economic dilemma solidified conservative opposition in congress, and unbridled inflation corroded his popularity among urban voters as well. With the approach of the next election, the influential journalist and politician Carlos Lacerda raised a tremendous stir by denouncing the corruption that Vargas, while holding himself to strict financial probity, had always tolerated in his inner circle. Frustrated and cornered, Vargas committed suicide. The suicide became the most efficacious of the spectacular gestures that marked Vargas's four-decade career. He left a brief political testament condemning his enemies, whom he identified as those opposed to the country's authentic national independence and antagonistic to the well-being of the people. Declaring (a bit forgetfully) that he had fought these enemies throughout his public life, Vargas portrayed his suicide as a sacrificial surrender to their vengeance. The day after the suicide, Brazilians took to the streets by the hundreds of thousands in response, reinvigorating the populist coalition that had seemed on the verge of disintegration a few days before.

The presidency of Justelino Kubitschek, elected in 1955 with the support of the political heirs of Vargas, signaled the onset of postwar Brazilian developmentalism. In the context of his very traditional home state of Minas Gerais, Kubitschek had appeared progressive, but in the larger context of Brazil as a whole, his sole emphasis on economic growth represented a retreat from the commitment to nationalist and social issues that had characterized the final, populist phase of Vargas. The new president declared that his economic development programs would constitute a great leap forward, bringing Brazil half a century's progress in five years. The complement of his economic initiative was another equally grandiose scheme, the transfer of the national capital from Rio de Janeiro to a remote spot on the central plateau, supposedly as a prologue to the effective incorporation of the vast and sparsely inhabited interior reaches of Brazil into the country's national economic life. It is hardly surprising that, five years later, in 1960, Kubitschek's exorbitant predictions had not been realized. True, the Brazilian economy had shaken off the stagnation of the early 1950s and achieved one of the highest rates of growth on the planet, but the new capital at Brasília had not brought the hoped-for population shift to the interior, and the process of rapid expansion had itself created new imbalances in the national economy. In addition, Brazil's export sector (which had retained the prosperity of the immediate postwar years longer than the export sectors of other Latin American countries) was now suffering intense competition from coffee producers elsewhere, and Kubitschek's huge expenditures had stimulated rampant inflation.

By the time of the presidential election, developmentalist policies seemed unlikely to bring further advances and had, at any rate, failed to garner the continued loyalty of the populist coalition. The opportunity of the moment was seized with masterful skill by a colorful politician from São Paulo, Jânio Quadros, who mobilized themes deriving partly from several decades of anti-Vargas opposition to capture the presidency in 1960. Brazilian electoral law allowed a rival of Quadros to become his vice president as a result of the same election. Vice President João Goulart was a political heir of Vargas closely identified with the labor movement, which had continued its gains during the 1950s. The national political influence of labor had even attracted rural and oligarchical forces to its banner in more than one Brazilian state. Despite the strength of organized labor, the Quadros victory announced the end of the populist hegemony that had lent stability to Brazilian politics since World War II. Although the erratic behavior of the new president somewhat muddied the clarity of the transition, the deterioration of the populist coalition marked a political turning point like that of 1930.

In the three decades since 1930, the Brazilian economy had undergone a startling (if incomplete) metamorphosis, evident, for example, in the state of organized labor in the 1960s. Brazilian unionization had been carried out from the top down, following the example of fascist Italy. However, unlike the Italian case, where official unions had been violently imposed on workers with long traditions of labor militancy, Brazil's official unions had often constituted the workers' first experience of labor organization. Surprisingly, when compared with workers' attitudes elsewhere, the Brazilian rank and file found their unions valuable precisely because of their connections with the state, but their attitude was not out of keeping with the political history of popular urban sectors in Brazil. Even in the great urban centers of the Brazilian southeast, where the process of socioeconomic evolution had advanced furthest, social and cultural patterns had altered less than one might imagine, partly because the extremely rapid rate of rural to urban migration outstripped the changes associated with industrialization.

In this setting, political labels became deceptive descriptions of the movements they designated. Labor parties were not necessarily dominated by industrial workers, and they often demonstrated characteristics quite different from those of labor parties elsewhere. Even more curiously, labor parties played a relatively minor role in heavily industrialized São Paulo, where a flamboyant local politician named Adhemar de Barros adapted familiar clientelist practices to the new urban context with huge success. Labor politics fared much better in the state of Rio Grande do Sul, where its leadership derived from the same class of powerful ranchers that had produced both Getúlio Vargas and his labor minister, João Goulart. As throughout Brazil, this oddly composed laborism often subsumed political clans and clienteles of long standing that had adopted the party label strictly for tactical purposes. Despite the nominal political strength of labor, then, and despite the apparent influence of urban middle-class votes in the victory of Quadros, the old structures of power in Brazil had altered less than many believed in 1960.

Argentina

Argentina's populist experience differed from Brazil's in a manner indicative of the larger contrasts between the two countries. Argentina was significantly more urbanized and more industrialized than Brazil in 1945. The impact of European immigration had been considerably greater in Argentina, though its rate of population growth remained slow enough to be a matter of perennial concern and the work force of the new industries located in the city of Buenos Aires had to come primarily from internal migration. (Until the end of World War II, most migrants to the city of Buenos Aires came from the surrounding pampean countryside; thereafter, the interior provinces supplied the majority. Never, however, did Argentina's internal migrants equal the seemingly inexhaustible supply produced by rural Brazil.) The basic facts of Argentine society resulted in the development of an urban working class that by the mid-twentieth century had already achieved salary levels historically comparable to those earned by workers on the European continent. In addition, the rural/urban balance of political power had tipped much further toward the cities in Argentina than was the case in Brazil. Along with the confrontational style of Juan Perón and of the popular movement that formed around him, these factors explain the far more abrupt and decisive advent of populist power in Argentina, contrasting with the incremental growth of populist influence in Brazil during these years.

Perón

In the second half of 1945, Perón occupied the posts of vice president, minister of war, and secretary of labor, but his candidacy for president had failed to gain the support of Argentina's traditional political establishment. The government of which he formed a part seemed increasingly under siege by an opposition tide that united landowners and industrialists with urban middle sectors impatient at their political marginalization since the 1920s and encouraged, now, by the wartime triumph of liberal democracy. Perón's response was to appeal increasingly to the working class for electoral support, and it was a demonstration mobilized, for the most part, by veteran union organizers that rescued him when elements within the army attempted to remove him from the political scene. Perón had long anticipated the coming of the general election, and he had prepared for it better than his adversaries. His forces, composed of dissident factions of various traditional parties, were scarcely formidable in institutional terms, but Perón's personal popularity had become surprisingly intense in a

brief time. As recently as 1944, much of the support for his policies as
secretary of labor had been organized by union leaders, but the fervent
multitude that acclaimed him on 17 October 1945 afterward com-
memorated the Day of Peronist Loyalty as a moment of political
definition linking them directly to Perón. The union organizers who
had helped Perón cobble together his Labor party had little choice but
to accept the personal ascendancy of "the Leader." The unswerving
loyalty of the working class did not, by itself, assure Perón's election as
president, but the candidate soon revealed an instinctive mastery of
electoral politics rivaled in Argentine history only by Hipólito Yrigoyen himself. Many local-machine politicians, particularly dependent on state patronage and aware that times were irremediably changing, correctly predicted a Peronist triumph and realigned themselves
to take advantage of it. The new movement gained momentum as the
political clienteles of such local bosses transferred their loyalty directly to Perón. As a result, the Peronists won a narrow victory in the
1946 election against a coalition whose electoral center of gravity lay
in the middle and upper classes, though it also included the Radicals
and various parties of the left.

Once in office, Perón used the power of the state to consolidate his
political supremacy and meld together an increasingly disciplined
following. He nationalized the Central Bank, created a public corporation to oversee Argentina's foreign trade, restaffed the university and
the judiciary with loyal personnel, and established nearly exclusive
control over the press and the radio. The constitutional reform of 1949
institutionalized the authoritarian cast of his administration and guaranteed his first reelection. Gradually, the last shreds of autonomy were
crushed out of the organized labor movement, and the diverse forces of
Peronism were gathered into a single party. The impressive unity of
the movement can be explained, in part, by its rapid expansion among
formerly unpoliticized groups without preexisting party allegiances to
conflict with their new Peronist loyalties. Under Perón, labor unions
rapidly doubled in size with the addition of new members for whom
the very meaning of political militancy was defined by fidelity to the
Leader. Perón's wife Eva was instrumental in maintaining his relationship with the unions, and she brought other, previously unorganized
groups into the Peronist fold. Eva Perón cultivated the support of
women by advocating their right to vote and by creating a special wing
of the party for them. She reached out to "the humble" by creating a
Social Welfare Foundation to minister paternalistically to their needs.
As a result, in future elections Peronist electoral majorities depended
less on labor unions.

Still, Perón's working-class base of support placed real limitations on him in the late 1940s. The legitimacy of his government depended on periodic elections, since the army had indicated its unwillingness to support him otherwise, and Perón could not obtain convincing electoral validation of his continued rule without the backing of organized labor. This circumstance produced certain political and economic difficulties. Although his government systematically sacrificed the economic interests of the rural sector to those of the industrial sector, Perón's identification with labor militancy kept Argentina's industrialists politically hostile to him. In order to woo his working-class following, Perón effectively subsidized the needs of urban consumers at the expense of rural producers, thereby creating consumer expectations impossible to maintain as the situation of the Argentine export sector deteriorated. International prices declined from their immediate postwar high even as the country's urban workers—flush from recent gains in living standards—increased their demand for affordable food. To make matters worse, Argentine agriculture suffered an increasing technological disadvantage in competing with foreign agricultural producers who were better able to afford the new techniques and, at least in the United States, often benefited directly from substantial government credits and subsidies. Economic pressures finally put an end to the improvements in working-class living standards as inflation rose, the value of the Argentine peso fell, and the rate of industrial growth slowed.

By 1951, Perón was attempting to extricate his regime from the requirements of its working-class constituency by augmenting the centralized, authoritarian power of the state. Although many viewed the death of Eva Perón in that year as a defining moment in her husband's change of heart, the fact was coincidental. Essentially, the transformation responded to a new political economy, anticipating the basic outlines of the sort of developmentalism applied in many countries a few years later. In order to reduce the country's oil imports and thereby improve its balance of trade, Perón loosened state restrictions on the exploitation of Argentine oil fields. For a regime that had proudly raised the banner of economic independence a few years before, this tactical retreat signaled a weakness and an opportunity for the opposition. A second opportunity was created by an anticlerical campaign that he initiated as part of his drive to consolidate all power in the hands of the state. This measure provoked resistance in the military, never totally in Perón's camp even at the height of his influence, and in September 1955 a fairly small group of officers was able to overthrow the populist leader and send him into exile. From Panama,

Venezuela, the Dominican Republic, and, finally, Madrid, the exiled Perón remained a power in Argentine politics for nearly two decades. Purges of the officer corps after his fall turned the Argentine military permanently against him, but he retained the undying loyalty of about a third of the country's electorate as well as influence deriving from the continued Peronist orientation of the labor movement. Most helpful of all in maintaining Perón's popularity in Argentina during his long exile was the persistence of the same quandaries that had brought the end of his government but that now undermined those of his successors as well.

The first of these was Gen. Eduardo Lonardi, associated with the conservative Catholic currents that had helped precipitate the fall of Perón. Believing that Lonardi was encouraging Catholic attempts to coopt Peronist labor unions, the military quickly replaced him with another general, Pedro Eugenio Aramburu, who favored the total obliteration of all traces of Peronism from Argentine life. Aramburu proscribed the Peronist party, purged the leadership of organized labor, and introduced electoral reforms (such as proportional representation) in hopes of accomplishing his goal. By 1957, he had clearly failed. Peronist control of the labor unions was quickly being reestablished, and in the election for a new constituent assembly, more than a quarter of the electorate followed Perón's instructions from exile and voided their ballots. Radicalism, the only force capable of mounting an effective resistance to Peronism at the polls, had split into two competing parties during the campaign for the constituent assembly. Unless something changed soon, the Peronists would inevitably control the upcoming presidential election. Arturo Frondizi, the leader of the smaller and more ideologically progressive of the Radical factions, took the opportunity to cut a deal. Before his party's disappointing showing in the recent elections, Frondizi had hoped to make it the heir of Peronism, but now he was content to guarantee the future rights of Peronist organizations in return for Perón's endorsement for president. Frondizi had failed to capture directly the loyalty of the workers, but having borrowed it temporarily through his agreement with their exiled chief, he strove to gain the backing of their industrial employers as well. Together, he calculated, they might form a coalition strong enough to subdue the export-oriented landowning and mercantile interests as Perón had been unable to do.

Frondizi was also prepared to tackle the central economic problem of the moment. Argentina's agricultural export sector had lost its economic dynamism, if not its political gravitation, and industry had been unable to take its place as the driving force of the national economy. Recent attempts to invigorate industry through government investment in construction of gas pipelines and a steel plant had done more to revive Peronist labor unions than to restore the lost momentum of Argentine industrialization. Previous governments had also tried, without success, to stimulate the export sector using monetary manipulations and foreign investment. Frondizi renewed the assault more resolutely than his predecessors. General salary increases were followed by an unprecedentedly drastic currency devaluation (designed to stimulate the export sector) and an energetic campaign to recruit North American investment capital for various industries (partially offsetting the negative impact of the devaluation on urban incomes). The industrial sector responded encouragingly, but the agricultural sector failed to revive, partly due to unfavorable conditions on the international market. As inflation surged, Frondizi faced mounting skepticism. Most damaging was the wide public mistrust of his brusque transformation from spokesperson of the anti-imperialist, anti-Peronist left to conservative developmentalist and ally of Perón. Frondizi's flirtation with Peronism gave particular pause to the country's determinedly anti-Peronist military leadership, and his leftist past became more worrisome to them, too, after the coming of the Cuban Revolution in 1959. At the end of the period under consideration, the Frondizi administration found itself politically besieged and reduced to immobility.

In both the preceding cases, then, political mass mobilization was sponsored in the democratic climate of the postwar years by national leaders who needed a new constituency to offset the power of their political adversaries, but the advance of populism had halted in both Brazil and Argentina by 1960. Although mass mobilization occurred in a number of other countries as well, the tendency to identify populist regimes all over Latin America may reflect no more than the desire to impose an artificial neatness to the confusing lines of heterogeneous political realities. The postwar reform movements of Peru, Venezuela, and Guatemala were all more unequivocally democratic than in populist Brazil or Argentina. In the Peruvian experience, to which we turn now, postwar democratization was made possible by the advance of mass-based opposition forces barely tolerated by those in control of the political system.

Peru's party of the masses, the Popular American Revolutionary Alliance (APRA), took advantage of the postwar political climate to rebuild its strength. Temporarily, at least, the country's military and civil authorities had resigned themselves to the electoral victories that granted their Aprista nemesis a decisive role in choosing the next president and virtual control of the national congress in 1945. While Aprista unions carried out strikes in Lima and on the plantations of the northern coastal strip, the traditional ruling classes of Peru fortified their influence in the army and retained nearly total control of the commanding heights of the Peruvian economy and the mass media. To break the impasse, APRA called on President José Luís Bustamante y Rivero but found him reluctant to recognize his political debt to the party that had helped him win office. Frustrated again by the intransigence of their powerful adversaries, the Apristas turned to direct action, culminating in a 1948 insurrection. Although they had significant backing in the Peruvian navy, the army stood against them and the rebellion eventually collapsed after a bloody fight in the port of Callao. Bustamante y Rivero now outlawed APRA once more, but he also refused to modify his economic policies to favor the export sector, and in punishment a military coup removed him from power and installed a member of its own ranks.

The next president, Gen. Manuel Odría, took the official persecution of Aprismo to new extremes. When Aprista leader Víctor Raúl Haya de la Torre sought political asylum in the Colombian diplomatic mission, Odría preferred to hazard an international confrontation rather than permit him to leave the country, keeping him besieged in the embassy for years. In many ways, Odría's government returned to the political model of Peruvian regimes in the 1930s. Convinced of its inability to win free elections against APRA's popular majority, it chose to locate its base of support in the military instead of the electorate. The economic policies of the new military government were even more anachronistic. At a moment when nearly all the large or middle-sized nations of Latin America maintained close control of their foreign trade, Peru returned to a wide-open laissez-faire model reminiscent of the golden years of the oligarchical republic at the turn of the century. Anachronistic or not, the arrangement allowed the Peruvian economy to thrive for a number of years. Meanwhile, Odría appeared willing to take a leaf from the book of Peronism, granting the vote to women—among whom his wife, María Delgado de Odría, did her best to drum up new supporters for her husband—and assiduously courting the political favor of the rapidly growing marginal population in the outskirts of Lima. The oligarchical backers of Odría's regime were not amused by these gestures at populism, in which they divined an attempt to cultivate an alternative base of political support. So when prosperity of the export economy faded in the mid-1950s, they began to withdraw their support from the regime.

This was the moment for which the Apristas had been waiting.

During his sequestration in the Colombian embassy and afterward in exile, Haya de la Torre had retooled the party to make it more moderate in style as well as in ideology. Because of the inveterate rivalry between Peruvian Communists and Apristas, he could sincerely announce his support of the United States in the cold war. Having become convinced of the futility of insurrections and the adamant opposition of the military to any Aprista government, Haya de la Torre was more willing than ever to make compromises and enter political coalitions that included his formerly irreconcilable adversaries in the oligarchy. In 1956, APRA backed a coalition candidate, Manuel Prado, who won the presidency without the large majority that had characterized Aprista electoral participation in the past. Clearly, the party's search for moderation was to have its cost. In fact, a second progressive politician, Fernando Belaúnde Terry, did almost as well in the election without any party organization worthy of the name, revealing that the tactics of Haya de la Torre could be imitated advantageously by those unburdened by the specter of a radical past. As APRA lost its earlier majority in Lima, Belaúnde made gains there. He also had strong support in his native Arequipa and in the southern highlands where the Apristas had never made much headway.

Although a candidate backed by APRA now became president, the party itself lost ground everywhere except for its traditional northern stronghold. Prado continued the economic policies initiated by Odría, presiding now over a boom in the exportation of fish meal, while the party of Haya de la Torre concentrated on defending the interests of its working-class clientele in the northern region and in the labor movement. As Aprista participation in the government undercut the party's tradition of radicalism, the more militant labor leaders reoriented their political allegiances increasingly toward the Communists. Within the youth organizations of APRA, many believed that the party had sold its revolutionary soul for a pittance, and a small but belligerent minority of dissidents soon made itself felt. From its remote Leninist roots, the party had retained the habit of providing theoretical justifications for its tactical zigzags, and the resulting internal debates began to appear to be theological disputations on the recent pronouncements of Haya de la Torre, whose leadership was called increasingly into question. APRA's search for moderation had stabilized its position in the Peruvian political system at the cost of its internal unity and its ability to grow.

In Venezuela, postwar democratization depended on an alliance between long-repressed social and political forces from below and a national leadership—Rómulo Betancourt and his Democratic Action

party—that had only recently gained control of the state thanks to a
barracks revolt led by middle-ranking officers. Democratic Action far
overreached the expectations of its army sponsors when it plunged
ahead with an ambitious program that enormously expanded government social welfare programs, rewrote labor legislation, and organized
a mass political base among peasants and workers. In 1947, the resulting electoral juggernaut placed Rómulo Gallegos, Venezuela's most
celebrated man of letters, in the presidency and provided him with a
congress totally dominated by Democratic Action. Afraid that they
might thus be reduced to permanent irrelevance, the country's other
political parties watched complacently as the startled military overthrew Gallegos the next year. The coup was received favorably also by
oil interests and by the U.S. State Department, which, soon after 1945,
had begun to mitigate its support of elected, constitutional governments that did not also comport with the anti-Communist impera-
tives of U.S. strategy in the cold war.

At first, the new military government hoped to return power to
civilian leaders of Democratic Action's rival parties, but Col. Marcos Pérez Jiménez, who emerged to make himself president in 1952,
thought otherwise. Resorting to massive fraud in order to win the
election, Pérez Jiménez implanted a rigid dictatorship. Meanwhile,
Venezuelan oil production (which had climbed steadily even through
the years of worldwide depression) was creating an economic bonanza
greater than anything the country had ever known. The dictatorship
spared no expense in its efforts to create public works worthy of a great
capital in Caracas, where upper- and middle-class neighborhoods expanded rapidly. The shantytowns of the city outskirts grew as well, due
to an exodus from rural areas that gained speed as the government
abandoned the attempts of Democratic Action (now outlawed along
with the Communist party) to improve conditions in the countryside.
Concern with economic diversification evaporated within government circles interested primarily in securing solid support among the
oil interests and building political capital with the resulting patronage.

In exile, Rómulo Betancourt, still the head of the Venezuelan
opposition, came to the same conclusion reached by Peru's Haya de la
Torre at about the same time. Political democratization was definitely
possible in Venezuela, and social reform, while more difficult, remained feasible as well. However, Betancourt had begun to doubt that
truly revolutionary change lay within the realm of immediate possibility, especially when it challenged the political and economic hegemony of the United States. The Venezuelan army might open the
door for some kind of modernizing reforms, but its support would

always be conditional. Consequently, reform could be achieved only as long as rivalries among players in the democratic arena could be kept within mutually acceptable bounds. In other words, Democratic Action had to adopt goals more moderate than those that had inspired its overwhelming electoral triumphs just after 1945. The fruits of this more prudent approach ripened only slowly, however. Still suspiciously "pink" in the eyes of U.S. cold warriors, Betancourt barely managed to avoid expulsion from his refuge in Puerto Rico, while the dictatorship of Pérez Jiménez hosted the 1954 OAS meeting that sounded a new alarm regarding Communist threats to the hemisphere.

Unfortunately for Pérez Jiménez, however, the stability of his dictatorship depended on the vigor of the Venezuelan oil boom, and by 1958, when the dictator had scheduled his next reelection, the expansion of oil production in the Middle East had begun to drive down prices and reduce the country's market share as well. Furthermore, though Venezuela had become a leading producer of iron ore, the excessively generous terms awarded to North American concessionaires resulted in disappointing earnings from the Venezuelan point of view. In an effort to recapture the economic euphoria of a few years before, Venezuela proposed to form a state monopoly of the petrochemical industry—a suggestion that quickly alienated the affections of foreign oil companies that had been, until that time, staunch backers of Pérez Jiménez. Bereft of its former support, the dictatorship tottered during three weeks of popular uprisings and succumbed to a military coup in January 1958. The coup leaders called elections, and the president of the junta, Adm. Wolfgang Larrazábal, came close to winning them. In addition to his prestige at having overthrown the dictator, Larrazábal made (necessarily discreet) anti-U.S. sentiments an important part of his campaign and even received the endorsement of the Communists. The admiral won the most votes in Caracas, but the rural areas of Venezuela remained loyal to the memory of Democratic Action, carrying the day nationally for Rómulo Betancourt. Painted by Larrazábal as the preferred candidate of the United States, Betancourt returned to power at the head of a party resigned to a new moderation. By eschewing the radicalism of its earlier phase, Democratic Action gained allies among conservative groups but lost them at the popular level and became increasingly limited by the social color of its new alliances. This explains why the leaders of the Cuban Revolution, scanning the Latin American horizon for areas in which to extend their influence after 1959, found what seemed to be promising prospects in Venezuela.

In Guatemala, postwar political events began in much the same

way, with a revolt of junior army officers who called elections and ush- *Guatemala*
ered in a period of ebullient reform. The reformer in this case was Juan
José Arévalo, an intellectual just returned from a long exile in Argen- *José Arévalo*
tina to become president of Guatemala in 1945. Even more important
than the projects of reform-minded Guatemalan politicians, however,
were the initiatives of worker and peasant organizations that had
suddenly gained a freedom of action previously unknown. Real wages
rose dramatically, and the labor legislation enacted in the capital
received unusually effective enforcement, thanks in part to the efforts
of Guatemalan Communists who possessed the kind of grass roots
organization needed to implement the social reforms. Despite their
achievements, though, the Guatemalan reformers had not succeeded
in mobilizing a broad and coherent base of political support comparable to that constructed by Venezuela's Democratic Action in 1945–48,
and their primary stay remained in the officer corps. When the time
came to elect Arévalo's successor, two army officers vied for leadership
until one was killed suddenly in circumstances that his followers
found suspicious, and their suspicions focused on the other contender,
Col. Jacobo Arbenz, who won the election of 1950.

Partly as a way of escaping his dependence on the officer corps, *Jacobo*
Arbenz increased the government's efforts to mobilize popular politi- *Arbenz*
cal support. His extension of the agrarian reform into new regions of
Guatemala dangerously intensified conservative opposition. Less radical than the Mexican legislation that had inspired it, the Guatemalan
agrarian reform law of 1952 threatened to expropriate only unculti-
vated lands, but it happened that these lands belonged to some of the
most powerful landowners in the country. Most notable among these
was the United Fruit Company, which also objected to the government's projected construction of a highway and port that would destroy United Fruit's transportation monopoly in Guatemala's Atlantic
lowlands. At this point the U.S. secretary of state, John Foster Dulles,
whose close personal connections with United Fruit doubtless informed his perspective, decided to put an end to the reformist experiment, less because of Communist participation in the reforms, it
would appear, than because of the Arbenz government's refusal to join
the United States' anti-Communist crusade. Dulles was correct in
believing that if a tiny country like Guatemala were able to ignore
with impunity his calls for Pan-American unity, U.S. political hege- *CIA overthrow*
mony over the hemisphere would be severely compromised. *of Arbenz*

The overthrow of Arbenz by the U.S. Central Intelligence Agency
and disaffected elements of the Guatemalan army was followed by the
destruction of the worker and peasant organizations that had contrib-

uted such vitality to the ten years of social reform since 1944. Col. Carlos Castillo Armas, the chief of a small dissident faction of (still somewhat reformist) military officers, ruled until 1957, when a true representative of the pre-1944 order, Gen. Miguel Ydígoras Fuentes, became president, completing the restoration of the status quo ante: the traditional formulas of oligarchy and dictatorship. Developments after 1960 would show that the old formulas could no longer be maintained by the sporadic and small-scale brutalities of the past. Instead, the regimes restored by U.S. initiative in 1954 would encounter ever sharper resistance and eventually make massacres routine.

In Costa Rica, where a process of social reform had already begun by 1945, the cold war context had a very different impact. Costa Rica's ruling National Republican party, of enlightened oligarchical extraction, had begun to defend the interests of public employees and other salaried members of the dependent middle class. The numerous small coffee growers, who constituted a Costa Rican peculiarity within the general Central American picture, had benefited much less, and they became the backbone of a new Social Democratic party that made an electoral alliance with the conservative opposition in 1948. Refused the fruits of their victory at the polls, the opposition forces rebelled. Communist organizers raised worker militias on coastal banana plantations to defend the government, but Social Democratic leader José Figueres rallied supporters in the coffee-growing areas for the revolution and triumphed militarily. As head of the resulting junta, Figueres not only promoted infrastructural and agricultural development but also nationalized banks and actually abolished the Costa Rican army. The anti-Communism of Figueres (who banned the party in Costa Rica) allowed him to proceed with his ambitious social reforms without interference from (and even occasionally protected by) the U.S. State Department. The constituent election of 1949 brought the conservatives briefly to power, but Figueres's Party of National Liberation achieved a crushing electoral majority in 1952.

As the cumulative result of the 1948 revolution and the ensuing string of innovations, Costa Rica became something of a tropical welfare state. The National Liberation program included higher income taxes, industrial protectionism, sanitation, pensions, hospitals, and schools. It reached out to small entrepreneurs and workers on the United Fruit plantations of the Atlantic coast, formerly marginalized from Costa Rican national life. Although the conservatives continued to alternate in power because of the electorate's ill humor at an occasional economic downturn or at a particularly infelicitous administration, they did not dare to alter the consensual socioeconomic

model instituted by the party of Figueres. The continued viability
of that model depended on the maintenance of economic prosperity,
but, at least in the period currently under consideration, Costa Rica's
staunchly anti-Communist alignment in the cold war assured it access to development funds controlled by the United States.

Postwar politics in Chile confirmed the recovery of that country's
proverbial constitutional stability, as well as its unequaled sensitivity
to European examples. The renewed international prestige of representative democracy brought nothing less than a revival of the Popular
Front, which, before World War II, had united Communists and radical
factions of various other parties in a mass-based movement for significant social reform. The candidate of the Radical party left wing,
Gabriel González Videla, received the most votes—though not an
absolute majority—in the election of 1946. As president, González
Videla tried to broaden his coalition by including some conservatives
in his cabinet, a tactic that first threatened to rob his administration of
its ability to act coherently and ultimately pushed it to the right. The
president's support on the left disintegrated as the Communists withdrew from the coalition, further precipitating the administration's
conservative turn. In a bid to retain the support that earlier Popular
Front governments had received from the United States, González
Videla aligned Chile firmly on the U.S. side in the emerging cold war.
Because of a general strike, the regime then outlawed the Communist
party, and many members, including the poet Pablo Neruda, a senator
at the time, were imprisoned or driven out of the country. The government that had begun as a Popular Front completed its ideological transfiguration by orienting its economic policies increasingly to
landowning interests and neglecting those of the urban working and
middle classes.

The constituencies thus orphaned by the regime now discovered
new attractions in the figure of Carlos Ibáñez, remembered for his
popularly oriented (if authoritarian) presidency of the late 1920s. In the
1950s, Ibáñez proposed to accelerate industrialization, end inflation,
carry out an agrarian reform, and perform other not inconsiderable
tasks sorely desired by Chileans feeling the pressures of a troubled
postwar economy. Anathematized by the political leadership of almost
all the country's established parties, Ibáñez nevertheless emerged triumphant in the 1952 presidential election, but the combative style of
the old caudillo did not serve him well in the new era, and his proposed
economic remedies fell flat. Chile's international trade situation worsened so much that Ibáñez had to retool his economic policies along
lines recommended by the International Monetary Fund, provoking a

violent popular reaction against the government. In an effort to mollify rising discontent, the beleaguered president permitted the gradual legalization of the Communist party. The Socialist party, which also gathered strength and recovered its unity in the mid-1950s under the leadership of Salvador Allende, reestablished its old alliance with the Communists.

In the decade and a half between the election of 1958 and the military coup of 1973, the division between the forces championed by Allende and those that opposed him was to be the most important cleavage in the Chilean political system. The left achieved this unprecedented prominence in Chilean political life because the country's socioeconomic stagnation had created a widespread desire for audacious solutions. The Socialists proposed to create a coalition uniting the parties of the left in a movement with clearly proletarian and revolutionary contours. Although the battle lines were clearly drawn, Allende's Socialists and their allies had, as yet, little chance of overcoming the powerful forces arrayed against them. For that reason their Communist rivals continued to insist on the need for a broader alliance across class lines to increase the chances of immediate electoral success. The Christian Democratic party, which blossomed in the reform-minded climate of the late 1950s, was the Communists' middle-class ally of choice. In the 1958 election, Allende took second place and Eduardo Frei, the Christian Democratic candidate, third. The winner, representing the traditional right and middle-class voters frightened by the steady corrosion of their standard of living, was Jorge Alessandri, son of the liberal agitator of the 1920s and conservative president of the 1930s. Alessandri had promised to restrain inflation and stimulate growth through a return to orthodoxy in financial management and a further opening of the Chilean economy to international trade. His anti-inflation campaign achieved a remarkable success, but the country's continuing economic slump and uncertain political future kept Alessandri from attracting the international investment he hoped would promote expansion of the export sector. Thanks to continuing economic stagnation, the denouement of Chile's ongoing national dilemma seemed no closer to 1960 than at the end of World War II.

Mexico, on the other hand, traversed the early postwar period on a steady course set by its governing elite in 1940. Without abandoning a rhetorical commitment to the social objectives of the 1910 revolution, the presidents from Manuel Ávila Camacho onward sacrificed those objectives in practice to the goal of economic growth. The leaders of popular organizations who had accepted the new emphasis as a temporary expedient during the war years turned out to have lost their influence in the government permanently. The removal of the left wing's most influential national figure, Vicente Lombardo Toledano, as head of the Mexican Workers' Federation exemplifies this changing of the guard. The new generation had not participated in the armed struggle of the revolution. Unlike his presidential predecessors, Miguel Alemán, the chief executive who took office in 1946, did not come from the army, which was henceforth to be the docile servant of a developmentalist state and no longer the proud standard-bearer of the revolution's epic past. The consolidation of the state was reflected in the absence of any challenge to each president's officially designated successor and the conversion of the subsequent "election campaign" into something more closely resembling the triumphal tour of an anointed heir. Under Alemán, the official party also signaled the nature of its internal evolution in an apt change of name, from the Party of the Mexican Revolution to the Institutional Revolutionary Party (PRI).

The PRI's emphasis on economic growth found a variety of expressions. The postwar Mexican state channeled much of its financial support to the private sector through a government development corporation originally created by Lázaro Cárdenas in the 1930s and now altered in character and enormously expanded. Official policy intensified industrial protectionism but also systematically encouraged surreptitious foreign investment in industrial endeavors. Spending on public works underwent a dramatic increase, especially for the construction of roads. An improved internal transportation network not only promoted the integration of the domestic market but also stimulated tourism, and tourist dollars from the United States (along with the money sent back by Mexicans working north of the border) helped alleviate the balance-of-payment problem suffered by so many Latin American countries. The necessarily close relationship between the Mexican economy and that of the United States was therefore an advantage to the PRI in the period under consideration.

The PRI also had exceptional freedom of action in designing and executing economic policies because of the superior degree of autonomy enjoyed by the Mexican state. The power of large landowners, so often an obstacle in other countries, had been decisively broken in Mexico during the revolution, and the country's popular organizations, once forces for social change, had become organs of state control over society, with the result that Mexican leaders took their policy decisions relatively unperturbed by the pressures of popular demands. Nor did they have reason to fear the kind of military intervention in politics that had become all too frequent elsewhere. Consequently, the portion of the national budget consumed by the Mexican armed forces was by far the lowest of any major Latin American country. The Alemán administration turned its structural advantages into impressive accomplishments. The advance of Mexican industrialization was among the world's most dynamic in these years, and the increase in agricultural production, faster yet. On the darker side, encouragement of growth in favored economic sectors was accomplished partly by government toleration of high inflation, eventually provoking a level of urban discontent further exacerbated by scarcely concealed official corruption. Once again, as in the 1920s, an orgy of improbity was fusing political and business leadership into a new national elite.

The next president, Adolfo Ruiz Cortinas, who succeeded Alemán in 1952, applied correctives to the problems of rampant corruption and inflation. Characteristically of the Mexican case, his solutions were not untypical of those attempted elsewhere, with the important difference that they succeeded. The attack on inflation, for example, began with a drastic devaluation of the peso of the kind applied almost everywhere, but rather than foundering after a few months, to be repeated uselessly ad infinitum, the Mexican anti-inflation measures fixed the exchange rate of the peso unalterably for twenty years. Foreign capital continued to flow into this reassuringly stable investment climate, and the rhythm of economic growth, while slower than in the feverish period under Alemán, remained quite satisfactory during the mid-1950s, lending credence to the official proposition that Mexico had entered a long period of "stabilizing development" destined to solve social as well as economic problems in the long term.

In 1958, the new president, Adolfo López Mateos, awakened hopes that the government might go beyond developmentalist nostrums to revitalize the promises of social justice inscribed on the banners of the Mexican Revolution. Such hopes were soon dashed, however, when the state brutally repressed an independent railroad strike launched to test the waters, meting out draconian punishments to the organizers and giving clear indication that any alteration in its labor policy would result from official paternalism rather than popular pressure. López Mateos made equally ambiguous gestures in the direction of agrarian reform. Aggregate figures from the time indicate the distribution of quantities of land surpassed in Mexican history only by the Cárdenas administration, but social justice hardly seems to have been the primary goal.

There were two separate processes under way. The first responded to rural population pressure and the need for expanded agricultural production in central Mexico. Coupled with low commodity prices that kept the recipients living at not much above the subsistence level, this land distribution served larger purposes by assuring adequate food supplies for the rapidly growing urban population. The second aspect of land reform in these years must be viewed in the context of economic transformations in the Mexican north. There, vast arid tracts had been irrigated in highly capitalized projects using sophisticated techniques. These lands produced a diverse array of crops, both for export and for upper- and middle-class domestic consumers no longer satisfied with the traditional Mexican diet. Ironically, through various forms of legal or illegal manipulation, the framework of land reform in the new lands of northern Mexico helped create replicas of U.S. agrobusiness enterprises.

In sum, the Mexico of 1960 boasted economic advances unparalleled in Latin America. Its performance was all the more impressive because of inherent difficulties in exploiting some of the country's resources and because the pace of population growth now tended to undercut the country's economic gains. For the time being, the developmentalist solution worked well enough to create political stability. Far from achieving the egalitarian society promised by the revolution, Mexico exhibited inequalities more marked than those of many other Latin American countries with avowedly conservative governments. However, if most Mexicans no longer believed the government's protestations of revolutionary commitment, the gradual improvement of majority living standards over the period of a generation was unusual enough in their historical experience to legitimate the regime for some years to come.

In Bolivia, considerations of cold war geopolitics allowed the consolidation of a revolution more radical than any discussed so far. The postwar history of Bolivia began with a surprising turn after 1946. The collapse of a nationalist military regime in that year had dragged down a number of reform forces with it, leaving the field open for a resurgence of the country's traditional oligarchical parties. These lost no time in reasserting their control over army officers and Communist organizers, who, in another of the odd tactical alliances typical of the time, had cooperated to bring down the dictatorship. The oligarchical restoration (which its adherents preferred to call "democratic") then postponed all social reforms as inherently threatening to the country's political stability. Bolivia's economic situation, temporarily buoyed up by its near monopoly on tin during World War II, now deteriorated as tin-mining areas formerly under Japanese control returned to the world market in the late 1940s. As the motor of the country's export economy slowed, so did the inflows of tax revenue, and the government returned to its inveterate practice of printing money to meet its expenses.

The National Revolutionary Movement (MNR) that had seemed so discredited in 1946 suddenly returned to life, throwing off its now dated quasi-fascist motifs and incorporating formerly Trotskyite labor organizations led by the miner Juan Lechín. In the 1951 election, MNR leader Víctor Paz Estenssoro received more votes than any other candidate but fell short of an absolute majority. Given the literacy requirements for suffrage at the time, the election indicated potentially huge support for Paz Estenssoro among the disenfranchised majority. The panicky civil authorities consequently arranged for themselves to be overthrown by generals whom they trusted to keep the situation in hand, but a contrary movement with minimal army support was joined by a miners' militia, and together they captured the city of La Paz and put the MNR in power. The revolution of 1952 made Paz Estenssoro president and radically changed the basis of political power in Bolivia by conferring the right to vote on the illiterate majority, reducing the army to a shadow of its former self, and making the miners' militias the foremost armed power in the country.

The new strength of the miners found an immediate echo in the nationalization of the large tin mines. Most former owners received generous indemnities and preserved their control over refining plants outside of Bolivia. As a result, they continued to dictate the price of tin within the country, thereby limiting the economic benefits of the miners' achievement. The miners, for their part, demanded improved working conditions that put the beleaguered tin industry permanently in the red, a situation that made the nationalization of tin practically irreversible. Worried about the consequences of a miners' hegemony in the new political landscape of Bolivia, Paz Estenssoro and other MNR leaders sought to offset their influence by encouraging the growth of peasant organizations in the countryside.

Agrarian reform, of course, was the most important incentive for peasant mobilization. Before the 1950s, peasant militancy had been notable only in Cochabamba and around Lake Titicaca, where commercial agriculture had already reduced the hold of traditional social relations. The initiatives of the MNR now politicized the vast areas of the country where traditional haciendas had maintained their sway over indigenous communities until the mid-twentieth century. Representatives of Bolivia's corporate peasant communities rose up, under the aegis of the MNR, to recover a mode of political power with deep roots in the colonial past. Vastly surpassing the miners' unions in membership, these peasant organizations were nevertheless too diffuse—and, at least occasionally, too distracted by ancient intercommunity rivalries—to challenge the dominant political role of the tin workers, but they did restore a measure of balance to the political system that had emerged from the revolution.

The support of peasant organizations became increasingly important as the MNR lost favor among the urban masses who had contributed decisively to its rise in 1952. In the long run, the government's agrarian reform and highway construction would redound to the benefit of urban dwellers, particularly by incorporating new lands on the eastern slopes of the Andes into the national market for agricultural products. In the short term, however, the revolution's efforts to dismantle the hacienda system disrupted the flow of food to the cities and the mines. Because of their influence in the government, the miners were able to secure preferential provisioning during the periods of shortage, exacerbating antigovernment sentiments in urban areas and enabling the semifascist Bolivian Socialist Falange to gain an electoral majority in the cities. The MNR survived the rapid erosion of urban political support partly because of its new rural constituency and partly because of the support it received, surprisingly enough, from the United States.

During the first years of the MNR government, the Eisenhower administration provided funds to attenuate the potentially destabilizing effects of Bolivia's international trade imbalance, thus acquiring, at a modest cost, a Latin American showcase of social change under U.S. auspices. As might be expected, this state of affairs did not long endure, though it appears that the Bolivian government's unorthodox financial policies worried its capitalist sponsor more than did the ideological radicalism of the MNR left wing. By the mid-1950s, the U.S. government began to push for more conservative economic policies, and Hernán Siles Suazo, who succeeded Paz Estenssoro as president in 1956, made every effort to comply. Although Siles Suazo made real progress in stabilizing the national economy, the internal contours of political power limited his room to maneuver. Most constricting was the continued dominance of the tin miners, who made further gains in the election of 1960, when Paz Estenssoro sought a new term as president, this time with Juan Lechín, the veteran unionist, as his running mate. Unfortunately for the MNR, Paz Estenssoro's electoral victory put the party's left wing in office just as the Cuban Revolution was heightening the anti-Communist preoccupation in U.S. policy toward Latin America. Also, there was a still-greater internal puzzle to be solved by the Bolivian revolution: how to create a market economy that could function within the social and political parameters created by the revolution of 1952.

no democratization Nicaragua Somoza dynasty

The democratizing wave of the immediate postwar period had less impact outside the countries already described. In Nicaragua, Honduras, and El Salvador, for example, it might as well never have existed. In Nicaragua, it failed to loosen the grip of the Somoza dynasty at all. Not even the assassination of Anastasio Somoza, Sr., in 1956 could succeed in doing that, since an election in the following year made Somoza's son Luis president of Nicaragua, and the enrichment of families close to the Somozas proceeded unabated. The most notable economic change was the introduction of new agricultural export enterprises, especially cotton. Appreciable democratization did not occur in Honduras and El Salvador, either. Instead, the dictatorships that had ruled both countries during the 1930s and 1940s simply relaxed into more or less stable oligarchical republics.

Honduras + El Salvador relaxing dictators

Ecuador

Velasco Ibarra

Ecuador saw the return to power, in 1944, of José María Velasco Ibarra, the popular leader who claimed, not without reason, that all he needed to become elected president of Ecuador was a balcony from which to address the crowd. The military had already once removed him from the presidency in the mid-1930s. Much as had occurred on that occasion, Velasco Ibarra's dictatorial actions soon gave the military an excuse to overthrow him again in favor of Galo Plaza—a less volatile representative of the country's economic elite and a man who, as an added benefit, had earlier held an influential position in the United Fruit Company. Soon Ecuador's dynamic coastal region became an important producer of bananas, exported by United Fruit but grown by a prospering class of middle-sized landowners whose presence changed the social landscape of that part of the country. However, nothing, it seemed, could prevent periodic incursions of Velasco Ibarra onto the national stage. In 1952, the aging Velasco Ibarra returned from Argentina, where he had learned a thing or two in the school of Peronism, and he won another presidential election with his durable mass appeal and antitraditionalist rhetoric. Once again, he quickly broke with the organizations that had helped him get elected and began to reveal his underlying authoritarianism. On this third try Velasco Ibarra at least finished his stormy term of office. The conservatives had helped make that possible by offering him their lightly veiled support in hopes of inheriting control of an intact constitutional framework at the end of his term, but they were dismayed to see the irrepressible Velasco Ibarra elected again in 1960.

To solve the riddle of Velasco Ibarra, one must see how the ineffectual redeemer promised, but repeatedly failed, to fill an aching void that had opened in Ecuadorian political life as the economic changes of the postwar period eroded the traditional bonds of social deference. The society of the coast was becoming too diverse to remain much longer under the sway of the liberal oligarchy that had dominated it since the late nineteenth century. The highlands, for their part, experienced the transforming pull of growing urban markets (especially Quito's), a stimulus to which the indigenous country people responded more effectively than did the conservative seigneurial class in decline. As the traditional political order lost its hold, no coherent force had emerged to take its place. The repetitious tragicomedy protagonized by Velasco Ibarra, for all its apparent incoherence, represents nothing less than the struggle of democratic forces to be born.

Paraguay's history between 1945 and 1960 presents more somber lines. The postwar winds of change found the Paraguayan government in the hands of the Colorado party and military officers of moderately reformist inclinations. The prestige of constitutional democracy, temporarily influential, encouraged a reemergence of the renovating political currents that had flowed in Paraguay during the late 1930s (shorn, now, of the corporatist trappings popular during that decade). A suppressed liberal and left-wing revolt in 1947 hastened the transfer of power into the hands of a civilian, Natalicio González, a Colorado who venerated the country's military and authoritarian glory days in the period leading to the Paraguayan War but also displayed interest in certain ideological motifs used by APRA in Peru. When González began to undercut the institutional power of the military too much, the army replaced him with another Colorado, Federico Chaves, who disappointed the army with his promotion of Peronist-style social policies not to their liking. In 1954, Gen. Alfredo Stroessner overthrew Chaves and began his long, highly repressive dictatorship. Stroessner's regime was essentially military, though the Colorado party continued to function as its political instrument. In many ways, Paraguay under Stroessner approximated a Central American model, with a strong emphasis on the construction of communications infrastructure to foster economic growth and a systematic neglect of festering social problems. A country of fewer than two million inhabitants, Paraguay lost 400,000 economic and political refugees in a steady flow to Argentina and Brazil before 1960.

Uruguay, on the other hand, had recovered its constitutional government well before the end of World War II, and the disappointments that it endured were of a different nature. Having joined the Allied cause with particular enthusiasm, Uruguayans had imagined that victory would bring an improvement in their daily lives. To the contrary, the cessation of hostilities seemed only to accelerate the country's troublesome wartime inflation. In the presidential election of 1946, the individual candidate who received the most votes was Luis Alberto de Herrera, a Blanco who drew on a number of Peronist themes. Because of Uruguay's unusual electoral system, however, the presidency went to the Colorados, who had won more votes as a party. The leading Colorado of this period was Luis Batlle Berres, nephew of the party's great reformist president of earlier in the century, but not alone in seeking to be the standard-bearer of Batllismo. His competition for that honor came from more conservative members of the family with strong influence in the Colorado party, including control of its most important newspaper. Batlle Berres was fortunate to be president of Uruguay at the outbreak of the Korean War, which provided a strong impetus to the country's economy, giving him an opportunity to apply successfully his approach to industrialization. Uruguay's postwar prosperity was not destined to last, but it left Montevideo with an impressive array of luxurious high-rise buildings and a series of consumer expectations that would be difficult to satisfy in the leaner years ahead.

The Uruguayan countryside, meanwhile, had been made to subsidize urban affluence through official price policies. Large-scale ranchers could partially escape their effects by sending their herds illegally across the border to market in Brazil, but farmers and smaller livestock producers did not have that option. The discontent of the "forgotten man" of the interior was crystallized by the radio programs of Benito Nardone, who became the leader of a rural protest movement and eventually guided it into the Blanco party. In 1958, the Blancos regained the presidency for the first time since 1865, but their euphoria soon vanished into disenchantment. The "parasitic" bureaucracy and the "artificial" industrialization that employed so many urban Uruguayans had made wonderful rhetorical targets for ruralist rhetoric, but serious moves against them were not politically feasible. For many years, Uruguay's electoral clienteles had distributed public employment, with 40 percent of them going to the opposition. The country's vaunted democratic institutions thus began to appear, upon closer inspection, inert and paralyzed, despite mass participation in the electoral process.

In Colombia, the years between 1945 and 1960 were dark, indeed, and the tempest struck with little warning. In 1946, Mariano Ospina Pérez, a conservative, recovered the presidency from the divided liberals, who had held it since the early 1930s, and set about rebuilding the solid conservative domination of the first three decades of the twentieth century. This conservative resurgence encouraged the most intransigent elements within the party to seize the initiative. Setting their sights on the presidential election of 1950, they drew on all the resources of the conservative government to crush the liberals' ability to mount an effective opposition. Jorge Eliécer Gaitán, the liberal whose oratory attracted huge crowds of urban dwellers, responded by leading thousands of followers on silent protest marches through the streets of Bogotá. Gaitán's assassination in 1948 set off the most devastating urban riot in the history of Spanish America, temporarily cowing the conservatives and encouraging the startled liberal elite, themselves a bit unnerved by the explosion of popular wrath, to make temporary peace with the conservative government. Once the emergency had passed, however, the spirit of elite consensus evaporated, the conservatives returned to their partisan offensive, and the liberals returned to their determined opposition.

Across large areas of the Colombian countryside, partisan bloodshed escalated in the next ten years to a level that took hundreds of thousands of lives in an orgy of killing remembered, in Colombia, simply as "la Violencia." Although channeled by party loyalties, the violence drew its devastating force from social tensions that had been accumulating in rural areas for decades, tensions that the liberals themselves had exploited during the 1930s in their efforts to break the patterns of oligarchical domination that undergirded early twentieth-century conservative political hegemony. In historical perspective, it is evident that, by accelerating the rural exodus to the cities, the violence resulted in a concentration of landholding for the cultivation of new commercial crops. At the time, however, the Conservative party's crusade to refashion Colombian political life along lines similar to those of Franco's Spain seemed most important in driving the conflict. This was especially the case when Laureano Gómez, the ultrarightist leader originally behind the conservative offensive, became president in 1950. Gómez extended government patronage to Catholic workers' organizations and extended systematic government persecution to include even Protestant missionaries and their congregations, in defiance of U.S. public opinion. Eventually, it became evident that the tenacious resistance of liberal guerrilla armies in a number of regions would be able to deny Gómez the definitive victory he sought. Although partially implicated in the campaign of official violence, the Colombian army was not committed to the crusade of the ultraright and wished to avoid deeper involvement. Alarmed by the threat of a prolonged civil war, the army finally ousted Gómez in

1953 and replaced him with one of their own, Gen. Gustavo Rojas Pinilla.

Contrary to general expectations, Rojas Pinilla took Colombian political life in a populist direction. A moderate conservative when he became president, he was welcomed initially with considerable enthusiasm by the liberals, who hoped for a restoration of the traditional political order. However, taking a leaf from the book of Peronism, Rojas Pinilla began to build a new, more personal political base that cut across old party lines to follow the socioeconomic cleavages that emerged ever more sharply in mid-twentieth-century Colombian cities, much as the liberal caudillo Gaitán had attempted a decade earlier.

Rojas Pinilla failed to reshape the political landscape in the way that Perón had done in more urbanized Argentina, but he did alarm both of the country's traditional parties. When it became evident that Rojas Pinilla did not view his presidency as a brief transitional phase, liberal and conservative leaders combined against him. The head of the Liberal party, Alberto Lleras Camargo, traveled to meet with the exiled conservative leader Laureano Gómez in Spain, and there the two agreed upon a plan of collaboration between their two parties. For the following sixteen years—four presidential terms—liberals and conservatives agreed to alternate in the control of that office and to divide representation equally in collective bodies such as the national congress. This National Pact, as it was called, had immediate consequences. Formal conservative antagonism to Rojas Pinilla brought the Catholic church actively into the opposition, and that move was followed by a general strike and universal lockout. In 1957, Rojas Pinilla finally abandoned his hopes for another presidential term and fled the country as the army, too, aligned itself with the National Pact.

Colombia's traditional parties had recovered the reins of power with relative ease, but the road ahead was plagued with difficulties. First, though the violent turmoil in the countryside declined and altered in character, it remained chronic in some regions. Second, during the 1950s Colombian cities had grown faster than ever as rural refugees sought to escape the bloodletting, and the traditional liberals and conservatives still seemed incapable of effectively incorporating new urban sectors into their political base. The liberal left wing that had cultivated these groups in the past hesitated to do so now for fear of disrupting the bipartisan spirit of the National Pact. Indeed, bipartisanism now began to undermine the polarities of partisan loyalty that had enabled the oligarchically dominated Liberal and Conservative parties to retain the loyalty of most Colombians for more than a century. The third difficulty was economic. By 1960, government-sponsored industrialization (another cause of rapid urban growth) was encountering structural barriers similar to those in other Latin American countries. To complete the disheartening prospect of 1960, it became plain that the coffee boom so helpful in attenuating the consequences of postwar political conflict would not last long enough to facilitate the return to constitutional rule.

It was the Caribbean, so often atypical of political patterns in the rest of Latin America because of its tighter and more enduring colonial and neocolonial links, that announced the end of the early postwar period for the region as a whole in 1959. The pivotal event, of course, was the triumph of the Cuban Revolution, which merits extended consideration and has no parallels in the Dominican Republic or Puerto Rico. Dominican history in the period 1945–60 can be reduced, in summary, to the consolidation of the Trujillo dictatorship and the increasing elaboration of the sugar plantation economy described in the preceding chapter. A more detailed preliminary discussion of Puerto Rico, on the other hand, will provide a useful counterpoint to the Cuban experience.

By the middle of the twentieth century, U.S. domination had finally begun to transform all areas of Puerto Rican life. Economic integration and migration were succeeding where early attempts to assimilate the island into North American culture through the educational system had failed. The occupation of the island's fertile coastal plain by U.S. sugar interests had created a monocrop economy almost as one-dimensional as those that had characterized other Caribbean sites in the heyday of sugar and slaves. After World War II, the U.S. connection began to resonate in Puerto Rican political life, still monopolized by a tiny urban elite and divided by three distinct positions vis-à-vis the United States, some arguing the advantages of continuing under the aegis of the United States as an autonomous commonwealth, others advocating U.S. statehood or the third alternative, total independence. The island's first political mass movement emerged under the leadership of an *autonomista*, Luis Muñoz Marín. Like many of his young collaborators, Muñoz Marín had been strongly attracted by the New Deal, and, following a pattern more influenced by the U.S. than the Latin American experience, he had renounced the socialist convictions of his youth to embrace a more moderate reformism in the postwar years. Turning away from the anticolonialist preoccupation of earlier Puerto Rican politics, the Popular Democratic party founded by Muñoz Marín concentrated instead on the issues of social reform and economic development.

In 1947, popular enthusiasm for the party's program enabled its founder to become Puerto Rico's first elected governor. (Previous governors had been appointed to the post by the president of the United States.) Once in office, Muñoz Marín obtained for the island the status of a commonwealth with administrative autonomy and full control over the educational system. The new situation protected Puerto Rico's Hispanic heritage from direct assimilationist threats but somewhat offset this effect by further tightening the economic bonds between island and mainland because the development program of the new government emphasized the need to attract investment capital from the metropolis. As its principal attraction, Puerto Rico offered a labor force too numerous to be overly demanding in terms of wages and working conditions, complemented by social legislation that followed mainland U.S. trends at a prudent distance. Substantial economic diversification did occur on the island, although not enough to absorb the island's extremely rapid demographic growth. Mounting federal subsidies and accelerating emigration to the mainland helped alleviate the demographic pressure at a cost (not yet fully appreciated by Puerto Rican leaders) of further economic dependency on the United States. In the short term, Puerto Rico's economic success seemed as impressive as Mexico's, and it brought an even more significant improvement in the standard of living of the rural and urban masses.

In consequence, the political fortunes of Muñoz Marín and the autonomistas soared, and neither the proponents of statehood nor the advocates of independence were able to make much headway beyond their respective—oligarchical and intellectual—core constituencies. Although never reconciled to the island's status as booty won by the United States in 1898, Latin American public opinion as a whole was impressed by the postwar experience of Puerto Rico. After all, U.S. domination had become so thoroughly a fact of life throughout the Caribbean and Central America as hardly to distinguish the Puerto Rican case. What did attract attention was the progress of social reform carried out in the framework of representative democracy by political leaders sharing many of the objectives of Latin American parties whose progress had been forcibly blocked in other countries. The Puerto Rican example was quickly eclipsed, however, when the revolution in neighboring Cuba returned anti-imperialist nationalism to center stage in the hemispheric drama.

The international resonances of the Cuban Revolution may obscure its origins in the specific historical experience of Cuba, where the patriotism of the wars for independence in the late nineteenth century flowed directly into the anti-imperialism of the mid-twentieth century. As a result of that continuity, the twin issues of national independence and anti-imperialism gained a centrality in Cuban political life unmatched in any other Latin American country. The expressions of Cuban nationalism had been powerful and varied, but also largely frustrated, until the time of the revolution. After its official establishment as a sovereign state in 1902, Cuba had remained, for thirty years, under the formal U.S. tutelage specified by the Platt Amendment. That amendment had been repealed in 1933, but North American hegemony had continued to make itself felt as powerfully as ever through the years of crisis and war. Such was the situation in 1944, when the international vogue for electoral democracy created conditions for Cuba's first government elected without fraud and coercion.

The chief executive who emerged from the election was Ramón Grau San Martín, the former president overthrown by the army with U.S. encouragement a decade earlier because of his combative attitude toward the United States and his taste for radical social reforms. Returning to office in 1944, Grau consolidated his electoral strength through systematic government corruption fueled by the temporary prosperity of the island's sugar economy in the early postwar period. Grau's reputation as a political purifier was quickly sullied, but the flush times of his administration contrasted sufficiently with the preceding lean years to win the 1948 presidential election for his minister of labor, Carlos Prío Socarrás. As the cold war began in earnest, Prío courted the favor of the United States by purging Cuban labor unions of Communist influence, but he gradually lost domestic support as the price of sugar dropped and, inevitably in a country still dominated by its export crop par excellence, the formerly rosy economic picture darkened. A boom in the tourist industry partially offset the deterioration of sugar prices, but tourism brought with it a rise in various undesirable activities, especially prostitution. Increasingly unhappy with the pervasive corruption that thrived in such circumstances (but spread its benefits less lavishly than during the recent sugar boom), Cubans responded to new calls for a moralizing patriotism. This time the spokesperson was a popular radio personality, Eduardo Chibás, candidate of the new Orthodox party. The Ortodoxos appeared to be the certain victors of the upcoming 1952 election even after their flamboyant leader committed suicide during one of his radio programs, to be replaced by a less charismatic figure.

Also seeking the presidency in 1952 was the former dictator, Fulgencio Batista. Since Batista did not have widespread support in the Cuban electorate, however, he cut his links with the Communists to appeal to U.S. policymakers and used the army to make himself dictator again. No longer able to clothe himself, as in the 1930s and 1940s, in the legitimacy of social reform, and confronted by massive opposition, Batista ruled much more repressively than in his previous dictatorship. Powerful currents of public opinion stirred up by the Ortodoxos found an ideal target in the dictator's venal and ideologically bankrupt rule and constituted an important barrier to its consolidation. In 1953 a young Ortodoxo named Fidel Castro began his revolutionary career by leading an attack on one of Batista's military barracks. The attackers hoped to spark a general insurrection, but their desperate tactic failed when the uprising did not occur. Their failure, and the brutal government response, discouraged other attempts to overthrow the dictator for a time. The next year Batista felt strong enough to run unopposed for president, and, in the warm glow of his electoral triumph, he made a number of benevolent gestures toward the opposition. As the result of one of these, Fidel Castro was allowed to leave his Cuban prison for exile in Mexico.

Immediately, Castro began to plan his return to Cuba. By 1956, he had put together a tiny guerrilla force that disembarked on Cuban shores, climbed into the Sierra Maestra Mountains in the thinly populated eastern part of the island, and began to rally popular support. Day after day, the rebels' radio transmitter broadcast their presence to the rest of Cuba, and the insurgents eventually gained international attention on the front page of the *New York Times*. Batista reacted with increasing savagery, and the revolution did not gain much momentum in the cities. When Castro called for a general strike, at one point, neither the Communist party nor the country's labor unions responded. However, in its mountain fastness the rebel army remained unbeatable, and the rural insurgency eventually began to expand its operations onto the plains rich with commercial agriculture. Then, as so many times before in the history of Cuba, the towering smoke of burning cane fields announced the government's inability to guarantee order. Among those who began to withdraw support from Batista at this point where his erstwhile allies in the U.S. government, who placed an embargo on the shipment of arms to his government. By mid-1958, when the insurgents began their final offensive, the dictator's forces were totally demoralized.

On New Year's Day, 1959, delirious crowds greeted the bearded guerrillas as they entered Havana in triumph. The Cuban people saw the revolutionaries of the Sierra Maestra as heirs of a long line of nationalist redeemers, thwarted time and again in the past by internal and external enemies. This specifically Cuban aspect of the revolution formed the trunk from which another, social revolution would spring,

taking definitive shape only after a decade of feverish experimentation. The eventual adoption of Soviet models had roots in patriotic,
anti-imperialist attitudes that signified implacable opposition to the
island's former hegemonic master through close identification with
its rival. The day of the revolutionary victory also marked the clear
ascendancy of Fidel Castro as the unquestioned leader of all forces of
the revolution, even without the existence of a unified command
structure. In the eyes of the excited crowd, Castro so effectively embodied the revolution that institutionalization of his leadership could
be postponed without confusion. In the meantime, a tremendous
amount of power was concentrated in his hands, foreshadowing the
authoritarian cast of a future regime that departed from Latin American norms only in the novel institutional form it gave, eventually, to
the entirely vernacular tendency of strong one-man rule.

The authoritarian outcome of the Cuban Revolution presents
much less an interpretive problem than does its rapid evolution into a
social revolution utterly unannounced by political developments in
Cuba during the period 1944–59. Contemporary explanations of this
evolution are less convincing when viewed from the perspective of
more than three decades afterward. Contrary to a formulation once
popular, the Cuban Revolution no longer seems a middle-class protest
that became radical because the island's economically dependent society lacked internal structures that might have channeled reformist
energies toward more modest goals. That interpretation, and all others
that seek the origins of the revolution in social conflict, must solve the
riddle of why a movement promising profound socioeconomic change
garnered so little support among those whom the reforms were intended to benefit. Why did the urban and rural working classes play so
modest a part in the military phase of the revolution? Why, furthermore, did the landowning sugar interests not lift a finger to oppose it?
The answer must be that in 1959 Cuba's was not yet a social revolution, that it became one only as it forged ahead more determinedly
than any previous movement on the moralizing nationalist and anti-
imperialist course set by earlier generations of Cuban revolutionaries.
This historical momentum carried through into the socialist phase of
the movement, though without the national unanimity evident at the
revolution's triumph in 1959. (To understand the genesis of Cuba's
social revolution at a moment of patriotic fervor, rather than socioeconomic conflict, one might recall that George Orwell hoped a revolutionary Britain might emerge in just that way from the national
crisis of World War II.) Finally, Cuba's socialist option might never
have succeeded without the skilled leadership of Fidel Castro, whose

*Soviet
alliance
preceded
the social
revolution*

wisely ambiguous comment to the effect that Cuba could be revolutionary only by becoming Communist becomes clearer if one keeps in
mind that the Soviet alliance preceded and conditioned the island's
social revolution.

The reforms implemented in 1959 fell far short of being revolutionary. Cuba's initial agrarian reform, for example, was based on
principles more moderate than those invoked in Bolivia or Mexico.
The rent-control measures implemented in urban areas resembled
those already adopted by other Latin American governments of widely
varying political orientations. Economic management was entrusted
to a team of young specialists who had done their apprenticeship in
international organizations and were eager to apply solutions that
Latin American economists in general did not consider radical. They
proposed to foment industrialization in ways then current in most
major countries of the hemisphere, using state-supplied credit and
investment to expand the internal market. The moderation of these
initiatives garnered broad support in Cuba, and, to the degree that he
remained personally identified with them, the initiatives strengthened Castro's hand.

During the early stage of the revolution, Castro was able to argue
that institutionalization would encumber, rather than consolidate,
the popular reforms so quickly put under way. Meanwhile, he maintained discreet control of the revolutionary army through its leadership: Ernesto "Che" Guevara, an Argentine doctor who had found his
vocation as a revolutionary with the Arbenz government in Guatemala and had joined Castro's insurgents in Mexico after the overthrow
of Arbenz; Camilo Cienfuegos, another bearded young commander,
who had risen in the revolutionary ranks thanks to his natural skill as
a fighter; and Raúl Castro, Fidel's brother and the only member of his
inner circle who maintained close relations with the Cuban Communist party. Well before the radicalism of the revolution could be gauged
by its final objectives, its leadership showed itself unwilling to observe
the limitations on political and economic action traditionally imposed by U.S. hegemony. This became plain immediately after the
triumphal entry into Havana, when revolutionary tribunals began
summary trials and executions of those the victors regarded as war
criminals.

The social and economic reforms implemented initially by the
Cuban Revolution challenged the United States only to the extent
that any vigorously nationalist economic policy in Cuba necessarily
tasted of defiance to a hegemonic power whose diplomatic representative on the island had viewed with alarm the creation of a separate

Cuban monetary system not many years before. It was Castro's reticence toward the U.S.-controlled Pan-American system, from which Cuba was eventually expelled, that really rankled in Washington, D.C., and his insistence that the United States take responsibility for funding development programs in Latin America infuriated the administration of President Dwight D. Eisenhower, which lost no opportunity to evince its dismay at the losses suffered by U.S. interests as a result of Cuban economic reforms. The suspension of Cuba's sugar import quota in the U.S. market, a tactic that had worked marvelously to bring the island into line in 1933, became a topic of renewed discussion in Washington. This time, however, the arrival of another player changed the dynamics of the game, when, in early 1960, the Soviet Union offered to provide an alternative market for Cuban sugar. Cuba's revolutionaries had found a way, seemingly the only way, to resist the suffocating hegemonic power of the United States. From that moment on, nothing would be the same in Cuba or in the rest of Latin America.

[margin handwriting: turn to Soviet Union for sugar market— only way out of U.S. hegemony]

CHAPTER VIII

A Decade

of Decisions

(1960–1970)

BY 1960 THE DEVELOPMENT STRATEGIES adopted in Latin America during the three previous decades seemed to have exhausted their potential, and the unpredictable socialist outcome of the Cuban Revolution suggested a new turn of events for the region. As both the developed capitalist countries and the countries of the socialist bloc enjoyed powerful and sustained economic growth, Latin Americans regarded the performance of their own economies with increasing disenchantment. To many, the decade of the 1960s constituted a cross-roads where the future course of the region's history would be determined. The mood of urgency within Latin America, which was now beginning to understand itself as part of the "Third" World, heightened the effects of a new interventionism from the "First" and "Second" Worlds, emboldened by their prosperity to take a more active role in Latin American affairs. In various ways, then, internationalism was in the air.

The creation, in 1960, of both the Latin American Free Trade Association and the Central American Common Market represents one aspect of the region's search for new options to overcome economic stagnation. The Free Trade Association, joined by all the major countries, wove its way carefully through a maze of sensitive sectoral interests in each to elaborate a modest list of tariff-free goods. After this initial success, however, the political pressures made it impossible to expand the list. The more compact Central American Common Market had a considerable impact on the isthmus for a few years before it, too, succumbed. As developmentalist programs lost momentum in the respective member countries, multinational corporations seemed likely to benefit most from these international trade agreements, which greatly facilitated their strategies of organization and marketing. The Andean Pact, a third regional trading group formed slightly later, made a concerted (though only moderately successful) effort to limit the influence of such corporations. However, with the exception of Mexico, where such corporations had begun their advance earlier and already constituted a basic element of the country's political economy, the failure of Latin America to keep pace with the growth of the world economy had little to do with the supposedly excessive influence of the multinationals. Partly owing to the climate of alarm within the region, foreign investors were wary, and their participation was, in fact, not strong enough to incorporate Latin America into the international economic boom, with its accompanying social costs.

The dilemmas of Latin American development were hardly new, of course, but the widely acknowledged failure of postwar developmentalism put those dilemmas at center stage in the 1960s. More and more, it appeared that the countries of the region could achieve their aspirations only by breaking out of an international framework that many had come to regard as a constraint on healthy economic development in Latin America. Hence the popularity of dependency theory, which explained Third World underdevelopment as a function of the subordinate role played by the affected national economies in the capitalist world order. The thinking of dependency theorists began with basic assumptions not far from those of Raúl Prebisch, whose lack of specific solutions they reproached without really being any more specific themselves. In a general way, however, the *dependentistas* all emphasized the need for radical economic restructuring and belittled the piecemeal modifications proposed by those who took Prebisch as their guide. The majority believed that if Latin America's chief problems were economic, the therapy was nevertheless political, and most recommended a socialist revolution.

The Cuban Revolution thus came at an opportune moment, in the view of those outside Latin America who wished to encourage socialist transformations there, and at a perilous moment for the international champions of capitalism. When policymakers in Moscow and Washington, D.C., spoke of a "Latin America at the crossroads," they both described this reality and indicated their own disposition to influence developments in the region. Their prolonged economic expansion of the postwar period daily seemed to push back the limits of the possible in all realms of human endeavor. In the United States and the Soviet Union, respectively, Lyndon Johnson announced the construction of a capitalist Great Society where poverty would be totally eliminated, and Nikita Khrushchev proclaimed that the millenarian moment, the transition to pure communism, was near at hand. The Catholic church, another important international actor in Latin

America, decided at the Second Vatican Council to confront pastoral challenges that had been building up for a century.

These forces not only took on a more activist attitude regarding Latin America but also modified their goals. Soviet willingness to sponsor the Cuban Revolution represented an important new direction in the foreign policy of the world's second superpower. Convinced that the dynamism of global socioeconomic change called for a new approach, the Soviets now abandoned the prudent conservatism that had characterized their international relations for more than a quarter century. As for the United States, the emergence of a socialist regime and, worse, a Soviet client state, in one of its nearest Latin American neighbors obviously explains its sudden activism in the region. Eisenhower's successor, John F. Kennedy, was determined to go well beyond a mere reestablishment of U.S. hegemony over Cuba and to strike at the root causes of social unrest—thereby preempting socialist revolution—in Latin America as a whole.

[margin note: JFK—preemptive strike at socialist revolution]

The proposals of the Kennedy administration were based partly on a general theory of development and partly on the experience of developing countries outside of Latin America. The theory had been enunciated in a slender book by one of the president's advisers, W. W. Rostow: *The Stages of Economic Growth: A Non-Communist Manifesto* (1968). For Rostow, the self-sustaining economic development already achieved by certain "mature" industrial societies was something more than a logical goal for the rest of the world. It was the culmination of the world-historical process and the ultimate solution to all of its conflicts and contradictions. For Latin America, more particularly, development was the effective antidote to revolution, making promotion of economic development in the hemisphere urgent. Accelerating the process of development actually increased the danger of revolution in the short term, however. To manage the volatile transitional period, Kennedy's advisers looked to the experience of Asian and African countries that had undergone rapid development since World War II to discern why a revolution occurred in some cases and not in others. For example, the agrarian reforms introduced in Japan, Korea, and Formosa had attenuated social tensions and removed obstacles to economic expansion, while the antirevolutionary strategies employed in Malaysia and the Philippines underlined the importance of deepening the institutional framework of state control among the masses.

[margin note: development seen as antidote for revolution]

The Alliance for Progress, as the resulting U.S. policy initiative for Latin America was entitled, consequently recommended vigorous pursuit of land reform, rapid and broad-based industrialization, and

[margin note: Alliance for Progress—U.S.-based development plan for L.A.]

expansion of the functions and resources of the state. It projected a U.S. contribution of twenty billion dollars in the first decade, half to come from the national treasury and the rest from private investment, to be matched by a similar amount from (mostly official sources) within Latin America. The architects of the Alliance for Progress hoped to reach a 2.5 percent annual growth rate in the per capita gross national product of the participating Latin American countries. Such feats of social engineering could only be accomplished by strong national states, so another facet of the program envisioned major tax reform to make the collection of public revenues more effective and shift the burden to wealthier social groups who had long avoided paying their share. The U.S. policy of strengthening Latin America's national states had an ulterior political motive that figured much less in public representations of the Alliance. Stronger governments allied with the United States could also more effectively combat the revolutionary contagion in the hemisphere.

Democratic states with strong counterinsurgency capabilities were the sort thought most suitable to the purposes of the Alliance for Progress. The Kennedy administration sought allies especially among those currents of moderate reform that had displayed unwavering fidelity to the United States in the cold war despite the systematic neglect—and even the hostility—of the Eisenhower administration. The creators of the Alliance intended to eschew dictators, no matter how faithful their anti-Communism, believing that only democratic systems with a significant degree of popular mobilization could tap and rechannel potentially dangerous pressures from below. Still, Kennedy wanted Latin American democracies to have powerful armies at their service, and a considerable portion of the U.S. funding for the Alliance took the form of military aid. For their part, Latin American militaries were expected to undertake civic action programs, promoting socioeconomic development and winning the confidence of the rural masses in the remote areas of the countryside where other institutions of state control hardly existed. These regions seemed particularly crucial theaters of counterinsurgency action in view of the Cuban promise to make the Andes into a Sierra Maestra–style guerrilla nucleus on a continental scale.

The Organization of American States (OAS) did not receive an important role in the Alliance for Progress, and, during the rest of the decade, the United States gave progressively less attention to the multilateral body that had been the centerpiece of its Latin American policy in the 1950s. The U.S. government's new preference for bilateral agreements was confirmed in 1965 when a U.S. proposal to create a permanent Pan-American military force met a rebuff in the formerly docile OAS. Bilateral contacts between Latin America and the United States tightened and proliferated, as a result, not only through normal ministerial and diplomatic channels but also between various administrative branches and even between nongovernmental organizations in the respective countries. For example, organized labor in the United States (politically allied with the Kennedy administration) broadened its contacts with Latin American unions to include distribution of Alliance funds for social welfare programs, as well as more familiar advisory functions, in the hope of winning working-class hearts and minds for the U.S. cause. The government of Peru strengthened its support in Lima by administering a housing program supported by the Alliance. Latin American politicians disposed to align themselves independently with the United States might also take advantage of this sort of aid. Carlos Lacerda, state governor and spokesperson for the Brazilian right, used a similar housing program to increase his own political capital along with that of his international sponsor. The ambitious goals of U.S. policy in Latin America during the 1960s thus led to a highly complex and differentiated U.S. presence in the region.

Aiming simultaneously to transform and to conserve, or, in the formula common in Latin America, to promote both development and security, the Alliance for Progress found it impossible, at times, to serve its dual objectives equally. In moments of crisis, highest priority invariably went to the conservative goal of preventing revolutions, and logically so, since socioeconomic transformation was the means, rather than the end, of U.S. policy. The preferential option for representative democracy was also eclipsed by security concerns, as may be observed in the U.S. response to Peru's military coup of 1962. The Peruvian elections in that year had been won narrowly by Víctor Raúl Haya de la Torre, a declared political ally of the United States, but U.S. defense of its democratic principles went no further, in this case, than a brief withdrawal of its diplomatic representative in Lima, after which normal relations were resumed. Following Kennedy's assassination, Lyndon Johnson returned explicitly to an older modus vivendi, whereby the United States would be a friend to its friends and not concern itself overmuch with how allied governments ruled internally. Consequently, the Brazilian military was able to plan its 1964 overthrow of constitutional president João Goulart in close coordination with U.S. diplomats, who even promised U.S. military support if needed. The Dominican intervention of 1964 offers a further demonstration of U.S. priorities. In that year, Dominican supporters of overthrown constitutional president Juan Bosch rose up against the military rulers who had taken power the year before. Fearing that the conflict would spark another socialist revolution in the Caribbean, Johnson sent a U.S. expeditionary force to quell the rebellion and to arrange for the election of a new Dominican government acceptable to the United States. Unilateral North American intervention on the island was subsequently camouflaged by the presence of peacekeeping forces from other OAS member countries, under the command of a Brazilian general.

Within Latin America, this new U.S. intervention in the Caribbean provoked a less unanimous response than that elicited by the gunboat diplomacy of the early twentieth century. Anti-imperialist sentiment, reawakened by the Cuban Revolution and reinforced by subsequent U.S. actions in the region, did gain an importance that it had not displayed in Latin American public opinion since before the official initiation of the Good Neighbor policy in 1933. However, there appeared, as well, a countervailing attitude that had no analog in the earlier period. As socialist revolution came to seem a real possibility in the hemisphere, conservative opponents of socialism in Latin America, many of them traditionally hostile to the United States, now identified themselves increasingly with U.S. anticommunism.

Chief among the fervent new allies of the United States were the officer corps of most Latin American armies. The fortification of state power promoted by the Alliance for Progress gave new prominence to the region's military establishments, with particularly dramatic consequences for small and middle-sized countries like Uruguay and Bolivia. The flow of U.S. funding obviously contributed to the new prominence of Latin American armed forces, but a more important source of prestige was their image as esteemed allies and (they liked to think) peers of the world's most powerful military. The bilateral contacts between U.S. and Latin American officers facilitated the diffusion of National Security Doctrine, which urged the armed forces of the hemisphere to take an active part in pursuing the twin goals of security and development. Beginning in the late nineteenth century, Latin American armies had frequently claimed a central role in the process of modernization. Universal military conscription, for example, had become a tool for extending literacy to social groups without access to schooling. Still, the modernizing role had been difficult to integrate with the explicitly defensive function of the armed forces taught by foreign military advisers before World War II.

By defining security as counterinsurgency, then linking counterinsurgency to the problem of economic development and presenting both as aspects of a heroic global crusade, national security doctrine provided the perfect ideological justification for military activism in national life. Latin American armed forces also drew inspiration from other sources less commonly recognized, particularly the French military experience. French martial traditions were historically closer to those of Latin America. French officers had done some of the same soul-searching as their Latin American counterparts concerning the validity and limits of those traditions, and the French army's protracted battles with national liberation movements in a disintegrating colonial empire, from Algiers to Indochina, had devolved in a framework more germane to the experience of Latin American militaries—as reflected, for instance, in the recourse to ecclesiastical authorization for the use of torture in counterinsurgency. Whatever the origin of personal or emotional justifications given to such methods, national security doctrine was the decisive institutional rationalization for them. U.S. advisers may not have provided basic instruction in the art of inflicting physical pain during interrogation, as their critics frequently alleged. (Indeed, the defenders of U.S. counterinsurgency training make the contrary claim that it taught alternatives to torture, and it is scarcely credible, at any rate, to regard the use of torture in Latin America as necessarily an exotic import.) Nevertheless, the emphasis on counterinsurgency made such violent tactics a legitimate topic of discussion in military circles, and the apocalyptic attitudes inherent in the cold war mentality tended to legitimate the most drastic methods.

Under the aegis of national security doctrine, the armed forces of Latin America acquired a stronger sense of corporate identity, both nationally and internationally. At times, high-ranking officers seemed to find their closest interlocutors in the armies of other countries rather than in the governments of their own, as when Argentine general Juan Carlos Onganía chose the occasion of the Fifth Conference of Latin American Armed Forces, meeting at West Point, to redefine the relationship between Argentina's constitutional authorities and its military establishment. On the national level, Latin American militaries adopted a substantially new mode of intervention in political affairs. Whereas in the past, ambitious generals and colonels had seized a national leadership role with the support of followers both inside and outside the ranks, armies now tended to intervene politically as corporate groups. The figures of individual military leaders became less important, often displaying very little autonomy vis-à-vis the military institutions that placed them in office.

This more institutionalized form of armed intervention in political life responded to the increasing fear of socialist revolution and to a growing sense of isolation in many military establishments regarding the national societies around them. As the perceived menace of imminent revolutionary cataclysm seemed daily to escalate, conservative groups became determined to keep those at the pinnacle of power—even generals ostensibly there to protect conservative interests—on a tight rein to avoid the unpredictable turns sometimes taken by individual leaders. At the same time, the cultural transformations of the 1960s began to affect broad reaches of Latin American societies. To the military leaders who envisioned themselves as embattled sentinels defending the ramparts of Western civilization against godless communism, these transformations signaled a dangerous softening and decay of moral fiber in societies about to undergo the supreme test.

The technological advances of the period (air travel, long-distance telephone links, motor scooters, and birth control pills, to name only a few of the most important) were opening the vistas of the 1960s cultural revolution then occurring in the developed world to Latin Americans long constrained by a suffocatingly narrow set of life choices. Proliferating technologies of communication spread the cultural ferment broadly, from the privileged upper crust with the most invested in the status quo to the middle and lower-middle classes from which most of the revolutionary challengers were to emerge. Viewing these changes as a foretaste of the final victory, young revolutionaries often proceeded more in a mood of celebratory anticipation than hard-bitten militancy, and upper-class young people sometimes joined, with surprising enthusiasm, in the festively iconoclastic spirit of their "class enemies." In 1973, French sociologist Alain Touraine would describe how, during the death throes of Chile's socialist experiment, the pampered youth of Santiago continued to celebrate the rites of hedonist liberation amid the icons of the international counterculture.

The optimistic spirit of the 1960s cultural revolution never could have become so widespread had Latin America's socioeconomic crisis been as grave as sometimes painted in retrospect. True, the developmentalist policies applied since 1945 had failed to provide the steady economic expansion and social melioration promised by proponents, sputtering along instead in fits and starts with a marked tendency to stagnation. A bitter disappointment of high hopes and an ever more frustrating gap between the models provided by the core countries and the capacity of peripheral countries to imitate those models were both sharply felt consequences of the period's irregular and unequal economic development. Despite the prevailing disillusionment, however, most Latin American countries had in fact experienced a real improvement in general standards of living, and, however unrecognized, that

improvement engendered a deeply felt optimism shared by the proponents and the adversaries of socialism—shared, that is, by those outside of the siege mentality of the armed forces, where such attitudes
were received with rising alarm. Military fury at this perceived fri-
volity would eventually be unleashed in a wave of savage repression at
the end of the decade.

reorientation of the Church

The military's siege mentality was compounded by the seeming
defection of its oldest ally among the defenders of order and tradition,
the Catholic church. Latin America had been among the less dynamic
regions of world Catholicism until about the time of the Second Vatican Council, which encouraged a more accessible liturgy, a more
modern curriculum for Catholic education, a larger role for the laity,
and an attitude of social engagement that came to be called a "preferential option for the poor." During the 1960s, this last element, the
reorientation of the church's mission more toward the poor, rose in
importance to become the central tenet of a distinctively Latin American religious phenomenon, liberation theology, a radical Christian
outlook paralleling and drawing importantly from the revolutionary
socialist critique already widely influential in the hemisphere. The
adherents of liberation theology were distinctly a minority in the
Latin American church, and many of their innovations would be repudiated eventually by the Pope, but for a decade they could be seen as
the vanguard of a general movement broadly affecting the Catholic
church in Latin America and naturally worrisome to military establishments that preferred the church to remain, as it had been for
centuries, a bulwark of the existing social hierarchy.

If the cultural crosscurrents of the 1960s muddied political confrontations in Latin America, so did developments in the core areas of
both the capitalist and socialist worlds. The most dramatic signs of
trouble were the stormy and enigmatic outbursts that occurred in
1968, from Prague and Paris to Mexico City, from Communist China
to many major U.S. universities. As varied, in some ways, as their
diverse geographic contexts, these upheavals had one thing in common. They expressed impatience with the unaccountable delay of the
peaceful yet radical transformations that had seemed so near at the
dawn of the decade. The stark light of these thunderous outbursts
revealed fissures not previously thought to exist in the political structures of the capitalist and socialist core areas.

1968 - new political fissures

The events of 1968 initially raised the expectations of Latin American revolutionaries, who only gradually understood the more discouraging—and more enduring—lessons of that year. Despite the weakened legitimacy of all the regimes that became the object of protests in

1968, none were overthrown. This fact had grim implications for the proponents of political change in Latin America, who had tended to view the weak legitimacy of their own governments as the surest sign of impending revolution. The protests that had occurred in the Soviet bloc further diminished their revolutionary élan by besmirching the international prestige of the socialist model. Although Latin America's social revolutionaries had never identified themselves closely with the Soviet-style communism as practiced in eastern Europe, it was now more difficult than before to see the Soviet system as even a rough approximation of the kind of utopia they sought. After 1970, the slow deterioration of the world economy also contributed to the un-raveling of revolutionary designs, as will become clear in the following chapter.

The Cuban Revolution set the tone of Latin American history in the 1960s, as Kennedy obviously realized when he directed his coun-terrevolutionary policy primarily at the South American continent rather than at Cuba itself. A U.S.-sponsored invasion of the island was not long in coming, but Kennedy did not initiate the plan. It was the Eisenhower administration that, before leaving office in 1961, had begun training and arming Cuban exiles for an expedition against the revolutionary government, and Kennedy's halfhearted support for the project contributed to its failure. When the counterrevolutionary force disembarked at the Bay of Pigs in April 1961, hoping to elicit popular support for its efforts to overthrow Castro, the response of the Cuban population demonstrated convincingly that, to the contrary, the revo-lution retained wide support and could easily crush a much stronger force than had invaded. The attack was pushed back into the sea even before most defending forces could be brought into play.

Smarting under this blow to its prestige in the hemisphere, the Kennedy administration switched its offensive to diplomatic terrain. At the OAS meeting of January 1962, the United States forced the ex-pulsion of Cuba from the hemispheric organization by gaining the sup-port of two-thirds of the members in spite of the opposition of the most important Latin American countries. At the same meeting, the United States imposed the establishment of a Consultative Security Committee in which many Latin Americans saw the beginnings of an international counterrevolutionary police force. Stiff, if ultimately unsuccessful, resistance to both measures contrasted with the docile reaction of the OAS to similar U.S. initiatives against Guatemala a decade earlier. The hegemony of the United States remained intact, but its institutions were working less smoothly than before.

Then, in October 1962, the United States denounced Soviet inten-

tions to install a missile base in Cuba and announced a naval blockade
to prevent further shipments of offensive weapons to the island. After
a short but sharp diplomatic confrontation, Soviet premier Nikita
Khrushchev agreed (much to the displeasure of the Cuban government) to dismantle the offending missile bases in return for Kennedy's promise not to sponsor another invasion of the island. Although minor incursions of Cuban dissidents and other hostile actions
against Cuba continued for years under U.S. auspices, worsening the
revolution's economic difficulties, the resolution of the Cuban Missile
Crisis ended the danger of frontal attack against Castro's regime.

The United States concentrated instead on economic and diplomatic sanctions. For a decade the U.S. economic blockade reduced to a
minimum Cuban trade with capitalist countries. The U.S. diplomatic
quarantine, for its part, isolated the Cuban Revolution from the rest of
Latin America, with the sole exception of Mexico, which maintained
relations with Cuba less in solidarity with the revolution than in
fidelity to its own tradition of diplomatic independence vis-à-vis the
United States. However, neither the economic blockade nor the diplomatic quarantine could prevent Cuba's example from having a huge
influence in the rest of Latin America. For all its overweening fury, the
United States had failed to break the independent will of a Latin
American government almost within sight of its shores, and that
example could hardly fail to encourage revolutionary movements elsewhere and undermine the discipline of the OAS.

The Cuban Revolution aspired to do more than provide a distant
example, however. Although limited by the modesty of its resources
and by the military vigilance of the United States, Havana tried to
match its actions to its internationalist words, supporting revolutionary change in the rest of Latin America. In doing so, it provided an
alternative to the gradualist policies and tactical alliances with moderate reform groups that old-line Communist parties had favored in the
hemisphere since 1935. The model suggested by Cuban revolutionaries was based on their own success in the late 1950s, when a small
group of guerrillas had established a nucleus of activity in a remote
rural area, then slowly extended operations into more central regions.
Foquismo, as this strategy was named (for the *focos*, or focal points,
where guerrilla activity began), offered a way to precipitate conditions
conducive to a general insurrection in countries where those conditions did not yet exist. Regis Debray, the French intellectual who
publicized foquismo in the international left, called it "a revolution in
the revolution."

Insurgent focos quickly appeared in a number of Latin American countries, often with Cuban inspiration and training, but less frequently with significant material backing from Cuba. Many of the focos were so remote from Cuban shores as to make such backing logistically impossible. The brunt of the island's material support for revolutionaries abroad went to Venezuela precisely because of the comparative ease of transporting it there. For the most part, Cuba's scarce resources were devoted to foreign projects only when required by the internal tensions or external alliances. The former condition obtained in 1962–63 and 1967–68, when frustrations at home were soothed by patriotic undertakings abroad, and the latter in the 1970s, when deference to the Soviet Union required that Cuba show the revolutionary colors in Africa.

Cuban influence had cultural dimensions as well. Despite U.S. attempts to seal off the island, its image remained powerfully present in the collective imagination of Latin America during the ferment of the 1960s. The literary awards distributed by Havana's Casa de las Americas became the first collective hemispheric equivalent of the Pulitzer prizes given in the United States, and Cuban posters provided the young celebrants of Latin America's cultural revolution with a colorful graphic counterpoint to the pop art productions of New York. Like the exportation of foquismo, Cuba's cultural projection in the rest of Latin America responded more to internal developments than to any concerted internationalist program. In effect, the diffusion of Cuba's revolutionary vision was suddenly abandoned after 1969, despite its impressive resonance, because the period of cultural efflorescence ended on the island itself. The internal processes of the Cuban Revolution are therefore essential to understanding Cuba's role in the hemisphere.

The consolidation of power in the hands of the bearded veterans of the Sierra Maestra insurgency continued steadily during the 1960s as dissenters from the revolution's new Marxist-Leninist ideology were weeded out, to be followed by members of Cuba's traditional Communist party, oriented too closely to the Moscow line. Hubert Matos, the last important opponent of socialism within the military ranks of the revolution, had been eliminated already by the first year of the decade. Cuban labor leaders who had not offered much support for the insurgency and then opposed its ideological evolution were also replaced in 1960. Having raised the banner of socialism, Castro next had to wrest it definitively from the old-style Communists who had carried it at the behest of the Soviet Union since the 1930s. A significant minority of the older Communists were technicians and professionals whose skills were in critically short supply because of the massive exodus of

Cuba's upper and middle classes to seek a haven from revolution in the United States. Castro therefore welcomed the old-line Communists into the revolutionary government initially, but their presence became increasingly threatening to the predominance of the Sierra Maestra veterans as Cuba moved into the orbit of the Soviet Union. As the Cuban economy encountered repeated setbacks in the early 1960s, old-line Communist technocrats offered tempting scapegoats for popular discontent, and the last remnant of their independent influence was eradicated in the 1968 campaign against the so-called "microfaction." Only then, after the disappearance of all other claimants to the legitimating mantle of social revolution, could Castro fully recognize Soviet leadership internationally.

The search for an original solution to Cuba's economic problems occupied tremendous energies, brought equally large disappointments, and led to repeatedly revised goals. The challenges to be faced were enormous. For a century, the Cuban economy had been oriented toward the United States, and those formerly close structural contacts had now been replaced with an economic blockade. Links with new trading partners in the Soviet bloc required entirely different principles of organization. Most disruptive of all was the legacy of false starts committed by the Cuban revolutionaries themselves as they attempted to accelerate radically the process of industrialization at the expense of the traditional agricultural mainstays. In effect, the revolutionary concentration of political power on the island enabled the Cuban leadership to implement quite rapidly the proposals advanced at that time by economists all over Latin America. After a few months of general prosperity, sugar production entered a severe crisis and efforts at industrialization flagged under the debilitating effects of the economic blockade. Eventually, the single-minded push for industrialization was replaced by an emphasis on formerly underexploited areas of primary production like fishing, cattle ranching, poultry farming, and nickel mining. Within a few short years, the economic strategy of the revolutionaries came full circle when they realized that, whatever future development was to occur in Cuba, the resources would have to come from the island's old economic dynamo, sugar. As early as 1963 Castro announced plans to reverse the systematic neglect suffered by the sugar industry during the first phase of the revolution, setting an ambitious goal of ten million tons—almost twice the production of any previous year—for the harvest of 1970.

Economic challenges encouraged a further radicalization of the revolutionary process. Strongholds of privilege like North American–style country clubs and private schools run mostly by the Catholic church were destroyed early in the decade. Progressively more sweeping innovations demonstrated the revolutionaries' commitment to social transformation. The second wave of agrarian reform affected all landholdings except the comparatively few small parcels owned by peasants, and even their meager agricultural production had to flow, from that point on, into the state-run distribution system. The huge majority of rural properties were expropriated and consolidated into state farms on the Soviet model. In urban areas, the swift nationalization of the industrial sector was followed quickly by the state takeover of retail commerce. Such transformations were carried out much more rapidly in revolutionary Cuba than in Eastern Europe after World War II. In part, Cuban revolutionaries were acting on a belief that their powerful enemies might make use of any uncontrolled sector of the economy to strike at the revolution. Their inspiration was also ideological, however. Although clearly informed by Marxism, the passionate rejection of all vestiges of the market economy seemed to draw particular intensity from the vernacular Cuban tradition of revolution as civic purification. The same tradition reinforced the tendency to view economic hardship—like the rationing begun in 1962—as an opportunity to instill an egalitarian ethic and practice civic virtues.

Whether the result of unrealistic goals, mismanagement by inexperienced personnel, or the unwieldy accumulation of ad hoc administrative improvisations, the economic failures of the early 1960s sparked a national debate over how best to build a socialist Cuba. One side proposed to continue resolutely rooting out all traces of a market economy to establish a pure socialist system in which idealistic devotion to the common good, rather than material incentives, would spur the productivity of the work force. The national figure most closely identified with the purists was Che Guevara, whose recent management of economic affairs had been admittedly much less successful than his military leadership during the insurrection. The other side, led by Carlos Rafael Rodríguez (the one leader of the old Communist party who had joined the revolution before its victory), argued for a more cautious and gradual approach. The gradualists believed that the sudden transformations demanded by the purists would provoke too much internal resistance and that, at any rate, Cuba did not yet have enough trained managers to administer a centralized, command economy. The debate was resolved in favor of Guevara, but only after he had left Cuba to promote the revolutionary cause elsewhere.

Central control of the economy was congenial to the revolution's ubiquitous "Maximum Leader," Fidel Castro, who wanted to be personally on the front line of every daily economic skirmish. The frequent reordering of priorities and the mobilization of "microbrigades" (workers and administrators taken from their normal occupations to do special jobs elsewhere) created an atmosphere of feverish activity doubtless more rewarding to the exultant leadership than to the working rank and file, and the results were far from satisfactory. Increasing scarcities and accumulating failures undermined the workers' will to forge ahead to ever greater efforts. As moral incentives lost their ability to motivate further gains in productivity, managers applied stricter discipline. Worker absenteeism reached epidemic proportions, and even sympathetic observers of the Cuban Revolution began to fear that only progressively drastic measures could compel the workers to the supreme effort required for the ten-million-ton sugar harvest set for 1970. Meeting that objective had become the acid test of the revolution's new model. As the deadline approached, all Cuba was drafted into one great "microbrigade," and a gigantic graph in Havana's Plaza of the Revolution registered the harvested tons. The final total far surpassed any previous sugar harvest in the island's history, but it fell more than a million tons short of the goal. The purist experiment had failed. From then on, the Cuban revolutionary leadership resigned itself to applying less exhilarating but more workable economic strategies based on models from the Soviet bloc.

Despite the bitter disappointments of its first decade, the revolution had created a more egalitarian social order and effectively identified its interests with those of the Cuban people. The exhaustion of popular support for unlimited economic experimentation was more than offset by gratitude for the triumphant vindication of a national sovereignty so long denied, and whatever the failings of certain individual officials, the revolution had also canceled the systematic government corruption that had been a defining characteristic of Cuban public life before 1959. Social welfare programs had achieved impressive advances in public health and, especially in rural areas, the availability of decent housing. In addition, early literacy campaigns had been followed by the creation of an educational system that opened to all Cubans professional opportunities formerly available only to the elite—opportunities that were all the more numerous in the 1960s because of the departure of so many middle-class professionals. If they breathed easier with the end of the revolution's most imaginative innovations in 1970, most Cubans had little desire to undo the accomplishments of the 1960s.

The decline of Cuba's revolutionary creativity had a very different meaning for the brilliant intellectual following that the decade of experimentation had inspired both at home and abroad. Already, during the 1960s, Cuban intellectuals had bridled at the regime's attempts to regulate individual life-styles and creative activities. Their resistance had led to the partial reversal of restrictions, but, by 1970, the cumulative result was a situation that no longer compared favorably with the limitations on artistic freedom in Eastern Europe. At the same time, the unflattering reports of some foreign observers made the revolutionary government rue the day it had invited so many sympathizers to witness the construction of Cuban socialism, and when an exasperated Fidel Castro denounced several of these erstwhile friends as CIA agents, the result was only to exacerbate skepticism abroad. The breaking point for many of the Cuban Revolution's intellectual and artistic admirers outside the country, was the 1971 case of the poet Heberto Padilla. Padilla's book *Fuera del Juego* had received a Casa de las Americas prize in 1968, but the poet's disenchantment (suggested by the title of the book) eventually became so irksome to the regime that it imprisoned him and obliged him to engage in an appalling exercise in "self-criticism." The desertion of so many Latin American and western European intellectuals does not seem to have worried the Cuban revolutionary leadership, which found more practical international support in its alliance with the Soviet Union, a relationship confirmed in 1968 by Castro's public justification of Soviet military intervention in Czechoslovakia.

1971- intellectual break w/ Cuba

Motivated by the practical desire to lift the diplomatic siege imposed in the early 1960s, the Cuban Revolution now showed more eagerness to reestablish contacts with Latin American governments of various political stripes than with the region's revolutionary muse. The normalization of relations with Cuba was also desirable to many of its prospective interlocutors, who hoped that reintegrating the island into the political framework of the hemisphere would reduce its appeal as their revolutionary antithesis, beacon of an alternative order that had exerted a polarizing effect on many Latin American countries during the decade just past.

In Brazil, the process of polarization led to a sharp confrontation out of keeping with the country's political traditions. Jânio Quadros, the president elected in 1960, hardly represented a radicalizing force in most respects. He opposed the powerful influence of organized labor and the trend toward economic interventionism that had characterized Brazil's dominant populist coalition since 1945, but he also claimed the right to develop an independent foreign policy, believing that his economic conservatism would earn him the tolerance of the United States in that regard. The plans of Quadros might have been acceptable to Eisenhower, but they were not to Kennedy, who took office

Brazil

the next year and who cared more about Pan-American discipline than about economic orthodoxy. Meanwhile, Quadros's unpredictable personal style began to alienate his internal political supporters as well. The Brazilian president's external and internal opponents joined in mutual horror and indignation when, in August 1961, he decorated the revolutionary hero Che Guevara, who happened to be passing through Brazil. Quadros responded to the chorus of opposition by quite suddenly resigning the presidency amid declarations powerfully reminiscent, in a number of ways, of the suicide note left by Getúlio Vargas in 1954. The similarities in language raised the suspicion that Quadros intended a political metamorphosis, mobilizing the forces of populism and returning triumphantly to office with a new base of support. If those were his intentions, they were roundly disappointed. Unnerved by the president's erratic behavior, the Brazilian congress quickly accepted the Quadros resignation in spite of the risks implied by the next man in line.

Vice President João Goulart was a direct political heir of Vargas, and he was closely associated with the Brazilian labor movement. In other words, Goulart represented the tendencies—further intensified with the polarizing impact of the Cuban Revolution—that most perturbed the "conservative liberals" who had voted for Quadros. When Quadros resigned, Goulart was traveling in the People's Republic of China, a country that at the time elicited an even more intense conservative loathing than did the Soviet Union, and for a few days it looked as though the Brazilian army would refuse to let him assume the presidency. The army was mollified when the congress introduced constitutional reforms that limited the power of the presidency by recasting the Brazilian system in a parliamentary mold. Goulart accepted the arrangement provisionally, until a plebiscite could be held to confirm or reject it in 1963. Goulart recovered his full presidential power as a result of that plebiscite. In the interim, while all of Brazil's political energies were absorbed by the crisis of succession, the country's economic problems had become critical.

Goulart prepared to address the long-postponed economic crisis with the aid of an impressive group of advisers, including Celso Furtado, one of the most prominent economists to emerge from the United Nations' Economic Commission for Latin America (ECLA). Furtado combined a short-term attack on Brazil's rampant inflation with long-term goals of economic modernization and agrarian reform following lines originally advocated by ECLA and subsequently endorsed by the Alliance for Progress. The Brazilian labor movement, which constituted the core of Goulart's political base within the populist coalition, adamantly opposed stabilization through wage controls, and Furtado had to resign. Soon after that, sectors of the population not previously mobilized began to enter the political arena with the president's blessing. Proposals to extend voting rights to enlisted military men and allow unionization of noncommissioned officers did nothing to endear Goulart to the hierarchy of the Brazilian armed forces. Progressive forces unleashed under the auspices of the Goulart administration also urged the extension of suffrage to illiterates in conjunction with the legalization of peasant leagues and the adoption of a vigorous program of land reform, which they hoped would together destroy, at long last, the traditional political influence of rural landlords. The immediate effect, however, was to turn the full force of that influence against the Goulart administration.

While Furtado and others affirmed that Brazil's rural masses had begun to stir spontaneously, that assessment may underestimate the effects of determined efforts at popular mobilization. The creation of the famous peasant leagues in the northeastern part of the country offers a case in point. Although the unstudied anger and frustration of the peasants undoubtedly played its part in these mobilizations, the northeastern peasant leagues were actually put together by Francisco Julião, a lawyer from Recife, who worked with the cooperation of the Catholic church to provide an alternative to Communist organizing in the region. Julião's remark that Cuba provided a model for the Brazil of the future offers a typical instance of the confusion of ends and means that occurred as reformers and revolutionaries competed to guide the whirlwind of change that all believed inevitable. Goulart himself contributed to the confusion with pronouncements of a highly revolutionary tenor that made him sound quite radical and further alienated the middle-class elements of the populist coalition. In early 1964, high-ranking military officers led multitudinous demonstrations of middle-class "Christian mothers" who declared their unreconcilable opposition to communism of the sort that they believed the president intended for Brazil. Meanwhile, Goulart's economic policies, intended primarily to augment his support among the poor, fueled the fires of inflation and further aggravated middle-class sensibilities.

On 31 March 1964, a military coup put an end to Goulart's transgressions and sent him into exile. The coup received public support from the governors of Brazil's most important states and, barely less publicly, from the U.S. embassy, which had closely followed the development of the military conspiracy. The Brazilian congress declared that the presidential office had been left vacant and hastened to entrust it to the head of the Chamber of Deputies. The Brazilian people—

and not only the middle class—reacted more favorably than the leaders of the coup had dared hope. One North American scholar of Brazil's urban slums found that the *favela* dwellers poured forth into the center of Rio de Janeiro on the day following the coup, not to initiate a desperate defense of the Brazilian revolution, but to join in the festivities. Most of the celebrants probably did not intend to approve the abolition of constitutional government and regarded the coup as one more of the brief military interventions that had punctuated the Brazilian political process without leading, in most cases, to prolonged dictatorships.

This time, however, the Brazilian military showed no intention of quickly returning to the barracks. By executive decree—the first of the military government's "institutional acts"—the armed forces initiated a purge of Goulart's congressional supporters and offered Field Marshal Humberto Castelo Branco, leader of the forces that had carried out the coup, as interim president. Pleased with the rout of their political adversaries, the remaining legislators elected the military president unquestioningly. High on Castelo Branco's agenda was the problem of inflation, which, in contrast to Goulart's approach, the military government attacked essentially by holding down wages, but a sharp recession and high unemployment (bitter but necessary medicine according to Roberto Campos, architect of the military's economic policy) resulted in setbacks for government candidates in the municipal and state elections of 1965. To retain its control of the political arena, the military government put forward its Second Institutional Act, authorizing the existence of only two political parties. The first of these, the National Renovating Alliance (ARENA), brought together supporters of the regime, and the other, the Brazilian Democratic Movement (MDB), united those members of the moderate opposition whom the military continued to tolerate. The Second Institutional Act also abolished direct presidential elections, leaving the selection of future national executives to the more easily controlled congress. The Third Institutional Act subsequently did away with the direct election of state governors and the mayors of state capitals as well.

To this point, the military government had strayed less from Brazil's constitutional tradition than had the Estado Novo created by Getúlio Vargas in the 1930s, nor had the armed forces' abuses of human rights, though they included the torture and unexplained permanent disappearances of political enemies, reached unprecedented levels. The military rulers who had taken power in 1964 departed from the Brazilian political tradition principally in two directions, both of which characterized Latin America as a whole during the stormy 1960s. First, the armed forces intervened in politics as an institution, not as the constituency of an individual leader; and second, they reacted to any internal challenge with a zealous extremism clearly indicative of the political climate encouraged throughout the hemisphere by the Cuban Revolution. Always preferring to do things by the book, the military government found its theoretical justifications in the writings of Gen. Golbery do Couto e Silva, whose embellishments of national security doctrine undergirded more than one creative institutional innovation. The election of Castelo Branco's successor in 1967 illustrates the emphasis on procedure characteristic of this military government. The initial electors were the generals on active duty, who submitted a list of eligible candidates to a conclave composed of the commanders of the country's military regions. The chosen name then went to the Brazilian congress, which provided the requisite constitutional investiture of the next president.

Gen. Artur da Costa e Silva had a good-humored common touch that contrasted notably with his predecessor's coldly austere style and seemed (misleadingly, as it turned out) to imply the possibility of a political thaw to accompany the long-awaited economic recovery. In 1968, as the Brazilian economy began a period of rapid expansion, the government was disposed to tolerate the signs of political opposition that became common in the country's major cities. Brazilian university students found themselves in the vanguard of the protest, and many national leaders of the pre-1964 era (from Goulart and Kubitschek on the left, to Quadros and Lacerda on the right) lent their support. Roused by the awakening of public opposition to the military government, the congress refused the president's request for the expulsion of several of its most outspoken and indocile members. The crackdown came in the form of the Fifth Institutional Act, which inaugurated a period of hard-line military rule more repressive than any other in Brazilian history, authorizing the dissolution of congress and the widespread nullification of political rights. Government purges of political and labor organizations were now extended to cultural and professional bodies, especially universities, where recent unrest had revealed hidden dangers. In 1969, Costa e Silva's poor health allowed the military government to replace him with Gen. Emílio Garrastazu Médici, a fervent hard-liner more in keeping with the new temper of the regime.

Political scientists have described the post-1968 Brazilian regime as a paradigmatic example of "bureaucratic authoritarianism," a political formula that insured the progress of industrialization after the populist and developmentalist formulas had lost their effectiveness. At the center of the bureaucratic authoritarian state was the military, guided by its "apolitical" patriotism, applying its technical expertise and its supposed administrative efficiency to the business of governance. In fact, bureaucratic authoritarian regimes tended to represent the interests of three very specific groups: the military hierarchy, the national economic elite, and the transnational corporations that played such a large part in this stage of Latin American industrialization. Such regimes maintained a carefully controlled pluralism within this three-way alliance and a strict authoritarianism in their treatment of all those outside it. In effect, the subordinate classes lost many of the rights of citizenship, and they underwent a steady process of depoliticization and disarticulation. The systematic repression exercised by bureaucratic authoritarians in defense of a capitalist industrial model reminded many observers of the fascist states of the first half of the twentieth century.

Comparisons with fascism reveal as many differences as similarities, however. The Brazilian military government of the 1970s sought to depoliticize and fragment the masses, whereas fascist states, to the contrary, had attempted to politicize and integrate them. In this aspect, the Estado Novo of 1937–45 had been much closer to the fascist pattern than were the bureaucratic authoritarians. While the Estado Novo had mobilized labor unions in its support, the military government of the 1970s preferred to demobilize them. The military government also maintained a careful scrutiny of any organization that might facilitate the political solidarity of socially subordinate groups, permitting only forms of popular association—like those connected with carnival parades or soccer clubs—that promised a distraction from political concerns. The similarities between bureaucratic authoritarianism and fascism lie instead in the wanton violence directed at any opposition or even any potential source of it. The repression experienced by Brazilians after 1968 was fully as systematic and probably more brutal than what Italians endured before 1943 under fascism. A small group of urban guerrillas led by Communist dissident Carlos Marighela posed the only resistance, and they were soon crushed amid a further escalation of government repression. For a few years in the early and mid-1970s, Brazil appeared in the eyes of world public opinion as the most ignominious Latin American example of official scorn for human rights.

At the same time, the renewed dynamism of the economy helped quiet other dissenting voices. Only two years after the reluctant beginnings of a recovery in 1967, the country's economic showing had

become impressive enough to be dubbed the "Brazilian Miracle" by its
boosters. In stark contrast to an economically stagnant Spanish America, Brazil expanded its gross national product at one of the highest
rates in the world. Moreover, the structure of Brazilian industrialization began to ramify and diversify in a way not seen before in any Latin
American country. Despite the continuation—indeed, the exacerba-
tion—of vast social inequalities, Brazil was developing a modern sector able to keep pace with the international rhythm of technological
advance within a still largely archaic Third World framework, and that
success seemed to favor the consolidation of the regime that had
fostered it.

Argentina, once Brazil's rival in economic terms, fell further behind in the 1960s as it attempted to apply a similar model of development. Both countries faced a critical situation at the start of the
decade, but Argentina's crisis was sharper and longer lasting. The postwar export boom had ended ten years earlier in Argentina, the Argentine political context was more fraught with contradictions and
ambiguities, and Argentine conservatives contemplated the Cuban
Revolution with even more unmitigated horror than did their Brazilian counterparts. Under such troubled circumstances, the developmentalist program launched by Argentine president Arturo Frondizi
was far less successful than the Brazilian analog sponsored by Kubitschek a few years earlier.

Frondizi's hands were tied by the military on one side and by the
Peronists on the other. Conservatives noticed with alarm that this
former head of the left wing of the Radical party did not share their
revulsion for the revolutionary process under way in Cuba. When he
tried to place officers loyal to constitutional principles in charge of the
three armed forces, the ominous dissatisfaction within the military
leadership led him quickly to back down, setting a precedent with
significant future consequences. Convinced that obedience to civil
authority constituted professional suicide, the Argentine officer corps
began to assert ever greater autonomy vis-à-vis the constitutional
government and to practice its own curious version of direct democracy. In what they termed a "deliberative mode," the military leadership began proudly to proclaim themselves representatives of the collective will of the ranks. Meanwhile, the Peronists, to whom Frondizi
owed his election, evinced increasing impatience with the conservative economic policies that resulted in hardships without producing a
vigorous recovery. As the country's labor unions regained some of the
strength they had lost after the fall of Perón, they became more effective opponents of efforts to rationalize and restructure state-owned

corporations (especially the railroads), leading Frondizi to use the army against strikers.

Stronger economic growth would have alleviated these political pressures, but it stubbornly failed to materialize. Most discouraging was the continued stagnation of the agricultural export sector, even after the government implemented a currency devaluation to stimulate it at the expense of other sectors. Nevertheless, Frondizi used every tactic at his disposal to prolong artificially the weak economic expansion that had occurred. He was hoping to gain enough electoral support to maneuver between the Peronists and the military, and various local elections during 1961 indicated that his efforts had not been in vain. Even though the Peronists were allowed to present their own candidates in these elections, the "intransigent" Radicals identified with Frondizi made impressive strides.

At the same time, the Argentine president was heartened by the installation of a new administration in Washington, D.C., one widely expected to show a greater sensitivity to Latin American problems. Believing that the Cuban crisis could ruin this opportunity by pushing Kennedy into a stance even more intransigent than Eisenhower's, Frondizi made a fatal attempt to mediate, meeting with revolutionary leader Che Guevara who happened to be in Argentina to visit his family. Efforts to keep the meeting a secret failed, and the Argentine military reacted furiously. In an attempt to placate the armed forces, the president broke diplomatic relations with Cuba, but he proclaimed his resolve to maintain the independence of Argentine foreign policy and promised a reckoning at the polls during the upcoming provincial and congressional elections of 1962. Frondizi's party did well in those elections but not as well as the Peronists, who received a full third of the votes cast and revealed themselves still to be the single most powerful electoral force in the country. Unwilling to countenance a Peronist comeback, the armed forces dissolved the congress and overthrew Frondizi, announcing their obedience to constitutional norms all the while.

The military installed a semiconstitutional interim president, José María Guido, to preside over a murky period of transition during which the army's internal conflicts twice erupted in fighting and economic conditions became so bad that, at one point, a third of the labor force stood idle. Another currency devaluation meant to stimulate the agricultural export sector only made matters more volatile in urban areas. Fearful of where their actions might be leading, the armed forces decided to let the electorate choose among carefully limited alternatives. At first they appeared willing to allow Peronist participation in a moderate electoral coalition, but, soon realizing that such a coalition would probably again become a vehicle for Frondizi's intransigent Radicals, they stipulated so many limitations that the Peronists decided to abstain. As a result, the Radical party's traditional centrist faction obtained an unexpected victory in the election.

The new president, Arturo Illia, was a politician of mostly local renown from Córdoba who could not have been in a weaker position. Thanks to the peculiar circumstances of the election, he entered office having won the votes of only a quarter of the electorate, and his standing with the military was equally shaky because of the Radical party's troubled past relationship with that institution. However, Illia was determined to assure the complete reestablishment of electoral liberties and to govern without appeal to military repression.

The only cause for optimism was the recovery of Argentina's export sector. In 1963, fifteen years after the end of the brief postwar boom and eight years after the first implementation of a variety of policies to favor them, Argentine agricultural exports began to grow once more. Rebounding from the sharp recession of the previous year, the result was the most vigorous period of economic expansion experienced in more than a decade. Although the recovery began to flag in mid-1965, the general situation remained far better than at any time in the recent past. Illia could not take credit for the recovery, but he did encourage it by replacing the brusque measures of earlier administrations with a careful gradualism. The slow currency devaluation introduced by Illia was similar to the "sliding peg" arrangement later celebrated as one of the secrets of the "Brazilian Miracle." This innovation did much to ease the shock of policies designed to shift resources between different sectors of the economy. In addition, Illia annulled certain oil concessions granted by Frondizi to foreign interests and generally moderated the government's formerly frenetic efforts to recruit international capital. Unfortunately for Illia, his economic policies were so evenhanded as to leave all of his prospective electoral allies equally dissatisfied. The opposition press ridiculed him unmercifully, sometimes with the financial support of the military, who feared that Illia's commitment to open elections would facilitate the advance of Peronism.

The Peronists had indeed rebuilt much of their political base by the mid-1960s. Their power was now more concentrated in the labor unions, which had survived the period of persecution better than had the Peronist party itself, and their success at enduring severe official repression gave them great expectations for the future. The obligatory payment of union dues also made some of the Peronist unions among the best-financed political forces in Argentina. The union leadership believed that the faction currently in control of the armed forces had accepted the Peronist presence as a fact of Argentine political life. By now, however, the labor leaders had begun to imagine a Peronism without Perón. They suspected that, although the military might be disposed to tolerate them, it was less likely to tolerate the return of the exiled Leader. Then, too, Perón's return would likely result in a loss of the independence that union leaders had won since 1955. In spite of this undercurrent of serious reservations on the part of the Peronist leadership, the return of Perón had tremendous popular appeal, and in 1964 Augusto Vandor, head of the powerful metal workers' union, launched "Operation Return" to make it happen. Perón himself believed the idea premature, but he reluctantly left his Spanish exile and boarded a flight to Buenos Aires to make the attempt. The flight stopped in Rio de Janeiro, where, acting on a request from Illia, Brazil's new military government forced Perón to turn around, and Operation Return ended anticlimactically with his return to Madrid.

Having demonstrated a decorous loyalty to the exiled chief and proved that his return to Argentina did not figure among the real political alternatives of the moment, Vandor felt himself free to concentrate on building Peronism without Perón. In the congressional elections of 1965, the Peronist candidates together received nearly 40 percent of the votes, with those controlled by Vandor polling more than 30 percent. Brimming with confidence, Vandor induced the country's General Confederation of Labor (CGT) to begin an aggressive campaign of strikes and sit-downs with objectives that avoided any hint of class struggle and even echoed some of the demands then being made of the government by the industrialists themselves. This bid for respectable political power worked so well that when the military decided to overthrow Illia shortly thereafter, it involved the Peronist union leadership in its planning. This strange pair of bedfellows led to another. From his vantage point in Madrid, Perón had recognized Vandor's intentions to take over the Peronist movement, and, deciding to reassert his control, he found a willing collaborator in President Illia.

When Perón sent his third wife, Isabel, to advance his cause in 1966, Illia's government did all it could to facilitate her mission in Argentina. The venue was an election in the province of Mendoza, where Illia's commitment to open, competitive elections provided an opportunity to test the divisions within Peronism. Isabel Perón went there to endorse, in the name of her husband, an obscure candidate for governor of Mendoza against the candidate supported by the union leadership, who, in addition to being locally influential, ranked among the most visible Peronists in the national congress. After ten years of absence, the image of Juan Domingo Perón flickered on Argentine television screens appealing to the voters, and his candidate easily carried the election. Illia's government had been hoping that Perón's counterendorsement would weaken Vandor's dissidents and expedite their accommodation into the post-Peronist order. The last thing the government had wanted was a resurgence of Perón's personal influence over the movement, but as a number of former Peronist dissidents rushed to pay homage to Isabel in the wake of the election, all signs pointed to an imminent reunification of the Peronist movement under its historic chief.

The threat of such an outcome in the 1967 congressional and provincial elections steeled the resolve of the remaining dissident Peronists and the military to oust Illia. Their common cause was reinforced by the expostulations of journalists in the service of the military hierarchy, who had taken to listing the armed forces and the labor unions (along with the church and associations of business leaders) as "the real factors of power" underlying the country's formal political structures. A wide consensus among these chief players did indeed support the military's coup against President Illia in June 1966. At the swearing in of the new president, Gen. Juan Carlos Onganía, the heads of the three armed forces and a radiant Augusto Vandor rubbed elbows with prelates, industrialists, and distinguished representatives of the most select Argentine society, and the country's political parties—with the exception of Illia's Radicals—beheld the turn of events with scarcely concealed satisfaction. However, Onganía was about to begin a campaign of ideological purification that would soon dissipate the mutual self-congratulation of the glittering assemblage.

The military government directed its offensive against the insidious cultural revolution under way in Argentina since 1955. Its first targets were the universities, considered hotbeds of subversive ideology and moral corruption. One month after Onganía took office, government intervention eliminated the autonomy traditionally enjoyed by the national universities. Next, the military purifiers directed their attention to the cultural and artistic life of Buenos Aires, which, in the highly charged climate of recent years, had become more intense and also increasingly, even militantly, frivolous. Beginning with the government of Onganía, the cosmopolites of Buenos Aires, accustomed to living in the vanguard of international cultural developments, gradually fell behind the inhabitants of other Latin American capitals whom they had once regarded as incurably provincial. The military project of cultural and ideological purification acquired its high profile in the absence of pressing socioeconomic and political problems. The Communist party, for example, did not become the special object of repression because it was not perceived as particularly threatening at the moment. As for Argentina's lingering sociopolitical issues, the military government avoided a direct approach, hoping instead to make them disappear through macroeconomic management.

In late 1966, Onganía named a new minister of the economy, Adalbert Krieger Vasena, to oversee a comprehensive restructuring of the Argentine economy, with sweeping social and political implications. Krieger Vasena abandoned the policies applied for over a decade to support the country's agricultural exports, now that the recovery of prosperity in that sector of the economy made them unnecessary, and directed his reforms to strengthening the fiscal position of the state. He introduced a new devaluation of the currency but immediately taxed away the exporters' increased earnings. The government therefore had less need to print money to meet expenses, and inflation came down, making fewer devaluations necessary in the future. The Krieger Vasena plan set the exchange rate of the new peso close to its level before the inflationary period began, hoping that such aggressive optimism would attract the foreign investment needed to maintain the new exchange rate and to allow a much-needed recapitalization of Argentina's deficient industrial plant, technically backward agriculture, and aging communications infrastructure. The plan achieved notable success in 1967 and 1968, and the government's hopes were high in spite of certain clouds on the horizon, such as the exorbitant interest rates necessary to attract foreign investment.

In early 1969, events in the city of Córdoba so changed the political landscape as to obscure permanently the impact that the economic reforms might have had in the longer term. A string of minor riots culminated in March of that year with a citywide upheaval, known as the *Cordobazo*, in which autoworkers were joined first by university students and then by a broad spectrum of the urban population, revealing the presence of tensions that the military government had done nothing to address. The military's erstwhile allies in the labor movement felt betrayed because, after having supported the coup that brought Onganía to power, they found the government first insisting on economic measures that the unions had long opposed, then promoting rival labor leaders who docilely accepted any and all official dispositions. Labor resistance to Onganía had started slowly, but the Cordobazo marked its full awakening. Even before the Cordobazo, Augusto Vandor had begun to explore the possibility of a return to an electoral system sponsored from within the military by the old anti-Peronist, Gen. Pedro Eugenio Aramburu. Vandor was soon assassinated amid the rising violence that affected much of the country in the wake of the cordobazo, without ending the coalescence of opposition forces around Aramburu. The deterioration of the political situation undermined Onganía's prestige among the high-ranking officers who had installed him in the presidency and crippled his efforts to retool the Argentine economy. Three months after the cordobazo, Onganía was forced to accept the resignation of Krieger Vasena, and his government limped on for almost a year in a state of semiparalysis.

The assassination of General Aramburu in 1970 dealt the coup de grace to the Onganía administration and definitively scuttled the project of democratic opening initiated by Vandor. Aramburu's death also signaled the arrival of a new political force, that of the group that had killed him: the Montoneros, a Peronist insurgent organization that based its tactics on a free reading of the lessons of the Cuban Revolution. As for the armed forces, they insisted on their own version of what they, too, called an Argentine Revolution, referring to the overthrow of Illia's constitutional government in 1966. Led now by Gen. Alejandro Agustín Lanusse, they unseated Onganía and held onto power as political tensions escalated vertiginously in a crescendo of violence that augured ill, indeed, for the coming decade.

Still comparatively tranquil in the early 1960s, nearby Uruguay continued to endure the gradual decay of the urban welfare state created by the Colorado party of José Batlle y Ordóñez in the prosperous early decades of the twentieth century. After the Blancos finally managed to win the presidency in the late 1950s by promising to champion the interests of the neglected countryside, they encountered fierce resistance in the urban labor movement. The Uruguayan population was, in fact, heavily urban, and no frontal assault on urban interests had much chance of success. In order to remain in power beyond the election of 1962, the Blanco government had to mollify city dwellers with an official generosity that necessarily accelerated inflation. The cost of electoral victory was a collapse of the country's banking system as the Uruguayan peso went into a free-fall. As importations ceased for lack of hard currency to pay for them and pay raises were neutralized in advance, the government found it impossible to appease its detractors and responded finally with outright repression. In the context of a still-functioning electoral system, that move sealed the fate of the Blanco government in the election of 1966.

Besides returning the Colorados to executive office, the 1966 election ended the country's experiment with a collective presidency whereby the representatives of various factions in each party had shared presidential power proportionately to their electoral strength. Rule by executive council, the Uruguayans decided at this point, had been more effective at distributing patronage than at taking decisive administrative action. Gen. Oscar Gestido, the new Colorado president, was a man whose essentially honest intentions won him authentic popularity, but the continued factionalism of the Uruguayan congress and the difficult economic situation tied his hands. At Gestido's death in 1967, Vice President Jorge Pacheco Areco began to revitalize a Colorado heritage older than Batllismo itself, the party's nineteenth-century military authoritarianism, in order to confront an armed challenge from the revolutionary left. The offensive of the Uruguayan left took various forms: a labor movement strongly linked to the Communist party; a student protest movement directed at the government's links to the United States; an electoral coalition uniting Communists, Socialists, Christian Democrats, and various Colorado and Blanco splinter groups; and, finally, the urban guerrillas who called themselves Tupamaros.

The Tupamaros were led by militant former labor and political organizers who scorned the moderate programs put forward by the left-wing electoral coalition. At first, this clandestine group provoked a widely positive response with its spectacular and largely bloodless operations. The popularity of the Tupamaros in the late 1960s revealed a deep disaffection of many Uruguayans with the status quo. The restoration of electoral politics after the dictatorship of the 1930s had not restored the collective political faith that Uruguayans had so convincingly demonstrated in the 1910s and 1920s, and postwar economic hardships had made the former Batllista welfare state plainly inviable. If Uruguayans showed some receptivity to the revolutionary proposals of the Tupamaros, it was because they yearned for a return to the general prosperity and social harmony of a lost golden age, not because they were ready for the violent confrontations implied by the revolutionary program and the response that it would inevitably provoke. As in so many other Latin American countries, the crucial decisions of the 1960s were being postponed until the 1970s.

As for Bolivia's "decade of decisions," it saw the gradual disintegration of the progressive regime installed by the 1952 revolution. In the late 1950s, President Hernán Siles Suazo had adopted cautious policies of economic austerity and political demobilization in order to curry favor with the United States and deal with the shaky economy. Víctor Paz Estenssoro, the original leader of that revolution, returned to the presidency in 1960, promising to accelerate the pace of social change. Like Siles Suazo, he found that the Bolivian economy provided few resources to work with, and his vice president, the veteran unionist Juan Lechín, backed by the country's powerful tin miners, became increasingly impatient. When the president proposed to amend the constitution in order to succeed himself in the next election, Lechín broke away and took a considerable portion of Paz Estenssoro's National Revolutionary movement (MNR) with him. At that point, Paz Estenssoro turned to the armed forces for support, designated Gen. René Barrientos as his running mate in the next election, and won a hollow victory marked by the abstention of the opposition. Outbreaks of protest on the part of miners and students and the exile of opposition leaders accused of conspiring against the government led to a military coup in November 1964. At the head of the coup was Vice President Barrientos, who sent Paz Estenssoro himself into exile and allowed the opposition leaders to return home. There followed a period of political reshuffling, during which Juan Lechín returned to exile and Barrientos finally emerged on top, winning the presidential election of 1966.

Barrientos proclaimed himself the heir of the 1952 revolution, but during his term in office the distinctive sociopolitical configuration of that revolution continued to fade, especially the crucial part played by the tin miners. The rift between the MNR governments and the miners concerning the management of the substantially nationalized Bolivian tin industry had begun to open in 1956, and it only got worse thereafter. In sum, the industry's margin of profitability was so narrow as to be inevitably undercut by the workers' modest gains in compensation and working conditions, and the unions refused to give up their hard-fought achievements. As successive administrations struggled to wring a profit out of the country's most important export activity, the tin miners became the principal nucleus of opposition to the government. Loss of support in the mines and urban areas pushed the MNR to retrench in the countryside, as we have seen, and to rebuild the Bolivian army into a force capable of overpowering the miners' militias that had helped accomplish the revolutionary triumph in 1952. In the late 1960s, the revolutionary government repeatedly ordered the military occupation of the mining region.

Meanwhile, the rest of Bolivian society was becoming more integrated. The agrarian reform and highway construction programs had done much to win the sympathies of the country's rural people for the revolutionary government, so that, even without the miners or strong urban backing, Barrientos won 60 percent of the popular vote in 1966. When Che Guevara selected a remote area of Bolivia to begin a Cuban-style insurgent foco in South America, he committed a grave error. The rural Bolivians of the area, well integrated in a framework of peasant unions, were indisposed to aid Guevara's insurgents. Without popular support of the sort that had sustained the foco of the Sierra Maestra, his small band was easily eliminated by Bolivian "Rangers" with U.S. counterinsurgency training. The better integration of the countryside had stimulated the national market economy, beginning the slow creation of new mercantile and entrepreneurial classes, even in parts of the country not affected by the agrarian reform. This occurred most of all in the eastern slopes of the Andes and the formerly isolated plains beyond, where the burgeoning city of Santa Cruz awakened from a colonial slumber to become the center of the country's most economically dynamic region. Bolivia's largest cities benefited, too, as modest industries developed to meet the needs of a more consolidated national economy chronically short of hard currency to pay for imports.

The revolution of 1952 had, indeed, transformed Bolivia, but it had itself been transformed in the process. Calls to "deepen" the original socialist aims of the revolution did not gain majority support, but neither did the orthodox free-market liberalism that was attracting adherents in some other Latin American countries by the end of the 1960s. In the absence of a clear path to follow, the government marked time and maintained a carefully cultivated ideological ambiguity.

In the northern Andes, Ecuador continued to struggle, amid the polarizing influences typical of the 1960s, toward a democratic redefinition of the terms of political conflict. For almost a generation, that process of redefinition had been thwarted by repeated attempts to express itself through José María Velasco Ibarra, the pugnacious caudillo about to become president once again in 1960. Velasco Ibarra had been elected at the head of a coalition dominated by the left, but, in his habitual manner, he alienated much of his electoral support soon after taking office when he tried to rid himself of his vice president, Carlos Julio Arosemena, a representative of important elements of that coalition. In 1961, the military stepped in to resolve the question and again consigned Velasco Ibarra to his now traditional Argentine exile. The military's antipathy for Velasco Ibarra had outweighed its distrust of Arosemena's orientation toward the left.

Once Velasco Ibarra was out of the picture, however, Arosemena's lack of enthusiasm for the U.S.-directed campaign against Cuba provided a signal for strong conservative opposition to rally against him. Encouraged financially, as well as morally, by the United States, conservative forces finally moved in 1963 to oust Arosemena and pulverize the growing power of the socialist left in Ecuador. As one of the first measures in this campaign, they closed the universities, where students had been staging pro-Cuban demonstrations. Three years later, a new constituent assembly returned Ecuador to a system of free elections that made possible—and therefore inevitable—yet another presidency of the irrepressible Velasco Ibarra, beginning in 1968. This time, though, the ideological polarization that affected so much of the hemisphere in the 1960s worked to keep the elderly caudillo in power. When, after breaking with his electoral supporters, as he inevitably did once in office, Velasco Ibarra reached for dictatorial powers, the military supported him. The long shadow of the Cuban Revolution had finally convinced them that Velasco was the only leader popular enough to maintain the established order against the revolutionary tide.

In the countries of Central America, the decade of the 1960s witnessed few dramatic political developments but several socioeconomic ones. The location of the isthmus—near Cuba and in the strategic "backyard" of the United States—made it unlikely to escape the ideological polarization of these years, but Guatemala continued to be more affected than the other countries. The creation of the Central American Common Market also had an uneven impact on the isthmus.

At the time of the Cuban Revolution, Guatemala seemed about to undergo a precocious recovery from the trauma of 1954. President Miguel Ydígoras Fuentes had allowed the beginnings of a democratic opening that benefited the political heirs of the overthrown revolutionary government, but the fall of Havana changed his mind. Guatemala would not be spared the worst polarizing impact of the cold war. In the early 1960s, when Ydígoras offered his country as a base for clandestine operations organized by the United States against Cuba, other Guatemalan army officers took up arms against his government and, invoking the Cuban model, began a rural guerrilla war in the Guatemalan mountains. Leftist opposition mounted in urban areas as well, setting off the terrorism of the right that would become a hallmark of Guatemalan political life in the late twentieth century. The military removed Ydígoras in 1963, then escalated its violent repression to a point that made its control of the country independent of the presidency. In 1966, the military allowed a civilian president, Julio César Méndez Montenegro, to take office after he promised not to defy the army and its conservative allies. Montenegro represented another attempt to renew the reform impulses of 1944–54, but he could accomplish little in the climate of fear daily augmented by new acts of right-wing terrorism that he proclaimed himself powerless to halt.

The terror had grown so great by the late 1960s that the military was able to impose its own candidate, Col. Carlos Arana Osorio, in the election of 1970. The unrestrained brutality suffered by Indian peasants and urban opposition elements during Arana's rule foreshadowed the inauguration of similar tactics by the right all over Latin America during the decade to come.

There was less political conflict in the rest of the countries of Central America. Only in Nicaragua did the Cuban Revolution figure directly, with the creation of a guerrilla foco in the mountains. Nevertheless, it would be many years before the guerrillas gained enough momentum to threaten the government. In the interim, the second president of the Somoza dynasty, Luis, managed the country and the family fortune with undeniable skill until his death in 1967, at which time the Nicaraguan presidency passed to his brother, Anastasio, Jr. The third Somoza soon demonstrated the characteristic rapacity of his line, but he lacked the political finesse of his predecessors, and his heavy-handed style began a gradual deterioration of the family's control over Nicaragua. In El Salvador, oligarchical dominance continued to be punctuated by military interventions. A coup in 1960 put reformers briefly in power until another removed them the following year. In mid-decade, the election of José Napoleón Duarte as mayor of the capital brought the rapid growth of his Christian Democratic party, but that party did not challenge oligarchical hegemony in the 1960s. Honduras, for its part, was ruled for much of the decade by a mildly reformist military government, while in Costa Rica, the political consensus established by the revolution of 1948 continued to allow for the peaceful alternation in power of the contending parties.

The dynamism of the region's economic growth, enhanced by the formation of the Central American Common Market in 1960, tended to upstage political developments in the isthmus during the early part of the decade. The new trading bloc especially stimulated industrial expansion in Guatemala and El Salvador, the two countries whose population and previous development enabled them to take best advantage of the expanded market, and it also accelerated the growth and diversification of agriculture, which became less dependent on bananas and coffee with the expansion of new crops like cotton. Unfortunately, the intensification of commercial agriculture, principally for export, had some deleterious effects. In El Salvador, the combination of rapid population growth and increasing concentration of landholding left larger and larger numbers of rural people without access to a livelihood, so that the number of landless peasants, 12 percent of the total in 1960, quickly tripled. The impact of a similar phenomenon in Nicaragua was attenuated by that country's much lower population density, but, as the production of food crops for internal consumption diminished, the living standards of the poor necessarily suffered there as well.

By the second half of the 1960s, the resulting social tensions put a strain on the Central American Common Market, slowing the process of integration begun so auspiciously a few years earlier. It had become evident that not all of the participating countries benefited equally and that the consolidated market had boosted the industries of Guatemala and El Salvador at the expense of industrial aspirations elsewhere. The most obvious sign of trouble was the so-called "Soccer War" fought between El Salvador and Honduras in 1969. Disturbances following a preliminary Salvadoran victory in that year's World Cup contest sparked the conflict, but it had deeper socioeconomic roots. As the expansion of export agriculture had proceeded throughout the decades, economic refugees from overcrowded El Salvador had poured into more sparsely populated Honduras. In the early 1960s, Honduras limited the number of Salvadoran employees that companies could legally hire, and the year before the war, another law prohibited acquisition of Honduran public land by Salvadorans. The Honduran government wanted to reserve its public land for distribution to its own nationals as part of the country's agrarian reform. The effect of its prohibition, however, was to eliminate a crucial escape valve for El Salvador's excess rural population. The good offices of the OAS put an end to the "Soccer War" after two weeks, but the buildup of rural tensions in El Salvador would vastly sharpen political confrontations in the decade ahead.

Panama, governed by a narrow oligarchy since its independence in the first decade of the twentieth century, entered a period of crisis in the 1960s. Owing to its banana plantations and, above all, to its interoceanic canal, Panama had become even more closely incorporated into the U.S. economy than had the five traditional Central American countries to the north of it. The oligarchy's orientation toward the United States had encountered no resistance more significant than that offered by a prodigal son of the oligarchy itself, Arnulfo Arias. Beginning in the 1930s (when, like so many other Latin Americans, he became interested in European fascism), Arias directed nationalist sentiments against the United States and also against the black descendants of West Indian immigrants who had come to Panama to work on the construction of the interoceanic canal. Neither the perennial popularity of Arias nor his frequent denunciations of official election fraud seriously threatened oligarchical control of the country before 1952.

In that year, the commander of the Panamanian National Guard, José Antonio Remón, permanently transformed the political landscape by replacing the civilian oligarchy with the plebeian military as the real locus of power in the country. Under what essentially remained military leadership despite a string of civilian figureheads, the Panamanian government began to challenge the perpetual sovereignty over the canal that the United States had acquired by treaty in 1903. Egypt's nationalization of the Suez Canal in 1956 did much to raise Panamanian aspirations to regain control of their own waterway. By 1964, the anti-Panamanian attitude of the foreign residents of the Canal Zone had led to anti-U.S. disturbances of unprecedented severity. Four years later, a National Guard junta assumed power under the direction of a new popular leader, Gen. Omar Torrijos. Torrijos showed more talent than any previous military leader at drumming up public support for his government, particularly among the formerly marginalized sectors of the population, and he used his political capital to push more vigorously for a redefinition of U.S. treaty rights over the canal and its surrounding zone. At the end of the 1960s, awareness of a nationalist awakening in Panama led U.S. diplomats to be so gingerly in dealing with the question of sovereignty rights that they largely refrained from sounding the trumpets of the cold war in spite of the Panamanian general's vaunted ideological eclecticism.

In the Dominican Republic, on the other hand, U.S. policy and, therefore, domestic political alternatives retained a familiar polarity, reinforced by events in neighboring Cuba. The decade opened with the assassination of the durable dictator Rafael Trujillo in 1961, followed the next year by the election of Juan Bosch, the most prestigious intellectual adversary of the dictatorship, accused by the Dominican military of conniving with the communists. In 1963, a military coup deposed Bosch, but other officers soon tried to restore him to power, and the resulting confusion brought the 1964 U.S. intervention. The unilateral U.S. presence in the Dominican Republic was soon converted into a more decorous multilateral OAS presence that arranged for presidential elections in 1966. These elections pitted Bosch against Joaquín Balaguer, formerly Trujillo's vice president. Balaguer won by a comfortable margin and set about building a level of political control so thorough as to threaten another lifetime presidency in the Dominican Republic. Balaguer's techniques were milder than those used by his former mentor, but they did not exclude prudent application of electoral manipulation and intimidation. His task was made easier by the division of the opposition into the followers of Bosch, increasingly drawn to the Cuban example, and more conservative politicians with whom Bosch's followers found it difficult to make common cause.

When the decade of the 1960s dawned in Venezuela, Rómulo *Venezuela* Betancourt and his party, Democratic Action, had returned to power after a decade of dictatorship. However, the situation in 1960 was far different from the postwar moment when Democratic Action had first erupted on the Venezuelan national scene. Democratic Action now governed in a coalition with the Christian Democratic party (COPEI), and its original revolutionary enthusiasm had been chastened by earlier reversals. Betancourt refused to recognize Latin American governments that did not result from free elections or maintain a representative system, and he reserved a special (and abundantly requited) animosity for Fidel Castro, whom he had once believed his political disciple.

Although the Democratic Action party had not abandoned its commitment to agrarian reform and labor's right to organize, it soon faced challengers from the left. As early as 1961, a small group of dissidents formed the Revolutionary Movement of the Left (MIR). Larger groups of impatient younger members broke away from Democratic Action in 1962 and 1967, while urban guerrilla activity began early in the decade and continued for years. Clandestine revolutionary violence received vocal support from university students and more active participation from the youth of the sprawling squatter settlements around Venezuelan cities. Both the government and the participants in the insurgent movements believed that Venezuela had begun to recapitulate the Cuban experience, and both sides regarded the presidential election of 1964 (which the guerrillas had vowed to scuttle) as a decisive test of strength. Therefore, a 90 percent turnout of Venezuelan voters in the election constituted a major triumph for the Democratic Action government, despite the fact that its candidate received only a third of the votes. The president-elect Luis Leoni, a faithful follower of Betancourt, had to enter a coalition with COPEI, which now emerged as a serious rival of Democratic Action. When COPEI withdrew from the coalition, Leoni's position became substantially more difficult, and he had to spend much of his energy combating the insurrectionary movement that threatened to spread, at mid-decade, from urban to rural areas. In foreign policy, Leoni found Betancourt's rigid policy of not recognizing de facto governments impractical as such governments became ever more common in the hemisphere.

In 1968, an important split in the ranks of Democratic Action helped give COPEI its first presidential victory in the person of Rafael Caldera, whose administration proved considerably more fortunate than Leoni's. By the last years of the decade, the political climate of disillusionment had begun to cool the revolutionary ardor of the Venezuelan left. Some even transferred their hopes to the rotund figure of the ex-dictator Marcos Pérez Jiménez, who won a senatorial election in 1970 only to see it annulled by the country's Supreme Court. This mutation from an insurrectionary impulse to a resurrectionary one had been born of the discontent of Venezuela's marginal urban poor, and both major parties responded to the challenge by extending their networks of clientele into the squatter settlements, quickly incorporating them into the respective partisan machines. Caldera also abandoned Betancourt's and Leoni's foreign policy line and reestablished diplomatic relations, right and left, with military dictatorships all over South America but also with the Soviet Union. Even Venezuelan relations with Cuba improved, though still informally.

Venezuela continued to thrive economically during the 1960s, coming to embody the most complete Latin American example of a consumer economy. It had been a prosperous decade for both the subsidiaries of multinational corporations (visible in the ubiquitous supermarkets of Greater Caracas, for example, as well as in the international oil companies) and for the national import-substitution industries systematically favored by protectionist legislation. In addition to its other strengths, Venezuela had become a major exporter of iron ore. The country's consumers and industrialists had benefited mutually from the constant expansion of mineral exports because the state reserved to itself the exploitation of many of these and, in tough negotiations that extracted progressively more advantageous conditions from the oil companies, aimed at eventual nationalization of petroleum as well. Indeed, a special key to the political stability of these years was the skill of government managers in spreading the benefits of economic growth widely among all of the influential sectors of the Venezuelan population.

In spite of its shaky beginning in the first years after 1958, then, Venezuela's electoral democracy rode the wave of prosperity to a new level of consolidation by the end of the 1960s, but the Venezuelan political experience did not win widespread prestige in a Latin America attracted to more dramatic alternatives. Probably, the unparalleled bounty and longevity of the country's export boom made the Venezuelan case seem too exceptional to serve as a model for Latin America as a whole.

Mexico

Mexico, another atypical case, seemed to be on an opposite trajectory from that of Venezuela, as its long-stable political system revealed signs of exhaustion in the 1960s. President Adolfo López Mateos, president at the outset of the decade, sponsored a constitutional reform to give the opposition a fixed number of seats in the Chamber of Deputies, but the official Institutional Revolutionary party (PRI) soon showed that it had no intention of allowing any real threat to its monopoly on political power. The test came under Gustavo Díaz Ordaz, who succeeded López Mateos as president in 1963: first, when the leaders of the PRI stonewalled all attempts at internal democratization; then, when the conservative National Action party (PAN) had the effrontery to win certain municipal elections in the Mexican north—elections that the government lost no time in annulling. Mexico's governing elite recognized the need for some kind of democratic opening, but it simply could not bring itself to sacrifice voluntarily its privileged position at the seat of power.

In reaction to this spectacle of intransigence on the part of the governing elite, universal resentment erupted in a mobilization of impatient secondary school and university students in Mexico City. The student movement produced powerful echoes throughout urban Mexico, particularly because at its vanguard were the sons and daughters of the professional middle classes who had risen under the aegis of the revolution and constituted the most progressive elements of Mexican society. The identity of the dissidents, however, did not attenuate the violence of the official repression in a year when Díaz Ordaz, soon to host the Olympic Games in Mexico City, was committed to demonstrating his government's solidity in the eyes of the world. His commitment took the bloody form of a massacre of protesters in the Tlatelolco district of the capital. The brutal repression ended the disorder in the city streets but contributed catastrophically to the alienation that most young Mexicans of the political class felt toward their government.

More than a response to the authoritarian style of the governing elite, Mexico's political crisis of the 1960s reflected the end of the long period of "stabilizing growth." The demands of the protesters were many. They wanted a new style and new faces in government, a more pluralist political scene, and a more overt discussion of the specific dilemmas facing Mexican society. They called for the implantation of a true rule of law and the elimination of the arbitrary exercise of power that, as the massacre of Tlatelolco illustrated, might be imposed even against members of the ruling classes. Although they talked less about it, they wanted a reform of the government's pervasive and equally arbitrary economic power as well. The protests of the late 1960s gave voice to a generalized but inchoate desire for change, and whether or not the demonstrators realized it, the sum of their demands was a sweeping political and economic renewal. Fortunately for the regime, the prevalent desire for change was not matched by any consensus concerning what specific new course to adopt, leaving the PRI considerable room to maneuver.

The regime had two basic alternatives. First, it could take up the banners of revolutionary egalitarianism and popular mobilization so unceremoniously shunted aside twenty-five years earlier in its headlong pursuit of economic expansion. Second, it could embrace a very traditional sort of political liberalism that satisfied almost all of the protesters' demands, despite the fact that the slogans ringing through the streets of Mexico City always framed those demands in the socialist terms then in vogue. Rigorously applied, both formulas meant dismantling the bastions of privilege constructed by the governing elite during the past two generations. Battling now for its survival, the regime opted to combine the two options so that each partially nullified the other, but with an accent on the appeal to a revolutionary heritage that it had always claimed to embody. The man chosen to implement this difficult task was Luis Echeverría, elected to succeed Díaz Ordaz in 1969.

As secretary of government at the time of the Tlatelolco massacre, and therefore more directly implicated in it than Díaz Ordaz himself, Echeverría appeared an unlikely candidate to orchestrate a rapprochement between the regime and its critics. His approach proved so efficacious, however, that it became standard practice in subsequent Mexican presidential successions. For the purposes of the regime's secure continuity, the new president had to be, as always, the handpicked successor of the departing president. The innovation was to make Echeverría his predecessor's most vociferous critic as well. Echeverría denounced the waywardness of Mexico's institutional revolution, and he promised to restore its legitimacy with the help of both the young elite protesters of Tlatelolco and the frustrated rural and urban masses who had seen their needs so long postponed. The rhetorical fanfare sounded by Echeverría produced even fewer results than the reforms of his predecessors. The conversion of Mexico City's most important daily newspaper into a truly independent publication, for example, met with thunderous presidential applause until some of its reporting infringed on matters that Echeverría considered rather too sensitive for public airing. Similarly, a few troublesome confrontations caused official purifiers to back away immediately from condemning corrupt labor leadership for the betrayal of rank-and-file interests.

In terms of economic management, on the other hand, the changes introduced by Echeverría had to be more than rhetorical. The formula of stabilizing growth had begun to belie its name as both industrial and agricultural expansion slowed in the late 1960s. The agricultural decline was especially worrisome because Mexico's self-sufficiency in food production, even as its population tripled, had constituted perhaps the most valid achievement of the institutional revolution. The demonstrations of 1968 had not spelled the imminent demise of the regime, but they had dissolved its aura of invulnerable permanence. In the 1970s, the PRI would begin to review its economic options with a careful eye to discovering the political implications of each, in the manner of other Latin American governments traditionally less stable and more at the mercy of public reactions.

For Peru, the polarizing impact of the Cuban Revolution meant a turn toward Alliance for Progress formulas with a distinctive twist. The rise of revolutionary socialism in the hemisphere pushed the leadership of Peru's reform party, the Popular American Revolutionary Alliance (APRA), further along the anti-communist, pro–North American path it had followed since World War II. At the beginning of the 1960s, it appeared that APRA's founder, Víctor Raúl Haya de la Torre, would win the upcoming presidential election as the result of a tactical alliance with Peruvian conservatives, but the election of 1962 proved indecisive, with each of the three principal candidates winning a sizable portion of the popular vote. In the absence of an absolute majority, the choice of president fell to the Peruvian congress, or rather, to the Peruvian army, which intervened at this point, alleging electoral fraud in favor of APRA and calling new elections for the next year. The 1963 election had a clearer outcome. Virtually all of the parties to the left of APRA supported Fernando Belaúnde Terry, the popular reformist who had become Haya de la Torre's chief rival in the previous decade. Belaúnde's language very consciously echoed Alliance for Progress formulas, including the promise of agrarian reform and better integration of Peru's isolated highland interior (both the sierra and the eastern Andean slopes known as the Montaña) with the national economy centered on the coast. As president, he would have an opportunity to test his ideas in practice.

Peru's socioeconomic panorama looked fairly bright at the opening of the decade but gradually darkened during its middle years. Before the 1963 election, the country's economy had prospered as the fish meal exports continued to do well and an approving United States awarded Peru part of the sugar import quota it had formerly reserved for Cuban production. However, both fishing and sugar cultivation took place in coastal Peru, and they attracted a flood of migration from the sierra, where traditional subsistence economies eroded amid escalating social conflict that led to the internal occupation of a number of highland regions by the Peruvian army. Belaúnde's agrarian reform project, intended to address this problem, was blocked in the congress by conservatives who resisted in principle and Apristas who wanted to see the failure of their rivals at all costs. Then the fish meal export boom began to fade as the catch declined. Successive currency devaluations to favor exporters were accompanied by accelerating inflation and falling presidential popularity. Belaúnde attempted to revive the economy by negotiating concessions with a North American oil company that had a long-standing dispute with the Peruvian state. The manner of the negotiations, as well as the content of the agreement, offended nationalist sensibilities, preparing the way for Belaúnde's overthrow, and the apparent certainty of an APRA victory in the 1969 elections clinched the matter.

In October 1968, a coup by the armed forces sent Belaúnde into exile and inaugurated an atypical sort of military regime. The experience of the Peruvian army in the disorders of the sierra had made a deep impression on the officer corps, who saw in the rising peasant mobilization both a threat to the established order and an opportunity for the military to shape a new Peru. They proposed to seize the momentum created by ongoing uprisings, impose their own stamp on the emerging movements, and extend their control over older popular organizations affiliated with APRA in coastal Peru. Far from forgetting the agrarian reform project of the deposed civil government, the military regime used it to secure grass roots political support, to promote the diversification of the economy, and to further the integration of national society. The military government also insisted on a redefinition of Peru's external relations that emphasized diplomatic and economic autonomy. Their first target, in that regard, was the issue that had partially justified their seizure of power: the question of sovereign control over the country's petroleum. More than a political expedient, the nationalization of oil marked the first of a series of measures revealing the new international stance of the Peruvian military regime.

Political observers in Peru and in the rest of Latin America found this government disconcertingly difficult to categorize. It applied the "security and development" formulas associated with the Alliance for Progress with greater dedication than any other regime in the hemisphere while simultaneously raising anti-imperialist issues reminiscent of the early days of APRA. It used familiar counterinsurgency tactics to control the outbreak of guerrilla activity in the sierra, but it otherwise refused to fit itself into a cold war mold. Like the leaders of the Mexican Revolution in the 1920s, the Peruvian military leadership of the 1960s demonstrated a willingness to tolerate the most intransigent revolutionary ideologies of the day, and it invited avowed radicals to take leading positions in the government's social welfare agencies. Moreover, it reestablished ties with the Soviet Union and Cuba. To the chagrin of Peru's left-wing opposition, Fidel Castro showed his appreciation by commending the profoundly revolutionary character of the Peruvian military regime. At the end of the 1960s, the future course of Peru was anyone's guess.

[margin note: Completely atypical & unpredictable regime by end of decade in Peru]

Colombia, another country that revealed the significant impact of Alliance for Progress ideas, presented a picture of political stasis keenly in contrast to Peru's puzzling new departure. The National Pact (which had ended the period of "la Violencia" between liberals and conservatives with an agreement for the two parties to alternate in power) lost popularity under the uninspired aegis of its second president, Guillermo León Valencia, a conservative. By the time of the 1966 election, more than half the electorate preferred not to participate in obediently electing Carlos Lleras Restrepo, the liberal next in line. Lleras Restrepo attempted to infuse new meaning into his presidency by identifying it with popular aspirations like agrarian reform. He knew that, in order to carry out an agrarian reform in Colombia, it would be necessary to bypass local party organizations through the direct, constant application of popular pressure. Rural Colombians turned out en masse to support the agrarian reform, but they did not constitute the irresistible force that Lleras Restrepo had anticipated (thinking, perhaps, of the more overwhelmingly rural Colombia of the 1930s, before la Violencia accelerated the exodus toward the cities). Urban Colombians, for their part, were disappointed when the president's emphasis on economic development failed to produce the desired results. By the time of the next presidential election in 1970, the urban electorate was disenchanted enough to vote in large numbers for the populist ex-dictator, Gen. Gustavo Rojas Pinilla. The National Pact candidate in that election, Misael Pastrana Borrero, carried the day by a narrow margin. A conservative, Pastrana Borrero had little interest in the reformist thrust of his liberal predecessor, and under his administration Colombia returned to the sociopolitical immobility that had characterized it early in the decade.

[margin note: Colombia]

[margin note: disenchantment with the National Pact]

Chile, more than any other single country, exemplified the politi-

Chile

*socialist
alternative
in every
election*

cal alternatives facing Latin America as a whole in the 1960s. The socialist alternative, offered to Chilean voters in every election of the decade, became the explicit competitor of the internal representatives of Alliance for Progress ideas in the election of 1964. The contours of the Chilean experience therefore constitute a fitting culmination of this discussion of Latin America's "decade of decisions."

In 1960, the president of Chile was Jorge Alessandri, a conservative who had edged out Salvador Allende's coalition of the left in the close election of 1958. That election had seen the rise of two centrist parties—the Radicals and the Christian Democrats—as swing groups, able to give predominance to the left or the right. Alessandri allied himself with the Radicals in his push to restore the country's economic health through orthodox financial management and free trade. An early spurt of growth (fueled partly by injections of credit from sources controlled by the United States, Alessandri's international ally) had spent itself by the second half of his presidency, significantly undercutting the appeal of the ruling center-right coalition. The left acquired further momentum as the traditional identification of rural Chileans with their landowners' parties, the essence of conservative hegemony in the countryside, gave signs of evaporating. In the senatorial election of 1963, a socialist candidate won a striking upset in Curicó, part of the country's rural and, until then, solidly conservative central southern region.

As the mood of many Chileans shifted in favor of social change, the parties on the right gave their passive support to the Christian Democratic candidate, Eduardo Frei, who seemed best able to contend with Salvador Allende in the next election. In order to achieve that effect, conservative landowners had to abdicate their traditional control over the voters of the countryside in favor of Christian Democratic organizers, who proposed to create farm workers' unions and carry out a moderate agrarian reform—two things the landowning class had successfully resisted for decades. Calling for a "Revolution in Liberty," the Christian Democrats promised to combine some of the social transformations also proposed by the Socialists and their allies with a comfortingly conservative ethos of social stability. For the election of 1964, the Christian Democratic party received monetary aid from sister parties in Europe and also from the Central Intelligence Agency. In order to make their reforms palatable to their conservative supporters at home and abroad, Frei's party framed its appeal in crudely anticommunist terms, a tactic that proved quite successful at the polls but created enduring hostility between the Christian Democrats and the parties of the left.

Eduardo Frei won such a convincing majority in the election of 1964 that his startled erstwhile supporters on the right bolted immediately to the opposition, where they proceeded, in an odd conjunction with their recent adversaries on the left, to obstruct the Christian Democrats' legislative initiatives in any manner possible. The midterm congressional elections reduced the influence of the right even further and opened a reasonably wide path for Frei's legislative proposals for social and political reform. His agrarian reform sought to create a new class of independent small farmers who would benefit from government-supplied technical assistance and political organizing provided by the Christian Democrats. The reform was touted as a way to improve Chile's low level of agricultural productivity, long recognized as a drag on the national economy, but the sponsors of the reform also hoped that the class of small farmers would replace the large landowners as the political center of gravity (beholden, of course, to the Christian Democrats) in the Chilean countryside.

A parallel reform aimed to remedy another economic problem, stagnation in Chile's important copper-mining industry. For decades, the state had absorbed most of the industry's profits through taxation and currency exchange policies, and the mining companies had reacted by abstaining from any further investment, much to the detriment of productivity. Frei's solution was the "Chileanization" of copper (as opposed to the nationalization of the industry demanded by the left). His plan called for the government to become a partner of the copper companies, supplying them with capital (to come from U.S. subsidies and credits) for modernization and expansion. In addition to stimulating the economy, then, the Christian Democrats hoped to reach beyond their urban, middle-class base and build a solid electoral majority by cultivating particular rural and industrial interests. On the last front in this campaign of political expansion, Frei's party directed solicitous attentions to the marginal poor who had gathered in Chilean cities as a result of the accelerated rural to urban migration of the postwar period and who had so far taken little part in national political confrontations.

Although the achievements of Christian Democracy during the Frei administration were indeed impressive, they fell short of their goals. The agrarian reform could not improve the country's agricultural productivity overnight, and the Chileanization of the copper industry went no further than the creation of a framework for future negotiations. As early as 1967, it became clear that Frei's economic initiatives could not so easily break through the larger structural impediments that had hampered previous attempts to stimulate eco-

nomic expansion in Chile. Nor had the Christian Democrats succeeded in turning the rural and urban poor into their faithful political
clients. Even had they been able to provide land, as planned, to 100,000
families, many more would still have remained landless, and the
actual number of plots distributed was only a third of that number.
The shortfall opened fertile ground for the parties of the left, whose
organizers quickly moved in to take advantage of the collapse of the
political hegemony of the landowners. Finally, the appeal to the urban
poor, carried out by Catholic charitable organizations associated with
the governing party, was limited by the modest resources dedicated to
such work and by the condescending paternalism of many of the
volunteers.

In both rural and urban settings, the left remained an effective
competitor in the struggle to win over the newly independent participants in Chile's political process. Within the left, the Socialists and
those inspired by the example of Cuba surpassed the influence of the
older Communist organizations closely tied to the labor unions. Accustomed to preferential treatment by all recent political coalitions,
whether oriented to the left or to the right, the Chilean middle class
found itself suddenly ignored, and it witnessed the political radicalization of the rural and urban poor with considerable alarm. Events in the
formerly tranquil realm of Chilean academia were also unsettling, as
university students protested against an old-fashioned academic elite.
This revival of a nineteenth-century political issue, symptomatic of
Chile's odd mixture of progressivism and traditionalism, had not been
on the government's agenda, but the Christian Democrats backed the
students, and the resulting conflict threatened quickly to get out of
hand.

Gradually, the resistance encountered by the Christian Democrats
led to a division in their ranks. Some wanted to forge ahead with
their project of economic and political transformation at any cost, and
the language that they used to describe their Revolution in Liberty
sounded more and more reminiscent of the revolutionary left. Other
Christian Democrats, President Frei among them, remained far more
cautious, still chiefly motivated by the wish to distance themselves
from the leftists. In the late 1960s, the more progressive wing of the
Christian Democratic party gained the upper hand. The party's candidate in the election of 1970 would be Radomiro Tomic, who used quite
radical rhetoric in his attempts to reach left-leaning voters and perhaps also to offset the liability of recently having been Chile's ambassador in Washington, D.C. The increasingly progressive stance of the
Christian Democrats and the partial achievement of their reforms

made radical politics seem less threatening to many Chileans. A vivid illustration of this development occurred in the congress, where the conservative opposition, still in a tactical alliance with the parties of the left, supported the election of Salvador Allende as president of the senate.

With the approach of the election of 1970, the left had again become a viable electoral alternative. Understandably, however, the possibility of victory accented ideological differences and heightened long-standing rivalries among the parties that occupied that end of the Chilean political spectrum. The Communists, in particular, believed that, no matter how near the opening might seem, Chile was not ready to begin its transition to socialism. They persisted in advocating a broad, interclass coalition of progressive forces, and under certain circumstances were willing to ally themselves with the Christian Democrats. The Socialists (especially their vocal radical faction) angrily rejected Communist incrementalism, called for a class-oriented alliance of proletarian parties, and made increasing use of insurrectional rhetoric. A united front of parties of the left finally coalesced behind Salvador Allende, who, as head of the more moderate Socialist faction, could alone bring together the disparate pieces of the fractious coalition, but three previous defeats in presidential elections made the prospects of Allende's candidacy seem less than overpowering.

Only in the feverish final weeks of the campaign did observers begin to anticipate Allende's victory. When the votes were counted, Allende had won 36 percent, while Jorge Alessandri, again the candidate of the right, won 34 percent. The margin was slender but wide enough to open the way for what came to be called the "Chilean Way to Socialism," a path that Allende promised to tread in strict accord with the country's constitutional traditions in spite of fearsome obstacles that he well understood. It was a paradoxical ending for a decade during which the great political challenges had been defined by the Cuban model of insurgency and the image of Che Guevara. Salvador Allende, a veteran politician whose career spanned three decades, stood in striking contrast to the bearded young guerrilla. In 1970, Guevara was dead and Allende was about to show the extent of his dedication to the dream of a socialist Chile. The three years of his presidency would finally resolve the revolutionary question hanging over Chile—and all of Latin America—during the 1960s.

CHAPTER IX

LATIN

AMERICA IN

OUR TIME

REFORMIST AND REVOLUTIONARY impulses had not disappeared by the end of the 1960s, but after 1970 changes in the international context created a substantially new situation in Latin America. During a quarter century of unprecedented economic expansion and political stability, the United States had exercised an overwhelming hegemony over the other industrialized core countries of the world economy, and these, in turn, over the developing world. However, the international order that had appeared so well consolidated during the first postwar decades proved more vulnerable than anyone had imagined. Consequently, the evolution of the international context constitutes the best starting place for our discussion of recent Latin American history.

The world economic order changed rapidly after 1970. The end of the long postwar economic boom in the capitalist core came clearly into sight by 1971, when U.S. president Richard Nixon suspended the parity of the dollar (that is, its convertibility for a fixed amount of gold, established by the Bretton Woods Accords of 1944) in an attempt to adapt to his country's loss of absolute economic predominance over other industrial powers. In so doing, he removed the monetary standard that had undergirded the international monetary system during its decades of steady prosperity, and two years later the first oil shock sent the destabilized international economy reeling. Arab countries, who had first exercised their substantial control over world oil supplies in 1967 (when they used it as a political weapon against Israel) subsequently discovered another, far more useful, outcome of their concerted actions: a startling rise in the international price of oil. In the 1960s, developments in Latin America had seemed cumulative, and the ultimate direction of events, clear. None of that would be true in the 1970s.

The oil shock of 1973 brought a sudden and dramatic corrective to

(margin note: 1971 - boom over)

(margin note: 1973 - oil)

a situation that had taken shape as the economies of the world's most developed countries had grown more rapidly, for the most part, than the production of the food and raw materials they consumed. The prices of most food products and raw materials exported by the developing world had risen only slowly. In the case of oil, steady expansion of production had kept up with the frantic increase in consumption and maintained surprising price stability until the creation of the Organization of Petroleum Exporting Countries (OPEC). The adoption of new production limits by OPEC led to a sudden jump in oil prices that caused inflation in the world's heavily industrialized economies and slowed their expansion. At least in the case of oil, the supposedly inherent disadvantage of primary-product exporters regarding the industrialized core countries—a maxim shared in Latin America by developmentalists and dependency theorists—seemed no longer to apply. However, the new situation did not prove directly beneficial to most of the world's developing countries because the slowdown of economic growth in the most developed countries tended to reduce imports of food and raw materials other than oil.

Another result of the oil shock was a massive flow of "petrodollars" from the countries that imported petroleum to those that exported it. Far too great to be absorbed into the economies of the petroleum exporters, this capital went in search of immediate investment at extremely low rates of interest. The economic slowdown in the most industrialized nations prevented them from absorbing all the petrodollars, and consequently it became easy for poorer countries in both the Third World and the Soviet bloc to borrow money during the 1970s. Because interest rates were so low, however, banks carefully limited these to short-term, or at most middle-term, loans, in order to take advantage of higher rates in the future.

The relative position of the world's major powers was affected by the new facts of international economic life. The United States, which still produced most of the oil it consumed, suffered less than Europe or Japan, a circumstance that slowed the gradual, but already evident, deterioration of U.S. economic and political hegemony. The U.S. decline was also softened by its ability to manipulate the exchange rate of the dollar to favor its balance of trade. Europe was the hardest hit by the oil shock, while Japan continued its steady economic advance without yet threatening the hegemonic position of the United States. As for the Communist countries, their command economies faltered as well, after having maintained quite respectable growth rates in the first postwar decades. The growing complexity of their economic structures had made them more and more unwieldy, and the elites

who had built their own social position along with those structures
were reluctant to experiment. After a few fitful gestures at reform, the
Soviet Union settled deeper into political and economic immobility,
while its Eastern European satellites sought any opportunity to renew
their financial contacts with the capitalist world.

All of the most developed capitalist countries had to deal with
dangerous levels of inflation in the late 1970s. In 1978, U.S. financial
managers tried to curb inflation by imposing a drastic increase in
interest rates. The measure reduced earnings and increased unemployment but failed utterly to halt inflation. The second oil shock in 1979
reinforced the inflationary trend and made combating it a priority for
governments all over the industrialized world. Conservative administrations like those in Great Britain and (beginning a bit later) the
United States turned the anti-inflation campaign into an assault on
the social welfare programs that had proliferated during the postwar
boom, and even governments far more committed to maintaining
a welfare state, such as the socialist administrations of France and
Spain, saw a need for retrenchment in that regard. The world's developing countries, particularly those that had borrowed heavily in
petrodollars, found themselves doubly disadvantaged by the economic
policies applied by the industrial core countries in their efforts to
defeat inflation. The rapidly rising interest rates and the resulting
recession worked simultaneously to choke off the flow of loans to the
developing world and make repayment of the outstanding ones far
more onerous. The situation of capital-hungry developing countries
worsened when successive budget deficits led to massive and sustained borrowing by the U.S. government, keeping interest rates up
and absorbing much of the investment capital available on the international market.

In this way, the United States temporarily escaped the consequences of its growing economic insufficiencies by spreading the impact over the rest of the world, but addressing those insufficiencies
would only become more painful and more costly later on, as the
United States began to lose its formerly unquestionable industrial
preponderance in the world economy. Although the countries of the
European Community remained economically stagnant through the
1970s and into the 1980s, Japan demonstrated a seemingly inexhaustible capacity for sustained economic expansion during this period, and
smaller Asian countries like South Korea, Formosa, Hong Kong, and
Singapore began to perform the difficult feat of "peripheral industrialization," competing with U.S. industries even in a number of activities unrelated to their comparative advantage of inexpensive labor

costs. In Latin America, the Brazilian and Venezuelan steel industries showed a similar vitality. As a result, the distinction between developed and developing countries tended to blur somewhat during the 1980s. Overall, however, heavily indebted Latin American countries were not in a position to take advantage of the more fluid world economic picture.

In addition, the geopolitics of the period after 1970 appeared to close down alternatives earlier open to Latin American governments. The hegemonic influence of the United States appeared more powerful than during its moment of trial in the preceding decade. During the 1970s, the Soviet Union renounced any aspiration to rival U.S. influence in Latin America and indicated little interest in promoting Latin American revolutions of the Cuban type, preferring to promote diplomatic and commercial contacts with regimes of whatever political stripe. The countries of western Europe had little to offer economically, and they hesitated to do anything politically that might offend the United States—still their most important military ally and trading partner. Even the alternative perspectives formerly contemplated within the hierarchy of the Catholic church were repudiated by the Vatican, as Pope Paul VI's search for an equilibrium between continuity and innovation gave way to Pope John Paul II's reassertion of unalloyed ecclesiastical traditionalism. Strong papal disapproval severely diminished the political consequences of the currents of liberation theology that continued to exist in the Latin American church.

U.S. supremacy in the Western Hemisphere seemed less embattled than it had during the 1960s and was therefore exercised less vigorously. Relations with Latin America no longer constituted a priority for U.S. administrations, beginning with that of Richard Nixon, who preferred that the United States assume a "low profile" in inter-American affairs. Gone was the dramatic emphasis of the Kennedy years but not the willingness to use whatever means necessary to achieve U.S. policy goals, as Nixon confirmed through repeated attempts to forestall and then to "destabilize" Chile's socialist experiment of the early 1970s. When Jimmy Carter was elected in reaction to the abuses of the Nixon presidency, he extended his moralizing mandate to include a foreign policy emphasis on human rights. The new accent on human rights did not imply a renunciation of more traditional goals, and it provided a new legitimating rationale for U.S. international involvement, rather in the manner that Great Britain's campaign against the slave trade legitimated and consolidated its hegemony in the Atlantic world during the nineteenth century. Nevertheless, Carter's foreign policy did have a beneficial effect in Latin

America. A considerable number of Latin Americans probably owe their lives to his efforts—something that cannot be said of any other U.S. president—and he is no doubt the only former chief executive of that country ever to be greeted cordially by ordinary citizens on a private visit to the streets of a Latin American city, as occurred in Buenos Aires in 1984.

Nevertheless, all of the Latin American regimes condemned for violating human rights outlasted the Carter presidency, and his foreign policy was perceived by many within the United States as an abdication of the country's defense of its own national interests. When, after a few years, the public revulsion for Nixon's *realpolitik* had dissipated, U.S. conservatives began to equate Carter's moral qualms with those of the antiwar demonstrators who, in their view, had brought about the humiliating U.S. debacle in Vietnam. The U.S. Senate debate over ratification of a treaty conceding to the Panamanians full sovereignty over their national territory and eventual control over the interoceanic canal showed the popularity of conservative calls for a more aggressively nationalist foreign policy. It was during these debates that Ronald Reagan, soon to succeed Carter as president, began to display nationally the political talents that he had already used so successfully in California. The effects of the resurgence of conservative U.S. nationalism could be observed in Carter's policy toward Nicaragua as the moribund Somoza dictatorship tottered under the Sandinista-led final offensive of 1979. Declining to seek the negotiated solutions unacceptable to the increasingly mobilized Republican right, the Democratic president aided Somoza more resolutely than Dwight Eisenhower had aided the Cuban dictator Fulgencio Batista twenty years earlier.

The Reagan victory of 1980 put the right wing of the Republican party in the White House, banished human rights to rhetorical obscurity, and returned anti-insurgency and the struggle against communism to top priority in U.S. foreign policy. The military dictatorships that had been the chief targets of Carter's criticisms now became particularly intimate allies. The U.S. ambassador to the United Nations, Jeane Kirkpatrick, justified these alliances by explaining that merely authoritarian regimes like Anastasio Somoza's or the Shah of Iran's constituted preferable alternatives to totalitarian Communist regimes. Misplaced Democratic scruples had led Carter to desert these essential tactical allies, according to Kirkpatrick, but Reagan would not make the same mistake. In its zest for opposing Communist expansion with resolute shows of force, the Reagan administration focused its Latin American policy on the region where the United States had often used force before, and it viewed inter-American relations as a whole through the narrow lens of Central America and the Caribbean, a habit that could lead to important misunderstandings. Argentine participation in training Reagan's counterrevolutionary Nicaraguan insurgents, for example, led the military government in Buenos Aires to assume incorrectly that the United States would in turn refrain from aiding Great Britain against Argentina in the Malvinas Islands War of 1982. Subsequently, the Reagan administration's preference for military solutions kept Nicaragua and El Salvador at the center of its Latin American policy even during such significant developments as the redemocratization of much of South America, the consolidation of a major guerrilla movement in Peru, and the coalescence of new opposition within the formerly docile Organization of American States.

There was more than a revival of cold war anti-Communism driving U.S. policy toward Latin America in the 1970s and 1980s. The need to recover a sense of national pride, discussed previously in connection with the Panama Canal Treaty, came even more clearly to light in the 1983 military expedition against Grenada. How else to explain the almost delirious enthusiasm with which the North American public hailed the conquest of a practically defenseless Antillian ministate by the greatest military force on earth? Was it not the same need for showy self-vindication that made the dignified electoral denouement of Sandinista rule in Nicaragua something of an anticlimax for those who had prosecuted Reagan's "Contra War" with such unflagging zeal? While these concerns took center stage, other important issues enjoyed less-sustained attention. Such was the case with the proliferating drug trade (that had far-reaching and multifaceted effects on U.S. relations with countries as diverse as Colombia, Bolivia, and Paraguay) and with the massive illegal migration of Mexican workers to the southwestern United States.

In each case, the government of the United States found addressing thorny domestic problems less congenial than dealing with their international manifestations. If solutions that treated external symptoms seldom cured internal social ills, they at least provided U.S. policymakers with the satisfaction of implementing their prescribed treatment. Unlike public opinion at home, Latin American public opinion posed no political obstacle and could easily be brushed aside along with the protests of governments powerless to resist the will of U.S. administrations. The Mexican leadership dared to do little more than politely express its concern when the United States attempted to cut off totally a flow of undocumented migration that functioned as an escape valve for explosive social tensions in Mexico, while the augmentation of drug interdiction efforts led to the reappearance of a U.S. military presence in the Andean countries, again without vigorous protest from the affected governments.

The lack of outcry against policies imposed in Latin America without reference to the needs of the region did not necessarily reflect a strengthening of U.S. hegemony there. Nor can it be explained solely by the natural reluctance of debtor governments to antagonize the creditor with whom they must engage periodically in endless renegotiations of their debts. Rather, the nationalist and anti-imperialist motifs that had mobilized broad sectors of Latin American public opinion in the 1960s and early 1970s were losing their ability to do so by the 1980s, and this was but one indication of a more general change in the public mood, as the exhilarating ideological alternatives of the "decade of decisions" now faded on the political horizon. The notion, so influential in the 1960s, that Latin American problems derived inevitably from the nature of dependent capitalist economies and that socialism offered the antidote began to seem insufficient as Taiwan and South Korea turned their versions of dependent capitalism into industrial success stories, while Communist Poland and Rumania lapsed into stagnation. Even more important in the general change of spirit was the decisive defeat of the movements that had responded to the revolutionary vision in different parts of the hemisphere. For a discussion of Latin America in our time, the essential first point of reference, analogous in influence to the Cuban Revolution for the 1960s, is the catastrophic experience of Chile.

Although Salvador Allende received the largest number of votes in the Chilean presidential election of 1970, those votes did not constitute an absolute majority, nor did his Popular Unity coalition command a majority in congress. Therefore, Allende's government, which took office only after satisfying the congress of its intentions to work strictly within constitutional limits, was a delicate political balancing act. If the new president's intention to respect the country's institutional traditions was sincere and augured well for the trials ahead, other events of the transition to the Popular Unity government foreshadowed a darker outcome. In an attempt to prevent an Allende presidency, right-wing elements kidnapped (and later killed) the head of the army, Gen. René Schneider, and blamed the kidnapping on leftist extremists. They failed in their attempt to abort the government of Popular Unity, but the incident provided a bitter foretaste of future efforts to resist the "Chilean Way to Socialism."

The first months of Allende's administration were unexpectedly easy. The nationalization of the country's large-scale copper mines passed the congress with virtual unanimity. The opposition got its way in refusing to broaden existing agrarian reform legislation, but the reforms already under way gained momentum without provoking alarming tensions in the countryside. This surprisingly placid political climate can be traced to the economic prosperity of the moment as the government undertook a massive redistribution of income that had the immediate effect of augmenting consumer demand. After a brief flurry of panic on the part of the propertied classes, business boomed, inflation actually declined, and Chilean factories began to produce at full capacity. The impact on the political fortunes of Popular Unity can be gauged by the results of the municipal elections of 1971, in which the left won an absolute majority of the votes for the first time. The government's halcyon days were short-lived, however. Domestic prosperity quickly skewed the balance of trade by swelling importations of foreign goods, and a fall in the international price of copper made the imbalance worse. In addition, a capital flight began as industries stopped reinvesting in their Chilean plants and remitted their profits abroad to escape the expropriations that would inevitably accompany the promised transition to socialism.

The ideological orientation of the Popular Unity government had international costs as well. The most important of these was the implacable hostility of the United States, first expressed in an inordinately extreme reaction to the nationalization of copper and then, more damagingly, in a commercial and financial blockade. This caused major economic dislocations, and though the countries of western Europe declined to join the blockade, neither did they rush to fill the void that it had created in the Chilean economy. The Soviet bloc, on the other hand, did supply considerable aid, but after a little over a year it began to show signs of unwillingness to do so indefinitely.

The change of economic circumstances produced a sudden heightening of social and political tensions. Proliferating scarcities of food and consumer products inspired popular organizations to set up a surveillance of retail stores to prevent speculation and hoarding. A rash of industrial conflicts led the government to put many factories under state supervision, applying emergency legislation little used since the 1930s. Popular Unity soon lost whatever minority support it had enjoyed among the urban middle sectors, which henceforth mounted a solid and vociferous opposition to the government. In response, the largely middle-class Christian Democratic party moved rapidly to the right but, even so, suffered a hemorrhaging of its political base in favor of the stalwartly conservative National party, home of the country's traditionalist right wing, rabidly and unalterably hostile to Popular Unity.

Economic dislocation and political polarization fed each other in a self-perpetuating cycle. The government reorganized the agrarian reform to include small subsistence plots farmed by individual families as well as larger tracts farmed in common by the recipients (intended to provide food sold through government channels). Given the vastly higher prices available on the black market, substantial amounts of this produce flowed into extralegal channels of commercialization, exacerbating economic distortions and worsening the political situation. Independent truck drivers became crucial operators in a parallel economy that affected a larger and larger number of products. When Allende nationalized the trucking industry, the independent truckers responded, in October 1972, with a strike that put them in the vanguard of the ever more militant opposition and caused the government immense difficulties. The army refused to break the strike by force, and material aid to the strikers from within the Nixon administration made them immune to any economic pressure. Although Allende's Popular Unity retained the solid support of the working class, the peasants, and the marginal poor, the opposition gained the practically unanimous backing of the middle and upper classes. Consequently, government and opposition found themselves beyond hope of compromise in a confrontation that had taken on the rawness of open class conflict.

The mobilization of the Chilean masses had outrun the government's capacity to control, and differences within the coalition of the left were increasingly expressed in action. The Communist party showed itself typically cautious and—as the rhythm of events became more precipitous—it began to lose influence over workers, many of whom transferred their allegiance to less-restrained groups. The most aggressive of these were the radical wing of Allende's own Socialist party and the Revolutionary Movement of the Left (which took its inspiration from the Cuban experience and had only provisionally renounced armed struggle). As Chilean society divided into warring camps, these groups had taken the initiative in organizing cordones populares, areas effectively dominated by committed revolutionaries well to the left of the official policies of the Popular Unity, in industrial and working-class neighborhoods around Santiago.

In late 1972, the extreme left was preparing for a final battle over the fate of socialism in Chile, while President Allende did everything possible to avoid that battle. By taking military officers into his cabinet, he reinforced the authority of the government enough to hold it together until the congressional elections of March 1973, in hopes of containing the conflict within constitutional bounds. As a result of those elections, the parties of the left lost the absolute majority that they had briefly claimed in 1971, but their 43 percent of the vote was still substantially more than Allende had won in 1970. The mixed outcome did not resolve the ongoing political crisis, and Allende sought other avenues of peaceful settlement—among them, an accord with the Christian Democrats and a plebiscite on the constitutional reform proposed by Popular Unity—promising to resign if the reform were not approved. However, the opposition, not in a transactional mood, did everything possible to counteract Allende's efforts. It obstructed the government's ministerial appointments, encouraged further strikes (including another truckers' strike), and even began to make open use of terrorist violence, the favorite tactic of the extreme right.

In August 1973, the military forced the resignation of Gen. Carlos Prats, an officer identified with the constitutional principle of political neutrality for the armed forces. As both head of the army and a member of Allende's cabinet, Prats had constituted a check on the influences calling for a coup. Prats's replacement, Gen. Augusto Pinochet, had no such qualms. On 11 September, the armed forces attacked the house of government, where Allende had gone to await them, determined to sacrifice his life upholding his constitutional trust as legitimate president. The death of Allende was followed by devastating repression in factories and working-class neighborhoods. The soccer stadiums, transformed into huge open-air prisons, became the scenes of numerous executions, while in rural areas more killings erased all trace of recent mobilizations in support of Popular Unity. The Battle of Chile was over, and the left had suffered a crushing defeat. The savagery of the coup shocked the world, which did not expect such a spectacle in one of Latin America's model democracies.

Even many Chileans who approved of the coup expected a quick return to constitutional government, but Pinochet soon made it clear that the military government intended to remain, to govern by force, and to disallow any participation by the political parties. How can the duration and degree of repression following the 1973 Chilean coup be explained? Beneath the personal ambition of Pinochet and the institutional ambitions of the Chilean armed forces (piqued by the establishment of military rule in other Latin American countries) lay the class conflicts exposed by the Allende experience. Sobered by the shortages of food and dismayed at the plebeian insolence of the social forces awakened by the Popular Unity, Chile's middle and upper classes had glimpsed cataclysmic consequences ahead. For years after the coup, the evidence of those convulsive years would weigh more heavily on their minds than any nostalgia for a less ruthless style of government.

The intense crisis that Chile underwent during the final stage of its socialist experiment helps account for several aspects of the dictatorship that continued afterward for almost two decades. Like military governments in Argentina and Brazil, the military government of Chile absolutely prohibited any form of popular mass organization. The Chilean armed forces also benefited from a mobilization of the middle and upper classes that made itself felt at critical junctures for at least ten years following the coup. Events preceding military takeovers in Argentina and Brazil, where the danger of real social upheaval was more a matter of collective fears than immediate possibilities, had not created that level of middle- and upper-class commitment to their respective dictatorships. Unlike the generals who served as presidents in Argentina and Brazil, Augusto Pinochet was a political leader in his own right, with a loyal personal following among the civilian population, and not simply a representative of the military institution who maintained his position by astute manipulations of the officer corps. Principally for this reason, the rule of the Chilean armed forces alone tended to operate as a personal dictatorship at variance with the bureaucratic-authoritarian model.

The Chilean dictatorship of the 1970s and 1980s also broke with the bureaucratic-authoritarian paradigm (most clearly exemplified by Brazil) in renouncing a central emphasis on industrialization. No doubt, this decision was influenced partly by the political threat presented by ever larger conglomerations of industrial workers in a country with strong traditions of militant labor organization, but the abandonment of developmentalism as the guiding economic philosophy of military governments in Chile, Argentina, and Uruguay had to do as well with the size of their respective populations, which amounted to merely a fraction of Brazil's. In effect, changing technologies had increased the size of the internal market required to achieve the developmentalist goal of industrial diversification characteristic of the core countries. Chile's relatively small population put that goal out of reach and thus provided the disciples of Milton Friedman with an opportunity to apply their theories of free-market liberalization at the behest of the dictatorship.

Overcoming the inflation that had raged in the last months of Allende's government was the first order of business. The impotence of the terrorized working class and the obedient resignation of the

middle class made the requisite recession politically painless for the
dictatorship, while the privatization of the assets placed under state
control by Allende offered handsome opportunities for the groups
close to the levers of power, not excluding (it was widely believed)
some of the economic advisers who had come to oversee the liberalization of the Chilean economy.

The restructuring proposed by the neoliberal economists was indeed ambitious. Of all the places where their theories were applied,
only Chile undertook genuinely to "shrink the state" in order to
"enlarge the nation," that is, the private sector. Turning away from
industry (which they thought basically inappropriate for Chile) and
away from mining (which they thought necessarily crippled by excessive oscillations of international price and demand), the neoliberals
put export agriculture at the center of the restructured Chilean economy. They left in place the land distributions made under the first
stage of agrarian reform, in the confidence that market forces (as well
as large operators' privileged access to credit) would gradually produce
a reconcentration of landholding. As that process of reconcentration
occurred, the rural poor flooded into urban *callampas*, the Chilean
term for the ubiquitous shantytowns that grew rapidly in the outskirts
of Santiago and other cities. In the countryside, however, conditions
had been created for a flowering of agricultural export expansion that
would gradually reduce the influence of the unstable mining economy
and allow the propertied classes eventually to reap the sweetest fruits
of their victory.

This process of economic restructuring was imperiled, at the outset, by a few years of windfall prosperity in the mid-1970s. The Chilean coup had occurred at the time of the first oil shock, and the
subsequent international plethora of petrodollars found an attractive
investment opportunity in Chile's newly liberalized economy. The
major influx of hard currency kept the exchange value of Chilean
currency quite strong, provoking a disastrously high rate of consumer
imports and making the country's export products less competitive.
The resulting trade imbalance was palliated with additional credit,
and by the end of the decade the urban physiognomy of Santiago had
been transformed by a frenzy of construction and a vast proliferation of
retail and service activities. The middle- and upper-class inhabitants
of this formerly austere and quiet capital were becoming the opulent
victims of all of the normal scourges affecting affluent consumer
societies, such as the rush-hour traffic jams that persisted in spite of
the new highway network. The seductively easy credit terms of the
mid-1970s led to massive indebtedness all over Latin America—and

not just among the converts to neoliberalism—but as a result of that orientation in Chile, the credit flowed more narrowly into consumer spending than elsewhere. In 1983, the foreign debt contracted by the inhabitants of Greater Santiago (apart from the public debt contracted by their government) was estimated at thousands of dollars per capita.

Rising interest rates rapidly inflated Chile's already swollen debt in the late 1970s and early 1980s. New international credits were very difficult to obtain after 1981, and some of the largest Chilean banks soon tottered on the edge of insolvency, to be rescued only by government intervention. If pursued methodically, the ensuing economic salvage operation would have involved the military government as deeply in the economy as had the nationalizations carried out by Popular Unity. True to the spirit of free-market liberalization, Pinochet used government resources to shore up only a few key enterprises and allowed a wave of bankruptcies to engulf the rest. It is perhaps unsurprising that the economic shambles of the early 1980s formed the backdrop for the first serious political crisis to confront the Chilean military regime.

Pinochet's seizure of power in 1973 had been received initially with applause from all of the opponents of Popular Unity, who expected to inherit control of the government after a brief military interlude. In the mid-1970s, seeing that the armed forces had other plans, the Christian Democrats moved circumspectly into the opposition, while the Catholic church intensified its protests against the atrocities committed by the military during and after the coup. The large number of Chileans in exile overseas (where refugees of the left were soon joined by members of the emerging moderate opposition) had a significant impact on European and North American public opinion in this period, putting the issue of human rights in the international spotlight for the first time in Latin America. The Pinochet regime reacted to its critics abroad with characteristic attempts to exterminate them, the most famous example being the 1976 assassination in Washington, D.C., of former diplomat Orlando Letelier by agents of the Chilean secret police. Criticisms of Pinochet became frequent in Europe and the United States, and relations with Washington turned frigid by 1977, but as long as Chile retained its high credit rating these international snubs did the regime little damage. For a while, the government even managed to turn foreign disapproval to its advantage. In a 1978 plebiscite it invited Chileans to choose between support of General Pinochet and national dignity, on the one hand, and an unnamed alternative symbolized by a black flag, on the other. So satisfactory was the outcome of this trial balloon that the

regime scheduled another plebiscite in 1980 to approve an unabash-
edly authoritarian constitution that extended Pinochet's presidential
mandate for at least another nine years.

Successful institutionalization of the Pinochet dictatorship did
not save the Chilean regime from severe political difficulties when
prosperity vanished in the early 1980s. Even the heads of the other
military branches began openly to demur at the prospect of a perpetual
Pinochet presidency. In 1982 and 1983, a moderate opposition alliance
between the Christian Democrats and the Socialists offered a "safe"
alternative to the military dictatorship and threatened to undercut its
support. General Pinochet reacted with his normal slyness, suddenly
extending his political toleration to include the far left. The left's old
working-class base had narrowed with the decline of industrialization,
but the peripheral callampas, which now housed more than half the
population of Greater Santiago, provided an opportunity for a larger
base. When the noisy beating of pots and pans, formerly used by the
privileged classes to protest against Allende, resounded again in Santiago's affluent Barrio Alto, an ominous echo arose from the sprawling
slums. Street demonstrations, repeated each month for more than a
year, also revealed the participation of all social classes. Although
the ranks of the opposition remained divided, the voice of the extreme
left was heard again. Pinochet had invited his old middle- and upper-
class supporters to recall the political implications of Chile's class
divisions.

By the late 1980s, Chile was the only country of the Southern
Cone that had not yet returned to democratic rule. Atypical in that
regard, Chile nevertheless exemplified with unparalleled, almost paradigmatic, clarity the social forces underlying the process of military
dictatorship and redemocratization in South America's most developed countries.

Uruguay's passage through military dictatorship and redemocratization exhibited a markedly lower level of social conflict and polarization. In the 1960s, even the country's tiny urban guerrilla group, the
Tupamaros, had limited itself to largely bloodless stunts intended
more to sway public opinion than to overthrow the government. By
1970, however, the Tupamaros began more drastic actions, such as the
kidnapping of Dan Mitrione, a U.S. adviser to whom the guerrillas
attributed the increasing use of torture by the Uruguayan police. The
eventual killing of Mitrione by his captors allowed Colorado president
Jorge Pacheco Areco to set a tone of epic struggle against sinister forces
of subversion in his prosaic daily encounters with protesting university students and labor unions.

In the elections of 1971, the year in which the Chilean left won an absolute majority of the votes, the Uruguayan left received the support of only one-fifth of the electorate, almost entirely in Montevideo, with much of the rest going to other opposition elements, most notably the majority faction of the Blanco party, now led by Wilson Ferreira Aldunate, whose irreproachably conservative past did not prevent him from becoming an energetic critic of the government's authoritarian drift. Citing the perils of a national emergency, Juan M. Bordaberry, Uruguay's new president by the narrowest of margins, turned to the army for the decisive mandate that the election had failed to provide. In 1973, the army liquidated the Tupamaros with a fulminating efficacy that raised suspicions about the possible intentionality of their earlier failures, and when the civil opposition then unanimously called for the military to withdraw from the political scene, the response was a presidential coup dissolving congress and setting up a National Security Council dominated by the armed forces to make key governmental decisions.

After two weeks of strikes and disturbances in Montevideo, Uruguay succumbed to its new, essentially military, government. Following a familiar pattern, the regime repressed labor unions and independent political organizations, as well as all unauthorized cultural and ideological expression. It used systematic imprisonment, frequently accompanied by torture, as its method of civic discipline. By the end of the military period, a fifth of all adult male Uruguayans had been incarcerated, if only temporarily. Compared to the other dictatorships of the Southern Cone, Uruguay's was distinguished by its exaggerated legalism and the tendency to make its adversaries disappear into prisons rather than unmarked graves, in contrast to the preferred usage of the Argentine and Chilean militaries. Some leaders of the Uruguayan opposition escaped prison at home only to disappear permanently after fleeing to exile in Buenos Aires.

The easy international credit of the 1970s did not produce the same degree of artificial prosperity evident in Chile, and no sector of Uruguayan society offered the regime the kind of backing that Pinochet received before 1980. Instead, long lines began to form in front of the U.S. consulate in Montevideo during the early-morning hours of each weekday, as a generation of young people was driven to seek economic opportunity through emigration. At one point, Uruguayans emigrating to Australia chartered entire ocean liners. Even the country's landowners, hoping to recover economic well-being under military rule, found that the strength of the Uruguayan peso, buoyed up by modest inflows of international credit, undercut their profit margins.

With the end of the anemic prosperity induced by the international surfeit of petrodollars, the military leadership began to search for ways to return the country to the control of its traditional political parties.

An eventual return to democratic traditions had always interested Uruguay's military more than that of Argentina or Chile because the Uruguayan left had never threatened the status quo electorally. When, in 1976, President Bordaberry proposed to do away permanently with the Blanco and Colorado parties, the armed forces did away with Bordaberry, instead. A more modest proposal to establish the military as a cogoverning force alongside the traditional parties was rejected by Uruguayan voters in 1980, giving the movement toward redemocratization further momentum within the armed forces. In 1981, under the direction of a new military president, Gen. Gregorio Alvarez, the government allowed labor union activity to recommence. The next year, the Blanco and Colorado parties, as well as a third party representing the Catholic right, were reorganized, with elements strongly opposed to the dictatorship taking the lead in each of the two traditional parties. Frankly in retreat, the military legalized all parties and began to negotiate the terms of transition. Most importantly, the armed forces refused to allow participation in the upcoming presidential elections by Gen. Líber Seregni, the preferred candidate of the Broad Front coalition of the left, or by Wilson Ferreira Aldunate, their longtime nemesis among the Blancos. A failed attempt by Ferreira Aldunate to impose unconditional democratization by making a dramatic illegal return from exile only encouraged the acceptance of the military's terms by the other parties, not eager to compete electorally with a popular leader who could claim to have ousted the military single-handedly. As a result, the Blancos and the coalition of the left fielded less attractive second choices in the 1984 election, and the Colorado candidate, Julio María Sanguinetti, carried the day. The relative strength of the various parties in 1984 almost exactly replicated the last presidential election in 1971.

[margin note: a return to the same results before the dictator]

Uruguay's restoration of the political status quo ante was more complete than anyone could have imagined during the dictatorship. This surprising return to the situation of 1971 threw the period of military rule into sharp relief, making painfully explicit how little had been accomplished, and also suggested the advisability of concessions such as granting amnesty to those guilty of atrocities in order to prevent any reentry of the armed forces into political life. Through the 1970s and into the 1980s, continued economic and demographic involution had combined with violent repression to sap the dynamism of the country's social forces and cow the impatient demands of those

who returned to the political arena in 1984. Consequently, Sanguinetti's government was able to maintain consistent economic policies
in the following years, bringing slow but sustained growth and gradually curbing inflation. Ruled again by a moderate Colorado government in the late 1980s, the Uruguayan republic harkened back with
imperishable fidelity to the epoch of its early twentieth-century reformer, José Batlle y Ordóñez, though the attempt to recover the
modest social miracles of Batllismo was becoming an almost archae-
ological undertaking.

Argentina Argentina's path through dictatorship and redemocratization was
more turbulent than any other. Between 1970 and 1985, Argentines
witnessed the long-awaited return of Juan Perón, a widening schism
among his followers, the proliferation of political violence, and a war
with Great Britain that disgraced and finally put an end to one of the
most brutal military regimes in the annals of Latin America.

In 1970, the Argentine armed forces were gradually resigning
themselves to relinquishing control of the national government that
they had seized four years earlier. Four guerrilla movements, three of
them Peronist in orientation, had begun to build up their battle chests
with the ransoms from repeated kidnappings (provoking ominously
little public outcry) when another uprising in Córdoba, an aftershock
of the 1969 Cordobazo, confirmed the generals' decision to withdraw
in 1971. Gen. Alejandro Agustín Lanusse, who had determined the
prudence of that course earlier than most of his colleagues, was put in
charge of organizing the elections. Lanusse faced a complicated task
because, although the military still refused to allow the return of Juan
Perón from his long exile in Madrid, most other important political
actors in the country were finally convinced that no lasting settlement
could be made without the personal participation of Perón and that the
armed forces themselves now presented the gravest danger to the
country's traditional political institutions.

public acceptance of violent leftist tactics Meanwhile in Spain, Perón warmly embraced the Peronist guerrilla organizations and exhibited an ideological transformation that
brought him into convergence with the radicalized Peronist Youth, a
course that the aging leader described as a mere generational passing of
the baton. The violent tactics recently adopted by the clandestine
Peronist organizations still met, at this time, with a public indulgence
that explains the willingness of other political forces to join the inter-
generational Peronist alliance. By November 1972, Lanusse's efforts to
prevent the return of Perón had been thwarted, and the illustrious
exile arrived to preside with triumphant congeniality over a series of
crowded banquets where even the most committed erstwhile anti-

Peronists gathered to lift a glass. Perón maintained his long-standing truce with the Radical party while organizing a "Justicialista" coalition that encompassed a wide array of smaller political groups. Perón also personally selected candidates for the upcoming March 1973 elections, including his nomination for president of Héctor J. Cámpora, a veteran Peronist legislator of legendary docility. The roster of Peronist candidates revealed the lingering impact of the labor unions' earlier attempt to create a Peronism without Perón. Carefully limiting labor influence in his nominations, Perón distributed candidacies generously to the far left. The Peronist Youth (the political wing of the Montonero movement) alone received as many legislative slots as the Peronist labor unions, and figures of the left were named to the ticket for a number of important provincial governorships, including that of Buenos Aires.

Perón returned to Madrid confident of victory, and he was not disappointed. In spite of a last-ditch revision of electoral laws by the leaders of the armed forces, Cámpora came so close to winning an absolute majority of the votes that the other parties renounced the option of a runoff election, and the Justicialista candidates achieved comfortable majorities in both houses of congress. The strength of the Peronist showing was not, in fact, much different from what it had been in the country's last election in 1965. What had changed was the attitude of the rest of the political powers of the country toward Peronism. Their new acceptance assured Perón's Justicialista coalition of enough allies to win the 1973 election, and, more importantly, given the Peronists' frustrated electoral victories of the past, it guaranteed their acquiescence in the results.

The triumphant Peronists still faced immense difficulties. The conflicts within the movement between the labor unions and the radical youth groups were not likely to be papered over easily, and Perón created a third competing faction around his former private secretary, José López Rega, an ex-policeman who had combined the functions of chamberlain and court astrologer to the exiled caudillo, henceforth minister of social welfare in Cámpora's cabinet. The Peronist Youth made itself felt publicly through incessant street demonstrations and privately through the influence it enjoyed in the administration of President Cámpora as well as a number of provincial governments, and that high-level influence did more than earlier strings of kidnappings to awaken a general mistrust of and resistance to the Peronist far left.

Seemingly oblivious to the growing climate of apprehension, the Peronist left prepared to affirm its new predominance within the movement by organizing a huge demonstration to welcome Perón on the occasion of his definitive return to Argentina. They intended to stand around him at the podium as he spoke to millions of Argentines upon his arrival at the airport, thus consecrating themselves as his new apostles. They did expect some resistance from other Peronist factions, but the events of 20 June 1973 took them quite by surprise. As it turned out, the largest multitude ever assembled on Argentine soil gathered at the airport to witness a pitched gun battle between the Peronist left and its rivals, who counted among them right-wing Peronist veterans of the pre-1955 security forces, forces associated with the Peronist labor unions, and bands of gunmen improvised by López Rega at the ministry of social welfare. The left was routed and never even saw Perón, whose plane was warned away from the airport and landed elsewhere.

Perón now made a tactical change of course, praising the boldness of the victors and denouncing the vanquished as an alien force that had infiltrated the movement and perverted its legitimate aspirations. So devoted were his youthful followers on the left that they preferred, for a time, to interpret the condemnations of their venerated leader as evidence of the sinister influence of López Rega, but Perón's statements signaled the political isolation of the insurrectionary Peronist left, and a purge of the Justicialista coalition's left-wing elements now began. Meanwhile, Cámpora stepped down to allow Perón to become president. Despite a certain lack of public enthusiasm for the caudillo's choice of his own wife as running mate, the Perón-Perón ticket swept the election of October 1973 with a two-thirds majority. Perón's new presidency marked another step in the escalation of political violence in Argentina, as the terrorism of the left was joined by the terrorism of the right, organized, in the view of many, by López Rega. By May 1974, the Peronist left had realized the gulf that divided it from the president, and during the May Day celebration of 1974 the breach became open, as the Peronist Youth and the sympathizers of their associated clandestine branches left the gathering amid noisy insults. The insurrectionary left now posed less a challenge to Perón than did organized labor.

Soon after taking office in 1973, the Peronist government had begun a massive redistribution of income and adopted rigid wage and price controls along with the slogan, "Zero Inflation." This redistribution had immediately stimulated consumer demand, but the resulting economic expansion was short-lived, and inflation surged anew. As the government doubled the amount of currency in circulation through unrestrained emissions, it resorted to frequent readjustments of its official wages and prices, without managing to prevent the deterioration of living standards. Only a few weeks after his rupture with the Peronist left, a saddened Perón found himself pleading with an angry crowd of workers to relax their impatient demands. He explained that otherwise he would resign his office and give up the attempt to restore a measure of concord to the divided country. Although he did not know it, the speech was his melancholy farewell to the workers who had followed him faithfully for so long. Perón's death in July 1974 temporarily created the mood of reconciliation that his last administration had been unable to foster, as all political forces in the country rallied expectantly around the vice president, María Estela (usually called Isabel) Martínez de Perón.

As chief executive, Isabel Perón abandoned any effort at concord and imposed the solutions of the Peronist right. Right-wing terrorists launched a virtual war of extermination against the left, and the insurrectionary movements responded in kind. Going beyond kidnappings for ransom, they began to murder industrialists who resisted labor demands. Gradually, the disparate elements of the left joined forces against their common enemies. Various clandestine groups of the Peronist left united with the Montoneros and, adopting a tactic of the (Trotskyite) Revolutionary Army of the People, began indiscriminate attacks against military officers. Their objective was to provoke a coup against Isabel Perón by showing her incapable of maintaining order, and they were aided by a worsening economic situation. When the government adopted an anti-inflation plan that called for a recession and a lowering of real wages, the labor unions fought it desperately and succeeded in paralyzing the stabilization program. By early 1976, inflation neared 1,000 percent. The leaders of the military, who had been waiting until conditions worsened enough to subdue any resistance to a coup, decided that the moment had arrived.

In March 1976, a junta composed of the heads of the three armed forces deposed the president and began an open-ended project of "National Reorganization," the first stage of which was to annihilate the insurrectionary groups. Their aims went beyond the destruction of the Montoneros, which was already well under way, having begun in the months before the coup. Rather, the Argentine military hoped to mete out exemplary punishments, to devastate the country's young rebels so thoroughly as to provide an unforgettable object lesson to their sympathizers.

The largely decentralized "Dirty War" provided ample opportunities for a certain process of political feudalization notable in the Argentine military government of 1976–83. This time, more clearly than in the coup of 1966, the military had taken power as an institution, and the divisions among the three arms caused more than a little friction. The junta administered the country with the help of a nine-member advisory legislative commission equally representing the three services, and this unwieldy group was supposed to reach unanimous decisions. Similar arrangements characterized the middle levels of the military government as well. In practice, factional fault lines within the regime led to severe internal contradictions, prevented any effective check on the thousands of tortures and disappearances, and encouraged an abdication of responsibility for abuses of all kinds, including the satisfaction of personal greed. A notable example was the refusal of various branches of the armed forces to collaborate with the efforts of the government's own minister of the economy, José Alfredo Martínez de Hoz, in his efforts to privatize state-owned enterprises under military control.

Overall, the Argentine dictatorship's efforts to restore health to the economy under Gen. Jorge Rafael Videla, the first president designated by the junta, were less successful than its repression of the left. Once the idea of privatizing the state-owned enterprises had been frustrated, the principal remaining instrument of economic reform was monetary manipulation. During two years of unmitigated government-imposed austerity, the steady advance of export agriculture succeeded in redressing Argentina's trade deficit and initiated an interlude of modest prosperity. Martínez de Hoz hoped that a strong peso would accomplish his goal of industrial reform indirectly, making imports more accessible and creating ruinous competition for the country's older, less efficient industries, while the more recently established capital-intensive industries were protected by high import tariffs. The strong peso soon undercut the agricultural export expansion that had helped buttress it, however, and the flow of Argentina's international trade then turned chronically negative. Only the constant influx of foreign credit, easily available through the late 1970s, maintained a satisfactory balance of payments. The commercial and financial sectors of the Argentine economy expanded frenetically in these years, absorbing some of the workers and managers who left industrial activities, while a substantial emigration of professionals and skilled workers held down unemployment.

In 1978, the economic picture was moderately bright, and the bloodiest years of terrorism and repression had passed. On the last day of the World Cup soccer championship held that year in Argentina and won by the Argentine team, Videla received a cordial welcome from the crowd. It was the apogee of the military regime. Divisions at the highest levels of the government continued, however, and Videla was not easily able to secure his chosen successor as president, Gen. Roberto Viola. In addition, the military leadership now had to confront the consequences of the atrocities that had marked their consolidation in power. In 1979 a mission from the Organization of American States prepared a devastating report on the human rights situation in Argentina. By 1981, the drying up of international credit markets had set off an extremely serious banking crisis in the country and provoked changes in the regime. President Viola, a proponent of cautious political opening, was replaced by a hard-liner, Gen. Leopoldo Galtieri. Galtieri's rise had been promoted by the Argentine navy in return for his promise to use force to reclaim the Malvinas Islands, occupied by Great Britain since 1833.

The Argentine military government hoped to use the Malvinas War of 1982 to alleviate its internal difficulties. The sudden economic downturn had awakened new discontent that the regime, now subject to international scrutiny, dared not douse with more tortures and disappearances. A military victory, though, promised to drown all internal opposition in a wave of nationalist fervor. Galtieri's calculations concerning the domestic political impact of a war with Great Britain were correct, and the initial Argentine capture of the Malvinas Islands met with an explosion of popular enthusiasm even more intense than anticipated, but the military government had sorely miscalculated international reactions. Instead of accepting the trivial loss of its remote island possessions as a fait accompli, London prepared for war, and the United States gave no sign of favoring Argentina as the generals (faithful supporters of Ronald Reagan's revival of cold war priorities in the hemisphere) had imagined would be the case. As the British fleet made the long voyage to the South Atlantic, Argentine negotiators remained intransigent, and the government searched frantically—but unsuccessfully—for international support. The battle, once joined, ended in a matter of days. The Argentine military was disgraced (only the air force showing itself at all efficacious in the fighting), and the surrender of the country's expeditionary force in the Malvinas quickly brought down General Galtieri.

The military catastrophe deprived the regime of any ability to negotiate favorable terms for its electoral departure. Argentines finally began to hear the clamor of the women who had gathered for years in the main square of Buenos Aires to protest the official murders of the government's Dirty War, and the "Mothers and Grandmothers of the Plaza de Mayo" found themselves surrounded, rather suddenly, by the solicitous attention of their compatriots. The shocking awareness of what had occurred, now almost universal, evolved quickly into an equally widespread conviction that Argentina needed a new beginning, a break with the period stretching back to the first military takeover in 1930. The politician who best expressed the country's mood was Raúl Alfonsín, who stepped forward as presidential candidate for the Radical party so closely linked to the country's pre-1930 political traditions. Alfonsín was opposed by the military, the labor unions, and the Peronists, whom he accused of having dominated Argentina, together or in discord, during most of recent memory. For once, the Peronists were unable to work their electoral magic, and Alfonsín was elected by a comfortable margin.

Becoming president in 1983, Alfonsín tried to make Argentina democratic and pluralist without making structural changes in the social and institutional forces that had grown up over the last half century, but those forces (ranging from the labor unions to the military) stubbornly resisted being forced into the new mold. The president seems to have hoped that the military would purge itself of the worst human rights offenders, but the presidential commission charged with investigating the thousands of disappearances encountered stiff opposition, as did the prosecutors of the military leaders who held ultimate responsibility. Meanwhile, Alfonsín's administration became entangled in a chronic dispute with organized labor. His efforts to appease the labor unions by raising and maintaining wage levels (in the midst of a debt crisis bequeathed to him by the military government) led to inflation levels that, by mid-1985, were approaching those of Isabel Perón's last weeks as president. Alfonsín's package of anti-inflationary measures, the Austral Plan, received widespread support, but, without the reform of the state-owned enterprises whose deficits had continued to grow during the military government, long-term success remained elusive.

In the late 1980s, the lack of a decisive new socioeconomic course for Argentina and a new surge of inflation brought the Peronists to power once more. Although the Radicals had not succeeded in restructuring the country's political forces and sporadic, localized military mutinies continued to create occasional alarm, the survival of democracy did not appear immediately threatened. Furthermore, the evolution of Argentine society gradually sapped the power of the colliding forces of the preceding period—such as the labor unions, which, by refusing to allow the more efficient reorganization of state-owned enterprises, assured their own gradual decline along with these strongholds of their influence.

Brazil's military government of the same period left a less over-

whelmingly negative legacy. During the late 1960s and 1970s, the Bra- *Brazil*
zilian economy grew at astounding speed, entering the ranks of the
world's largest national economies by the 1980s. Nevertheless, in the
aftermath of dictatorship, Brazil struggled with the most severe economic problems in all of Latin America, and, for the first time in
recent memory, Brazilians no longer looked to the future with optimism. To see how that situation was created, we must look back to
1969, when hard-liner Emílio Garrastazu Médici, who had made his
career in military intelligence, became president in response to an
awakening of civilian opposition to the government.

The presidency of Médici indicated the temporary failure of the
regime to fulfill the vision of the leader of the 1964 coup, Humberto
Castelo Branco, who had originally aspired to create a controlled representative system in alliance with civilian conservatives. The right's
failure to win elections under conditions carefully prepared by the
military government had convinced the hard-liners to dissolve the
congress in the late 1960s. However, even hard-liners like Médici did
not talk of the permanent installation of a military dictatorship, and
the congress was reconvened in 1970 when the most extreme faction
within the military was at the height of its influence. Perhaps a thirst
for international respectability, or the desire to distance themselves
from what they viewed as a Spanish American tradition of dictatorship, helped persuade the Brazilian generals to eschew the permanent
institutionalization of their power, but there were also practical limitations. The hard-liners were a relatively young group who were not,
for the most part, at the top of the military hierarchy. Any attempt to
remake the system in their image was bound to provoke a challenge
from above. Médici therefore declared his intentions to restore Brazil
to civilian rule, while at the same time accelerating the country's
transformation into a police state. A general climate of repression
silenced the opposition and assured the regime of electoral victories
(outside the major urban centers, at least) in the congressional elections of 1972.

The onset of impressive economic growth in 1969 also did much to
help the military regime through its political difficulties. The prosperity of the "Brazilian Miracle" was quite intentionally uneven, and
the biggest losers were those at the broad bottom of the social pyramid
who had scarcely begun to influence the political process before the
military takeover. For many of those who had formerly supported alternatives of the left, the economic prosperity provided benefits sufficient, if not to win their allegiance, at least to inspire their patience.
Workers in the new capital-intensive industries favored by the military

government saw their real wages increase, while Brazil's progressive middle class discovered the tantalizing delights of consumer culture, and even the intelligentsia could divert its attention from the obscurantism of the military regime to the proliferation of professional opportunities at previously unthinkable levels of remuneration.

The economic expansion of the period also satisfied the requirements of Brazilian industrialists vis-à-vis the multinational corporations that grew more rapidly than the economy as a whole. The military government took a large part in the management of an economy that had become the eighth largest in the capitalist world by the end of the 1970s, and the leaders of purely domestic industrial enterprises did not fail to make themselves felt in the government. Few intra-elite tensions could not be alleviated by a steady annual economic growth rate of nearly 10 percent. In fact, one of the most influential proponents of dependency theory, Fernando Henrique Cardoso, introduced the term "associated development" to emphasize the part played by Brazilian entrepreneurs in reasonably harmonious conjunction with state and multinational enterprises.

Beyond the effects of military repression and relative economic abundance, there were larger structural causes for the political calm that settled over Brazil as the country's social forces flowed into major transformative changes in the 1970s. Brazilian industries now began to produce some of their own machinery and capital goods, while those manufacturing consumer goods made a much larger variety of them, reaching beyond the limited goal of industrial self-sufficiency to export ever larger amounts of their production, from shoes to high-tech armaments. In central Brazil, and most especially in São Paulo, a new generation of industrial workers became thoroughly acclimated to urban life, and large-scale commercial farmers (organized in powerful cooperatives) transformed the rural south with new crops like soy beans, of which Brazil became the world's largest exporter. Vertiginous population growth was absorbed not only by continued rural to urban migration, but also by the advancing frontiers that had always characterized Brazilian agrarian history. The migration of poor pioneers to the frontier relieved the dangerous compression of some areas of notoriously high social tensions, like the northeast, while destroying Indian populations to clear the way for the wealthy interests who reaped the real profits of agricultural expansion.

Brazil's economic dynamism had its weaknesses, of course. Many of these transformations actually increased social inequalities, creating, in urban areas, contrasts of wealth and poverty that were difficult to ignore. Moreover, the Brazilian economy remained extremely vulnerable to the fluctuations of global markets. Over half of the country's exports now consisted in manufactured products, and even its agricultural exports were no longer dominated so overwhelmingly by the coffee crop, but, on the other side of the ledger, imports of heavy machinery and capital goods also increased apace. As a result, Brazil's balance of payments remained so delicate that a drop in the international price of coffee could still wreak havoc. A massive growth in the number of motor vehicles and miles of highway made oil the imported commodity most dangerous to the balance of payments. In the mid-1970s, the sudden jump in the price of oil was temporarily offset by feverish borrowing at low interest as petrodollars flooded the international credit market. The external debt rose alarmingly, but as long as the economy maintained a respectable growth rate (about 7 percent in 1974–78) and inflation remained manageable, the Brazilian military regime could make favorable comparisons with other major Latin American countries that also borrowed heavily without equivalent expansion of industrial plant and infrastructure.

Brazil's military government began to encounter more political opposition as a result of its own moves toward political opening. The hard-liners had lost influence when Gen. Ernesto Geisel became president in 1974, though the military intelligence establishment remained under their control. Geisel's initiatives were frustrated not so much by the hard-liners as by a new failure of the regime's civilian allies to subdue the opposition in a more open political environment. In the legislative elections of 1974, the opposition came close to winning a majority in the Chamber of Deputies. The furious hard-liners then used the intelligence agencies to crack down on opposition leaders, such as Waldimir Herzog, a well-known São Paulo journalist who died under torture. The Herzog case inspired further defiance by Cardinal Evaristo Arns, archbishop of São Paulo, formerly less inclined to militant attitudes.

The rise of Arns as a figure of resistance to the regime constituted a clear sign of the changing nature of the opposition. Certain elements of the Catholic church had always defied the military repression, but with the leadership of Arns, ecclesiastical resistance became respectable. Earlier, the tone had been set by the social radicalism of liberation theology and Dom Helder Câmara, bishop of Pernambuco. In the latter part of the 1970s, however, Catholic opposition to the military regime evolved, in a movement parallel to Latin American public opinion generally, away from the revolutionary hopes of the 1960s and toward a renewed appreciation of the once-despised "bourgeois" civil liberties and rights that, as the official murder of Herzog so vividly illustrated, could be matters of life and death. When opposition to the military government became disassociated with revolutionary socialism, it rapidly spread to some of the most traditionally conservative sectors of Brazilian society—the law schools and lawyers' professional organizations, for instance.

As economic conditions grew more difficult later in the decade, Brazilian industrialists and entrepreneurs had their own reasons to look less sympathetically on the military regime. The external debt loomed ever larger, and the government's hugely expensive and not terribly promising Amazonian development projects (like its gargantuan hydroelectric dams) began to suggest the drawbacks of an economically activist and excessively autonomous state. Even though supportive of the government's attempts to explore alternative energy sources and thus make Brazil less dependent on imported oil, Brazilian businesspeople began to chafe at authoritarian limitations on their own influence over economic policy. Now that a decade and a half of rapid expansion had strengthened their hand and the labor unions no longer seemed so threatening, Brazilian entrepreneurs pondered the advantages that might accrue in their relationships with the multinational corporations and the state in a less restrictive political order.

A revival of opposition in the press reflected the new mood of the Brazilian elite and middle classes. The fading memory of class tensions before 1964 permitted a revival of publicity concerning social causes that the military government would previously have refused to countenance. The long suppression of organized labor meant that the specific demands of workers no longer automatically predominated among these causes. Instead, workplace-centered issues now competed for public attention with a variety of others—like environmentalism and neighborhood movements to address the problems created by rapid urbanization—that were less class-specific. Protests at the return of rampant inflation had a particularly broad appeal. Even the military regime endorsed the new acceptability of social causes when, ostensibly bowing to pressures from the Brazilian women's movement, it legalized divorce as a way of punishing the Catholic hierarchy for political disloyalty. Organized labor, for its part, returned to the national news in 1978 with the spectacular São Paulo metal workers' strike that turned their leader, Luís Inácio "Lula" da Silva, into an international celebrity with strong support in the mainstream opposition.

President Geisel struggled to contain the awakening of Brazilian civil society within the institutional framework that had been created by the military regime, successively modifying that framework to compensate for the government's loss of support. The prospect of opposition governments in several key states, for example, inspired the regime to amend the constitution so that state governors would no longer be popularly elected. Geisel's undemocratic manipulation of representative institutions enabled him to resist the hard-liners, who would rather have done away with them altogether. In 1979, he was able to turn the presidency over to his chosen successor, Gen. Euclides Figueiredo.

Brazil's democratic opening received little support from the Carter administration in the United States largely because of the regime's gestures at an independent foreign policy. After the collapse of the Portuguese empire in Africa, Brazil had established cordial relations with Marxist governments that arose in several of the new states, and the military government also persisted in a nuclear policy that did not follow the nonproliferation guidelines set by the United States. Even fervent Brazilian opponents of the military tended to approve of this independent foreign policy, impeding any wholehearted support for the Carter administration's policies. The Brazilian opposition was, in fact, so reluctant to align itself with the United States that it even refrained from echoing Carter's campaign for human rights despite its obvious applicability to their situation in Brazil.

During Figueiredo's term, the political opening begun by Geisel took on new momentum even without U.S. backing. The military hard-liners made their last stand with an anonymous terror campaign conducted by the intelligence services in 1980 and 1981, and afterward the more conciliatory tendency associated earlier with Castelo Branco emerged definitively triumphant. Figueiredo filled his cabinet with proponents of redemocratization and gave special prominence to Gen. Golbery do Couto e Silva, the political theorist who had helped institutionalize the regime in the 1960s and who now played an active role in its final stages. Couto e Silva modified the government's electoral guidelines to allow multiple opposition parties, an innovation that afforded the opposition greater liberty and simultaneously sapped its strength as it fanned out in several directions. Most political opponents of the government remained in the official Brazilian Democratic movement, but others joined the Workers' party (centering on the country's new labor movement) or the Democratic Labor party (a remnant of pre-1964 populism). The fragmentation of the opposition took some of the pressure off the military's supporters, who had to deal with economic difficulties as well as political ones.

The rise of international interest rates in 1979 had finally put an end to Brazil's long period of economic expansion. With the onset of recession, labor conflicts became more frequent, and inflation rose as well. The situation called for unpalatable medicine that was likely to make matters worse in the short term. With the approach of elections in 1982, however, the government wished to do anything but increase the ill humor of the electorate, and its economists abandoned all prudence in their attempts to engineer momentary improvements, contracting new loans and renegotiating the old ones at higher interest rates that vastly accelerated the accumulation of Brazil's external debt. The effect of these palliatives was to return the economy to slow growth just in time for the decisive congressional election.

The 1982 congressional elections were especially important because they coincided with the city and state elections that the government had postponed during the recession. Moreover, in order to get the opposition to accept the postponement, the government had restored the direct popular vote for mayors and governors. The several opposition parties together obtained a clear electoral majority, but divisions among them allowed the government to retain control of the legislature. On the other hand, opposition candidates won almost all the major gubernatorial and mayoral contests. The fact that the government called these results "favorable" indicates how modest its ambitions had become. Above all, the existing armed forces wanted to retain control of the congress and thereby determine how Figueiredo's successor would be chosen. Having achieved this, the government gave up its desperate efforts to avoid a deeper recession, finding it impossible to secure further loans in a credit market on the verge of panic. A default on payment of Brazil's international debts suddenly appeared imminent, and the economic debacle speeded the process of redemocratization. Dissatisfaction with the government naturally increased, but as long as the disheartened military proceeded steadily with its withdrawal from the political scene, the opposition declined to raise economic issues that might disrupt the process.

Opponents of the regime put their energies instead into a campaign to have the next president chosen in direct elections rather than by a more easily manipulated electoral college. The call for direct elections took on a festive atmosphere as much of the Brazilian political elite climbed onto the band wagon—where prelates, lawyers, and industrialists were joined by sports heroes and television actors. Television and the popular idols it created, a ubiquitous part of Brazilian life since 1964 (partly for economic reasons and partly because of the military's efforts at general depoliticization), now became a vehicle of mass mobilization. The campaign fell just short of winning the over two-thirds congressional majority necessary to institute the direct election of the president, but the steady defection of former government supporters in congress augured ill for the official candidate, even in indirect elections. The hopes of the military regime were further dashed when its preferred candidate proved so unpopular within the official party that an appreciable number of government legislators bolted to the opposition. In January 1985, the opposition ticket triumphed by an overwhelming majority in the electoral college, bringing the end of two decades of military rule.

President-elect Tancredo Neves, an aging politician from Minas Gerais, died before he was able to assume power. The man who took office in his place was José Sarney, who had led the mass defection from the military regime's official party to the opposition only a year before. Sarney's congressional alliance with the opposition had made victory possible, but his longtime association with the military regime did little for his popularity as president, especially given Brazil's continuing economic difficulties. Inflation continued to worsen and the external debt was held at bay only through repeated renegotiations that made it ever larger. In addition, the atmosphere of political restraint that reigned during the delicate process of political opening vanished once democracy had been reinstated, allowing a wide range of economic demands and conflicts to surface. The new government's agrarian reform project, for example, soon bogged down when landowners resisted it furiously, using an effective combination of local violence and national political maneuverings.

At the same time, the appeal of some of the issues and personalities associated with the opposition to the military government now diminished. When Fernando Henrique Cardoso, whose brilliant work as a sociologist had long inspired Brazilian intellectuals of the left, entered the mayor's race in the city of São Paulo, he was defeated by Jânio Quadros, the erratic ex-president of the early 1960s, whose campaign combined crude anticommunism with law-and-order themes appealing to a middle class aghast at the soaring levels of street crime. Contrary to what might have been expected, the former foes of the dictatorship made little attempt to turn the human rights violations perpetrated during the preceding two decades into a major political issue, partly out of reluctance to jeopardize redemocratization, partly because Brazilians seemed eager to leave the past behind. In sum, despite a wide range of tensions and conflicts evident in postauthoritarian Brazil, the country showed little inclination to return to the volatile political polarization so marked in the years before 1964.

Brazil's economic picture remained dark in the late 1980s. While the external debt had been repeatedly renegotiated to avoid default, it continued to drain dynamism from the economy, and inflation showed no signs of abating. The indexation system introduced by the military government as a way of living with inflation had clearly, by this time, begun to perpetuate and even accelerate it. In 1986, only months after the implementation of Argentina's Austral Plan, President Sarney introduced an analogous Cruzado Plan in Brazil. The Cruzado Plan was meant to stabilize the country's monetary situation by attacking both the root problem (the government's use of currency emissions to finance public spending) and the multiplier effect of indexation. Because the official value of the new currency was held artificially stable while its internal exchange value declined, however, Brazil's international balance of trade suffered. In 1987, amid a deep recession, Brazil defaulted on its external debt. The optimism that had been for so long a constitutive element of Brazilian national life, resistant to the sharpest political conflicts and the most disruptive cycles of economic boom and bust, seemed sadly undermined with the approach of the end of the twentieth century.

México

Mexicans, whose national mood often revealed a fatalistic melancholy more characteristic of Spanish America than Brazil, also had quite specific reasons for discontent in the 1970s and 1980s. As Brazil had transformed itself into one of the world's largest economies during these years, Mexico had achieved less despite enjoying the advantage of large oil reserves. Furthermore, the increasing fragility of sociopolitical order was much on the minds of the Mexican elite. The heirs of the Mexican Revolution had not yet found new formulas to replace those that, while functioning fairly well for half a century, gave clear signs of exhaustion by 1968.

Luis Echeverría, Mexico's new president in 1970, tried to coopt the critical spirit of 1968 by becoming himself the most prominent critic of the institutions he administered, but he could get only limited political mileage out of windy fulminations against "dark forces." A more substantial remedy for the discontents evinced by Mexican professionals and intellectuals was government investment in costly scientific institutions and universities that offered them expanded professional opportunities, an approach that recalls developments then occurring in Brazil, despite the very different ideological color of the two regimes. In an attempt to redefine the government's relationship to the masses, Echeverría embraced the Cardenista heritage of the 1930s, only to find that it did not easily apply to a Mexico that needed outside investment to continue its process of industrialization and foreign loans to attenuate grave social problems. Mexico's unprecedented need for international borrowing seemed particularly ominous but could not be avoided now that the country imported more and more of its staple food, which the government subsidized to compensate for the steady deterioration of real wages. Meanwhile, Echeverría's rhetorical radicalism alienated both international investors and Mexico's own propertied classes, while his showy displays of independence from the United States in foreign policy matters further undercut the kind of outside support he very much needed. When it came to actions requiring major resources, therefore, Echeverría could do little more than make the kind of minor adjustments that kept crisis at bay.

In the early 1970s, the imbalances in Mexico's external sector eroded the strength of its currency and threatened to destroy the stable exchange rate with the dollar that had endured since the postwar period and provided an essential key to economic stability in a country whose economy was so closely linked to that of its gigantic neighbor. Only ever more international borrowing kept the peso afloat, but it also speeded inflation, further undermining the fixed exchange rate in the long run. Finally, official devaluation of the peso became unavoidable. A 60 percent devaluation set off such capital flight that another of 40 percent was soon required.

In the countryside, there were now more landless people than when Lázaro Cárdenas had begun his land reforms. A rural guerrilla force appeared in the state of Guerrero, and though the Mexican army destroyed it with brutal efficiency, the episode gave the elite new cause to worry about the destabilizing implications of the socioeconomic crisis. Echeverría's response was to identify himself publicly with the cause of the dispossessed. In the arid northern part of the country, where agro-industry had created rich oases since World War II, the landless people invaded irrigated properties with presidential approval. The largely rhetorical resurrection of Cardenista agrarianism had little impact on the plight of Mexico's rural population as a whole but severely exacerbated the political tensions, and for the first time in many years rumors of a military coup circulated in the capital city. The durability of Mexico's one-party government belied the rumors, however.

In 1976, Echeverría was replaced by his official successor, José López Portillo, following elections that revealed Mexican enthusiasm for the "institutional revolution" to have reached a new low. Following the precedent set by Echeverría himself six years earlier, López Portillo excoriated his predecessor (in whose cabinet he had served) as the corrupt and demagogic principal cause of the country's undeniable crisis. The new president repudiated the agrarian radicalism endorsed by the previous administration and sought a reconciliation with the

private sector, particularly the foreign sources of credit and investment. In light of the Mexican state's current penury, the resources
necessary to overcome the crisis would have to come from outside the
country, and López Portillo solemnly promised that his government
would serve the interests of international investors in Mexico and
allow them greater freedom of action than in the past. The institutional revolution had begun the difficult transition from populist
largess to conservative discipline and austerity, a shift usually accompanied in other Latin American countries by a dramatic change of
political regime.

At this point, a very pleasant surprise saved the Mexican political
elite from a humbling total subjection to bankers and investors. Explorations had shown that Mexico possessed larger reserves of oil than
previously believed, and the enormous increase in its international
price had made those reserves quite profitable to exploit. At least for a
while, petroleum redressed Mexico's balance of trade and provided it
with abundant credit.

López Portillo's government announced that it would use the oil
bonanza to address the underlying structural problems of the Mexican
economy, especially the low productivity of its agricultural sector. It
reformed the rules governing the ejido, allowing ejidatarios to form
partnerships with private investors for the purpose of modernizing the
technology of production. The reform constituted a major ideological
departure, but its effects were slight because the Mexican government
continued to hold down the prices of the crops as a way of subsidizing
the living standards of the urban poor, and few investors showed
interest in an activity whose profits were so systematically limited.
Easy access to international credit enabled the importation of sufficient food and thus made this thorny question easy to postpone.
Continued migration to the cities, also encouraged by the booming
economy of the late 1970s, helped alleviate social pressures in the
countryside while creating difficulties of another kind. It was in this
period that the Mexican capital became the largest city in the world,
with all the problems attendant upon that distinction.

In this and other ways, Mexico's oil wealth shored up the status
quo rather than becoming the means of substantial change promised
by the regime. The political and economic elites continued to grow
together, as had been the case during earlier periods of expansion. The
state's petroleum monopoly, PEMEX, used its lucrative contracts to
favor labor leaders and chosen businesses, and the bounty to be distributed was great enough to defuse any resentment in the private
sector. In the political sphere, oil prosperity allowed the government

to proceed without haste in its efforts to reestablish the unshakable legitimacy of years past. López Portillo's approach was to open a larger space for opposition participation in the country's political life in the safest and most controlled way, not by honoring the results of free elections but by allotting a fixed number of seats in congress to any party that won a minimum level of electoral support. While the government clearly expected a challenge from the left, the most vigorous response came instead from the right.

The National Action party (PAN), linked to the church and conservative business groups, showed increasing strength as the economic euphoria of the 1970s disappeared in the 1980s. A drop in the earnings of Mexican oil exports combined with a rise in interest rates, surging inflation, the accumulated debt, a worsening balance of trade, successive devaluations of the peso, and massive capital flight spelled disaster for the economy and a renewal of the political ferment that the Institutional Revolutionary party (PRI) had managed to contain for almost a decade. Particularly in the northern part of the country, where economic growth had always been less dependent on state patronage and the local elite were therefore less beholden to the government, the PAN made gains that must be considered impressive for an opposition party in twentieth-century Mexico. In the presidential election of 1982, the government admitted that the PAN had won at least 14 percent of the vote nationwide (compared to 6 percent for a coalition including most of the parties of the left), and it appeared stronger yet in Mexico City, where the balloting was freer than elsewhere. The PRI's candidate achieved a majority that, even though it would be considered huge outside of Mexico, revealed some leakage in the official party's formerly airtight lock on power.

The new president, Miguel de la Madrid, a graduate of the Harvard University Business School, would need all his technical know-how to deal with Mexico's full-scale economic emergency in the mid-1980s. The country's national debt had been channeled through private banks that could not meet their obligations to foreign creditors after the collapse of the exchange rate. By nationalizing the insolvent banks, López Portillo had assumed their debts while appearing to revive the traditional economic nationalism of the PRI, a gesture that had won him some political credit despite the hard times. Hoping to gain enough breathing space in which to reactivate the economy, de la Madrid declined to make the external debt a symbol of conflict between the developed and the developing world (as other Latin American governments, including his predecessor's, had done) and instead approached Mexico's creditors with offers of cooperation and conciliation. He found them unwilling to provide any more leeway than strictly necessary to prevent default.

Undaunted, de la Madrid remained faithful to the program of austerities and fiscal discipline that he had charted upon assuming the presidency, progressively reducing government subsidies on basic commodities and watching as real wages plummeted and unemployment steadily worsened. The persistent inflation and successive devaluations of the peso also contributed to make this period the most difficult faced by the Mexican people during the last sixty years. After a grim half decade, the situation began to improve in 1987, mostly thanks to the rapid expansion of the *maquiladora* industries established along the northern border by multinational corporations. Attracted by Mexico's low wage levels, the maquiladoras used imported materials to create finished products for sale in the U.S. market. Hardly an unalloyed good, they constituted the most hopeful sign of the pervasive transition to a Mexican economy more open to free-market forces.

Within this painful panorama, Mexico's political institutions once more revealed their impressive resiliency. The new administration heaped blame on the preceding one without turning the universal ignominy of the departed president into a general purge of the country's political and economic elites and promised that, this time, it would really reform the political system. The lethargic official reaction to the earthquake that devastated Mexico City in 1985 sent public cynicism to new heights, and the United States, irritated at the Mexican government's lack of cooperation in Central America, gave increasingly open support to the PAN opposition, but neither circumstance seemed to portend an immediate political crisis. More worrisome, perhaps, was a certain resemblance to the last years of the Porfirian dictatorship, when, as in the 1980s, the power of the central government eroded along the northern border. In addition, many of those who now held power in Mexico City were technocrats, reminiscent of the Porfirian "científicos," a term that aptly describes both de la Madrid and his successor, Carlos Salinas de Gortari, whose paths to the presidency were more technical than strictly political. A lapse into technocracy can be dangerous for a regime whose strength has always rested on political skills, and that danger was frankly discussed by a dissident faction of the PRI at the time of Salinas de Gortari's selection as heir apparent. The candidacy of Cuauhtémoc Cárdenas, son of Mexico's most popular twentieth-century president, illustrated the preference of this dissident group within the PRI.

The PRI managed to impose its official candidate in the presidential elections of 1988, and though the Cárdenas challenge suggested future obstacles for the stability of one-party rule in Mexico, few observers were prepared to write the obituary of a political system that had survived extreme trials rather handily since 1968. That the durability of the PRI had little to do with the purity of its devotion to revolutionary objectives became patent once again in the 1980s, when the political elite itself led the capital flight that had such negative consequences for the majority of the Mexican people. More likely, the heirs of the Mexican Revolution maintained their hold on the country during most of the twentieth century because of the political sensitivity rightly pointed out by the dissidents of 1988.

Cuba's socialist regime also showed itself capable of enduring significant disappointments and difficulties after 1970, the period following the failed ten-million-ton sugar harvest. During the 1970s, the Cuban government at last gave up the dream of creating an alternative socialist model and institutionalized itself politically and economically along lines pioneered in the Soviet Union, the ally that had provided the resources to insure the survival of the Cuban Revolution. The constitution finally promulgated in 1975 placed all aspects of Cuban life under the guidance of the Communist party, while leaving a space for the economic incentives that the Cuban revolutionaries had earlier rejected.

There were several significant changes of direction in the 1970s. Leaving behind the disruptive experimentation of the 1960s, the Cuban economy began to grow again as mechanization and technological improvements at last produced a sustained rise in the economic productivity of both labor and land. The island's sugar production amply exceeded prerevolutionary levels, but that very success accented Cuba's dependence on a commodity whose future market possibilities seemed ever darker. In diplomatic terms, the Cuban leadership adopted a much more circumspect approach. While receiving Salvador Allende's election in Chile with unabashed enthusiasm, Fidel Castro made a concerted effort to reestablish relations with the other countries of Latin America irrespective of ideology. In the second half of the 1970s, when the growth of the economy began to slow, the Cuban Revolution projected its influence across the Atlantic, where the Ethiopian Revolution and the independence of former Portuguese colonies presented a new field for international action. Cuba's technical and military aid to African revolutionary regimes became a source of patriotic pride and provided Castro with an opportunity to exercise a powerful military establishment that remained far from superfluous in light of continuing tensions with the United States.

The additional participation of Cuban doctors, teachers, and technicians provided an outlet for the frustrated professionals that the Cuban Revolution had cultivated (perhaps too abundantly) following the emigration of so many middle-class professionals in the early 1960s.

By the end of the 1970s, the revolutionary government felt secure enough to seek if not a reconciliation, at least a less hostile relationship with the large Cuban émigré population in the United States. Although few Cuban émigrés modified their rancor toward the regime that now invited them to tour their lost homeland, many took advantage of the visit to dazzle their envious friends and relations on the island with the fruits of U.S. material prosperity. Their presence sharpened doubts about the gigantic revolutionary experiment that, while achieving significant progress in standards of living, seemed to have lost its dynamism after assuring the satisfaction of no more than the most basic needs. When an incident caused the removal of police guards outside the Peruvian embassy in Havana, more than ten thousand people crowded onto its grounds within a matter of hours, seeking asylum. Fidel Castro declared his readiness to let them leave Cuba, along with other "undesirables," and opened Mariel Beach to whatever vessels the Cuban community of Miami could provide to evacuate them. More than 100,000 people made the passage before the startled U.S. government closed the golden door. Castro, who had contributed to the U.S. decision by facilitating the departure of numerous residents of Cuba's prisons and mental hospitals, could now tell the enemies of his regime that the United States was once again responsible for their inability to leave.

Although the end of the Mariel boatlift thus appeared as a small Cuban victory, the mass exodus had included a worrisome number of the revolutionary elite. The Castro regime sought to address the causes of discontent, this time not by intensifying its ideological vigilance over the population but by legalizing an informal free market for food and agricultural products—as the Soviet Union had already done but the Cubans had resisted doing because of their commitment to the moral purity of the revolution. Their efforts encountered further obstacles as the international sugar market continued to deteriorate, and the country's foreign debt, acquired during the period of easy credit that had seduced so many Latin American governments, imposed a heavy drag on the economy. As Cuba depended more and more on the Soviet bloc for trade and capital, the impatience of the Soviets at a situation entering its third decade was expressed in ever more lightly veiled criticisms of Cuban economic management.

Given these difficulties, it is easy to understand why Havana preferred to sidestep the confrontations repeatedly sought by the Reagan administration in Central America. Cuban reluctance to participate more actively in the Central American revolutionary crisis of the 1980s can be attributed partly to the turbulence then beginning within the Soviet bloc and to the warmer U.S.-Soviet relations that seemed unlikely to benefit Cuba. However, Cuban prudence in Central America also expressed the weary attitude of leaders sobered by the dimming prospects of their own revolution, no longer the object of the fond hopes it had once awakened around the world. While such disillusionment may be natural in light of the exorbitant initial goals of the Cuban Revolution, it is fairer to place Cuba in the context of late twentieth-century Jamaica, Haiti, or the Dominican Republic, in whose company the achievements of Cuba's socialist revolution remain enviable, indeed.

Despite the economic difficulties of the period, the other states of the Spanish Caribbean also experienced substantial institutional stability in the 1970s and 1980s, often including an alternation in power. In the Dominican Republic, Joaquín Balaguer, president since the mid-1960s, was finally persuaded to step down in 1978 by the Carter administration when he appeared ready to ignore the results of recent balloting won by opposition candidate Antonio Guzmán. It fell to Guzmán to administer the wholesale collapse of the Dominican economy. During the 1970s, the Dominican Republic had looked to tourism and foreign borrowing as a way of overcoming the stagnation of its export economy based on sugar, with predictably disastrous consequences when the international financial climate altered so radically. In the 1980s, the catastrophic devaluations of the Dominican currency and the rioting in the streets of the island nation surpassed in intensity their South American counterparts, and clandestine emigration to the United States offered the last resort to the fast-growing population. The consequent universal discontent enabled a blind and aging Balaguer to make a comeback in the late 1980s, without much hope that an effective solution to the country's problems would soon be found.

Puerto Rico's economy fared little better during this time. Having shaken loose from the grip of sugar monoculture, the Puerto Rican administration was disappointed at the results of its attempt to industrialize the island. Despite its close association with the economy of the U.S. mainland, to which it offered an abundant and inexpensive labor force, Puerto Rico encountered overwhelming competition from newly industrializing areas in Asia. The island's tourist trade likewise met with vigorous competition, this time from the other Caribbean nations. As in the case of the Dominican Republic, Puerto Rico's burgeoning population increasingly sought an outlet in emigration to the United States. The U.S. government's subsidies to the Puerto Rican poor and unemployed also became more essential during the 1970s and 1980s. As a result, the relationship between the commonwealth and its metropolis drew ever closer. Even the nationalism that had constituted a barrier to assimilation lost that function somewhat as Puerto Ricans became one among many minority groups in the emerging multi-ethnic society of the late twentieth-century United States.

dwindling nationalism

Puerto Rico's political picture did not undergo major changes as economic growth slackened, though the Reagan administration's cutbacks in social programs—at the very moment when they were more needed on the island—naturally produced tensions. The movement for Puerto Rican independence, which tended to embrace a socialist option inspired by the Cuban experience, made slight headway after 1970. Its electoral bids continued to have minimal appeal, and the U.S. government continued to repress the movement's clandestine arm through drastic, but indubitably effective, methods. The statehood option seemed to gravitate more strongly as the impact of the larger U.S. context became increasingly important to Puerto Rico. In more than one general election on the island, the pro-statehood New Progressive party was able to defeat the Popular Democratic party that had guided the island's destiny during much of the period since World War II, but it owed such victories apparently more to the overall discontent of the Puerto Rican electorate than to the specific appeal of statehood. Puerto Rico thus exemplified the tendency, common throughout Latin America in this period, to alternate political parties within a fairly stable institutional framework.

Venezuela

On the southern shore of the Caribbean Sea, Venezuela also demonstrated remarkable stability after the fragile democracy restored in 1958 had weathered the stormy 1960s. It may be, however, that the strength of Venezuelan democracy in the period after 1970 stemmed less from the solidity of its institutions than from the relatively light impact of the debt crisis on the country's oil-rich economy.

Venezuela took a leading role in the formation of OPEC, and the nationalization of its petroleum industry was already well advanced in 1973 when the world's oil producers began to enjoy their great bonanza. In that same year, the Democratic Action party that had done so much to reestablish constitutional rule in the country recovered the presidency from the Christian Democratic party (COPEI). Democratic Action's founder, Rómulo Betancourt, now in the autumn of his

career, threw himself into the campaign with youthful vigor, presenting the party's candidate, Carlos Andrés Pérez, as the son he never had.
As president, Pérez disappointed his mentor by seeking a reconciliation with Cuba (still Betancourt's *bête noire*) and by showing little
restraint in the administration of Venezuela's oil boom. The expansion
of the state's economic activities in the 1970s involved not only further nationalization of its mineral wealth and public projects on the
monumental scale of the steelworks at Ciudad Guayana but also
government favors conceded to equally ambitious private-sector projects in a climate of disorderly improvisation that raised widespread
suspicions of corruption.

The skepticism expressed by Betancourt and other veteran political leaders concerning the conduct of the Pérez government did nothing to inhibit the fever of flush times in Venezuela, but the prosperity
of the 1970s raised the costs of maintaining the current political order.
The constant challenge (not always successfully confronted) to the
ethical standards of the ruling elite was only one of these costs. The
increasingly lavish style of partisan politics, with presidential campaigns handled by U.S. public relations firms, was another. Given the
level of expectations in a country where imported Scotch displaced
local rum even among the general population, the systematic dispen-
sation of favors that maintained the networks of political clienteles
also became correspondingly more expensive. The greatest price of
affluence, however, was the inflation of people's expectations of the
government, resulting in progressive expansion of the bureaucracy to
provide employment for the middle class, the provision of more numerous subsidies to guarantee the profits of the entrepreneurial elite,
and an increasing expectation, on the part of Venezuelan society as a
whole, that the government should guarantee the levels of consumption to which it had become accustomed.

Thanks to this unbridled spending, Venezuela joined Mexico in
accumulating an external debt at the very moment when other oil-
producing countries were flooding the international market with their
excess capital. It was left to COPEI's Luis Herrera Campins, who
succeeded Pérez as president in 1979, to face the economic difficulties
that appeared in the early 1980s. Although Venezuela's debt crisis did
not reach overwhelming proportions, the irked electorate returned
Democratic Action to power in 1984. In Venezuela, then—as in Puerto
Rico and elsewhere in the 1970s and 1980s—the institutional framework of political life gained solidity, becoming, by the end of that
period, the only arrangement ever known by more than half of the
population, while voter dissatisfaction expressed itself in an alterna-

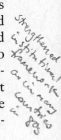

tion of parties in power. By the end of that period, the former revolutionaries of the 1960s had become totally reabsorbed into mainstream politics, while the key to the relationship between the constitutional government and the military, which, in the past, had played such a large part in Venezuelan politics, constituted one of the country's most valuable and best kept political secrets.

Paraguay

Paraguay's stability, on the other hand, still rested in the hands of a military dictator. Completing thirty years in power in 1984, Gen. Alfredo Stroessner ranked among the most durable heads of state in Latin American history. The heart of the Paraguayan regime remained the alliance between the army and the Colorado party. That alliance flourished by opening the doors to a peripheral participation in the dynamism of Brazilian economic expansion in the 1970s, particularly at the gigantic hydroelectric dam of Itaipu, located on the border between the two countries. The construction of Itaipu provided temporary employment for thousands of Paraguayan laborers and left a permanent legacy of regular Brazilian payments for the nominally Paraguayan portion of the electricity generated by the dam. Moreover, the extension onto Paraguayan soil of Brazil's expanding agricultural frontiers led to the profitable opening of sparsely settled northeastern areas of the country. Most important, however, has been Paraguay's new function as the informal economic back door to both Brazil and Argentina. The Stroessner regime reserved to itself and to its loyal retainers the profits of an immensely lucrative contraband trade and only eliminated illegal drugs from among the chief commodities of that trade when forced to do so by the United States.

Even this most classic of late twentieth-century Latin American dictatorships was unable to shut out political ferment completely. An incipient peasant movement, supported by some members of the clergy, had begun by the mid-1980s. Some opposition leaders from the traditional parties (as well as from the proscribed Communist party) maintained activity as well, much of it in exile. None of these challenges seemed too much, however, for an apparatus of repression that, though less systematic and brutal than in the past, seemed to have lost none of its old efficacy and retained some of the longest-held political prisoners in Latin America.

Many Latin American countries (running the gamut from democracies like Venezuela to old-style dictatorships like Paraguay) weathered the economic difficulties of the early and mid-1980s with their political institutions intact or even returned to constitutional rule (like Brazil and Argentina) during those difficulties. The experience of Latin America after 1970 thus disproved the notion of a necessary correlation—so widely accepted during the 1960s—between socio-economic and institutional crises in the region. In Central America and the Andes, however, the economic crisis of the 1980s did go hand in hand with a crisis of political institutions.

Of the Andean countries, Ecuador was the least affected by the crisis. Although institutional changes occurred there during the period, they did not appear more dramatic than those of the preceding decades. When the decade of the 1970s began, perennial president José María Velasco Ibarra ruled at last with the support of Ecuador's generals, who considered him preferable to left-wing alternatives until 1972, when, inspired by the reformist military coup in Peru, they themselves decided to provide that alternative. The Ecuadorian military junta that assumed control at that point adopted a program copied from the Peruvians and hoped to finance it using the proceeds from concessions awarded to several multinational oil companies in the Amazon lowlands. In their eagerness to secure as much as possible of the country's oil wealth, the Ecuadorian generals fixed a production volume and price out of keeping with the standards set by OPEC, and the oil companies punished the military government's audacity by systematically marginalizing Ecuadorian production in the international petroleum market. Ecuador's chastened military government then modified its oil policy and began to lose its reformist ardor, particularly as the Peruvian example itself lost prestige. The upshot of its efforts, in the end, was a limited program of agricultural and industrial modernization. Losing confidence in their ability to build a more integrated society and a more stable political order, the Ecuadorian military soon acquiesced to pressures for a return to constitutional rule.

The elections called for in 1978 were no longer haunted by the specter of Velasco Ibarra, but the military now identified a new populist leader, Assad Buccaram, a wealthy merchant of Guayaquil, as too dangerous to be president. The proscribed Buccaram's son-in-law, Jaime Roldós, ran in his place and won handily. President Roldós proved an able political leader, pushing for an expansion of rural development (especially in the country's tropical lowlands) and for a more independent foreign policy. He was, if anything, too successful for his father-in-law, who tried to reclaim a leadership role by obstructing the Roldós initiatives in congress. The president's untimely death in a 1981 helicopter accident transferred power to his vice president, Osvaldo Hurtado, a Christian Democrat who did not have a personal following strong enough to carry out the reforms promised by his predecessor. By the early 1980s, Ecuador was, at any rate, entering a period of debt crisis that would make all ambitious government projects impossible for the time being. Consequently, Hurtado was able to do no more than implement a series of austerity measures that assured a victory for the opposition in the next election.

The 1984 victory of conservative presidential candidate León Febres Cordero inaugurated a brief and stormy neoliberal economic experiment in Ecuador. So powerful was the negative reaction provoked by the laissez-faire policies of Febres Cordero that his government soon lost any ability to implement them. The midterm elections in 1986 brought a crushing defeat of the president's conservative coalition, and his relations with the military deteriorated until the president was sequestered by a faction within the armed forces that enjoyed considerable sympathy in congress. Febres Cordero recovered his freedom only after making exorbitant promises that permanently compromised his presidential authority. Ecuador's political turbulence naturally impeded its ability to deal with the debt crisis, which grew worse as the decade advanced, particularly after a 1987 earthquake damaged the oil pipeline connecting the country's petroleum-producing Amazon lowlands with its export facilities on the Pacific coast. By the last presidential election of the 1980s, all signs indicated that the conservatives would be replaced by a representative of the moderate left. Although the future course of the smallest Andean nation remained quite uncertain, its democratic institutions had recently demonstrated a resilience somewhat surprising in view of their shallow roots in Ecuadorian political traditions.

During the 1970s and 1980s, the other Andean republics faced more challenging socioeconomic transformations and were also more affected by the trade in illegal drugs, which reduced the control exercised by their respective governments over significant portions of each country's national economy and society. Governments thus weakened were less able to confront the sociopolitical crisis that affected so much of Latin America at this time. The impact of the drug trade was most salient in the case of Colombia.

Colombia entered the period still mired politically in the fixed-party alternation established by its National Pact of the late 1950s. Conservative Misael Pastrana Borrero's undistinguished term, beginning in 1970, was the last in the sequence of four accorded by the pact. In 1974, Colombian voters chose Alfonso López Michelsen, former leader of the Liberal party's dissident left wing and son of the president who had helped revitalize Colombian liberalism in the 1930s, but the presidency of López Michelsen was as barren of renovating impulses as the preceding one. In 1978, the election of Gabriel Turbay Ayala, another Liberal, at last interrupted the pattern of presidential alternation. Turbay, who represented the traditional currents within his party, obtained the narrowest of victories over Conservative candidate, Belisario Betancur. During Turbay's highly unpopular administration, the pulse of Colombian politics became yet more lethargic. In 1982, the conservatives again nominated Betancur, whose obvious personal dedication, persuasive campaign, and vigorous presidency temporarily reenergized the country's political life.

President Betancur vowed to attend to neglected problems created by rapid urbanization, to search for solutions to agrarian conflicts, and to reincorporate Colombia's several durable guerrilla movements into the political system. Betancur had great popularity among the general population, but he could count on little support from the political establishment to achieve his goals. Neither the Conservative party nor the dissident liberal faction that had also backed him in the election had the will to carry out ambitious social programs like the proposed housing construction for low-income groups that raised high hopes before collapsing in disappointment. Betancur's negotiations with the clandestine revolutionary movements were less than totally successful, and the guerrillas were, at any rate, only partly responsible for the wave of violence that threatened to engulf the country. So effective were the thugs organized by landowners against peasant protest and against the government's agrarian reform efforts that the president and members of his cabinet found themselves unable to visit certain areas of the country safely, in spite of military protection.

The rural violence of the 1980s reflected the expansion of large-scale tropical agriculture at the expense of displaced peasants and partook of a general weakening in the authority of the Colombian state—clearest in connection with the country's drug trade, which gained prominence in Colombia earlier than elsewhere in the region. The drug trade developed in well-defined and often isolated areas of the country and had little impact in its early stages on a national state that, in turn, refrained from interfering aggressively in those areas. As the illegal trade loomed larger and larger within the Colombian economy as a whole, marijuana and cocaine surpassed coffee as the country's most important export products, and Colombian drug lords began to take on a high public profile that belied the social stigma supposedly attached to the criminal origin of their fortunes. Soon, some of them spent vast sums to garner popularity and finance meteoric political careers. Caught between the drug mafias, the guerrilla armies, and the private posses of the landowners, Colombia's national state quickly lost the monopoly on the exercise of violence that it had

consolidated later and less completely than other national states in
Latin America.

The violence of the drug mafias increased in the 1980s just as the
violence associated with the insurgent movements seemed about to
decline. At the beginning of the decade, some proposed legalizing the
trade as a way of limiting its ravages, but that solution was unacceptable to the U.S. government, which preferred to deal with its domestic
drug problem by attacking the overseas supply. When the Colombian
government began to put more pressure on the illegal trade, the mafias
responded with a shocking wave of murders that rekindled the other
smoldering sources of social conflict in the country. In the middle
years of the decade, so many groups were killing each other, and webs
of enmity and alliance became so intricate, that responsibility for
individual incidents of violence became difficult to assign to a single
cause. For example, when the M-19 guerrilla movement seized the
Supreme Court building in Bogotá, they set a fire that, suggestively,
destroyed the files laboriously accumulated by the court in its efforts
to prosecute the drug traffickers. The army quickly retook the building in a bloody operation that cost the lives of most of the hostages as
well as their captors, hindering President Betancur's efforts at political
pacification. Ultimately, Betancur was unable to galvanize Colombia's
political forces to the kind of action needed to overcome the crisis. He
succeeded only in curtailing the violations of human rights that had
characterized the counterinsurgency tactics of the Colombian army.

At the conclusion of Betancur's term, the presidency passed to
Virgilio Barco, a representative of traditional elements in the Liberal
party whose election would have augured a return to political routine
had that been possible in the late 1980s. In fact, the situation had
deteriorated beyond any hope of salvaging an earlier modus vivendi. As
the Reagan and Bush administrations continued to press the Colombian government to combat the prohibited trade, the government's
measures seemed only to infuriate the drug lords, who reacted by
liquidating hundreds of officials and judges, including one member of
the presidential cabinet. Gradually, the reign of terror was extended to
journalists who published information or opinions that the mafias
considered indiscreet. Colombia's spiral of violence could not be explained simply in terms of political or social tensions. Thanks in large
measure to its illegal exports, the Colombian economy actually performed well during this period, and the impact of the debt crisis was
unusually light. Future observers will have to look elsewhere to explain how Colombia regressed so perilously close to a Hobbesian state
of nature in the late twentieth century.

In the Peruvian case, turmoil grew from an already-existing socio- *Perú*
political crisis only aggravated by the drug trade. The largest of the
Andean countries necessarily underwent a painful process of social
and cultural unification as a continued rural exodus and rapid urban
growth at last brought about an intimate confrontation between the *melding*
two Perus: the Indian nation of the central and southern highlands and *of the two*
the Creole, African, and mestizo nation of the coast. The melding of *Perus*
Peru's national split personality would have been difficult enough
without the profound dislocation of rural highland society, which
surpassed the attraction of the cities in motivating internal migration
in the 1970s and 1980s. The current period began with the ambivalent
legacy of the reformist military government established in 1968.

Agrarian reform was one of the basic instruments with which the
military hoped to restructure Peruvian society. For political reasons, it
began with the sugar and cotton plantations of the Pacific coast, where
the military reformers hoped to undercut the political influence that
the Popular American Revolutionary Alliance (APRA) had exercised
for decades. They largely failed to dislodge the dominance of APRA,
especially in its northern coastal stronghold, but their reforms did
considerably improve the lot of the rural laborers who became members of the new cooperatives. Still, much of the rural population of the
coast was left out of the agrarian reform, and, despite the availability of
funds for agronomical improvements, patterns of production on the
affected properties changed relatively little. The more varied land
tenancy of the highlands posed an even greater challenge, one which
the reformers skirted, for the most part, by concentrating on the
elimination of large and middle-sized haciendas. There was little public investment in technical innovations, and the productivity of highland agriculture and rural living conditions improved hardly at all. To
the contrary, a new state-run system of commercialization actually
disrupted access to traditional markets, increasing social tensions and
rural out-migration. The military government used the name of Tupac
Amaru, the eighteenth-century rebel, to symbolize its commitment to
the downtrodden Indian people, but overall the impact of the government's redistributive measures in the rural highlands was slight, or in
some cases, even negative.

The programs of Peru's reformist military government were more
successful in the sectors of the economy that had already undergone
significant modernization. Industrial wages were raised immediately,
and the government advanced plans to give workers a majority share in
private companies and multiply the number of publicly owned companies. Initially, state enterprises extended their activities into areas

where private initiative was inadequate, like the steel industry, and into other areas considered too essential to be left in private hands, such as petroleum extraction and even large-scale fishing (the source of the country's most recent export boom). Publicly owned companies were intended to subsidize the costs of production for the domestic market and reinvest their profits more systematically than private companies. Unfortunately, the carefully targeted nationalization of particular industries frightened foreign companies, leading to a general withdrawal of international capital and leaving gaps that then forced overexpansion of state enterprises. Plans for worker ownership also failed to develop as hoped, partly because of the cool reception of workers themselves, who recognized that the scheme would divert some of their income into forced savings for reinvestment.

In fact, a lack of popular enthusiasm and mobilization characterized the Peruvian military's attempt to create a social revolution from above. The fairly positive economic conditions of the first years following 1968 offered the best opportunity for popular mobilization, and the government took a first step in that direction with the creation of its National System for the Support of Social Mobilization, under the direction of former leaders of the radical left. In order to succeed, however, such efforts required a coherent set of guiding political ideas, and the officer corps of the armed forces was too ideologically heterogeneous to provide it. The reformist officers could agree only on particular measures and on the importance of continuing the process under military control. Their attempts at mass political mobilization therefore made little headway, and the Peruvian "revolution" of 1968 never acquired the kind of popular base that eventually might have made it self-sustaining. This state of affairs at least made the reforms less threatening to the middle and upper classes, who were content, for the most part, to poke fun at the process and reacted tepidly even in the face of such provocative measures as the government's suppression of university autonomy, its interference with the publication of major opposition newspapers, or its dissolution of the National Agrarian Society (representing the interests of the landowning class). The government's reforms thus proceeded without high levels of class confrontation or official repression.

By the mid-1970s Peru's military regime was in trouble. The reformist officers had not lacked the enthusiasm notably absent among the Peruvian people at large, but their ardor had been coupled with a dangerously large measure of inexperience in economic management. For this reason, many of the regime's ambitious projects turned out to be spectacular failures. The nationalization of the fishing industry had disastrous consequences when an overzealous maximization of short-term earnings practically exterminated the anchovy. Then an extremely expensive petroleum pipeline, constructed to carry crude oil from Amazonian wells over the Andes to the coast, disappointed the military's high expectations when the country's oil reserves proved smaller than they had believed, and so on. In addition, evidence of corruption began to undermine the regime's claims to selfless patriotism. Costly failures and accusations of malfeasance soon revived the political opposition, which came initially from organizations of the left.

Discouraged by their failures and concerned by the rising potential for social conflict, the military regime had two alternatives. It could begin to exercise the kind of political repression that it had so far avoided, or it could begin an orderly withdrawal from power. In 1975, a change in personnel at the top indicated that the generals had chosen to beat a gradual retreat, as the activist Gen. Juan Velasco Alvarado was removed by his colleagues. The new line included more conservative economic policies. Peru's foreign debt, accumulated partly as a result of the military government's arms-buying binge, demanded attention, and the generals had to woo the International Monetary Fund in order to attract further foreign credit and investment. The generals scheduled a constituent convention, charged with returning Peru to constitutional government, for 1978.

The elections for the constituent assembly showed that APRA had held onto the support of a third of the Peruvian electorate during the decade of military rule. The socialist left—which the military had encouraged to undercut the influence of APRA at the outset of its period in power—also made an impressive showing, winning collectively about a third of the votes. The right, represented by a populist ex-mayor of Lima, mustered less support than either of the other forces, and the generals began to brace themselves for an Aprista victory. That outcome was easier for them to accept, perhaps, because APRA's relationship with the military government had improved during the 1970s. Pleased to have their existence legally recognized for the first time by the armed forces, the Apristas had muted their opposition in what turned out to be a fatal error. By the time of the presidential election scheduled for 1980, APRA had come to seem too friendly to the exiting regime, and its venerable figurehead, Víctor Raúl Haya de la Torre had died. The electoral victory went instead to Fernando Belaúnde Terry, the president whom the military had overthrown originally to seize power in 1968. As the victim of the military government's original sin and the one major candidate who had refused to participate in the constituent assembly, Belaúnde was best able to ride the wave of resentment against the now vastly unpopular armed forces.

President Belaúnde began his new term with strong support in the congress, but he had the ill fortune to return to power on the eve of the economic catastrophes of what came to be called Latin America's "lost decade." Problems with the export sector and the external debt grew rapidly worse. An attempt to impose neoliberal austerity measures produced social costs that the Peruvian population could hardly afford and also led to a protracted battle with organized labor. The gradual rise of Peru's illegal economy, centered on the cultivation of coca leaves, softened the general downturn but brought another set of difficulties in its train. By the midterm elections of 1983, Belaúnde's Popular Action party was collapsing, while APRA showed new signs of vitality and the United Left, which had acquired a charismatic leader in Alfonso Barrantes, made notable gains among urban voters in Lima.

Another threat gradually overshadowed the others—a Maoist movement that proposed, in its name, to "Advance along the Shining Path of Mariátegui," referring to the Peruvian Marxist thinker of the 1920s. The ideologue of the group was an ex-professor from the University of Ayacucho, and many of his followers were students. The educational reforms of the military government had given many young people of modest origin the chance to attend universities. Unlike the young Aprista activists of previous decades, whose social origins lay in the impoverished provincial aristocracy and the middle class of Lima, this new generation of radical university students were not viewed as outsiders by the rural masses of the Peruvian highlands, and they were much more successful than the Apristas at political mobilization there. The guerrilla force that came to be known simply as the Shining Path took hold in the southern highlands around Ayacucho with surprising speed. The reforms carried out by the military government also contributed to the spread of the Shining Path. By removing the hacendado class from the scene in many parts of the rural highlands, the army's agrarian reform had made officials of the national state the chief representatives of authority and agents of social control in highland communities. The presence of this clear and singular political target facilitated the identification of highland peasants with the guerrilla struggle, especially after the Shining Path had demonstrated its ability to withstand repeated attempts to eliminate it.

The conflict between highland Indians and representatives of the state was reminiscent of colonial times, but the insurgency soon extended to the modernized coast. By the late 1980s, Lima had more than six million inhabitants (a third of the national population), most of whom had arrived in successive waves of migration from the highlands, fleeing poverty. Many were from Ayacucho, one of the highland areas nearest the capital, and the increase in political violence added to the flow of refugees from the center of guerrilla activity. By 1982, the Shining Path was making itself felt powerfully in the teeming shantytowns of Lima and attracting the attention of the capital with disruptive strikes. On more than one occasion, dynamited power pylons created temporary blackouts, allowing the urban dwellers to see, glowing on the darkened hillsides inhabited by rural newcomers, the shape of a gigantic hammer and sickle formed by innumerable torches. By the end of Belaúnde's term in 1985, the Peruvian army regarded Ayacucho as enemy territory, where government repression and insurgent reprisals became increasingly savage and wanton, while the inhabitants of the capital city had begun to live under curfew. Importantly, the labor unions and other urban organizations of the left declined to identify themselves with the violent methods and murky ideology of the Shining Path, and the government and army, eager to prevent such an identification from developing, carefully abstained from striking indiscriminately at the left. The left was therefore able to become a major contender in the election of Belaúnde's successor, allowing APRA to carry the day as the safer alternative.

Alan García, the first president to represent his half-century-old party, brandished the hoary anti-imperialist banners of APRA's origins. His praise of the Sandinista government of Nicaragua, then under covert attack by the United States, and his defiant promise to limit service on Peru's national debt to 10 percent of the country's export earnings won him the benevolence of the left, and his rejection of Belaúnde's austerity measures, followed by a general rise in wages and a flurry of consumer spending, provided the young president with unprecedented initial support. Not even the early failure of negotiations with the leaders of the insurgency or a subsequent massacre of guerrillas imprisoned in Lima (calling into question García's vaunted dedication to the cause of human rights) could dampen his popularity. García's popularity began to decline only with the ebb of economic prosperity, as the pent-up demand and unused manufacturing capacity that had accumulated during Belaúnde's austerity drive were finally exhausted.

The political climate became considerably stormier when García tried to address the fading economy by proposing the nationalization of important banks. This initiative stimulated the rise of a new populist right that extolled the virtues of free enterprise and found an eloquent spokesperson in Mario Vargas Llosa, Peru's acclaimed novelist. At the same time, new centers of Shining Path guerrilla activity were appearing in the south, near the Bolivian border, and in the Upper Huallaga Valley of the central north, where the insurgents collaborated with drug smugglers to undermine state control; also, a second guerrilla movement, naming itself after Tupac Amaru, began to vie with the Shining Path for predominance in Lima. By the late 1980s, Peru had sunk into a social and political crisis of an intensity that would inevitably test the country's constitutional framework.

In Bolivia, the drug traffic combined after 1970 with the ongoing sociopolitical conflict to create an upheaval so permanent as to exceed the meaning of the word *crisis*. The sociopolitical conflict stemmed from the unfinished revolution of 1952. Gen. René Barrientos, who had tried to steer the revolution onto a more conservative course during the second half of the 1960s, died at the end of that decade. His successor, Gen. Alfredo Ovando, appeared ready to reconstruct the original revolutionary alliance by courting the miners' unions and the urban left. The failure of his initial attempts to rebuild the power of the National Revolutionary movement (MNR) prompted radical elements within the military to replace him in 1970 with Gen. Juan José Torres, a man who they believed could succeed where Ovando had not. Torres called an Assembly of the People, where the various forces of the Bolivian left debated the most radical proposals imaginable, but the Assembly of the People so alarmed more conservative elements of the armed forces (which had never backed Torres unanimously) that a military coup deposed him in 1971.

There followed the longest dictatorship in twentieth-century Bolivia. Col. Augusto Banzer, head of the 1971 coup, kept himself in power until 1978 thanks to favorable international economic conditions and to his ruthless repression of political dissent. The availability of foreign credit and the expansion of Bolivia's oil production energized the urban economy, which, in turn, stimulated domestic agriculture. Although no permanent economic growth occurred as a result, the temporary prosperity facilitated partial dismantling of the politically sensitive tin-mining industry (with its perpetual deficits) and made the opposition to Banzer's dictatorship less intense than it might otherwise have been. Not until the dictator turned over power to his chosen political heir by means of scandalously fraudulent elections did the long-quiescent opposition revive, and its revival was forceful, indeed. A pair of generals occupied the presidential palace in quick succession as the armed forces arranged for new elections.

The elections of 1979 revealed the now-irreparable split in the revolutionary coalition and initiated an extremely agitated train of events in the next two years. The two largest factions of the MNR had become the nuclei of rival groups, each headed by a former president and veteran leader of the movement: Víctor Paz Estenssoro and Hernán Siles Suazo. Since neither received an absolute majority of the popular vote in 1979, the election was thrown into the congress, where the two sides were again too evenly balanced for a decisive outcome. The military tried to settle the impasse by taking power itself but gave up the attempt in the face of fierce popular resistance, in which the miners once again played an important role. Congress solved the dilemma by naming Lidia Gueiler, a revolutionary of 1952 and now head of the legislative branch, interim president in charge of new elections to be held the following year. This time Siles Suazo emerged clearly the victor, only to face yet another coup. With the aid of Argentine military advisers, Gen. Luís García Meza imposed a brief but brutal regime clearly linked to the drug trade, the only sector of the economy that showed any vitality in 1980. Irrepressible popular mobilizations forced García Meza out the next year, finally leaving Siles Suazo to assume the presidency to which the recent election had entitled him.

After purging the officer corps of its most volatile elements, Siles Suazo turned his attention to the disastrous economic situation. The intractable forces that had characterized Bolivian political life since mid-century opposed all of the president's efforts to combat an inflation that reached nearly 1,000 percent toward the end of his second year in office. By that time, Siles Suazo had discovered his inability to control the drug traffic and abandoned any attempt to maintain payments on the national debt. He soon gave up on the political situation as well, calling early elections before the end of his term. The economic shambles had inspired a certain nostalgia for the ex-dictator Banzer, who had presided over the modest economic well-being of the 1970s, and Banzer actually received the highest number of popular votes in the election called by the discouraged Siles Suazo. The second highest number of votes went to Paz Estenssoro, and the margin was so narrow that the decision again passed to the Bolivian congress, who preferred Paz Estenssoro over Banzer.

By the mid-1980s, the international cocaine trade had established itself firmly in Bolivia, encouraged by the complicity of numerous members of both the military and the civil government. Furthermore, the trade was fiercely defended by the country people who depended on the cultivation of coca for their livelihoods, an aspect of the situation that affected democratic governments more strongly than authoritarian ones. Under strong pressure from the United States, Paz Estenssoro stepped up efforts to curb the activities of traffickers, even authorizing the presence of U.S. military forces in Bolivia's coca-producing zones. Although the much-publicized U.S. raid on clandestine cocaine laboratories was not very successful, it provoked rather less protest within Bolivia than one might have expected, aside from a predictable outcry on the part of the political opposition.

Indeed, the economic crisis had become so overwhelming that other political topics could not command the public's full attention for very long. Inflation reached a point where Paz Estenssoro eventually resulted to tactics not very different from those recommended by Bolivian conservatives. Severe cutbacks in government spending—combined with the continued inflow of money from the illegal economy—did begin to stabilize the currency but at the cost of reductions in the salaries of public employees that were simply unsustainable in the long run. Another cost-cutting tactic, a reduction of government subsidies to the tin-mining industry, encountered the overpowering resistance of the militant miners' unions.

Bolivia's socioeconomic dilemma of the 1980s was, of course, similar to the one faced throughout Latin America, but it had more volatile implications because of the country's unfinished revolution, in which the contending social and political forces had not found a new equilibrium. Instead, the various heirs of the revolution of 1952 asserted themselves in a seemingly endless cycle of military occupations of the mining zone, peasant mobilizations against both the military and the miners, and urban protests against the political influence of the peasants. Meanwhile, gradual transformations, like the growing integration of the rural and urban economies, bound these contending forces more closely together. A unified Bolivian nation was undergoing its painful birth in a territory where ethnically divided groups had lived side by side for centuries. Although it left many problems unresolved, Bolivia's 1952 revolution impelled the rapid advance of this necessarily conflictive process, which proceeded at a crawl in neighboring Peru. Significantly, while Peru's armed forces returned to the barracks in the late 1970s because of their own failure, the Bolivian military was ejected from power by repeated popular mobilizations, an outcome almost unimaginable before 1952.

After 1970, Central America paralleled the Andean situation in regard to the disruptive impact of rapid socioeconomic change and the weakness of state structures. The diversification of export agriculture in Central America, particularly intense during the 1960s, had sharpened social inequalities in the countryside. Urban areas were ill-able to absorb the resulting rural exodus when the evanescent prosperity of the Central American Common Market disappeared and the urban economies of the isthmus lost their dynamism. As in the Andes, the tensions resulting from socioeconomic transformations might not have led to such violent confrontations in more strongly consolidated national states. Not only were state structures still developing in both the Andes and Central America, but they encountered new obstacles in the period under consideration. Where Colombia, Peru, and Bolivia underwent the corrosive effects of a booming illegal economy, the republics of Central America suffered the intrusion of a world power when the Reagan administration chose them as battlegrounds for its eagerly sought showdown with international socialism.

During the 1970s, Guatemala was already the scene of a protracted struggle between ruthless military governments and tenacious guerrilla armies with their roots in Indian communities. The Guatemalan Indians had managed to survive the late nineteenth-century assault on their common lands by serving as hired labor on the haciendas of the coffee planters until, by the second half of the twentieth century, the advances in agricultural productivity returned economic viability to indigenous communities. At that point, Indian property took on renewed attractiveness in the eyes of outsiders, and rural insurrections became occasions for land expropriations that, in turn, fueled further insurrections. Many of those who benefited from the expropriations of Indian lands were army officers, making the military's "antisubversive" campaigns into a kind of ferocious entrepreneurial activity. This activity was accompanied in urban areas by indiscriminate repression, as death squads recruited among the military and police murdered leaders of the political opposition, of labor unions, and of student groups, as well as ideologically suspect professionals and intellectuals.

In 1982, a military coup installed President Efraín Ríos Montt, a fervent convert to evangelical Protestantism, who halted the official terrorism against urban opposition and concentrated on winning the conflict with Guatemala's rural guerrillas. His army did make headway in the war, though its systematic brutality against the Indian population swelled the flow of refugees into Guatemalan cities and across the border into Mexico. The triumphant army officers, frustrated at the president's prohibition of urban death squads and outraged to find him serious about cleaning up administrative corruption, overthrew Ríos Montt in 1983. They replaced him with Gen. Oscar Mejía Víctores, who permitted them to derive their customary booty from the conduct of the anti-insurgency war and from their control of the state apparatus generally.

The redemocratizing wind that blew across Latin America in the mid-1980s did reach Guatemala, but its effect was anything but conclusive. In 1985, a candidate who did not represent the dominant current within the armed forces was allowed to win a presidential election for the first time in twenty years. However, Christian Democrat Vinicio Cerezo clearly recognized the limits of his freedom of action vis-à-vis the military. While he maintained a precarious institutional equilibrium between civil and military power, and while the urban opposition began a cautious revival of open activity, the violence in the countryside continued unabated, and the Guatemalan right urged its allies and the armed forces not to let things slip beyond their control.

El Salvador

The crisis of the 1970s and 1980s in El Salvador had an obvious antecedent as early as the rural uprising of 1932, but Central America's smallest republic had exhibited little political conflict during the intervening years, despite the buildup of strong socioeconomic tensions in densely populated rural areas. Matters began to come to a head, however, as a result of the presidential election of 1972, when the oligarchical-military alliance refused to recognize the victory of Christian Democrat José Napoleón Duarte, who was imprisoned, tortured, and finally exiled as a result. With the emergence of an armed clandestine movement later in the 1970s, the Salvadoran regime applied a Guatemalan-style official terrorism against the urban opposition, and the level of confrontation rapidly escalated. In 1979, the threat of civil war led army officers to establish a junta promising drastic reform. The Salvadoran right responded by escalating its terrorist campaign against the opposition, thereby heightening contractions with the fragile reformist government, which fell securely into conservative hands with the departure of its more progressive members.

In order to retain the aid of the Carter administration, the Salvadoran regime continued to talk of democratization and reform, but all true renovating impulses had now gone out of the movement begun in 1979. José Napoleón Duarte, a man personally committed to reform, was invited in as a figurehead, but his hands were tied by the reactionary consensus within the government and the army. As Duarte tried to carry out the promised land reform, the forces of the right murdered thousands of Salvadorans who participated in the opposition, including Oscar Romero, the archbishop of El Salvador, shot down while saying mass because he had raised his voice repeatedly to protest the massacres. These tactics were largely successful in suffocating the urban opposition, though they did bring discredit to the government, especially when the victims were from the United States.

The murders of North American nuns (whose efforts on behalf of the poor where judged overzealous by the Salvadoran right) provoked considerable revulsion in U.S. public opinion. But the success of the leftist guerrillas, who were gradually gaining control of the entire eastern third of the national territory, prevented the cutoff of aid by a U.S. government guided, after 1980, by the anti-Communist priorities of the Reagan Administration.

Elections for a constituent assembly had been scheduled for 1982, but by that time the opposition had been effectively eliminated from the political arena, and most of the leaders of the left who had survived the onslaught of the death squads were now working with the guerrillas. Unsurprisingly, the parties of the right won the elections, and Roberto D'Aubuisson, the man widely believed to have ordered the assassination of Archbishop Romero, became president of the constituent assembly. If the excesses of the Salvadoran right had begun to trouble the Reagan administration, it nevertheless continued to regard the defeat of the guerrillas as the only acceptable outcome of the conflict. Consequently, a total of several billion dollars in U.S. aid to the Salvadoran government went increasingly to sustain the army. While able to contain the territory under insurgent control to the eastern third of the country, the army was unable to defeat the guerrillas there, nor could it prevent them from blowing up bridges and power lines in areas supposedly under government control.

The stalemate allowed Duarte's Christian Democrats to regain momentum at mid-decade. Winning the presidential election of 1984, Duarte persuaded the Salvadoran generals to reduce their collaboration with the radical right and made an effort to negotiate with the guerrillas. The activity of the death squads declined enough to allow a revival of political participation by the left, and El Salvador's public life emerged, somewhat, from the reign of terror. At the same time, however, uncertainty surrounding the frustrated land reform disrupted agricultural production, and the continued fighting combined with the generally unfavorable context of the 1980s to create extreme economic difficulties. As the army's unwillingness to make the concessions demanded by the insurgents led to a failure of the negotiations and the war dragged on, discouraged Salvadorans began to withdraw the majority support from President Duarte. The army reinforced this trend by lending its influence to the right in the rural areas under its control. In 1988, the right triumphed in elections for the assembly and municipal governments, further hardening the army's resolve to achieve a military victory. As the decade moved toward its close, U.S. policy in El Salvador seemed to have been frustrated by its contradictory goals: simultaneously to strengthen the democratic process and to bolster a military establishment ill-disposed to tolerate that process.

In the 1970s, Nicaragua suffered an intra-elite conflict in addition to the kind of socioeconomic tensions evident in other parts of Central America. The development of profitable large-scale cotton cultivation and the expansion of ranching in Nicaragua had occurred at the expense of subsistence farming in the period since World War II, creating an agrarian problem that demanded attention. Meanwhile, many of the richest rewards of this economic growth had been reserved for the friends, family, and political allies of the ruling Somozas. Anastasio, Jr., proved less adept than his predecessors in dealing with the members of the Nicaraguan elite who had no privileged participation in the division of the spoils of modernization. The Nicaraguan upper class was thus seriously divided as it faced the socioeconomic challenge of the countryside, and the anger of traditional elite sectors against the ruling group had few outlets since elections were tightly controlled by the regime. The earthquake that devastated Managua in 1972, followed by scandalous official misuse of the international relief aid, heightened resentment against the Somoza government and led to an escalation of opposition to it. The regime responded with its habitual brutality. The 1978 assassination of Pedro Joaquín Chamorro, a member of the country's traditional elite and editor of the opposition newspaper *La Prensa*, marked the point at which anti-Somoza sentiments acquired a critical mass.

The long-awaited moment had arrived for the small, dedicated insurgent movement that had existed in Nicaragua since the 1960s without seriously threatening the stability of the Somoza dictatorship. Unified since 1961 in the Sandinista National Liberation Front (FSLN), the guerrillas included various organizations of Marxist-Leninist inspiration, as well as an equally audacious but ideologically more moderate group led by Edén Pastora. As had occurred twenty years earlier in Cuba, a wave of nearly universal repudiation began to swell against the dictatorship, and a tiny force of committed insurgents found themselves at the crest. The general insurrection that followed was hard-fought and bloody. Analogies with the Cuban case continued in the aftermath of the victory, as the revolutionary vanguard, determined to carry out its program, marginalized the uprising's less radical participants, such as Pastora and Violeta Chamorro (wife of the murdered editor). The leading director of the Sandinistas during the 1980s would be Daniel Ortega Saavedra, formally elected president in 1984 with a convincing 67 percent of the votes.

The Nicaraguan Revolution also contrasted with the Cuban experience in important respects. It occurred long after the evaporation of the international climate of optimism that had given impetus to the Cuban Revolution. The fighting had been more destructive and left a more militarized situation in its aftermath. Not an island like Cuba, Nicaragua had borders that were difficult to defend, making counterrevolutionary invasion a permanent threat for the Sandinistas. The defeated remnants of Somoza's national guard soon gathered along Nicaragua's northern border with Honduras, while Edén Pastora's dissidents operated on the southern border with Costa Rica. As social conflicts sharpened within revolutionary Nicaragua, these groups gained counterrevolutionary recruits. Moreover, Nicaraguan society in 1980 was quite different from Cuban society in 1959. Not only was Nicaragua much more rural, but the lower-income urban sectors were characterized by an abundance of small, independent entrepreneurs ill-prepared for the introduction of socialist economic structures.

With a prudence applauded by their revolutionary mentors in Havana, the Sandinistas announced that they would create a mixed economy that reserved an important role for the private sector. They hoped that the property expropriated from the Somozas' inner circle would provide the revolutionary state with most of the raw material out of which to construct a new public sector for the Nicaraguan economy. In this they were generally disappointed since it turned out that the expropriated industries and businesses, having prospered mostly because of Somocista corruption, lacked the economic potential that the Sandinistas had imagined. Even major export agriculture, the one nationalized activity that possessed inherent economic strength, was beset by a political weakness since the decision to preserve the large-scale organization of state farms frustrated the aspirations of country people hungry for land distribution. The decision to maintain the large state farms, along with the Sandinistas' gingerly efforts not to alienate small and middle-sized private properties, undercut the support that the revolution might otherwise have won among the rural majority.

These economic challenges were aggravated (as well as partially concealed) by the sustained military attack on the Sandinista regime carried out indirectly by the U.S. government after 1981. The direct agents of the counterrevolutionary struggle, celebrated as "freedom fighters" by the Reagan government in the United States but better known as the Contras, took their officer corps directly from Somoza's former national guard. Over the years, their ranks swelled or thinned alternately as a function of internal tensions in Nicaragua and external support from the United States. The Contras' terrorist tactics won them an unenviable reputation in Nicaragua, and resistance to them in the U.S. Congress occasionally endangered the continuation of their external support, but in the long run they succeeded in exacerbating the economic difficulties that ultimately proved fatal to the popularity of the Sandinista revolution.

The Contra onslaught led the Sandinistas to tighten their links with Cuba and the Soviet bloc, when the moral support originally offered by Mexico and the moderate left governments of Europe proved materially insubstantial, and to harden their stance vis-à-vis the internal opposition. When the opposition paper *La Prensa* accepted a subsidy from the United States (which had recently undertaken the clandestine mining of Nicaraguan harbors), the Sandinistas closed it. They also did little to avoid an open break with a Catholic hierarchy upset by the presence within the revolutionary government of a number of brilliant but indocile Catholic priests and by the promotion, against ecclesiastical orders, of prorevolutionary currents of liberation theology. Pope John Paul II even made a point to visit Nicaragua, where he reiterated strong criticisms of the Sandinistas. While sharpening the Sandinistas' sense of purpose and identity, their turn toward the socialist bloc revealed disappointing limits in the effective solidarity that they could expect from that quarter—limits too narrow to make radicalization of the revolution as successful an international strategy as it had been for the Cuban revolutionaries of the early 1960s. As for the ongoing counterrevolutionary attack, it never came close to overthrowing the Sandinista government, but the Contras' external support and Honduran bases made them impossible to annihilate. By the mid-1980s, both Moscow and Havana encouraged their Nicaraguan protégés to negotiate an end to the conflict with the United States, and the Sandinistas adopted a less confrontational course.

Negotiations bore fruit more rapidly than might have been expected because of the general clumsiness of U.S. Central American policy. Even before their moderate reorientation, the Sandinistas were able to enter freely into the negotiations favored by the Contadora Group (Mexico, Colombia, Venezuela, and Panama) in the confidence that the Reagan administration would make the outcome purely theoretical. A few years later, when the president of Costa Rica proposed a specific peace plan and, fearing that the crisis might be internationalized, the presidents of Central America unanimously approved it, the U.S. government was taken somewhat aback. The Nicaraguan government allowed *La Prensa* to reopen and went further than El Salvador and Guatemala in implementing the portion of the plan that required each signatory to negotiate with insurgent groups. The process was speeded up after 1987 by discredit brought upon Reagan's Central American policy because of the revelation that secret arms sales to Iran had been used to finance support of the Contras during a period when the U.S. Congress had expressly prohibited it. When the U.S. Congress began to put its weight behind the peace process and made Managua's participation a condition for a continued cutoff of aid to the Contras, the resolution of the crisis rapidly began to take shape.

Iran-Contra Scandal

As the 1980s drew to a close, the greatest obstacles to a negotiated solution in the Nicaraguan conflict came from the lack of unity in the various opposition forces, not from the Sandinistas, who seemed ready to adopt a more pluralist political style. A number of fissures appeared within the various forces arrayed against the government. The internal opposition parties (whose earlier attempts to disassociate themselves from the insurgents had been largely ignored) now loudly asserted that they, and not the Contras, were the proper interlocutors for the government. The position of the Contras was further undercut when the church hierarchy, represented within the country by Cardinal Miguel Obando y Bravo, offered itself as mediator and showed a sincere commitment to a negotiated settlement. Moreover, a division within the ranks of the Nicaraguan insurgents became evident. The former national guard officers who had initiated the armed movement and continued to lead it because of their training, seniority, and close links with the distributors of U.S. aid had little desire to see a successful conclusion of the negotiations. So unsavory was their image within Nicaragua that they feared to return there except as military victors. On the other hand, most of the volunteers who had joined the Contras during the course of the war were eager to return to Nicaragua as long as the Sandinistas made certain concessions.

The role played in the unraveling of the conflict by Oscar Arias, the president of Costa Rica, whose peace proposals had hastened the conflict toward a conclusion, reflected his concern that if something were not done to stop the fighting, Costa Rica would sooner or later be engulfed by it. Involvement in the conflict had been almost inevitable, since both the Sandinistas and, later, their adversaries had used Costa Rican territory to launch their operations in Nicaragua. As the 1980s advanced, however, the function of base camp for Nicaraguan insurgents passed increasingly to Honduras, partly because Costa Rican democracy offered less suitable conditions for clandestine operations and partly because the anti-Sandinista rebels who used Costa Rica as their base lacked the steady U.S. support given the Contras based in

Costa Rica

Honduras. Even so, the conflict in Nicaragua indirectly menaced the stability of Costa Rica by creating an unwonted level of ideological polarization in a country generally characterized, since 1948, by political consensus. In the presidential elections of 1986, the Costa Rican right lost by a narrow margin, and Arias, the winning candidate, set out immediately to promote the peace plan that eventually merited him a Nobel prize.

Honduras suffered much worse political polarization as a result of its proximity to the Nicaraguan conflict. Although the radical left had never been strong in Honduras, the country nevertheless became the scene of right-wing death squads of the kind deployed against revolutionary mobilization in El Salvador and Guatemala. The conversion of Honduras into a base for massive U.S. military operations had the greatest impact of all. The Honduran army supported this development with notable enthusiasm, and the civilian authorities, who had recovered control of the government from the military only in 1981, dared not stand in the way. The U.S. military presence offered very tangible economic benefits to the Honduran officer corps and to other select groups, and though the effect on Honduran society as a whole was not wholly positive, this poorest of Central American countries had few promising economic alternatives. As a result, the U.S. embassy in Honduras recovered the proconsular influence of an earlier period in partnership with the Honduran army, with whom U.S. officials often preferred to deal directly, while the constitutional government came to seem more and more irrelevant. In the late 1980s, the Honduran government regarded the unfolding peace process with considerable ambivalence, and not solely because of its natural reluctance to antagonize the United States. In addition, the Hondurans feared that a negotiated settlement might leave the well-armed Contra army stranded indefinitely in Honduras, where it would be a match, in many ways, for the forces of the government.

Panama was one more site of the Reagan administration's attempt to reaffirm U.S. hegemony over the Caribbean and Central America. During the 1970s, Gen. Omar Torrijos had worked to create a popular base for rule by the country's National Guard. Late in the decade, after securing a favorable treaty with the United States that promised to return to Panamanian sovereignty control of the canal and its surrounding zone, Torrijos felt confident enough to offer freer rein to the opposition parties. Torrijos's death in a helicopter accident left this project of political liberalization in the hands of the new national guard commander, Gen. Manuel Noriega, who turned it into something of a parody. Noriega continued the populism of his predecessor, though in a cruder vein, and he also sought to maintain the balancing act implied by diplomatic nonalignment in a tiny country situated at a crossroads of international activity. Specialization in financial and commercial services difficult to obtain in more strictly regulated environments created huge opportunities for corruption in Panama, and that corruption had worsened under the rule of the national guard. Noriega took it to new heights—most notably through his participation in the benefits of Panama's privileged position in the international *Noriega* drug trade.

Under Noriega, Panama became, almost openly, a busy entrepôt and center of financial operations for drug traffickers. The Panamanian opposition made this transformation a central point of contention, and tensions increased in 1984 when one of their most vigorous spokespersons, Hugo Spadafora, was murdered in circumstances that only the Noriega government claimed to find mysterious. From that point on, political opposition among the country's professionals and entrepreneurs, who suffered particularly from the unequal competition of Noriega's inner circle, grew steadily. In 1987, Panama appeared ripe for the sort of democratizing process that the Reagan administration had regarded with skepticism earlier in the decade. In this case, though, such an initiative held attractions for groups across the political spectrum in the United States. The far right yearned for confrontations that might modify the U.S. commitment to withdrawal under the 1978 canal treaty, and the entire Republican party could celebrate the downfall of a Caribbean government that maintained cordial relations with Cuba. As for the Democrats, they welcomed an opportunity to call attention to Noriega's role as an erstwhile ally of the Republican administration and hoped to further explore his role in illegal arms shipments to the Contras. Finally, the new prominence of drug-related problems in U.S. cities infused the crusade against Noriega with a moral righteousness satisfactory to all.

However, neither the unanimous repudiation of U.S. public opinion nor the charge of drug smuggling leveled by the U.S. Department of Justice seemed to impress General Noriega, and efforts to dislodge him by Panamanian president Arturo del Valle led to the destitution of del Valle instead of Noriega. Del Valle hoped to recover his presidency through the support of the U.S. government, which continued to recognize him as Panama's legitimate leader. In an attempt to oust Noriega, the United States began a commercial and financial blockade with predictably devastating effects in a country that used the U.S.

dollar as its official currency. Unfortunately for the anti-Noriega forces, however, the blockade proved most injurious to the economic interests of the opposition, strongly based in the country's entrepreneurs, merchants, and financiers. As the 1980s drew to a close, U.S. hegemony in Latin America had encountered another small but stubborn obstacle.

THIS END POINT to a survey of two centuries suggests a desperate immutability underlying the dizzying superficial variations, a view of Latin American history close to the one persuasively crafted by the practitioners of "magical realism." The enduring ravages of the current economic crisis, more prolonged and bitter than the depression of the 1930s, can only intensify that fatalistic mood. Nevertheless, the Latin America of today is not that of a century—or even a decade—ago. In the short lapse since the completion of the manuscript for this new edition, the region has continued to undergo changes that in fact reach deep below the surface. Some unavoidably tentative suggestions on the current direction of these changes constitute the only fitting conclusion for a contemporary history of Latin America.

As always, the influence of the core areas of the world economy has been decisive. Developments within Latin America appear essentially reactive, although (perhaps owing to the bitter lessons of the recent past) the reactions have increasingly taken the form of adaptation rather than resistance. This is very much the case in economic matters, as the hopes placed for so many years on the prospect of self-sufficient development have been abandoned. Latin American countries are now eager to establish closer links with the international economy, but the return to strategies that stress comparative advantages in the world market has been frequently blocked. While the solutions proposed in the 1940s and 1950s by the Prebisch school proved elusive, the problems caused by the diminished dynamism of the primary-export model are still very much in existence. In addition, the search for new solutions to the old dilemma is made more difficult by a permanent state of flux in the international economy itself.

The international scene did not appear promising even before the spontaneous breakdown of eastern Europe's socialist system made matters worse. In the late 1980s, the countries of western Europe enjoined Latin America to open its economy while they protected their own producers, and even those of former colonies, against Latin American competition. The United States, an even more enthusiastic crusader for free trade, used the protectionism of the European Community to justify its own. Japan, for its part, hardly appeared ready to abandon its selective, but frequently extreme, protectionist policies. This time, the industrialized nations had no need to fear the demands for reciprocity and eventual reprisals that had been possible in the 1930s. As the creditors with whom debt-burdened Latin America had to seek repeated concessions to avoid bankruptcy, they enjoyed an overwhelmingly advantageous bargaining position on trade matters.

In the early 1990s, the debt crisis has become less acute. This has occurred partly through renegotiation and limited repayment and partly through the lending institutions' gradual shifting of bad loans from the credit to the debit column in their internal bookkeeping. The time bomb threatening the stability of the world banking system has thus been defused, but a heavy burden remains on Latin American economies. The legacy of the crisis is aggravated by the inability of Latin American countries to find an adequate niche in the international trading system, and the wave of economic instability that currently threatens to engulf the world's developed economies makes the search almost pointless. Latin American leaders simply cannot know into what world economic order they must strive to integrate their countries.

Is the world economy moving toward ever closer unification? Or can we expect a division into rival trading blocks corresponding to three superstates, as envisioned by George Orwell in *1984*? As a third alternative, are we perhaps returning to a strongly national framework with results that, while disastrous for the world economy as a whole, may not be equally detrimental to all Latin American countries? Despite accumulating evidence of severe tensions in the process of economic unification, the overall logic of recent developments still favors it. Having set their course in that direction, Latin American leaders can only gamble that there will be no return to a strictly national economic focus. They well know that, despite the crucial importance of these developments to Latin America, the region can exert but little influence on the larger course of events.

As usual, the changes in the world political context join their effects to those of the current economic turbulence. With the sole exception of U.S. policy toward Cuba, the end of the cold war has removed the framework that for decades defined the relationship between Latin America and the United States. Paradoxically, the breakdown of the socialist system in eastern Europe, by allowing the United States to exercise influence more broadly, may lessen the weight (though not the effectiveness) of its hegemony over Latin America. As the 1991 Persian Gulf War illustrated, Latin America is no longer the only area of the world where the United States can, without fear of reprisals, demonstrate its political resolve through military force. Consequently, the U.S. government may exercise more tolerance toward the smaller threats to its interests within the Western Hemisphere, and, now that the United Nations has become a reliable instrument of U.S. policy, the world's remaining great power may show more forbearance for the rather formalistic gestures toward diplomatic independence in which the Organization of American States occasionally indulges. This does not preclude U.S. interventions such as the recent one in Panama, which, by capturing Gen. Manuel Noriega (and randomly killing a large number of innocent Panamanian bystanders), removed what had become a serious embarrassment to Washington, D.C. Notwithstanding occasional backsliding, however, U.S. policymakers have favored a peaceful solution to the protracted civil war in El Salvador and have accepted with comparative good grace Nicaraguan president Violeta Chamorro's policies of national reconciliation, under which the Sandinistas have retained significant influence. Of course, the progress toward peace in Central America also came from the forces of the left, as the spectacular collapse of Soviet and Eastern European socialism decisively sapped their will to win and "Victory or Death" no longer seemed the only alternatives.

Relations between north and south may now escape the bleak and predictable rut of the past decades, though the new developments in that relationship will not necessarily be harmonious. In facing future conflicts, Latin America will not be as defenseless as its current predicament would appear to indicate. Although the United States has risen by default to the position of sole political and military superpower, that lofty status has done little to slow the gradual but steady deterioration of its position in the world economy. Only a radical reformulation of economic policy can detain this alarming trend, and it is revealing that, upon awakening from a decade of complacent inaction in this regard, a deeply conservative U.S. administration pinned its hopes for revitalization on a free-trade agreement including Canada and Mexico, despite evidence that some negative effects will be felt in the United States. To minimize the prospects of a negative impact in the United States, proponents of the free-trade agreement are fond of pointing out that the U.S. economy dwarfs Mexico's. Since 1900, however, the population of Mexico has risen from less than a fifth to almost a third that of the United States, and that upward trend will continue in the foreseeable future.

We glimpse here one of the manifold consequences of the demographic explosion that, although finally contained in the larger Latin American countries, will level off only at roughly double the present population of the region. Population growth is, without doubt, the most important internal factor in Latin America's future development. In 1950, the populations of Latin and Anglo-America were roughly equal, but the former now outnumbers the latter by almost two to one. A rate of growth exceeded, in recent decades, only in sub-Saharan Africa holds obvious dangers for the future, but it has not so far appeared to be an obstacle to economic growth. To the contrary, the economic expansion of all major Latin American countries has far outstripped population growth in the period since World War II. While their populations have doubled, tripled, or almost quadrupled, their economies have grown ten-, twenty-, or thirty-fold. In the 1980s, Mexico's per capita gross national product (GNP) is sixteen times what it was in the 1940s, and the corresponding figures for Brazil and Argentina have increased by multiples of ten and eight, respectively. The populations of Colombia and Peru are three times larger than in the 1940s; their per capita GNP, eighteen times greater. Growth of both kinds has changed the relative weight of Latin America in global affairs. The debt crisis of the 1980s, for example, attracted worldwide attention less because of its effects at home than because of its sheer magnitude and its potential to disrupt the international financial system. Similarly, Latin America has always been Catholic, but now the majority of the world's Catholics are Latin American. Within the United States, President Ronald Reagan began to feature teeming masses of prolific, brown-skinned refugees to the United States among the most dreadful prospective consequences of the revolutionary menace in Central America.

Demographic growth is also shifting the centers of economic dynamism and the relationships among social groups within the region. Brazil and Mexico have acquired the scale necessary for fully integrated industrial development, the elusive goal set by developmentalists in so many Latin American countries just after World War II. Aside from these two giants, however, other former economic leaders of the region, particularly Argentina, find that goal more remote than ever. The countries in the vanguard of Latin American economic expansion during the first century of independence have, in general, lost ground to those whose economies dominated the late colonial scene. Mexico City's recovery of first place among the hemisphere's urban centers symbolizes that reversion. In addition, Indian populations, decimated by European invasion in the sixteenth century and gradually recovering since the late eighteenth, are at last breaking down the barriers that marginalized them. The effects vary greatly according to national context—from the quiet transformation of the Peruvian capital into an Andean metropolis, to the always decisive participation of Indian peasants in the shifting coalitions of postrevolutionary Bolivia, to the tragedy of Guatemala, where the heirs of the conquerors have responded to indigenous initiatives with another wave of conquest and subjugation as savage as the first.

Here is no simple reversion to the past but rather a complex and innovative interweaving of many disparate elements of Latin America's heritage as the region faces the challenges of the present and the future. Andean miners continue to recognize the mountain spirits placated by their ancestors for four centuries while giving firm loyalty to their Trotskyite labor union, and Andean peasants graft similarly modern ideologies onto community social structures of pre-Columbian origin, reforged in the fires of the colonial experience. It is in Latin American cities where the ambiguous articulation of past and present may be best observed. In the 1980s, the process of urbanization no longer promises to reduce Latin America to a generic modernity indistinguishable from European or North American models. The rural origins of so many of Latin America's city dwellers decisively affect their political perceptions (formed in a strongly authoritarian and paternalistic context) and their social strategies (powerfully structured by family and group solidarities), as well as their struggle for a livelihood (populating poor neighborhoods with domestic animals by the thousands). Recent hard times saw a huge growth in the informal sectors that, in cities like Lima, for example, account for a very significant portion of economic activity.

These developments of the late twentieth century do not point to the emergence of a definitive social and cultural profile. Latin America is still young and unpredictable. On the other hand, they do suggest that, whatever the region's future, the road there will run not through predetermined, universally valid stages of development, but rather along the zigzagging path of Latin America's incongruent and contradictory historical experience. In retrospect, the naive promises of definitive solutions to the region's historical dilemmas, repeatedly announced during recent decades, serve as a warning that the next bend in the road is unlikely to be the last. Truly, no future course can be clearly charted, for the line of advance cannot be less enigmatic than the vast interior forces that create it.

GENERAL WORKS

Several college primers go beyond their pedagogic task to offer thoughtful and well-structured general views of the history of Latin America. They are Benjamin Keen, *A History of Latin America* (Boston, 1992), and Thomas E. Skidmore and Peter H. Smith, *Modern Latin America* (New York, 1984). A multivolume history that will no doubt continue serving as a source of authoritative information and interpretations for some time in the future is Leslie Bethell, ed., *The Cambridge History of Latin America*, 7 vols. to date (London, 1984–91). Among the few books that cover the whole span of Latin American history for specific subjects is Nicolás Sánchez-Albornoz, *The Population of Latin America: A History* (Berkeley, 1974).

NATIONAL HISTORIES

Until a few decades ago, histories of specific Latin American nations available in English were mostly translations of books written for high school use in the respective countries. More recently, the Latin American Histories Series published by Oxford University Press has included some truly distinguished national histories, among them Herbert S. Klein, *Bolivia: The Evolution of a Multi-Ethnic Society* (New York, 1982); John V. Lombardi, *Venezuela: The Search for Order, the Dream of Progress* (New York, 1982); Brian Loveman, *Chile: The Legacy of Hispanic Capitalism*, 2d ed. (New York, 1988); and Louis A. Pérez, Jr., *Cuba between Reform and Revolution* (New York, 1988). Not included in the series, but worth mentioning, is David Rock, *Argentina, 1516–1982: From Spanish Colonization to the Falklands War* (Berkeley, 1985).

INTERPRETATIVE STUDIES

Both Stanley J. Stein and Barbara Stein, *The Colonial Heritage of Latin America: Essays on Economic Dependence in Perspective* (New York, 1970), and Richard M. Morse, *El espejo de Próspero* (Mexico City, 1982), develop in novel ways viewpoints rooted in the long and far from constantly happy common historical experience of Latin and Anglo-America.

David Brading's massive *The First America: The Spanish Monarchy, Creole Patriots and the Liberal State, 1492–1866* (Cambridge, 1991), offers a fascinating and richly detailed overview of the trajectory of Spanish American ideas and ideologies from the conquest to the rise of mid-nineteenth-century liberalism.

During the vogue of dependency theory, two books won ample popularity. André Gunder Frank, *Capitalism and Underdevelopment in Latin America: Their History in Chile and Brazil* (New York, 1966), which provides the ideological and conceptual framework for the more anecdotal and highly popular *Open Veins of Latin America: Five Centuries of the Pillage of a Continent* (New York, 1973) by Uruguayan Eduardo Galeano, and has aged less well than Fernando Henrique Cardoso and Enzo Faletto's more nuanced and historically aware *Dependencia y Desarrollo en América Latina* (Mexico, 1971), translated as *Dependency and Development in Latin America* (Berkeley, 1979). Cardoso and Faletto's work as well as Celso Furtado, *A economia latino-americana (formacão histórica e problemas contemporâneos)* (Rio de Janeiro, 1969), translated as *Development of Latin America: Historical Background and Contemporary Problems* (London, 1970), reflect the influence of the structuralist approach to Latin American economic problems developed by the United Nations Economic Commission for Latin America under its first chairman, the Argentine economist Raúl Prebisch. From an independent position, Albert Hirschman has provided extremely acute analyses and comments on Latin American economic issues and policies. See especially *Journeys towards Progress: Studies of Economic Policy-Making in Latin America* (New York, 1963).

The recent wave of authoritarian repressive regimes inspired the ambitious global interpretation of the Latin American historical experience argued by the Chilean Claudio Véliz in *The Centralist Tradition in Latin America* (Princeton, 1980).

The Colonial Legacy

More than a quarter century after its publication, Charles Gibson, *Spain in America* (New York, 1966), still provides the best general introduction to the colonial experience in Spanish America. C. R. Boxer, *The Portuguese Seaborne Empire, 1415–1825* (London, 1969), which places the Brazilian colonial experience within the framework provided by Portuguese expansion, is now complemented by James Lockhart and Stuart B. Schwartz, *Early Latin America: A History of Colonial Spanish America and Brazil* (London, 1983), which explores in novel ways the commonalities between Spanish and Portuguese colonization in the Americas.

While much innovative work is currently being done on the early and mid-colonial decades, it only exceptionally offers insights relevant to the history of postindependence Latin America. Specific studies covering the whole span from conquest to independence are still comparatively rare. Among them, Charles Gibson, *The Aztecs under Spanish Rule: A History of the Indians of the Valley of Mexico, 1519–1810* (Stanford, 1964), still takes pride of place. More recent works with a similarly ambitious chronological scope include Nancy M. Farriss, *Maya Society under Colonial Rule: The Collective Enterprise of Survival* (Princeton, 1984); Stuart B. Schwartz, *Sugar Plantations in the Formation of Brazilian Society: Bahia, 1550–1835* (Cambridge, 1985); and Brooke Larson, *Colonialism and Agrarian Transformation in Bolivia: Cochabamba, 1550–1900* (Princeton, 1988).

Many students of the late colonial era either implicitly or explicitly consider the connection with the following revolutionary cycle. This is the case with most studies of the Spanish imperial reforms in the second half of the eighteenth century, including Mark A. Burkholder and D. S. Chandler, *From Impotence to Authority: The Spanish Crown and the American Audiencias, 1687–1808* (Columbia, Miss., 1977), as well as the following works. Two monographs on the impact of the introduction of intendencies in specific viceroyalties are John Lynch, *Spanish Colonial Administration, 1782–1810: The Intendant System in the Viceroyalty of the River Plate* (London, 1958), and J. R. Fisher, *Government and Society in Colonial Peru: The Intendant System, 1784–1814* (London, 1970). Studies on the military aspects of the reform include Lyle N. McAlister, *The "Fuero Militar" in New Spain* (Gainesville, 1952), and Leon Campbell, *The Military and Society in Colonial Peru, 1750–1810* (Philadelphia, 1978). The local impact of the reforms is examined in Brian R. Hamnett, *Politics and Trade in Southern Mexico, 1750–1821* (Cambridge, 1971), and the rebellions that greeted them, in John L. Phelan, *The People and the King: The Comunero Revolution in Colombia, 1781* (Madison, 1978), and Steve J. Stern, ed., *Resistance, Rebellion and Consciousness in the Andean Peasant World, 18th to 20th Centuries* (Madison, 1987). David Brading's two influential studies of Bourbon Mexico, *Miners and Merchants in Bourbon Mexico, 1763–1810* (Cambridge, 1971), and *Haciendas and Ranchos in the Mexican Bajío: León, 1700–1860* (Cambridge, 1978), both offer much more than their titles suggest.

For Brazil, Dauril Alden, *Royal Government in Colonial Brazil, with Special Reference to the Administration of the Marquis of Lavradio, Viceroy, 1769–1779* (Berkeley, 1968), concentrates on a crucial decade of the reform era, while Kenneth R. Maxwell, *Conflicts and Conspiracies: Brazil and Portugal, 1750–1808* (Cambridge, 1973), achieves an exceptionally complex and subtle presentation of the interplay between metropolitan initiatives and colonial reactions.

From Independence to 1850

John Lynch, *The Spanish-American Revolutions, 1808–1826* (New York, 1973), offers a comprehensive narrative of the revolutionary process and a judicious discussion of its historical roots and assessment of its consequences. David Bushnell and Neill Macaulay, *The Emergence of Latin America in the Nineteenth Century* (New York, 1988), provides a well-organized overview of the nineteenth-century efforts to create a new political and social order in both Spanish America and Brazil, from the immediate aftermath of the emancipation struggle to the heyday of liberalism in the 1880s. Emilia Viotti da Costa, *The Brazilian Empire: Myths and Histories* (Chicago, 1985), reviews the core issues of the period in Brazil with a decidedly more skeptical eye, while Tulio Halperín Donghi, *The Aftermath of Revolution in Latin America* (New York, 1973), notwithstanding the title, restricts its coverage to Spanish America until mid-century. The early attempts at postwar reconstruction are thoroughly explored for Gran Colombia in David Bushnell, *The Santander Regime in Gran Colombia* (Newark, Del., 1954), and more succinctly for Bolivia in William Lofstrom, *The Promise and Problems of Reform: Attempted Social and Economic Change in the First Years of Bolivian Independence* (Ithaca, 1972). Charles Hale, *Mexican Liberalism in the Age of Mora, 1821–1853* (New Haven, 1968), offers a lucid analytical presentation of the ideological climate during the postindependence decades in Mexico that provides clues for parallel developments in the rest of Spanish America. Also useful is Simon Collier, *Ideas and Politics of Chilean Independence, 1808–1833* (Cambridge, 1967). A very successful synthesis on the subject for Spanish America can be found in Frank Safford, "Politics, Ideology and Society," in Bethell, *Cambridge History of Latin America*, vol. 3. Not surprisingly, state and institution building in the postindependence era is better explored for Brazil than for Spanish America. See Fernando Uricoechea, *The Patrimonial Foundations of the Brazilian Bureaucratic State* (Berkeley, 1980), and Thomas Flory, *Judge and Jury in Imperial Brazil, 1808–1871: Social Control and Political Stability in the New State* (Austin, 1981). In Spanish America, glimpses of the haphazard progress of state building and institutionalization can be gleaned mostly from studies in political history and even political biographies, such as John Lynch's admirable *Argentine Dictator: Juan Manuel de Rosas, 1829–1852* (Oxford, 1981). Carlos Marichal, *A Century of Debt Crises in Latin America: From Independence to the Great Depression, 1820–1930* (Princeton, 1989), deals with an issue that reached a critical stage for the first time in this period.

In the new international context created for Latin America after the breakdown of the Iberian empires, the all-important British link has been studied mostly in its economic dimension in D. C. M. Platt, *Latin America and British Trade, 1806–1914* (London, 1973), which, however, adopts a decidedly British perspective. H. S. Ferns develops a less narrow approach in *Britain and Argentina in the Nineteenth Century* (Oxford, 1960), which offers abundant information on the first half of the century, while Alan K. Manchester, *British Preeminence in Brazil: Its Rise and Decline* (Chapel Hill, 1933), puts its emphasis on political history. On British investment, the brief and purely descriptive presentation in J. Fred Rippy, *British Investments in Latin America, 1822–1949* (Minneapolis, 1959), is still useful. The political connection with the United States, which became decisive only late in the nineteenth century, has been explored from early in the century in A. P. Whitaker, *The United States and the Independence of Latin America, 1800–1830* (Baltimore, 1941), and Dexter Perkins, *A History of the Monroe Doctrine*, rev. ed. (Boston, 1963).

For this period, the study of the economy is closely linked with that of economic policies. For Argentina, see Myron Burgin, *The Economic Aspects of Argentine Federalism, 1820–1852* (Cambridge, Mass., 1946), which offers many still-valid insights on the political impact of economic antagonisms. Paul Gootenberg's more recent *Between Silver and Guano: Commercial Policy and the State in Post-Independence Peru* (Princeton, 1989), an exploration of the manifold vernacular roots of the trend toward free-trade policies, is rich in suggestions equally relevant to other Latin American areas. The best general presentation of Cuba's separate path of economic growth can be found in Manuel Moreno Fraginals' masterwork, *The Sugarmill: The Socioeconomic Complex of Sugar in Cuba, 1760–1860* (New York, 1976). Franklin W. Knight, *Slave Society in Cuba during the Nineteenth Century* (Madison, 1970), and Hugh Thomas, *Cuba or the Pursuit of Freedom* (London, 1971), which, while concentrating on the republican period, also covers the early and mid-nineteenth century, should also be mentioned.

While most studies of social conflict in the countryside concentrate on later periods, John Tutino, *From Insurrection to Revolution in Mexico: Social Bases of Agrarian Violence, 1750–1940* (Princeton, 1986), explores the successive stages of social decompression and compression during the whole century from the Hidalgo insurrection to the Mexican Revolution.

THE NEOCOLONIAL ORDER

William P. Glade, "Latin America and the International Economy, 1870–1914," in Bethell, *Cambridge History of Latin America*, vol. 4, offers a powerfully structured and richly detailed synthesis of economic change during the heyday of the export economies, and in the same volume, Rosemary Thorp, "Latin America and the World Economy from the First World War to the World Depression," stresses the often-ignored signs of exhaustion of most export economies in the 1920s. Roberto Cortés Conde, *The First Stages of Modernization in Latin America* (New York, 1973), explores several national experiences. Roberto Cortés Conde and Stanley J. Stein, eds., *Latin America: A Guide to Economic History, 1830–1930* (Berkeley, 1977), offers bibliographies, preceded by introductory essays, for Argentina, Brazil, Chile, Colombia, Mexico, and Peru and is complemented by Roberto Cortés Conde and Shane Hunt, eds., *The Latin American Economies: Growth and the Export Sector, 1880–1930* (New York, 1985), a collection of essays on some central episodes and issues. Among the few national economic histories covering the period that are available in English, see William Paul McGreevey, *An Economic History of Colombia, 1845–1930* (Cambridge, 1971), and Markos J. Mamalakis, *The Growth and Structure of the Chilean Economy from Independence to Allende* (New Haven, 1976). Carlos Diaz-Alejandro, *Essays in the Economic History of the Argentine Republic* (New Haven, 1970), and Rosemary Thorp and Geoffrey Bertram, *Peru, 1890–1977: Growth and Policy in an Open Economy* (New York, 1978), emphasize issues of economic policy and continue their exploration into more recent times.

The social impact of the development of primary sectors serving the overseas or national market offers the main theme for a vast and growing literature. While no satisfactory general overview of the process in Porfirian Mexico is available in English, John Coatsworth's innovative and original *Growth against Development: The Economic Impact of Railroads in Porfirian Mexico* (De Kalb, Ill., 1981), deals with an essential aspect of it, and several monographs have begun to explore the process in a regional framework, among them Mark Wasserman, *Capitalists, Caciques and Revolution: The Native Elite and Foreign Enterprise in Chihuahua, Mexico, 1854–1911* (Chapel Hill, 1984), and Allen Wells, *Yucatán's Golden Age: Haciendas, Henequen and International Harvester* (Albuquerque, 1985). David J. McCreery offers more than what the title suggests in *Development and the State in Reforma Guatemala* (Athens, Ohio, 1983). For El Salvador, the process is presented from a geographical perspective in David Browning, *El Salvador: Landscape and Society* (Oxford, 1971), and from that of economic history in Héctor Lindo Fuentes, *Weak Foundations: The Economy of El Salvador in the Nineteenth Century* (Berkeley, 1990). Marco Palacios, *Coffee in Colombia, 1850–1970: An Economic, Social and Political History* (Cambridge, 1980), and Catherine Le-Grand, *Frontier Expansion and Peasant Protest in Colombia* (Albuquerque, 1986), explore similar changes in Colombia, while William Roseberry, *Coffee and Capitalism in the Venezuelan Andes* (Austin, 1984), treats the subject in Venezuela. In *Plantation Agriculture and Social Control in Northern Peru, 1875–1933* (Austin, 1985), Michael J. Gonzales offers a detailed and lucid analysis of the rise and transformation of plantation society in coastal Peru, while Florencia E. Mallon, *The Defense of Community in Peru's Central Highlands: Peasant Struggle and Capitalist Transition, 1860–1940* (Princeton, 1983), provides a methodologically and conceptually ambitious presentation of the survival and transformation of the peasant community under the impact of capitalist inroads. For Bolivia, besides the relevant sections of Brooke Larson's work mentioned above, see Erick D. Langer, *Economic Change and Rural Resistance in Southern Bolivia, 1880–1930* (Stanford, 1989). Arnold J. Bauer, *Chilean Rural Society from the Spanish Conquest to 1930* (Cambridge, 1975), concentrates on the period opened by the brief agricultural export boom of the mid-nineteenth century. For Argentina, Hilda Sabato, *Agrarian Capitalism and the World Market: Buenos Aires in the Pastoral Age, 1840–1890* (Albuquerque, 1990), has joined James R. Scobie, *Revolution in the Pampas: A Social History of Argentine Wheat, 1860–1910* (Austin, 1964), among the few studies on the Argentine agricultural export economy available in English. For Brazil's coffee economy, see Stanley J. Stein, *Vassouras: A Brazilian Coffee County, 1850–1900* (Cambridge, 1957), and the following studies that reach the postemancipation period: Warren Dean, *Rio Claro: A Brazilian Plantation System, 1820–1920* (Stanford, 1976), and Thomas H. Holloway, *Immigrants on the Land: Coffee and Society in São Paulo, 1886–1934* (Chapel Hill, 1980). In *The Amazon Rubber Boom, 1850–1920* (Stanford, 1983), Barbara Weinstein studies the atypical social changes unleashed in the Amazon by the short-lived rubber boom, and in *The Sugar Industry in Pernambuco, 1840–1910: Modernization without Change* (Berkeley, 1974), Peter L. Eisenberg examines the survival of an old export economy during the era of export-induced growth.

In Brazil as well as in Cuba, the vicissitudes of plantation economies were of course closely linked with those of the crisis of slavery as an institution, starting with the gradual strangulation of the slave trade and concluding with abolition. For Brazil, see Leslie Bethell, *The Abolition of the Brazilian Slave Trade: Britain, Brazil and the Slave Trade Question, 1807–1869* (Cambridge, 1970), and Robert Conrad, *The Destruction of Brazilian Slavery, 1850–1888* (Berkeley, 1972). For Cuba, David Murray, *Odious Commerce: Britain, Spain and the Abolition of the Cuban Slave Trade* (Cambridge, 1980), and Rebecca J. Scott, *Slave Emancipation in Cuba: The Transition to Free Labor, 1860–1899* (Princeton, 1985), cover similar subjects.

Recent studies have shown that in country after country, against received wisdom, primary-export-based expansion did not preclude some significant measure of industrialization. After Stanley J. Stein's pioneering *The Brazilian Cotton Manufacture: Textile Enterprise in an Underdeveloped Area, 1850–1950* (Cambridge, Mass., 1957), Warren Dean returned to the subject in *The Industrialization of São Paulo, 1880–1945* (Austin, 1969). Henry W. Kirsch explored the subject for Chile in *Industrial Development in a Traditional Society: The Conflict of Entrepreneurship and Modernization in Chile* (Gainesville, 1977), and Stephen H. Haber did the same for Mexico in *Industry and Underdevelopment: The Industrialization of Mexico, 1890–1940* (Stanford, 1989).

While this was a period of significant urbanization, studies in urban history are still scarce. See Richard Morse's classic *From Community to Metropolis: A Biography of São Paulo* (Gainesville, 1958) and James R. Scobie's *Buenos Aires: Plaza to Suburb, 1870–1910* (New York, 1970).

Leopoldo Zea portrays the ideological climate of the period in *The Latin American Mind* (Norman, Okla., 1963), which provides concise presentations of influential intellectual figures in the transition from romanticism to positivism in Spanish America. João Cruz Costa follows the same transition for

Brazil in *A History of Ideas in Brazil* (Berkeley, 1964), while Richard Graham, *Britain and the Onset of Modernization in Brazil, 1850–1914* (Cambridge, 1968), is rich in suggestive insights on the same subject. Frank Safford subtly explores one of the avenues of this transition in Colombia in *The Ideal of the Practical: Colombia's Struggle to Form a Technical Elite* (Austin, 1976). In *The Transformation of Liberalism in Late Nineteenth-Century Mexico* (Princeton, 1990), Charles Hale offers insights valid beyond Mexico.

The political aspects of the process are also unevenly and, on the whole, skimpily covered in recent historiography. For Mexico, Laurens Ballard Perry, *Juárez and Díaz: Machine Politics in Mexico* (De Kalb, Ill., 1978), follows the rise in the restored republic of political uses later systematized by the Porfiriato. For Colombia's intricate political history, see Helen Delpar, *Red against Blue: The Liberal Party in Colombian Politics* (University, Ala., 1981); James W. Park, *Rafael Núñez and the Politics of Colombian Regionalism, 1863–1886* (Baton Rouge, 1985); and Charles Bergquist, *Coffee and Conflict in Colombia, 1866–1910* (Durham, 1978). Chile's difficult political transitions are the subject of Maurice Zeitlin's controversial *The Civil Wars in Chile (or the Bourgeois Revolutions That Never Were)* (Princeton, 1984). Political and other dimensions in the agony of Spanish Cuba are the subject of Louis A. Pérez, *Cuba between Empires, 1878–1902* (Pittsburgh, 1982). For Brazil, the most important studies have dealt with regional politics within the loose federal framework of the old republic. Among others, Joseph L. Love, *Rio Grande do Sul and Brazilian Regionalism, 1882–1930* (Stanford, 1971), offers as an introduction a masterly analysis of the political system at the federal level, and Linda Lewin, *Politics and Parentela in Paraíba: A Case Study of Family-Based Oligarchy in Brazil* (Princeton, 1987), brilliantly reconstructs the social roots of local politics. Two studies explore the political impact of messianic movements: Ralph della Cava, *Miracle at Joaseiro* (New York, 1970), which examines the movement that under the leadership of Father Cicero achieved a successful integration into the local and national political network, and Robert M. Levine, *Vale of Tears: Revisiting the Canudos Massacre in Northeastern Brazil, 1893–1897* (Berkeley, 1992), which reviews another movement that conspicuously failed at such an integration.

For Spanish America, the available studies deal mostly with the democratizing processes of the twentieth century, starting with the Mexican Revolution, for which we now have a superb narrative and analytical presentation in Alan Knight, *The Mexican Revolution* (Cambridge, 1986). Friedrich Katz, *The Secret War in Mexico: Europe, the United States and the Mexican Revolution* (Chicago, 1981), provides not only a thorough study of the revolution but also a pioneering exploration of the social context for the rise of the rival revolutionary factions. John Womack, Jr., *Zapata and the Mexican Revolution* (New York, 1968), is a sympathetic biography of the most significant agrarian leader, and David Brading, ed., *Caudillo and Peasant in the Mexican Revolution* (Cambridge, 1980), gathers excellent contributions on the agrarian dimension of the revolution, examined in a regional framework. For the religious conflict in the 1920s, see Jean A. Meyer, *The Cristero Rebellion: The Mexican People between Church and State, 1926–1929* (Cambridge, 1973).

For Uruguay, see Milton I. Vanger, *José Batlle y Ordóñez of Uruguay: The Creator of His Times, 1902–1907* (Cambridge, Mass., 1963) and *The Model Country: José Batlle y Ordóñez of Uruguay, 1907–1915* (Hanover, N.H., 1980), and Göran Lindahl, *Uruguay's New Path* (Stockholm, 1963), which describes the new political balance that emerged after the 1916 constitutional reform. For Argentina, see David Rock, *Politics in Argentina, 1890–1930: The Rise and Fall of Radicalism* (Cambridge, 1975). For Peru, see Peter F. Klarén, *Modernization, Dislocation and Aprismo: Origins of the Peruvian Aprista Party, 1870–1932* (Austin, 1973).

The history of labor and the trade union movement has been even more unevenly covered. Hobart A. Spalding, Jr., *Organized Labor in Latin America: Historical Case Studies of Urban Workers in Dependent Societies* (New York, 1977), is more focused on the early stages of labor organization, for which it offers abundant information, than the more ambitious contributions in Charles Bergquist, *Labor in Latin America: Comparative Essays on Chile, Argentina, Venezuela and Colombia* (Stanford, 1986), and Ruth B. Collier and David Collier, *Shaping the Political Arena: Critical Junctures, the Labor Movement, and Regime Dynamics in Latin America* (Princeton, 1991), a political science study grounded on a painstaking historical reconstruction of national experiences. Among the few studies that deal with single countries are Ramón E. Ruiz, *Labor and the Ambivalent Revolutionaries: Mexico, 1911–1923* (Baltimore, 1976), and Peter De Shazo, *Urban Workers and Labor Unions in Chile, 1902–1927* (Madison, 1983).

Finally, the study of the external relations of Latin America and the gravitation of powers is more developed concerning the political-diplomatic dimension than the economic dimension, on which most of the available information is to be gleaned from studies that do not share an international focus. Most of the literature on international relations focuses on the actions of the outside powers, among which, of course, the United States soon wins pride of place. Among them are Lester D. Langley, *Struggle for the American Mediterranean: United States–European Rivalry in the Gulf-Caribbean, 1776–1904* (Athens, Ga., 1976) and *The United States and the Caribbean in the Twentieth Century* (Athens, Ga., 1982). See also works dealing with a single country or episode, such as Otis Singletary, *The Mexican War* (Chicago, 1960), and studies of episodes of U.S. intervention in and occupation of Caribbean countries, such as Bruce J. Calder, *The Impact of Intervention: The Dominican Republic during the U.S. Occupation of 1916–1924* (Austin, 1988). Studies that bring to the theme a Latin American perspective include Thomas F. McGann, *Argentina, the United States and the Inter-American System, 1880–1914* (Cambridge, Mass., 1957); E. Bradford Burns, *The Unwritten Alliance: Rio Branco and Brazilian-American Relations* (New York, 1966); and Robert N. Burr, *By Reason or Force: Chile and the Balancing of Power in South America* (Berkeley, 1965).

AFTER 1930

For more recent times, the growing complexity and contemporary relevance of the issues have favored, side by side with a proliferation of studies at the national and even subnational level, an explosive growth of research projects on trends of change in a Pan–Latin American framework, in which the contributions of other disciplines besides history become more important than for the earlier postindependence period. Among the latter, it is only in the study of international relations (concentrated more and more on relations between Latin America and the United States) that the historical approach appears still dominant. This is the case in Bryce Wood's classic studies, *The Making of the Good Neighbor Policy* (New York, 1961) and *The Dismantling of the Good Neighbor Policy* (Austin, 1986), and in David Green, *The Containment of Latin America: A History of the Myths and Realities of the Good Neighbor Policy* (Chicago, 1971), which is as critical as the title suggests of the motivations and results of that policy.

For the decades after World War II, the historical approach is less dominant, and the practical-political motivations are stronger. This applies to works by historians, such as Samuel L. Baily, *The United States and the Development of South America, 1945–1975* (New York, 1976), no less than to those by journalists, such as Jerome Levinson and Juan de Onís, *The Alliance That Lost Its Way* (Chicago, 1970), or political scientists, such as Abraham F. Lowenthal, *Partners in Conflict: The United States and Latin America* (Baltimore, 1990). The same is true for regional studies or analyses of single episodes, such as Walter LaFeber, *Inevitable Revolutions: The United States and Central America* (New York, 1983), and Richard H. Immerman, *The CIA in Guatemala: The Foreign Policy of Intervention* (Austin, 1982).

For the economy as well as for politics, the contributions of political economists and political scientists become clearly dominant. In the economic sphere, the publications of the United Nations' Economic Commission for Latin America (ECLA), created in 1947 under the leadership of Raúl Prebisch, offer abundant information and controversial interpretations and policy suggestions. For a representative sample, see ECLA, *The Economic Development of Latin America in the Post-War Period* (New York, 1964). On the 1930s, see Rosemary Thorp, ed., *Latin America in the 1930s: The Role of the Periphery in World Crisis* (London, 1984). On postwar issues and problems, see Albert Hirschman, ed., *Latin American Issues* (New York, 1961), and Werner Baer and Isaac Kerstenetsky, *Inflation and Growth in Latin America* (New Haven, 1964). On more recent times, see Rosemary Thorp and Laurence Whitehead, eds., *Inflation and Stabilization in Latin America* (New York, 1979); Alejandro Foxley, *Latin American Experiments in Neo-Conservative Economics* (Berkeley, 1983); Miguel S. Wionczek, ed., *Politics and Economics of External Debt Crisis: The Latin American Experience* (Boulder, Colo., 1985); and Joseph Ramos, *Neoconservative Economics in the Southern Cone of Latin America, 1973–1983* (Baltimore, 1986). For contributions by political scientists, see Michael L. Conniff, *Latin American Populism in Comparative Perspective* (Albuquerque, 1982); Alain Rouquié, *The Military and the State in Latin America* (Berkeley, 1987); David Collier, ed., *The New Authoritarianism* (Princeton, 1979); and Guillermo O'Donnell, Philippe C. Schmitter, and Laurence Whitehead, eds., *Transitions from Authoritarian Rule: Prospects for Democracy* (Baltimore, 1986).

Of course, most recent research falls within a national framework. For Mexico, see Nora Hamilton, *The Limits of State Autonomy: Post-Revolutionary Mexico* (Princeton, 1982), which is based on painstaking research and provides a complex portrait of the social and political actors during the Cárdenas years; Roger D. Hansen, *The Politics of Mexican Development* (Baltimore, 1971), which remains the classic presentation of the revolutionary regime in the era of "stabilizing development"; and Pablo González Casanova, *Democracy in Mexico* (New York, 1970), an unenthusiastic assessment of the social impact of half a century of revolution.

For Central America, see Victor Bulmer-Thomas, *The Political Economy of Central America since 1920* (Cambridge, 1987), and R. N. Adams, *Crucifixion by Power: Essays on the Guatemalan National Social Structure, 1944–1966* (Austin, 1970), which reflects the early—and still comparatively benign—stages of Guatemala's protracted sociopolitical crisis. The underlying agrarian issues are explored in Thomas Melville and Marjorie Melville, *Guatemala: The Politics of Land Ownership* (New York, 1971), and Elizabeth Burgos-Debray, ed., *I, Rigoberta Menchu: An Indian Woman in Guatemala* (London, 1984), offers a moving personal testimony of its impact. On El Salvador, Thomas P. Anderson has dealt with two critical moments in an equally tormented history in *Matanza: El Salvador's Communist Revolt of 1932* (Lincoln, 1971) and *The War of the Dispossessed: Honduras and El Salvador, 1969* (Lincoln, 1981). Enrique Baloyra, *El Salvador in Transition* (Chapel Hill, 1982), provides a less bland assessment than the title would suggest. For Nicaragua, see Neill Macaulay, *The Sandino Affair* (Chicago, 1967); D. C. Hodges, *The Intellectual Foundations of the Nicaraguan Revolution* (Austin, 1986); Forrest D. Coburn, *Post-Revolutionary Nicaragua: State, Class and the Dilemmas of Agrarian Policy* (Berkeley, 1986); and Carlos M. Vilas, *Sandinista Revolution: National Liberation and Social Transformation in Central America* (New York, 1986), a more positive but guarded assessment. For Costa Rica, see a positive presentation of the political order in Charles D. Ameringer, *Democracy in Costa Rica* (New York, 1982), and a social study of the rural sector in J. C. Cambranes, *Coffee and Peasants* (Stockholm, 1985).

For Cuba, see Samuel Farber, *Revolution and Reaction in Cuba, 1933–1960* (Middletown, Conn., 1976), which covers the years between the 1933 revolution and Castro's victory; Ramón L. Bonaechea and Marta San Martín, *The Cuban Insurrection, 1952–1959* (New Brunswick, N.J., 1973); Andrés Suárez, *Cuba: Castroism and Communism* (Cambridge, Mass., 1967); and K. S. Karol, *Guerrillas in Power: The Course of Cuban Revolution* (New York, 1970), which looks at the revolution from the vantage point of the critical late 1960s.

The exhaustively informative political science study by Jorge I. Domínguez, *Cuba: Order and Revolution* (Cambridge, Mass., 1978), looks at the revolution in a Tocquevillean vein as the culmination of a process of institution building. The economic surveys by Carmelo Mesa-Lago offer objective assessments of the revolution's achievements and shortcomings in this area, the most recent being *The Economy of Socialist Cuba: A Two-Decade Appraisal* (Albuquerque, 1981). A more recent and generally sympathetic exploration of the revolution's impact on Cuban life is Sandor Halebsky and John M. Kirk, eds., *Cuba: Twenty-Five Years of Revolution, 1959–1984* (New York, 1985).

On Colombia, Alexander Wilde offers an incisive view of the political regime in "Conversations among Gentlemen: Oligarchical Democracy in Colombia," in Juan J. Linz and Alfred Stepan, eds., *The Breakdown of Democratic Regimes in Latin America* (Baltimore, 1978). On "La Violencia" unleashed in the late 1940s, see Charles Berquist, Ricardo Peñaranda, and Gonzalo Sánchez, eds., *Violence in Colombia: The Contemporary Crisis in Historical Perspective* (Wilmington, Del., 1992). Leon Zamosc, *The Agrarian Question and the Peasant Movement in Colombia: Struggles of the National Peasant Association, 1967–1981* (Cambridge, 1986), offers an astute analysis of the eclipse of agrarian issues from the political agenda, with suggestions valid beyond Colombia.

On Peru, François Bourricaud, *Power and Society in Contemporary Peru* (New York, 1970), provides an astute socioeconomic and cultural analysis of the political development of the country, written on the eve of its experiment with radical military reformism. Abraham Lowenthal, ed., *The Peruvian Experiment: Continuity and Change under Military Rule* (Princeton, 1975), offers a perhaps excessively positive contemporary assessment of that experiment; a more critical retrospective view can be found in Cynthia McClintock and Abraham Lowenthal, eds., *The Peruvian Experiment Reconsidered* (Princeton, 1983). E. V. K. Fitzgerald, *The State and Economic Development: Peru since 1968* (Cambridge, 1976), stresses the limits in the transformative process. On Bolivia, James Malloy, *Bolivia, the Uncompleted Revolution* (Pittsburgh, 1970), is still the best overview of the impact of the 1952 revolution, and Dwight B. Heath, ed., *Land Reform and Social Revolution in Bolivia* (New York, 1969), covers the rural dimension of the revolution. Domitila Barrios de Chungara, *Let Me Speak!* (New York, 1978), chronicles the struggle of the tin miners to protect the gains from the revolution, from the viewpoint of an organizer of the miners' wives' protest movement.

On Brazil, two books by Thomas L. Skidmore, *Politics in Brazil, 1930–1964: An Experiment in Democracy* (New York, 1967) and *The Politics of Military Rule in Brazil, 1964–85* (New York, 1988), follow the political history of the period, and Peter Flynn, *Brazil, a Political Analysis* (London, 1978), explores the underlying trends. Alfred Stepan, ed., *Authoritarian Brazil: Origins, Politics and Future* (New Haven, 1973), as well as his authoritative *The Military in Politics: Changing Patterns in Brazil* (Princeton, 1971), and R. M. Schneider, *The Political System of Brazil: The Emergence of an Authoritarian*

Modernizing Regime, 1964–1970 (New York, 1971), look at the military era during its heyday. Peter Evans, *Dependent Development: The Alliance of Multinational, State and Local Capital in Brazil* (Princeton, 1979), explores the complex socioeconomic forces behind the military regime. For the later transition, see the relevant sections in Scott Mainwaring, *The Catholic Church and Politics in Brazil, 1916–1983* (Stanford, 1987); Maria Helena Moreira Alves, *State and Opposition in Brazil, 1964–1984* (Austin, 1988); and John D. French, *The Brazilian Workers' ABC: Class Conflict and Alliances in Modern São Paulo* (Chapel Hill, 1992).

On Chile, Alan Angell, *Politics and the Labour Movement in Chile* (Oxford, 1972), pays proper attention to the impact of the legal-institutional framework. Brian Loveman, *Struggle in the Countryside: Politics and Rural Labor in Chile, 1919–1973* (Bloomington, Ind., 1976), explores the rising social conflicts in the countryside and their political impact. Barbara Stallings, *Class Conflict and Economic Development in Chile, 1958–1973* (Stanford, 1978), places the Allende policies in their historical sequence; Stefan De Vylder, *Allende's Chile* (Cambridge, 1976), provides a sympathetic but critical assessment of Popular Unity's economic policies; and Peter Winn, *Weavers of Revolution: The Yarur Workers and Chile's Road to Socialism* (New York, 1986), is a poignant story of the Allende years and their aftermath from the vantage point of a militant faction of the working class. The economic policies of the Pinochet regime have pride of place in the books by Foxley *Latin American Experiments* and Ramos *Neoconservative Economics* mentioned above; for the political aspects, see Samuel Valenzuela and Arturo Valenzuela, *Military Rule in Chile: Dictatorship and Oppositions* (Baltimore, 1986). For the twilight of the military regime and the transition to democracy, see Paul W. Drake and Ivan Jaksic, eds., *The Struggle for Democracy in Chile, 1982–1990* (Lincoln, 1991).

On Argentina, Robert A. Potash followed the trajectory of the military in *The Army and Politics in Argentina, 1928–1945: Yrigoyen to Perón* (Stanford, 1969) and its sequel, *The Army and Politics in Argentina, 1945–1962: Perón to Frondizi* (Stanford, 1980). Joel Horowitz, *Argentine Unions, the State and the Rise of Perón, 1930–1945* (Berkeley, 1990), and Daniel James, *Perónism and the Argentine Working Class* (Cambridge, 1988), examine the course of organized labor. The best synthetic presentation of the Argentine predicament is Juan E. Corradi, *The Fitful Republic: Economy, Society and Politics in Argentina* (Boulder, Colo., 1985). In *Bureaucratic Authoritarianism: Argentina, 1966–1973, in Comparative Perspective* (Berkeley, 1988), Guillermo O'Donnell offers a brilliant analysis of a critical period, and in *Authoritarianism and the Crisis of the Argentine Political Economy* (Stanford, 1989), William C. Smith explores the links between the vicissitudes of political strife and those of economic policy. Jacobo Timerman's memoirs of jail and torture under the post-1976 military regime, *Prisoner without a Name, Cell without a Number* (New York, 1981), won a worldwide audience.

TULIO HALPERÍN DONGHI is Professor of History at the University of California, Berkeley. This book is a translation of *Historia Contemporánea de América Latina* first published in Spain in 1969. His other works include *El Pensamiento de Echeverría, Un Conflicto Nacional: Moriscos y Cristianos Viejos en Valencia, Tradición Política Española e Ideología Revolucionaria de Mayo, Historia de la Universidad de Buenos Aires,* and *Argentina en el Callejón.*

JOHN CHARLES CHASTEEN is Assistant Professor of History at the University of North Carolina, Chapel Hill.